P9-DMO-806

10/2/16

DRINKING AND DRIVING
Advances in Research and Prevention

The Guilford Substance Abuse Series

EDITORS
HOWARD T. BLANE, Ph.D.
Research Institute on Alcoholism, Buffalo

THOMAS R. KOSTEN, M.D.
Yale University School of Medicine, New Haven

DRINKING AND DRIVING: ADVANCES IN RESEARCH
AND PREVENTION
R. Jean Wilson and Robert E. Mann, Editors

ADDICTION AND THE VULNERABLE SELF: MODIFIED
DYNAMIC GROUP THERAPY FOR SUBSTANCE ABUSERS
Edward J. Khantzian, Kurt S. Halliday, and William E. McAuliffe

ALCOHOL AND THE FAMILY: RESEARCH AND CLINICAL
PERSPECTIVES
R. Lorraine Collins, Kenneth E. Leonard, and John S. Searles, Editors

CHILDREN OF ALCOHOLICS: CRITICAL PERSPECTIVES
Michael Windle and John S. Searles, Editors

GROUP PSYCHOTHERAPY WITH ADULT CHILDREN OF
ALCOHOLICS: TREATMENT TECHNIQUES AND
COUNTERTRANSFERENCE CONSIDERATIONS
Marsha Vannicelli

PSYCHOLOGICAL THEORIES OF DRINKING AND
ALCOHOLISM
Howard T. Blane and Kenneth E. Leonard, Editors

ALCOHOL AND BIOLOGICAL MEMBRANES
Walter A. Hunt

ALCOHOL PROBLEMS IN WOMEN: ANTECEDENTS,
CONSEQUENCES, AND INTERVENTION
Sharon C. Wilsnack and Linda J. Beckman, Editors

DRINKING AND CRIME: PERSPECTIVES ON THE
RELATIONSHIPS BETWEEN ALCOHOL CONSUMPTION
AND CRIMINAL BEHAVIOR
James J. Collins, Jr., Editor

DRINKING AND DRIVING
Advances in Research and Prevention

Edited by

R. JEAN WILSON
ROBERT E. MANN

THE GUILFORD PRESS
NEW YORK LONDON

© 1990 The Guilford Press
A Division of Guilford Publications, Inc.
72 Spring Street, New York, NY 10012

All rights reserved

No part of this book may be reproduced, stored in a retrieval
system, or transmitted, in any form or by any means, electronic
mechanical, photocopying, microfilming, recording, or otherwise,
without written permission from the Publisher.

Printed in the United States of America

This book is printed on acid-free paper.

Last digit is print number: 9 8 7 6 5 4 3 2 1

Library of Congress Cataloging-in-Publication Data

Drinking and driving : advances in research and prevention / R. Jean
    Wilson, Robert E. Mann, editors.
      p. cm. – (The Guilford substance abuse series)
    Includes bibliographical references and index.
    ISBN 0-89862-170-4
    1. Drunk driving–Prevention.   2. Drinking and traffic accidents.
  I. Wilson, R. Jean.   II. Mann, Robert E.   III. Series
  HE5620.D7D7   1990
  363.12′57 – dc20   90-39768
                                                                          CIP

CONTRIBUTORS

LISE ANGLIN, BA, Addiction Research Foundation, Toronto, Ontario, Canada

ROSS HOMEL, PhD, School of Behavioural Sciences, Macquarie University, Sydney, New South Wales, Australia

BRIAN A. JONAH, PhD, Road Safety Directorate, Transport Canada, Ottawa, Ontario, Canada

KNUT-INGE KLEPP, PhD, Research Center for Health Promotion, University of Bergen, Bergen, Norway

MICHAEL KLITZNER, PhD, Pacific Institute for Research and Evaluation, Vienna, Virginia

JOHN H. LACEY, MPH, Mid-America Research Institute, Chapel Hill, North Carolina

JAMES W. LANDRUM, MA, Social Science Research Center, Mississippi State University, Mississippi State, Mississippi

ROBERT E. MANN, PhD, Addiction Research Foundation, Toronto, Ontario, Canada

BRENDA A. MILLER, PhD, Research Institute on Alcoholism, Buffalo, New York

WOLF-R. NICKEL, Dipl-Psych, MA, Technischer Uberwachungs—Verein, Hannover, Federal Republic of Germany

CHERYL L. PERRY, PhD, Division of Epidemiology, University of Minnesota, Minneapolis, Minnesota

KATHRYN STEWART, MA, Pacific Institute for Research and Evaluation, Vienna, Virginia

JEFF S. TOPPING, PhD, Department of Psychology, Mississippi State University, Mississippi State, Mississippi

EVELYN R. VINGILIS, PhD, Addiction Research Foundation, Toronto, Ontario, Canada

ROBERT B. VOAS, PhD, National Public Services Research Institute, Landover, Maryland

ELISABETH WELLS-PARKER, PhD, Social Science Research Center and Department of Psychology, Mississippi State University, Mississippi State, Mississippi

R. JEAN WILSON, PhD, Road Safety Directorate, Transport Canada, Ottawa, Ontario, Canada

MICHAEL WINDLE, PhD, Research Institute on Alcoholism, Buffalo, New York

PREFACE

The idea for this book arose during the Tenth International Conference on Alcohol, Drugs and Traffic Safety held in Amsterdam in September, 1986. At this conference, we heard presentations by specialists in such diverse fields as forensic science, medical pharmacology, psychology, public health, epidemiology, traffic safety, alcohol treatment, legal administration, and the citizen activist movement. We learned of a proliferation of new legislation and programs being implemented in several countries. Although many of these measures were too recent to have been evaluated at the time, some papers described favorable outcomes of recent interventions. Perhaps most notable among these was the apparent contribution of random breath testing programs to the reduction of fatalities in Australia. A number of other countries also reported decreases in alcohol-impaired driving during the mid-1980s, despite wide variations in countermeasures and cultural/situational contexts.

Those of us fortunate enough to attend these international conferences tend to be struck by the fact that we are indeed in the midst of a very exciting and rapidly progressing area of interest. We may perhaps derive some satisfaction from the knowledge that we are working toward a common goal of improved understanding of the drinking–driving problem and its control on an international level.

We are also struck, however, by the fact that much of the research on drinking and driving is not easily accessible, even to the researcher. Many important studies continue to appear as technical reports published in-house, rather than in scientific journals or books. For the practitioner or member of the general public, information sources would seem even more obscure or would require great persistence and patience to obtain. The European countries, particularly the Federal Republic of Germany, the Netherlands, France and the Scandinavian countries, are sources of much valuable research on drinking and driving. Unfortunately, for the majority of unilingual English-speaking researchers who dominate the field, this research is largely inaccessible, except when presented at international conferences. Conference proceedings, such as those published for the International Conference on Alcohol, Drugs and Traffic Safety, provide a useful compilation of the most recent research findings worldwide; however, it is difficult to discern an integrated overall picture of the state of knowledge, even if one reads through the entire proceedings.

In this book, we have attempted to identify major advances in understanding the drinking driver, in theoretical and conceptual formulations of the drinking–driving problem and in measures aimed at its prevention. The book is focused on developments that have occurred primarily within the past 10 years, reflecting the relative newness of this field. We have drawn upon the expertise of specialists from five countries; however, the book is not primarily concerned with international comparisons. Rather, it is intended to provide an overall understanding of the most significant advances in the area over the past decade. We hope that the book is successful in filling an identified need and in making research and program knowledge on drinking and driving more widely available to anyone with an interest in the topic.

We wish to extend our sincere appreciation, first, to the authors who contributed chapters to this volume. Not only did we depend on their knowledge of specific topics, but also on their enthusiasm and whole-hearted support for the project. We are especially grateful to the staff of Guilford Press for their continued patience, encouragement, and advice, without which this book would not have been possible.

Our colleagues in Ottawa and Toronto provided invaluable suggestions, comments, and help in a variety of ways. In Ottawa, Brian Jonah and Linda Lackey, and in Toronto, Lise Anglin, Evelyn Vingilis, Paola Greco, and Evangeline Howe deserve special mention for their many contributions.

CONTENTS

1   INTRODUCTION   1
     R. Jean Wilson and Robert E. Mann

PART I. UNDERSTANDING THE IMPAIRED DRIVER

2   PSYCHOSOCIAL CHARACTERISTICS OF IMPAIRED
     DRIVERS: AN INTEGRATED REVIEW IN RELATION TO
     PROBLEM BEHAVIOR THEORY   13
     Brian A. Jonah

3   ADOLESCENTS, DRINKING, AND DRIVING: WHO
     DOES IT AND WHY?   42
     Knut-Inge Klepp and Cheryl L. Perry

4   ALCOHOLISM, PROBLEM DRINKING, AND DRIVING
     WHILE IMPAIRED   68
     Brenda A. Miller and Michael Windle

PART II. DETERRENCE AND THE
DRINKING–DRIVING PROBLEM

5   A NEW LOOK AT DETERRENCE MODELS   99
     Evelyn R. Vingilis

6   DRUNK DRIVING ENFORCEMENT, ADJUDICATION,
AND SANCTIONS IN THE UNITED STATES   116
Robert B. Voas and John H. Lacey

7   RANDOM BREATH TESTING AND RANDOM
STOPPING PROGRAMS IN AUSTRALIA   159
Ross Homel

PART III. OTHER PREVENTIVE APPROACHES

8   ALCOHOL AVAILABILITY, PER CAPITA CONSUMPTION,
AND THE ALCOHOL-CRASH PROBLEM   205
Robert E. Mann and Lise Anglin

9   YOUTH ANTI-DRINKING–DRIVING PROGRAMS   226
Kathryn Stewart and Michael Klitzner

10 PROGRAMS FOR THE REHABILITATION AND TREATMENT
OF DRINKING-DRIVING MULTIPLE OFFENDERS IN
THE FEDERAL REPUBLIC OF GERMANY   250
Wolf-R. Nickel

11 MATCHING THE DWI OFFENDER TO AN EFFECTIVE
INTERVENTION STRATEGY: AN EMERGING RESEARCH
AGENDA   267
*Elisabeth Wells-Parker, James W. Landrum,
and Jeff S. Topping*

INDEX   290

INTRODUCTION

R. JEAN WILSON
ROBERT E. MANN

It has long been recognized that alcohol impairs perceptual and motor functions essential to the task of driving. Even in the early days of the automobile, almost anyone would acknowledge that the drunk driver was a hazard on the road. However, awareness of the full extent of the problems of drinking and driving has only recently come to the public's attention.

Not until the 1960s were even rough estimates of the extent of alcohol involvement in road accidents generally available. During the 1960s and early 1970s, two significant research advances helped to set the stage for the more visible and widespread developments of the 1980s. The first of these was the determination of the proportion of crashes involving drinking drivers and the second was the demonstration of the relationship of crash risk to blood alcohol concentration (BAC).

A number of studies measured the BACs of fatally injured drivers, with sample sizes ranging from less than 100 to over 5,000 (Filkins et al., 1970; Nielson, 1969; Perrine, Waller, & Harris, 1971; Traffic Injury Research Foundation of Canada, 1975). Despite methodological differences, these studies were remarkably consistent in finding between 40% and 55% of fatally injured drivers with BACs exceeding 100 mg%. Studies of drivers involved in nonfatal crashes were (and still are) much rarer. Two early studies indicated that between 5% and 15% of drivers in nonfatal crashes had BACs of 100 mg% or greater (Borkenstein, Crowther, Shumate, Ziel, & Zylman, 1964; Lucas, Kalow, McCall, Griffith & Smith, 1955).

This research provided the first reliable estimates of the extent of the alcohol–crash problem. However, its full significance became apparent only when results could be compared with data on the BACs of drivers *not* involved in crashes using the same roads at the same times. These case control studies (e.g., Borkenstein et al., 1964; Holcomb, 1938; Hurst, 1974; Lucas et al., 1955) demonstrated that the relative risk of a crash increases as blood alcohol level increases, and rises sharply at BACs greater than about 80 mg%.

These few epidemiological studies constitute a landmark in the state of knowledge about alcohol and traffic safety. However, this knowledge has not been widely available to the public. Because the research was largely government-sponsored, it tended to be published in technical reports with limited distribution. In North America, citizen activist groups may have been instrumental in exposing alcohol–crash statistics to the public eye, at least indirectly. The now familiar figure of "50% of fatal accidents attributable to alcohol or drunk-driving" was widely quoted by the news media, as well as incorporated into government-sponsored advertising campaigns aimed at curbing drinking and driving. The public appears to have been surprised and perhaps even shocked by these revelations. Previously, people had been willing to accept that either the drunk driver was an isolated case or, because most drinking-and-driving incidents were crash-free, it was a relatively benign activity. Perhaps this state of complacency and ignorance about drinking and driving was partly responsible for the paucity of scientific work on the issue until recent times.

Considering the number of lives ended or otherwise harmed by drinking and driving, research on the issue, in terms of volume and funding, continues to lag behind that of many other (and sometimes lesser) health and safety problems. This situation is inconsistent with the fact that drinking–driving fatalities currently account for between one-third and one-half of all road fatalities and between 20% and 30% of all alcohol-related deaths. However, there is some ground for optimism.

During the past 10 to 15 years, an extraordinary amount of effort has been devoted to the problem on many fronts, and significant strides have been made. These include not only advances in research-derived knowledge, but also the mobilization of public opinion (e.g., changes in the social acceptability of driving while impaired) and strengthening of political will to do something about the problem. The latter has resulted in widespread legislative reforms and stricter, more intensive enforcement of driving while impaired (DWI) laws. The ascent of drinking–driving to the status of a major social issue of the 1980s is, in itself, worthy of attention. Undoubtedly research-based knowledge has contributed to the visibility of this issue, particularly that documenting the extent of the problem (e.g., alcohol involvement in fatal accidents). Social and political developments have, in turn, kindled research interest in drinking and driving, especially as more public- and private-sector funds become available for research on the topic.

The recent flurry of concern and action over drinking and driving and its consequences is remarkable in several respects. The sophistication and innovation of approaches for dealing with this problem are unprecedented—agencies and organizations involved have multiplied and diversified. There has also been a growing appreciation for the complexity of the problem among those individuals who deal with it directly from day to day. Researchers, policy makers, and ordinary citizens may well look back over the decade and legitimately ask: Has all this "sound and fury" made a difference? Has progress been made in abating the drinking–driving problem; in particular has there been a reduction in alcohol-related crashes?

An answer to these apparently simple questions is neither straightforward nor free from argument. Difficulties arise in assessing trends over time in alcohol-related data for several reasons (see Chapter 8, this volume, for a discussion of some of these considerations). The paucity of data prior to 1970 severely limits any generalizations; however, data that have been examined (inherent biases considered) suggest that alcohol involvement in crashes, at least in some geographic regions, has steadily escalated in postwar years through the early 1980s (Mann, Smart, Vingilis, Anglin & Duncan, 1987). In the 1970s and 1980s, because of livened interest in the problem, better resources and methodologies for measuring alcohol involvement in traffic crashes became available. Then population indices soon revealed some exciting trends beginning in the early 1980s: the magnitude of the problem began to decline.

It is not yet clear how strong or permanent these reductions are. For example, Fell and his colleagues developed a procedure for estimating total alcohol involvement in U.S. traffic fatalities based on accident characteristics in which BAC was known (Fell & Klein, 1986). Using these procedures, Fell and Nash (1989) reported a decrease of 17% between 1982 and 1987 in the number of fatalities among drivers with BAC > 100mg%. On the other hand, Zobeck, Grant, Williams, and Bertolucci (1989) reported that very little change had occurred over the same period of time, when police reports of alcohol involvement were examined. However, both Fell and Klein (1989) and

Zobeck et al. (1989) reported declines in the involvement of younger drivers in alcohol-related accidents over recent years.

Similar trends seem to be occurring in at least some other parts of the world. For example, in Ontario the recorded occurrence of alcohol in fatally injured drivers reached a peak in 1981 at 58.7%; that proportion had fallen to 40.6% by 1987 (Ontario Ministry of Transportation, 1987). In the United Kingdom, Kendell (1984) examined the rate of drinking–driving convictions and found a more variable pattern; the rates rose steadily between 1970 and 1975, declined in 1976 and 1977, increased between 1978 and 1980, and declined from 1980 to 1982.

The general picture that seems to be emerging is of a problem that increased in severity until the mid-1970s and early 1980s, followed by stabilization, and then declined in at least some parts of the world. This apparent turnabout in the drinking–driving problem is, of course, excellent news. It is our opinion that very substantial progress has been made in the scientific understanding of the factors that promote and reduce drinking–driving and its consequences, and that this progress has contributed in important ways to the reductions in alcohol-related crashes.

WHAT IS NOT IN THIS BOOK

The principles guiding our selection of topics for this book were: (1) they should be relevant to trends in the drinking–driving problem discussed above, (2) they were likely to be of continuing significance throughout the 1990s, and (3) together, they would provide an integrated picture of the most influential and significant developments in understanding and reducing the problem of driving while impaired by alcohol. Based on these admittedly subjective criteria, a number of areas were overlooked because they did not have a notable impact on social trends or the extent of the problem at the time of writing.

For example, important advances have been made in understanding the pharmacological and behavioral effects of alcohol in humans (e.g., Beirness & Vogel-Sprott, 1984). The study of the influence of alcohol on human behavior has a long tradition, with much important work carried out in the 1940s and 1950s. The development of modern recording equipment has vastly improved the ability to measure behavioral effects—notably the driving task itself. However, the state of knowledge has advanced in large part as a result of the recent synthesis and integration of previous work (e.g., Moskowitz & Robinson, 1988). As a consequence of convergent evidence, it is generally accepted that impairment of driving-related functions may occur at blood alcohol concentrations as low as 30 mg%. This conclusion is now bringing into question current legal BAC limits, especially for certain categories of drivers such as young drivers and commercial vehicle drivers. Thus, in the 1990s there may be an empirically driven trend toward lowering illegal per se limits.

Advances have also taken place in the forensic sciences (e.g., methods of measuring alcohol in the body) and technological fields. Some examples include the Passive Alcohol Sensor (PAS), which precludes the need for police officers to obtain voluntary breath samples, performance and alcohol interlock systems, and drunk-driver warning systems to prevent or deter drivers from operating their vehicles while impaired (see Voas, 1988, for a review of this topic). However, there are many impediments to the adoption of new technologies that have legal implications. Justice systems are generally slow or reluctant to accept these new methods and devices, and their use, to date, is primarily experimental.

Other areas omitted from this book are server-intervention programs, designated-driver programs, and other such approaches directed toward controlling individual alcohol consumption. Early evaluations of some programs of this type have been favorable (Russ & Geller, 1987; Gliksman & Single, 1988). However, their introduction is too recent and small-scale to have influenced the problem in the past 10 years.

ORGANIZATION AND FOCUS OF THIS BOOK

The model that has guided the organization of this book can be described in general terms as an interactionist model (Bowers, 1973; Sadava, 1987; Vingilis & Mann, 1986). This model considers the contributions of the individual and the environment to drinking–driving behavior, and furthermore proposes a strong and unique interaction between these two sources of variance. Vingilis and Mann (1986) propose that countermeasures that address the person, the situation, and their interaction stand a better chance of success. While this proposal has not often been directly tested, it seems logical that an appreciation for the complexity of the drinking–driving problem will hasten advancement of its prevention.

Part I of the book, "Understanding the Drinking Driver," is devoted to the individual and his or her immediate environment. Early work has clearly demonstrated a relationship between impaired driving and a wide variety of individual characteristics. More recent studies have expanded on these important observations and attempted to place them in a theoretical context. In the first chapter, Brian Jonah provides a comprehensive review of the psychosocial characteristics of impaired driving and integrates the findings within a framework of Problem Behavior Theory (PBT) developed by Richard Jessor and his colleagues (Jessor & Jessor, 1977). This theory can be considered a special case of an interactionist model and appears to be admirably suited to explain drinking and driving. The second chapter by Knut-Inge Klepp and Cheryl Perry also employs PBT, in this instance to predict the onset of drinking and driving among adolescents. The authors describe important and original work that confirms the usefulness of PBT. It also suggests that adolescents are a natural focus for drinking–driving prevention efforts because such behavior is usually initiated during this developmental stage. The third chapter in this section, by Brenda Miller and Michael Windle, focuses on the prevalence and role of alcoholism and problem drinking among drinking drivers. The authors illustrate how the psychosocial characteristics of drinking–driving offenders are of primary importance in understanding the emergence of serious alcohol problems in this population. Furthermore, these characteristics may be influential in maintaining the drinking–driving cycle.

The largest effort to reduce the drinking–driving problem has involved the legal system, with the enactment of laws, the imposition of penalties, and the strengthening of law enforcement procedures. Part II considers the theoretical and empirical aspects of this extended social experiment. Evelyn Vingilis explores the classical model of deterrence and its shortcomings. She presents a reconceptualized model which takes into account many of the research findings advanced in the chapters that follow. The next two chapters present the respective experiences of two countries, the United States and Australia, in terms of their most significant deterrence-based developments for dealing with DWI offenders. Robert Voas and John Lacey describe the history and current status of DWI enforcement in the United States, the adjudication process and its limitations, and the role of sanctions. Ross Homel's chapter describes Australia's experience with random breath testing (RBT) and random stopping programs. The program in New South Wales serves as a model to the rest of the world, demonstrating that a countermeasure derived directly from deterrence doctrine can be highly effective in reducing the incidence of drinking and driving and its consequences. Consistent with the interactionist theme of this book, Homel's model incorporates environmental factors (the physical and social environment) and individual factors (differential deterrability) in predicting the outcomes of RBT.

The final section describes other strategies and programs to prevent driving while imparied which are not deterrence-based. Robert Mann and Lise Anglin review evidence linking alcohol availability and population consumption levels to the alcohol–crash problem. This link is a contentious one, but recent work discussed in the chapter suggests that controlling alcohol availability can reduce drinking and driving. Kathryn Stewart and Michael Klitzner provide a critical examination of strategies to prevent drinking and driving among youth. They argue that new prevention programs must break away from unsuccessful models of the past. Like Klepp and Perry in Chapter 3, Stewart and Klitzner note that the factors that predispose youth to drink and drive are similar to those risk factors associated with other adolescent health risk behaviors. They suggest that new approaches must be based on this understanding.

Wolf Nickel provides an overview of European efforts to rehabilitate DWI offenders, bringing together work that was previously unavailable to the English-speaking world. He then describes an intensive rehabilitation program for repeat DWI offenders in the Federal Republic of Germany and its evaluation. In the final chapter, Elisabeth Wells-Parker, James Landrum, and Jeff Topping review the emerging evidence on the heterogeneous nature of drinking–driving offenders. They propose that approaches that match offender subtypes to appropriate rehabilitation and treatment modalities are more likely to have successful outcomes. They present findings which support the "matching hypothesis" and outline future research needs. Their chapter illustrates how an interactionist model can be applied to the design of preventive programs.

This book is intended to provide an overall understanding of recent trends in drinking and driving from a causal and historical perspective. While some chapters focus on developments in particular countries, the issues are common to all Western democracies. The topics covered should be of interest to scholars, researchers, and practitioners throughout the world whose many disciplines touch on the drinking–driving problem. Because it suggests guiding principles and highlights significant developments, this book may be used by professionals involved in program design and delivery within the traffic safety and alcohol treatment communities. We also hope that the book might serve as an introduction for those less familiar with the topic. We have attempted to facilitate an appreciation of the problem by providing a theoretical framework which places the individual within an environmental context in which drinking and driving may be predisposed and reinforced. In Parts II and III, strategies and programs are described which outline shortcomings and pitfalls of the past, promising new approaches and critical research needs of the future. Finally, we hope that our efforts to analyze and integrate major advances in drinking and driving to date will stimulate much needed research and prevention efforts to curb this continuing and pernicious problem in the next decade and beyond.

REFERENCES

Beirness, D.J., & Vogel-Sprott, M. (1984). Alcohol tolerance in social drinkers: Operant and classical conditioning effects. *Psychopharmacology, 84,* 393–397.

Borkenstein, R.F., Crowther, R.F., Shumate, R.P., Ziel, W.B., & Zylman, R. (1964). *The role of the drinking driver in traffic accidents.* Bloomington, Indiana: Department of Police Administration, Indiana University.

Bowers, K.S. (1973). Situationism in psychology: An analysis and critique. *Psychological Review, 80,* 307–336.

Fell, J.C., & Klein, T. (1986). *The nature of the reduction in alcohol in U.S. fatal crashes.* (Society of Automotive Engineers Technical Paper 860038). Warrendale, PA: SAE.

Fell, J.C., & Nash, C.E. (1989). The nature of the alcohol problem in U.S. fatal crashes. *Health Education Quarterly, 16,* 336–343.

Filkins, L.D., Clark, C.D., Rosenblatt, C.A., Carlson, W.L., Kerlan, M.W., & Manson, H. (1970). *Alcohol abuse and traffic safety: A study of fatalities, DWI offenders, alcoholics and court-related treatment approaches.* Washington, D.C.: U.S. Department of Transportation, National Highway Safety Bureau, Contract Nos. FH-11-6555 and FH-11-7129.

Gliksman, L., & Single, E. (1988, May). *A field evaluation of a server intervention program: Accommodating reality.* Paper presented at the Canadian Evaluation Society Meetings in Montreal, Canada.

Holcomb, R.L. (1938). Alcohol in relation to traffic accidents. *Journal of the American Medical Association, 111,* 1076–1085.

Hurst, P.M. (1974). Epidemiological aspects of alcohol and driver crashes and citations. In M.W. Perrine (Ed.), *Alcohol, drugs and driving* (pp. 131–157). Washington, DC: National Highway Traffic Safety Administration, DOT-HS-801-096.

Jessor, R., & Jessor, S.L. (1977). *Problem behavior and psychosocial development: A longitudinal study of youth.* New York: Academic Press.

Kendell, R.E. (1984). The beneficial consequences of the United Kingdom's declining per capita consumption of alcohol in 1979–82. *Alcohol and Alcoholism, 19,* 271–276.

Lucas, G.W., Kalow, W., McCall, J.D., Griffith, B.A., & Smith, H.W. (1955). Quantitative studies of the relationship between alcohol levels and motor vehicle accidents. In *Proceedings of the 2nd International Conference on Alcohol and Road Traffic* (pp. 139–142). Toronto: Garden City Press.

Mann, R.E., Smart, R.G., Vingilis, E.R., Anglin, L., & Duncan, D. (1987). Alcohol related accident statistics in Ontario between 1957 and 1984 — Is the problem increasing or decreasing? In P.C. Noordzij & R. Roszbach (Eds.), *Alcohol, drugs and traffic safety—T86* (pp. 245–249). Amsterdam: Elsevier.

Moskowitz, H., & Robinson, C.D. (1988). *Effects of low doses of alcohol on driving skills: A review of the evidence.* Washington, DC: National Highway Traffic Safety Administration, DOT-HS-807-280.

Nielson, R.A. (1969). *Alcohol involvement in fatal motor vehicle accidents. California, 1962–1968.* San Francisco: California Traffic Safety Foundation.

Ontario Ministry of Transportation (1987). *1987 Ontario road safety annual report.* Toronto: Ministry of Transportation.

Perrine, M.W., Waller, J.A., & Harris, L.S. (1971). *Alcohol and highway safety: Behavioral and medical aspects.* Washington, DC: National Highway Traffic Safety Administration, DOT-HS-800-599.

Russ, N.W., & Geller, E.S. (1987). Training bar personnel to prevent drunk-driving: A field evaluation. *American Journal of Public Health, 77,* 952–954.

Sadava, S.W. (1987). Interactional theory. In H.T. Blane & K.E. Leonard (Eds.), *Psychological theories of drinking and alcoholism* (pp. 90–130). New York: Guilford Press.

Traffic Injury Research Foundation of Canada (1975). *Analyses of fatal traffic crashes in Canada, 1973. Focus: The impaired driver.* Ottawa, Canada: Traffic Injury Research Foundation of Canada.

Vingilis, E.R., & Mann, R.E. (1986). Towards an interactionist approach to drinking–driving behaviour: Implications for prevention and research. *Health Education Research, 1,* 273–288.

Voas, R.B. (1988). Emerging technologies for controlling the drunk driver. In M.D. Laurence, J.R. Snortum, & F.E. Zimring (Eds.), *Social control of the drinking driver* (pp. 321–370).

Zobeck, T.S., Grant, B.F., Williams, G.D., & Bertolucci, D. (1989). *Surveillance Report #12: Trends in alcohol-related fatal traffic crashes, United States: 1977–1987.* Rockville, MD: National Institute on Alcohol Abuse and Alcoholism, Division of Biometry and Epidemiology.

PART I

UNDERSTANDING THE IMPAIRED DRIVER

PSYCHOSOCIAL CHARACTERISTICS OF IMPAIRED DRIVERS: AN INTEGRATED REVIEW IN RELATION TO PROBLEM BEHAVIOR THEORY

BRIAN A. JONAH

Driving while impaired (DWI) has most often been studied within the relatively young (less than 30 years old) discipline of road safety. For the most part, road safety research has focused on the compilation of epidemiological information on traffic accidents, some experimentation, and the development and evaluation of programs designed to increase road safety. With a few notable exceptions (e.g., Wilde, 1982), theory building has received relatively little attention, most likely due to the action-oriented funding of road safety research. If road safety research is to transcend the descriptive and the pragmatic, researchers must begin to integrate present knowledge into models of road-user behavior, which would, of course, include driving while impaired. Vingilis and Mann (1986) wrote:

> Thus we have our current situation of a plethora of research and literature on this behavior of drinking–driving, but little formulation of the behavioral processes involved. Indeed, this area is singularly impoverished in psychosocial theories and paradigms by which to explain the behavior. (p. 273)

Jessor (1986) has advised road safety professionals (i.e., researchers and programmers) that if the same strides are to be achieved in the road safety field as have occurred in behavioral medicine, particularly the fight against heart disease, then greater attention must be devoted

13

to theories that explain the lifestyle behaviors underlying road accidents. Taking heed of these admonishments, an attempt is made in this chapter to place the available knowledge about the characteristics of DWI within a theoretical framework that can generate predictions about such behavior. Through the generation and confirmation of such hypotheses, we can advance our understanding of DWI behavior; it is only through such an understanding that we will be in a better position to develop measures to control it.

Most researchers in the past have focused on the demographic and psychosocial characteristics of impaired drivers, paying little attention to the environmental context in which the behavior takes place. Vingilis and Mann (1986) have recently advocated an interactionist approach encompassing personal as well as environmental factors. This approach, which stems from Lewin's (1951) "field theory," has been more recently expounded by Bowers (1973), Endler (1981), and Magnusson and Endler (1977). Often, one field of study can be advanced by drawing on theoretical models developed in other domains. Problem behavior theory (PBT) is a formal theoretical model of the "field" genre, complete with operational definitions of constructs and empirical support for them (Jessor, 1987a; Jessor & Jessor, 1977). Most importantly, this theory recognizes the possibility that many problem behaviors are interrelated, such that the personal and situational factors influencing one behavior may be the same as those influencing another behavior.

It has been demonstrated that many high-risk driving behaviors are interrelated (Evans, Wasielewski, & Von Buseck, 1982; Jonah, 1986; Jonah & Lawson, 1986). Indeed, Wilson and Jonah (1986) have recently proposed that a subgroup of impaired drivers of unknown size exhibits a high-risk behavioral syndrome such that impaired driving is only one of the high-risk behaviors engaged in. The fact that one risky behavior such as impaired driving is related to others suggests that it may be difficult to change a single driving behavior in isolation.

Although PBT was formulated to account for the deviant behavior of adolescents (i.e., 12–18-year-olds), it does have relevance for the explanation of problem driving behavior, particularly impaired driving among drivers of all ages. Problem behavior theory adopts an interactionist approach, postulating that problem behaviors are interrelated by virtue of their common functions. Consequently, PBT is drawn upon in this chapter to organize and synthesize the literature on the characteristics of impaired drivers and their social environments. Unfortunately, there is not a perfect fit between the constructs embodied in PBT and the factors that have been examined in the literature. Therefore, some latitude is exercised in the use of PBT as a heuristic tool for integrating previous research findings.

PROBLEM BEHAVIOR THEORY

Problem behavior theory is primarily comprised of three independent yet linked systems of psychosocial influence: the behavior system, the personality system, and the perceived environment system. Within each system, there are explanatory variables that reflect the motivation to engage in problem behavior or constraints on it, the net result being a proneness to engage in problem behavior. Jessor (1987a) defined problem behavior "as behavior that departs from the norms—both social and legal—of the larger society" (p. 332). The conceptual framework of PBT is depicted in Figure 2.1.*

The behavior system consists of a problem behavior structure that includes a constellation of behaviors such as heavy drinking, illicit drug use, and sexual precocity and have been extended to include risky driving behaviors such as impaired driving, nonuse of seatbelts, and speeding (Jessor, 1987b). These behaviors share the same functions, such as repudiating conventional norms, securing independence from parents or other authority figures, and gaining status among peers. Consequently, these behaviors are meaningful and instrumental rather than arbitrary or pathological. The behavior system also contains a conventional behavior structure, which includes behaviors oriented toward traditional institutions of society, namely, the church and the school or the job. Obviously, the problem behavior structure works in opposition to the conventional behavior structure. Based on the structure of this behavior system, one would expect that impaired driving would be related positively to other problem behaviors and negatively to conventional behaviors such as religiosity and steady employment or good school performance.

Jessor (1987a) argues that problem behavior is the result of a person–environment interaction whereby the personality system and the perceived environment system exert a joint influence. According to Jessor, the variables comprising the personality system are at "the sociocognitive level and reflect social meanings and developmental experience" (p. 332). Within this system, there are three structures:

---

*The two structures that deal primarily with the characteristics of the parents (i.e., demography–social structure, socialization) are not considered in this chapter.

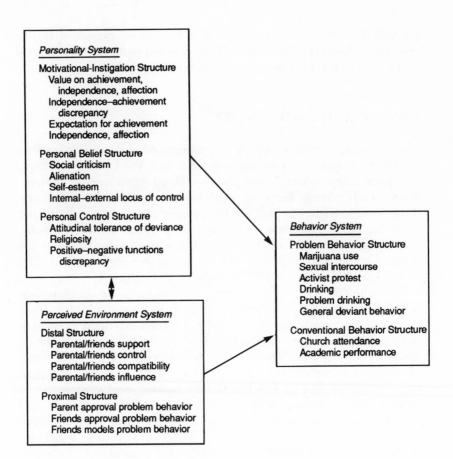

FIGURE 2.1. Conceptional framework of problem behavior theory. From "Risky Driving and Adolescent Problem Behavior: An Extension of Problem Behavior Theory" by R. Jessor, 1987, *Alcohol, Drugs and Driving, 3* (3–4), p. 3. Copyright 1987 by the Brain Information Service. Adapted by permission.

(1) the motivational-instigation structure, which embodies the goals for which a person strives (e.g., achievement, independence, affection) and the expectation that these goals will be achieved; (2) personal belief, which includes variables related to indirect or distal personal controls, such as acceptance of societal norms, values, and practices, alienation and isolation from others, self-esteem, and internal–external locus of control; and (3) personal control, which encompasses more proximal control concepts such as attitudinal

16

tolerance of deviance, religiosity, and the relative dominance of the reasons for engaging in problem behavior over the reasons for not engaging in the problem behavior. Hence, the likelihood of problem behavior increases with a lower value on academic achievement, a higher value on independence, lower expectations of attaining goals, greater social criticism, greater alienation, lower self-esteem, greater perceived external control and tolerance of deviance, less religiosity, and greater positive than negative functions of the problem behavior.

The perceived environment system refers to the "environmental characteristics—supports, influence, controls, models and expectations of others—that are capable of being cognized or perceived" (Jessor, 1987a, p. 334). Jessor argues that the perceived environment is more consistently related to behavior than the actual environment. Within this system, the distal structure, which is conceptually remote from the problem behavior itself, includes variables typifying the general social context within which the individual lives (e.g., whether the individual is more family-oriented or more peer-oriented, compatibility between influence of family and peers). The proximal structure characterizes the social environment in terms of models and supports for problem behavior per se. The perceived environmental proneness to engage in problem behavior is exemplified by lower family support and controls, lower peer control, lower family–peer compatibility, greater peer than family influence, lower family disapproval of problem behavior, and greater peer approval and models for problem behavior.

Taken together, the various theoretical constructs within the three systems are akin to psychosocial risk factors that increase or reduce the likelihood of a given problem behavior.

DEFINITIONAL AND METHODOLOGICAL CONSIDERATIONS

In pursuing this review, the terms *driving while impaired* and *impaired driving* will be used interchangeably. Impaired driving is defined as the operation of a motor vehicle while the driver's blood alcohol concentration (BAC) is over the legal limit, and impaired drivers are the people who engage in such behavior irrespective of whether they have ever been apprehended by the police. While this definition may at first appear to be objective, one should recognize that there are differences in this behavior between and within countries by virtue of there being different legal limits. For example, while many American states have a 100 mg% limit for driving under the influence, Canada and Great Britain have an 80 mg% threshold for impaired driving, and the Scandinavian countries and most Australian states have a 50 mg% limit. Since driving with a BAC above a specified limit is illegal, this definition is clearly consistent with Jessor's notion of problem behavior.

Past research on DWI characteristics has relied on a variety of samples of impaired drivers. While a few studies have focused on impaired drivers who were injured, fatally or otherwise, many more have been based on those drivers charged with and/or convicted of impaired driving offenses. Too few researchers have relied on night-time roadside surveys to gather information about the characteristics of impaired drivers or have interviewed drivers sampled from the general driving population. Considering that drivers involved in DWI accidents may be different from those charged by the police (Clay, 1974; Zylman, 1975) and that the latter may be somewhat different from self-admitted DWIs who have never been apprehended (Jonah & Wilson, 1986), it must be recognized that integrating characteristics across such diverse samples is a difficult task.

REVIEW OF THE LITERATURE

The literature differentiating impaired drivers from other drivers is organized according to the three systems of PBT, namely, behavior, personality, and perceived environment.

Behavior System

The basic premise of this system is that problem behaviors serve meaningful psychosocial functions and hence are related. This section examines the research bearing on the relationships among impaired driving and other driving behaviors, drinking behavior, drug use, health-compromising behavior, criminal behavior, and conventional behavior.

Driving Behavior

A number of researchers have established an association between driving while impaired and the nonuse of seat belts. Lawson and colleagues (1982) noted that drivers not wearing seat belts were more likely to have blood alcohol concentrations over 80 mg%. Similar observations have been made in other roadside surveys (Lawson & Stewart, 1986; Ontario Interministerial Committee on Drinking-Driving, 1980; Smith, Wolynetz, & Wiggins, 1976; Stewart & Lawson, 1987). Whether this relationship is the result of the effect of alcohol on the perceived risk of being injured in a car crash and hence the perceived need to wear a seat belt, or whether the two behaviors are functionally related by virtue of both being embedded in the problem behavior system, cannot be determined from these roadside surveys. The latter interpretation is more tenable, however, because social surveys have demonstrated that drivers reporting more frequent impaired driving also report less frequent use of seat belts (Biecheler-Fretel & Danech-Pajouh, 1986; Jonah & Wilson, 1986; Maron et al., 1986; Warren, 1986; Wilson & Jonah, 1985, 1988).

Jessor's (1987b) study of high school students revealed that those students who reported frequently taking risks while driving were more likely to report having driven after "a good bit to drink" during the past six months. Biecheler-Fretel and Danech-Pajouh (1986) noted that young drivers reporting that they had driven while impaired were less likely to respect speed limits and other traffic laws.

While some researchers have asked drivers to report the incidence of accidents or traffic citations during an interview or in a questionnaire, others have examined the actual records of drivers. Perrine (1975) noted that during a 3-year period, convicted impaired drivers had more crashes after drinking, more crashes in general, and more license suspensions and traffic violations on their record than did a group of general drivers renewing their licenses at a Vermont Department of Motor Vehicles office. Donovan, Queisser, Umlauf, and Salzberg (1986) compared the driving records of convicted impaired drivers with those of drivers drawn from the general driving population for a period of 3 years subsequent to the DWI group's conviction. Although statistical tests were not performed, it was obvious that the impaired drivers as a group had a higher incidence of accidents and traffic violations, particularly alcohol-related ones.

An investigation of the records of 9,273 British Columbia drivers revealed considerable overlap between impaired driving convictions and other types of driving offenses (Mercer, 1986). Mercer factor-analyzed the entries on drivers' records, isolating two factors that he labeled "reckless driving" (e.g., speeding, failure to stop at signs or lights) and "drinking and driving" (e.g., BAC over 80 mg%, failure to provide breath sample, 24-hour license suspension for having a BAC between 50 and 80 mg%). Using factor scores, two new composite variables called "drinking and driving" and "reckless driving" were derived. Mercer ascertained that 82% of the drivers scoring in the upper third of the drinking-and-driving variable also received a score in the upper third of the scores on the reckless-driving variable. Conversely, 75% of those scoring high on the reckless-driving variable also scored in the upper third on the drinking-and-driving variable. Furthermore, 50% of the drivers scoring high on the drinking-and-driving variable, compared to 13% for those who scored low, had accidents on their record, and 50% of the drivers involved in a fatal or injury accident had high drinking-and-driving scores.

Other researchers have examined self-reported accidents and violations. Farrow (1985) reported that young drivers (aged 16–19) who drove after drinking were more likely to report traffic citations such as speeding. Wilson and Jonah (1985) noted that self-admitted impaired drivers reported considerably more traffic violations per distance traveled than did those drivers who drove after drinking but not while impaired or those who never drove after drinking. In a subsequent study (Jonah & Wilson, 1986), convicted impaired drivers were shown to have had more total accidents, more accidents where they were at fault, and more traffic violations than either admitted (never convicted) impaired drivers or non-DWIs, but these differences may have been a result of greater driving exposure. More recently, Wilson and Jonah (1989) ascertained that violations were more common among convicted impaired drivers compared to a sample of control drivers.

Drinking Behavior

Perhaps no other behavior has been more closely associated with impaired driving than alcohol consumption. Obviously, the more frequently one drinks and the more one consumes per occasion, the more opportunities one has to drive while impaired. While many researchers have studied the drinking patterns of convicted impaired drivers, others have examined those of admitted DWIs as determined through social surveys.

Having reviewed the literature on the incidence of alcoholism among convicted impaired drivers, Vingilis (1983) concluded that 30–50% of impaired drivers can be classified as alcoholics, depending on the specificity of one's definition of alcoholism. Zelhart, Schurr, and Brown (1975) compared the reported drinking habits of a group of convicted impaired drivers participating in an Alberta rehabilitation program with those of institutionalized alcoholics, high-risk drivers (i.e., high number of demerit points), and police officers who were identified by scores on the Michigan Alcoholism Screening Test (MAST) as being normal social drinkers or borderline alcoholics. In terms of normal drinking days per week, the alcoholics drank more frequently but the other groups did not differ substantially among themselves. However, alcoholics *and* impaired drivers reported drinking more per sitting than did the other groups, and they were more likely to indicate that they had experienced problems due to their drinking and had sought help for these problems.

Selzer and Barton (1977) differentiated the drinking characteristics of convicted impaired drivers, alcoholics undergoing treatment, and a group of licensed drivers who were willing to complete the questionnaires (50% refusal rate). In rating their own level of alcohol consumption, impaired drivers fell between alcoholics and the general drivers. Although impaired drivers drank as frequently as the sample of licensed drivers, both groups drank significantly less often than the alcoholics. Impaired drivers, however, consumed more alcoholic beverages per occasion than did the general drivers but less than the alcoholic sample. Using the short MAST, 68% of the impaired drivers were classified in the alcoholic range. Similar results were reported by Selzer, Vinokur, and Wilson (1977). It is unclear whether these intermediate average consumption levels reflect more moderate drinking on average by DWIs compared to alcoholics or whether they reflect the fact that a significant proportion of DWIs are alcoholics (Vingilis, 1983).

Recently, Donovan, Queisser, Salzberg, and Umlauf (1985) compared the drinking habits of convicted impaired drivers with those of a group of high-risk drivers (four or more violations/accidents within 1 year) and those of a group of general licensed drivers. Impaired drivers scored higher than the other groups of drivers on self-rated drinking, frequency of drinking, and drinks per occasion; they also reported greater problems resulting from their drinking. On drinking measures, high-risk drivers had levels that were between the impaired drivers and the general driver group.

Jonah and Wilson (1986) examined the drinking patterns of convicted impaired drivers, admitted but never convicted impaired drivers, and nonimpaired drivers. The three groups did not differ in terms of the number of drinks consumed during the past week, but the convicted DWIs reported *fewer* days drinking during the same period. In contrast, the convicted group reported drinking almost twice as many drinks on the last drinking occasion compared to the other groups, and the admitted group tended to drink more per occasion than the non-DWI group. The convicted DWIs reported more alcohol-related problems (e.g., at work, with family) and more physiological symptoms of alcohol abuse (e.g., blackouts, delirium tremens) than did drivers in the other groups, although the admitted DWIs were intermediate between the convicted and non-DWI groups.

Wilson and Jonah (1989) compared convicted impaired drivers with high-risk drivers (i.e., involved in three or more reportable accidents within the past 3 years or had accumulated nine or more demerit points in the past 3 years) and with a sample of licensed drivers matched for age and sex. They noted that convicted impaired drivers reported more drinks consumed both in the last 7 days and on the last drinking occasion than either of the other two groups, which did not differ among themselves. The convicted impaired drivers also experienced more trauma events, which Skinner, Holt, Schuller, Ray, and Israel (1984) have argued are indicative of problem drinking. The DWIs also scored higher on scales of drinking for stress reduction and alcohol addiction.

The vast majority of studies just reviewed have compared the drinking patterns and problems of *convicted* impaired drivers with those of other groups of drivers. To the extent that convicted DWIs differ from those who drive while impaired but have never been caught, the conclusions about the drinking patterns of impaired drivers relative to other drivers might be distorted by relying on convicted DWIs alone. Fortunately, other studies have included subjects who are more representative of the general impaired-driver population. Smith and colleagues (1976) and Lawson and Stewart (1988) reported that drivers found to be impaired as determined by a breath test given during a roadside survey reported a higher number of drinks consumed either during the year prior to the survey or the 7 days prior.

Other researchers have conducted social surveys either by mail, by telephone, or face-to-face in order to gather information concerning impaired driving and drinking habits. Irgens-Jensen (1975) found that the proportion of Norwegian students who reported impaired driving increased with yearly alcohol consumption; almost 50% of women and men who drank 70 liters or more reported one or more instances of impaired driving. Also, students who reported more drinking-related problems—such as drinking first thing in the morning, having studies adversely affected by alcohol, or seeking advice about their drinking problem—were more likely to report driving while impaired. Norstrom (1983) asked Swedish drivers to return a mailed questionnaire that measured yearly alcohol consumption based on the frequency and quantity of alcohol consumption and driving while impaired. Alcohol consumption had a stronger relationship to impaired driving than did any other variable measured (e.g., moral attachment toward impaired driving).

Canadian respondents who admitted to driving while legally impaired during the past 30 days also reported consuming more than twice the number of drinks during the past 7 days and drinking a greater amount during their last drinking occasion than nonimpaired drivers (Wilson & Jonah, 1985). The estimated BAC based on length of time drinking on last drinking occasion, number of drinks consumed, and body weight on that occasion was 100 mg% for reported impaired drivers and about 56 mg% for those respondents who did not report driving while impaired. Wilson and Jonah (1988) reported that drinking quantity was significantly correlated with the frequency of reported DWI instances at high BACs (i.e., greater than 150 mg%).

American respondents were asked to indicate the largest number of drinks they had consumed prior to driving their car in the past year (Berger & Snortum, 1986). Using body weight, the researchers estimated whether the respondents had a maximum blood alcohol estimate (MBAE) over 100 mg% prior to driving. Monthly alcohol consumption was reported to be the major predictor of MBAE, accounting for about 15% of the variance. Beer drinkers were more likely to have an MBAE over 100 mg% than respondents who said they preferred to drink wine or liquor.

Heavy alcohol consumption is more common among young drivers who have been convicted of impaired driving or report driving while impaired (Beirness & Simpson, 1988; Farrow, 1986; Guppy, 1986; Wechsler, Rohman, Kotch, & Idelson, 1984).

In summary, it is clear that as alcohol consumption increases, so too does the incidence of driving while impaired. In the majority of studies that examined both frequency and quantity of consumption, quantity per occasion appears to be the more important factor. Whether frequency of drinking or consumption per occasion is more important in predicting impaired driving seems to depend on the definition of impaired driving (i.e., the legal limit) as well as the nature of the sample of impaired drivers (i.e., convicted DWIs versus self-reported DWIs). There is also an apparent correspondence between impaired driving frequency and the incidence of other alcohol-related problems. The level of alcohol consumption appears to decline as one goes from alcoholics through convicted impaired drivers, admitted DWIs, and high-risk drivers to drivers in general.

Use of Other Drugs

Selzer and Barton (1977) reported that convicted impaired drivers were intermediate between alcoholics and general licensed drivers in their use of prescribed drugs, such as sedatives and tranquilizers, but that they were more likely than either the alcoholics or general drivers to use stimulants and illicit drugs such as marijuana or LSD. When asked how often they used various methods of coping with depression and tension, DWIs were intermediate between alcoholics and the controls in the use of oral substances (excluding the "having a drink" item). These results were partially replicated in a subsequent study (Selzer et al., 1977).

Wilson and Jonah (1988) reported a significant correlation between number of drugs used and frequency of driving while quite impaired (i.e., BAC over 150 mg%). Wilson and Jonah (1989) noted that impaired drivers and high-risk drivers were similar in their use of marijuana, cocaine, amphetamines, and hallucinogens and that both groups were more likely than drivers in general to use these drugs. Irgens-Jensen (1975) showed that the use of barbiturates and tranquilizers was positively related to reported impaired driving among women but not among men and that marijuana use was unrelated to DWI for both sexes. Young drivers who used drugs such as cocaine, amphetamines, and barbiturates were more likely to report driving while impaired by alcohol (Beirness & Simpson, 1988; Farrow, 1986; Swisher, 1988; Wechsler et al., 1984). Jessor (1987c) has shown that for male high school students, "driving when you've had a good bit to drink" was significantly correlated with the frequency of marijuana use in the past 6 months but was unrelated for female students.

As part of a longitudinal study of youth, Elliott (1987) examined the relationship between drug use and alcohol-impaired driving, discovering that both the prevalence and frequency of DWI were highest among users of multiple illicit drugs. Indeed, driving under the influence of drugs other than alcohol was also highest among this group. Users of multiple illicit drugs reported driving while under the influence of alcohol over four times more frequently than those respondents who used only alcohol, and they reported driving under the influence of marijuana over three times more frequently than those who only used marijuana.

In summary, although the evidence on alcohol-impaired driving and the use of other drugs is limited, it suggests that impaired drivers are more likely to use other drugs. However, it should be recognized that in some of these studies, age may have been confounded with illicit drug use.

Health-Impairing Behavior

McGuire (1980) has noted that convicted impaired drivers with relatively high BACs at the time of their arrest were more likely to have tattoos, smoke heavily, and have respiratory, cardiovascular, and digestive problems compared to DWIs with low BACs. Beirness and Simpson (1988), Irgens-Jensen (1975), Jonah and Wilson (1986), and Wilson and Jonah (1988) reported that DWIs were more likely than nonimpaired drivers to smoke tobacco and to be heavy smokers. Jessor (1987c) has found that among adolescents who drink, driving while impaired by alcohol was significantly correlated with smoking of tobacco, frequent sexual intercourse, poor sleep patterns, and problem eating for males, and with smoking, poor sleep patterns, poor safety practices, and problem eating for females. Similarly, Beirness and Simpson (1988) noted that impaired driving decreased with positive health behaviors (e.g., dental checkups, regular exercise) and with average number of hours slept each night and increased with negative health behaviors (e.g., eating junk food). Although somewhat limited, these findings suggest that impaired drivers may be more likely to engage in activities that could be deleterious to their health.

Other Deviant Behavior

Irgens-Jensen (1975) reported that self-reported impaired driving among students was related to the tendency to admit to other offenses, such as vandalism, robbery, theft, and smuggling. Zelhart and colleagues (1975) found that convicted impaired drivers were distinguished from alcoholics and high accident/violation risk drivers by their greater involvement with legal authorities for reasons other than impaired driving (e.g., fighting, rowdiness). Elliott (1987) has shown that young drivers were much more likely to report driving under the influence of alcohol or marijuana if they had committed four or more delinquent or criminal acts during a 1-year period. Similarly, Swisher (1988) has noted that young drinking drivers were more likely to stay out all night without permission, shoplift, disrupt the classroom, and take things from others. Wilson and Jonah (1989) reported that DWIs were more likely to have been charged with a non-vehicle-related offense, such as assault or theft, than a group of control drivers. These few studies suggest a positive but weak association between impaired driving and involvement in other criminal activity.

Conventional Behavior

Selzer and colleagues (1977) found that impaired drivers were significantly less likely than control drivers to engage in church, club, or family activities. Farrow (1985, 1986), Swisher (1988), and Williams, Lund, and Preusser (1985) have noted that students reporting driving under the influence of alcohol had poorer academic performance than did students who did not report such behavior. Consistent with this latter observation are studies showing that, relative to other drivers, convicted DWIs have lower levels of education (Donovan et al., 1985; Jonah & Wilson, 1986; Selzer & Barton, 1977; Selzer et al., 1977), although reasons other than academic achievement may contribute to lower education.

Summary

Although there are relatively few studies relating impaired driving to other risky or conventional behaviors, the weight of the evidence is consistent with the notion that problem behaviors are part of a lifestyle of risk, or what Jessor calls a "problem behavior syndrome," that tends to facilitate the likelihood of engaging in deviant behavior. In a similar manner, this syndrome inhibits involvement in health-promoting and conventional behavior. Wilson and Jonah (1988) have conducted a factor analysis on a number of self-reported problem behaviors and found that there was a 1-factor solution with the following behaviors loading 0.35 or greater: drug use, competitive speed, driver aggression, drinking quantity, seat belt use, impaired driving, and trauma scale indicative of problem drinking. Further research should be initiated to ascertain whether a wider variety of problem behaviors and conventional behaviors are interrelated.

Personality System

Recapitulating the variables constituting the personality system of PBT,

> They are values, expectations, beliefs, attitudes and orientations toward self and others, and they are organized into three structures depending upon whether they constitute instigations to problem behavior or controls against it, and, if controls, whether they are relatively proximal to or distal from problem behavior. (Jessor, 1987a, p. 332)

Motivational-Instigation Structure

Jessor places considerable emphasis on the achievement–independence dimension of the personality system in attempting to account for the problem behavior of adolescents. Jessor's (1987c) male high school students were more likely to report having driven after having "a good bit to drink" if they placed a low value on achievement and a high value on independence. The net differential between the value placed on achievement and independence also correlated with reported incidents of DWI. No similar relationship existed for female students. Beirness and Simpson (1988) similarly reported that young impaired drivers had a lower attachment to traditional values such as academic achievement. No studies have assessed the relative value placed on achievement, independence, and affection by impaired drivers.

The motivational-instigation structure of the personality system needs to be operationalized in order to measure the values of people no longer in school as well as those of students. One approach could be the use of Rokeach's (1979) measure of terminal and instrumental values, which has been shown to have wide applicability among various age groups and cultures. Using a modification of Rokeach's instrument, Wilson and Jonah (1988) obtained a significant negative relationship between the value placed on responsibility and risky driving, which included impaired driving.

Personal Belief Structure

Considerable research has focused on a number of personality dimensions, some of which fall within the personal belief structure of PBT (i.e., social criticism, alienation, self-esteem, internal–external locus of control). Before turning to individual studies of personality characteristics, mention of some of the conclusions reached in previous review papers may be useful.

In a review of the characteristics of the convicted impaired driver, Moskowitz, Walker, and Gomberg (1979) concluded that "there are indications of psychosocial disturbances in his life and his drinking behavior appears to reflect stress and difficulties" (p. 17). Donovan, Marlatt, and Salzberg (1983) summarized the personality variables associated with increased driving risk, including DWI, as follows: emotional instability, irritability, impulsiveness, thrill seeking, expression of overt hostility, resentment, low frustration tolerance, feelings of frustration, oversensitivity to criticism, depression, feel-

ings of helplessness and personal inadequacy, low level of assertiveness, and external locus of control. Based on her review of the
literature, Vingilis (1983) has found that compared to control drivers,
impaired drivers are more neurotic, depressed, suicidal, paranoid,
irresponsible, and aggressive, as well as lower in self-esteem.

Turning to individual studies, McLean and Campbell (1975) compared the personality profiles of Australian convicted impaired
drivers with those of alcoholics and a control group of heavy drinkers.
On all but one scale of the California Personality Inventory, impaired
drivers scored between the alcoholics and the heavy drinkers. The
greatest discrepancies between the DWIs and the controls were on
the responsibility, self-control, socialization, well-being, intellectual
efficiency, tolerance, and achievement through conformity scales,
with the DWIs displaying lower levels on each. Selzer and colleagues
(1977) noted that the mean scores of convicted impaired drivers were
located between those of alcoholics and control drivers on the
following personality dimensions: self-esteem, depression, paranoid
thinking, and aggression. Convicted DWIs and alcoholics were
equally less responsible than the control drivers. In a subsequent
study (Selzer & Barton, 1977), convicted DWIs were found to be
situated between alcoholics and control drivers on the Eysenck
Neuroticism Scale. Additionally, the DWIs were between these two
groups in terms of self-esteem, self-control, and depression. On
measures of aggression and lack of responsibility, DWIs and alcoholics alike scored higher than control drivers.

Donovan and colleagues (1985) ascertained that convicted DWIs
and high-risk drivers were quite similar in regard to a number of
personality characteristics, both of these groups being more extreme
than the control drivers. These characteristics included depression,
emotional maladjustment, sensation seeking, external locus of control, assaultiveness, verbal hostility, irritability, and resentment.
Jonah and Wilson (1986) determined that DWIs (convicted or self-
admitted) compared to non-DWIs were more externally controlled,
resentful, verbally hostile, impulsive, and self-deprecatory, while the
convicted and admitted DWIs differed from each other only on
assaultiveness and depression. Recently, Wilson and Jonah (1989)
found that convicted impaired drivers scored higher on measures of
thrill seeking and assaultiveness than did drivers in general, but they
did not differ with regard to depression, verbal hostility, or external
locus of control.

Irgens-Jensen (1975) observed that the scores on a psychopathic
index (based on the Psychopathic Deviant Scale of the Minnesota

Multiphasic Personality Inventory) among students increased as a function of reported impaired driving, as did suicidal impulses among women. This psychopathology was typified by aggressiveness, impulsivity, and an inability to plan ahead. Boyd and Huffman (1984) found that among graduate students the frequency of driving while impaired decreased with emotional maturity.

These studies indicate that impaired drivers are more likely to possess personality traits indicative of maladjustment and social deviance than are drivers in general.

Personal Control Structure

This structure of the personality system encompasses attitudinal tolerance of deviance, religiosity, and the positive and negative functions of the problem behavior. Attitudes can be considered to be either proximal (i.e., attitude toward impaired driving or DWI countermeasures) or more distal (i.e., attitudes toward driving, alcohol use) in nature. Although high school students reporting DWI incidents were more likely than non-DWI students to be tolerant of deviance (e.g., offenses rated as less serious) and to exhibit "macho" attitudes toward alcohol use (Beirness & Simpson, 1988), other studies have failed to demonstrate a relationship between DWI and attitudes toward driving (Donovan et al., 1985; Perrine, 1975; Wilson, 1986; Wilson and Jonah, 1989).

With respect to proximal attitude measures, the scores of Swedish drivers on Norstrom's (1983) scale of moral attachment, which measures perceived acceptability of impaired driving, were significantly related to behavioral intentions to drive after drinking and to the reported frequency in the past 12 months of driving after consuming three beers or more. Berger and Snortum (1986) and Vayda and Crespi (1981) have reported similar relationships for American drivers. Goldfarb Consultants (1983) noted that Canadians who said they had driven after having too much to drink had more positive attitudes toward drinking and driving. Wilson and Jonah (1985) have reported that favorability toward increased police enforcement of laws against DWI was negatively correlated with frequency of impaired driving, as was willingness to moderate one's alcohol consumption when driving. Wilson and Jonah (1989) found greater tolerance for DWI among convicted impaired drivers than among high-risk drivers or drivers in the general population.

Although the number of studies is limited, these findings on attitudes suggest that while the more distal attitudes are generally unrelated to the incidence of DWI, the more proximal measures are related. This is consistent with Fishbein and Ajzen's (1975) notion that behavioral prediction improves as the specificity of the attitude measure increases.

Jonah and Wilson (1986) noted that self-rated religiosity was lower among self-admitted impaired drivers but not among those who had been convicted. A measure of traditional values that included religiosity was lower among young impaired drivers (Beirness & Simpson, 1988).

The more drivers believe they will be apprehended by the police or be involved in an accident while driving impaired, the less likely they should be to do it. Norstrom (1983) observed a relationship between perceived accident risk and DWI but was unable to detect any relationship between the perceived likelihood of being detected by the police while driving impaired and the frequency of driving impaired during the past 12 months. In contrast, Wilson and Jonah (1985) reported that impaired drivers and drinking drivers thought it was less likely than did nondrinking drivers that an average impaired driver would be stopped and charged by the police. Young self-admitted impaired drivers in Britain were shown to have a lower perceived likelihood of apprehension than did drivers not admitting to DWI (Guppy, 1986).

Summary

Very little research has addressed the role of the motivational-instigation structure underlying impaired driving. Concerning the personal belief structure, there is some support for the prediction derived from PBT that impaired driving is related to low self-esteem and a perceived external locus of control. Aside from the concepts included in PBT, there is strong evidence that impaired driving is related to aggressiveness, impulsivity, irresponsibility, and depression, as well as a general state of emotional maladjustment. Many impaired drivers appear to have a dysfunctional personal belief structure that provides them with less capacity to cope adequately with situations that could lead to DWI. With respect to the personal control structure, there is some evidence that attitudes toward the problem behavior (i.e., impaired driving) are related to DWI behavior, but more distal attitudes toward safety in general appear to be unrelated. The little research that has examined religiosity and positive–negative function discrepancy has yielded inconsistent results.

Perceived Environment

According to Jessor (1987a), adolescents prone to problem behavior have a perceived environment system that "consists of lower parental support and controls, lower friends controls, lower parent–friends compatibility, greater friends than parents influence, lower parental disapproval of problem behavior and greater friends approval for and models of problem behavior" (p. 334). Since PBT has not previously been applied to the understanding of impaired driving, it is not surprising that there are few studies available bearing on the constructs of the perceived environment system of PBT. Consequently, the studies reviewed in this section describe environmental influence in general and are not always defined in terms of the distal and proximal structures described in Figure 2.1.

Social Context

There have been a few investigations of the social context of drinking among DWIs, in particular the reasons for and the location of drinking. Donovan and Marlatt (1982) asked DWI arrestees to indicate which of 20 psychosituational factors best described the events surrounding the drinking episode that led to their arrest. According to Donovan and Marlatt, "the present DWI arrestees endorsed items suggestive of drinking within a gregarious social atmosphere. The majority of individuals reported drinking with friends in bars, taverns, cocktail lounges, or in homes of friends" (p. 425).

Snowden and Campbell (1984) asked clients in a DWI treatment program to rate their reasons for drinking generally but not necessarily at the time of their arrest for DWI. The major factors were family problems, fear and insecurity, isolation and drinking concern, social affiliation and relaxation, pain, and individual circumstances. Among university students, the major variables differentiating DWIs and non-DWIs in a discriminant analysis were drinking in a bar and drinking in order to get high or drunk (Beck, 1983). In a subsequent study using a self-completed questionnaire, Beck and Summons (1985) compared the social context of drinking for DWI offenders in rehabilitation courses and college students. A discriminant analysis revealed that college students were more likely to drink at a party, while DWIs were more likely to drink alone in their own homes. Moreover, college students appeared to drink for the enjoyment of the taste, in order to get drunk, and in order to get to sleep, while the

DWI offenders were more likely to drink to relieve stress. According to Beck and Summons, 74% of the respondents were correctly classified by these social context factors.

Selzer and colleagues (1977) compared the reasons for drinking given by alcoholics, impaired drivers, and control drivers. While alcoholics gave more overall reasons for drinking than the other two groups, only alcoholics gave more reasons expressing the desire for relief from tension than reasons expressing the desire for social relaxation. Impaired drivers gave more reasons expressing the desire for tension relief and social relaxation than did the control drivers. These findings were replicated by Selzer and Barton (1977). It is apparent that DWIs drink either for social facilitation or tension reduction or both, but the relative importance of these reasons is equivocal.

These studies on the social context of DWI incidents suggest two primary motivations for drinking: coping with life problems and peer pressure, each of which is examined in more detail below.

Life Problems

Several studies have demonstrated that many DWI offenders were experiencing difficulties in their lives and were unable to cope with them at the time of their arrest. Yoder (1975) reported that of 35% of DWI offenders taking part in a rehabilitation course had experienced some form of acute stress prior to the drinking episode that resulted in their offense and that 31% reported experiencing chronic stress. The most common source of this stress, be it acute or chronic, was interpersonal conflict. Selzer and colleagues (1977) asked alcoholics, DWIs, and controls to rate their family relationships, the frequency of family and job problems, and the level of distress experienced from these problems. Alcoholics reported poorer family relationships, more family and job problems, and greater distress than either the DWIs or the controls. Although DWIs and controls did not differ on any of the individual measures, DWIs had higher scores on a composite measure of distress. In a subsequent study, alcoholics experienced the highest incidence of family and job problems and the highest levels of concomitant distress, with DWI offenders reporting only greater family-related distress than the controls (Selzer & Barton, 1977). In a recent study, convicted impaired drivers and high-risk drivers reported more personal problems in their lives than did licensed drivers in general (Wilson and Jonah, 1989).

These results concerning family distress are consistent with the frequent observation that people who are divorced or separated tend to be overrepresented in the DWI offender population (e.g., Jonah & Wilson, 1986; Selzer et al., 1977). Although the weight of the evidence tends to implicate the role of stressful life events in the occurrence of impaired driving, it is unclear at this point how the effects of these events are mediated.

Social Influence

It is apparent from the studies reviewed earlier that many people drink to facilitate social interaction. Attention is now focused on the relevant others (e.g., family and friends) and how their attitudes and behavior may implicitly or explicitly influence the decision to drive while impaired. In Jessor's terms, the more distal environmental factors are addressed first.

Steer, Fine, and Scoles (1979) determined that about 20% of the DWI offenders in their sample had no father present as a role model when growing up and that an additional 14% had fathers who were heavy drinkers, thus serving as negative role models for drinking and perhaps DWI as well. Irgens-Jensen's (1975) Norwegian students were less likely to report driving after drinking if their parents were abstainers and, for women, drinking and driving decreased with the rated religiosity of their parents. Problem drinkers among a sample of youthful DWI offenders in Mississippi were more likely to come from families in which there was a problem drinker or from families that strictly prohibited the use of alcohol, suggesting a modeling effect in the former situation and a "forbidden fruit" effect in the latter (Lightsey & Sweeney, 1985). Homel (1986) found that reported pressure from friends to drink was significantly related to reported drinking and driving in Australia.

With respect to more proximal measures of social influence, Canadian drivers who indicated that they had ridden with someone whom they thought had consumed too much alcohol to drive or that they knew someone who had been stopped by the police for a DWI check were more likely than other drivers to report driving while impaired (Beirness & Simpson, 1988; Swisher, 1988; Warren, 1986; Wilson & Jonah, 1985). These observations suggest that impaired drivers may "hang out" together, thereby mutually reinforcing DWI behavior.

Berger and Snortum (1986) obtained a correlation between the maximum blood alcohol level attained prior to driving in the past year and the perceived attitudes of friends toward DWI. Jessor (1987c) has found that impaired driving for males (i.e., driving after having had "a good bit to drink") was significantly predicted by both parental influence and by the degree to which friends served as models for problem behavior; but only the latter measure was significant for females. Wilson and Jonah (1989) reported that convicted impaired drivers got along less well with their parents than did either the high-risk drivers or drivers in the general population. A weak but significant relationship between self-reported DWI and peer influence was noted among high school students by Beirness and Simpson (1988).

Summary

The few available studies provide consistent support for the notion that the perceived attitudes and behaviors of family and friends toward the consumption of alcohol and driving while impaired are important factors in the proneness to drive while impaired. Greater emphasis in the future should be placed on the constructs within the perceived environment system of PBT when studying the characteristics of impaired driving behavior.

SUMMARY AND CONCLUSIONS

Research performed to differentiate impaired drivers from other drivers in terms of behavior, psychosocial characteristics, and environmental influences has been reviewed and integrated within the conceptual framework of PBT. There is impressive support for the argument that impaired driving is embedded in a behavior system consisting of risky driving, excessive alcohol consumption, drug use, and, to a lesser extent, unhealthy behavior and illegal activity. Further study should attempt to expand the scope of the behavior system to include other driving and nondriving behaviors and to examine the nature of the linkage among these behaviors.

Evidence concerning the relationship between DWI and the personality and the perceived environment systems, while not conclusive, is consistent with PBT in a number of areas, including the personal belief structure (e.g., external locus of control, low self-esteem), the personal control structure (e.g., attitudinal tolerance, particularly proximal attitudes), and the influence of friends. There is also considerable evidence for a relationship between aggression, depression, impulsivity, and emotional maladjustment and impaired driving, and there is some indication that a stressful environment fraught with interpersonal conflicts may be an important antecedent of DWI in some cases. These latter dimensions have not to date been considered to be a part of PBT, but there is no reason PBT could not incorporate them.

Although the personality and perceived environment systems have been treated as independent entities, they may not be so in reality. For example, people may rely strongly on the perceived attitudes of their peers because they have relatively low self-esteem and hence are externally controlled. Further interactive linkages between the two systems should be explored in order to develop PBT further.

The observation that impaired driving is embedded in a constellation of high-risk behaviors suggests that impaired driving may be so tightly wedged into the behavior system that specific measures aimed at the elimination of DWI may be fruitless. Any change in DWI behavior may be countermanded by the pull of the other problem behaviors, all of which serve functional roles in the life of the individual. In order to eliminate impaired driving, at least among those drivers exhibiting a problem behavior syndrome, it may be necessary to persuade them to alter their lifestyles—no simple task. Rather than lifestyle change, perhaps the major focus should be early intervention. For example, educational activity on drinking, coping with stress, impaired driving, and risk taking should be conducted prior to the age when these problem behaviors usually appear among adolescents (i.e., ages 12–13). Such peer-led strategies have been successful in reducing smoking and drinking among adolescents (Perry, 1986).

Although our current knowledge of impaired driving is incomplete, efforts should be made to identify high-risk impaired drivers who are most likely to be involved in accidents. Prevention or rehabilitation programs should then be targeted to these high-risk drivers. Appropriate screening and rehabilitation programs similar to those now in operation in many parts of the world can reduce subsequent impaired driving (e.g., Nickel, Chapter 10, this volume; Siegal, 1985; Wells-Parker, Landrum, & Topping, Chapter 11, this volume) and have potential for reducing non-alcohol-related accidents as well. Programs based on sound psychometric measurement and effective rehabilitative counseling should be considered viable methods of driver improvement and control.

It is evident that much is known about the psychosocial characteristics underlying impaired driving. What had been lacking was a conceptual framework with which to synthesize our current knowledge in this area. Problem behavior theory lends itself well to the integration of this body of literature. The challenge that now faces researchers is to adopt the interactionist approach in general and PBT in particular in order to make predictions about impaired driving based on a constellation of variables drawn from its various systems. Furthermore, given that individual problem behaviors are embedded in a problem behavior structure, efforts should be made to predict the involvement of drivers in a variety of risky driving behaviors from the personality and perceived environment systems, as has been done by Jessor (1987b). Ultimately, PBT could be used to predict and explain risky lifestyles that incorporate not only driving behavior but also behavior in other domains, such as health and safety practices and criminal activity.

ACKNOWLEDGMENTS

The author gratefully acknowledges the comments of Brian Grant, Richard Jessor, and Evelyn Vingilis.

REFERENCES

Beck, K.H. (1983). Psychosocial patterns of alcohol abuse in a college population. *Journal of Alcohol and Drug Education, 28,* 64–72.

Beck, K.H., & Summons, T.G. (1985). Social context of drinking: DWI offenders and college students. In S. Kaye & G.W. Meier (Eds.), *Alcohol, drugs, and traffic safety: Proceedings of the Ninth International Conference on Alcohol, Drugs and Traffic Safety—San Juan, Puerto Rico 1983* (pp. 141–153). Washington, DC: National Highway Traffic Safety Administration, U.S. Department of Transportation.

Beirness, D.J., & Simpson, H.M. (1988). Lifestyle correlates of risky driving and accident involvement. *Alcohol, Drugs and Driving, 4* (3–4), 193–205.

Berger, D.E., & Snortum, J.R. (1986). A structural model of drinking and driving: Alcohol consumption, social norms and moral commitments. *Criminology, 24,* 139–153.

Biecheler-Fretel, M.B., & Danech-Pajouh, M. (1986, September). *Alcool, deplacements et insecurité routière chez les juenes automobilists: Resultats de l'enquete à domicile.* Paper presented at the International Symposium on Young Drivers' Alcohol and Drug Impairment, Amsterdam, the Netherlands.

Bowers, K.S. (1973). Situationism in psychology: An analysis and critique. *Psychological Review, 80,* 307–336.

Boyd, N.R., & Huffman, W.J. (1984). The relationship between emotional maturity and drinking-and-driving involvement among young adults. *Journal of Safety Research, 15,* 1–6.

Clay, M.L. (1974). *Characteristics of high risk drivers, alcoholic and otherwise* (Communication No. 304). Ann Arbor: Health Research Institute, University of Michigan.

Donovan, D.M., & Marlatt, G.A. (1982). Reasons for drinking among DWI arrestees. *Addictive Behaviors, 7,* 423–426.

Donovan, D.M., Marlatt, G.A., & Salzberg, P.M. (1983). Drinking behavior, personality factors and high-risk driving: A review and theoretical formulation. *Journal of Studies on Alcohol, 44,* 395–428.

Donovan, D.M., Queisser, H.R., Salzberg, P.M., & Umlauf, R.L. (1985). Intoxicated and bad drivers: Subgroups within the same population of high-risk men drivers. *Journal of Studies on Alcohol, 46,* 375–382.

Donovan, D.M., Queisser, H.R., Umlauf, P.M., & Salzberg, P.M. (1986). Personality subtypes among driving-while-intoxicated offenders: Follow-up of subsequent driving records. *Journal of Consulting and Clinical Psychology, 54,* 563–565.

Elliott, D.S. (1987). Self-reported DWI and the risk of alcohol/drug related accidents. *Alcohol, Drugs and Driving, 3,* 31–44.

Endler, N.S. (1981). Persons, situations and their interactions. In A.I. Rabin, J. Aronoff, A.M. Barclay, & R.A. Zucher (Eds.), *Further explorations in personality.* New York: Wiley.

Evans, L., Wasielewski, P., & Von Buseck, C.R. (1982). Compulsory seat belt usage and driver risk taking behavior. *Human Factors, 24,* 41–48.

Farrow, J.A. (1985). Drinking and driving behaviors of 16 to 19 year olds. *Journal of Studies on Alcohol, 46,* 369–374.

Farrow, J.A. (1986, September). *Adolescent drivers' analysis of dangerous driving situations involving alcohol: Comparison between DWI offenders, delinquents and high school drivers.* Paper presented at the International Symposium on Young Drivers' Alcohol and Drug Impairment, Amsterdam, the Netherlands.

Fishbein, M., & Ajzen, I. (1975). *Belief, attitude, intention and behavior: An introduction to theory and research.* Reading, MA: Addison-Wesley.

Goldfarb Consultants (1983). *Drinking and driving in Canada.* Toronto, Ontario, Canada: Insurance Bureau of Canada.

Guppy, A. (1986, September). *Drinking and driving in a sample of young English male drivers.* Paper presented at International Symposium on Young Drivers' Alcohol and Drug Impairment, Amsterdam, the Netherlands.

Homel, R. (1986). *Policing the drinking driver: Random breath-testing and the process of deterrence.* Report CR 42, Office of Road Safety, Australian Department of Transport, Canberra, Australia.

Hyman, M.M. (1968). The social characteristics of persons arrested for driving while intoxicated. *Quarterly Journal of Studies on Alcohol* (Suppl. 4), 138–177.

Irgens-Jensen, O. (1975). The relationship between self-reported drunken driving, alcohol consumption, and personality variables among Norwegian students. In S. Israelstam & S. Lambert (Eds.), *Alcohol, drugs and traffic safety* (pp. 159–168). Toronto, Ontario, Canada: Alcoholism and Drug Addiction Research Foundation.

Jessor, R. (1986, August). Summary comments presented at at the International Symposium on Dynamics of Social Change: Implications for Safety, Edmonton, Alberta, Canada.

Jessor, R. (1987a). Problem behavior theory, psychosocial development and adolescent problem drinking. *British Journal of Addiction, 82*, 331–342.

Jessor, R. (1987b). Risky driving and adolescent problem behavior: An extension of problem behavior theory. *Alcohol, Drugs and Driving, 3* (3–4), 1–11.

Jessor, R. (1987c). Unpublished data.

Jessor, R., & Jessor, S.L. (1977). *Problem behavior and psychosocial development: A longitudinal study of youth,* New York: Academic Press.

Jonah, B.A. (1986). Accident risk and risk-taking behavior among young drivers. *Accident Analysis and Prevention, 18*, 255–271.

Jonah, B.A., & Lawson, J.J. (1986). Safety belt use rates and user characteristics. In National Highway Traffic Safety Administration (Ed.), *Effectiveness of safety belt use laws: A multinational examination* (pp. 43–72). Washington, DC: U.S. Department of Transportation.

Jonah, B.A., & Wilson, R.J. (1986). *Impaired drivers who have never been caught: Are they different from convicted impaired drivers?* (Technical Paper Series, No. 860195). Warrendale, PA: Society of Automotive Engineers.

Lawson, J.J., Arora, H.A., Jonah, B.A., Krzyzewski, J.W., Smith, G.A., Stewart, D.E., & Hieatt, D.J. (1982). 1981 night-time surveys of drivers' alcohol use. In *Twenty-Sixth Annual Proceedings of the American Association for Automotive Medicine* (pp. 375–388). Arlington Heights, IL: American Association for Automotive Medicine.

Lawson, J.J., & Stewart, D.E. (1986). Alcohol in night-time driving by young drivers in Canada. In *Thirtieth Annual Proceedings of the American Association for Automotive Medicine* (pp. 45–53). Arlington Heights, IL: American Association for Automotive Medicine.

Lawson, J.J., & Stewart, D.E. (1988). Unpublished data.

Lewin, K. (1951). *Field theory in social science.* New York: Harper.

Lightsey, M.L., & Sweeney, M.E. (1985). Life problems experienced from drinking: Factors associated with level of problem drinking among youthful offenders. *Alcohol and Drug Education, 30*, 65–82.

Magnusson, D., & Endler, N.S. (1977). Interactional psychology: Present status and future prospects. In D. Magnusson & N.S. Endler (Eds.), *Personality at the crossroads: Current issues in interactional psychology.* Hillsdale, NJ: Erlbaum.

Maron, D.J., Telch, M.J., Killen, J.D., Vranizan, K.M., Saylor, K.E., & Robinson, T.N. (1986). Correlates of seat belt use by adolescents: Implications for health promotion. *Preventive Medicine, 15*, 614–623.

McGuire, F.L. (1980). "Heavy" and "light" drinking drivers as separate target groups for treatment. *American Journal of Drug and Alcohol Abuse, 7*, 101–107.

McLean, N.J., & Campbell, I.M. (1975). The drinking driver: A personality profile. In I. Johnston (Ed.) *Alcohol, drugs and traffic safety: Proceedings of Seventh International Conference on Alcohol, Drugs and Traffic Safety* (pp. 145–153). Melbourne, Australia: International Committee on Alcohol, Drugs and Traffic Safety.

Mercer, G.W. (1986). *Frequency, types and patterns of traffic convictions and frequency and type of traffic accidents.* Counterattack Program, Ministry of Attorney General of British Columbia, Victoria, British Columbia, Canada.

Moskowitz, H., Walker, J., & Gomberg, C. (1979). Characteristics of DWIs, alcoholics and controls. In *Proceedings of the 1979 NCA Alcohol and Traffic Safety Session.* Washington, DC: National Highway Traffic Safety Administration, U.S. Department of Transportation.

Norstrom, T. (1983). Law enforcement and alcohol consumption policy as countermeasures against drunken driving: Possibilities and limitations. *Accident Analysis and Prevention, 15,* 513–521.

Ontario Interministerial Committee on Drinking-Driving (1980). *The 1979 Ontario roadside BAC survey summary report.* Toronto, Ontario, Canada: Toronto Ministry of Transportation and Communications.

Perrine, M.W. (1975). The Vermont driver profile: A psychometric approach to early identification of potential high-risk drinking drivers. In S. Israelstam & S. Lambert (Eds.), *Alcohol, drugs and traffic safety: Proceedings of the Sixth International Conference on Alcohol, Drugs and Traffic Safety* (pp. 199–223). Toronto, Ontario, Canada: Addiction Research Foundation of Ontario.

Perry, C.L. (1986). Results of prevention programs with adolescents. In *Proceedings of the Fifteenth International Medical Advisory Conference,* Ottawa, Ontario, Canada: Medical Advisory Council.

Rokeach, M. (1979). *Understanding human values: Individual and societal.* New York: Free Press.

Selzer, M.L., & Barton, E. (1977). The drunken driver: A psychosocial study. *Drug and Alcohol Dependence, 2,* 239–253.

Selzer, M.L., Vinokur, A., & Wilson, T.D. (1977). A psychosocial comparison of drunken drivers and alcoholics. *Journal of Studies on Alcohol, 38,* 1294–1312.

Siegal, H.A. (1985). *Impact of driver intervention program on DWI recidivism and problem drinking.* Washington, DC: National Highway Traffic Safety Administration, U.S. Department of Transportation.

Skinner, A.A., Holt, S., Schuller, R., Roy, R., & Israel, Y. (1984). Identification of alcohol abuse using laboratory tests and a history of trauma. *Annals of International Medicine, 101,* 847–851.

Smith, G.A., Wolynetz, M.S., & Wiggins, T.R.I. (1976). *1974 national roadside survey: BAC of night-time Canadian drivers* (Technical Paper No. 1311). Ottawa, Ontario, Canada: Road Safety Directorate, Transport Canada.

Snowden, L.R., & Campbell, D.R. (1984). Reasons for drinking among problem drinker-drivers: Client and counselor reports during treatment. *Addictive Behaviors, 9,* 391–394.

Steer, R.A., Fine, E., & Scoles, P.E. (1979). Classification of men arrested for driving while intoxicated and treatment implications: A cluster-analysis study. *Journal of Studies on Alcohol, 40,* 222–229.

Stewart, D.E., & Lawson, J.J. (1987, June). *Results and inferences from the 1986 night-time surveys of drivers' alcohol use.* Paper presented at the Canadian Multidisciplinary Road Safety Conference, Calgary, Alberta, Canada.

Swisher, J.D. (1988). Problem-behavior theory and driving risk. *Alcohol, Drugs and Driving, 4,* 205–219.

Vayda, A., & Crespi, I. (1981). *Public acceptability of highway safety countermeasures* (Vol. 3) (DOT Publication No. HS-805-972). Washington, DC: National Highway Traffic Safety Administration, U.S. Department of Transportation.

Vingilis, E.R. (1983). Drinking drivers and alcoholics: Are they from the same population? In R.G. Smart, F. Glaser, Y. Israel, H. Kalant, R.E. Popham, & W. Schmidt (Eds.), *Research advances in alcohol and drug problems* (Vol. 7) (pp. 299–342). New York: Plenum.

Vingilis, E.R., & Mann, R.E. (1986). Towards an interactionist approach to drinking-driving behavior: Implications for prevention and research. *Health Education Research, 1,* 273–288.

Warren, R.A. (1986). Seat belt use and drinking and driving, *Canada Health Promotion Survey.* Ottawa, Ontario, Canada: Health and Welfare Canada.

Wechsler, H., Rohman, M., Kotch, J.B., & Idelson, R.K. (1984). Alcohol and other drug use and automobile safety: A survey of Boston-area teenagers. *Journal of School Health, 54,* 201–203.

Wilde, G.J.S. (1982). The theory of risk homeostasis: Implications for safety and health. *Risk Analysis, 2,* 209–225.

Williams, A.F., Lund, A.K., & Preusser, D.F. (1985). Driving behavior of licensed and unlicensed teenagers. *Journal of Public Health Policy, 6,* 379–393.

Wilson, R.J. (1984). *A national household survey on drinking and driving: Knowledge, attitudes and behavior of Canadians.* Ottawa: Road Safety Directorate, Transport Canada.

Wilson, R.J., & Jonah, B.A. (1985). Identifying impaired drivers among the general driving population. *Journal of Studies on Alcohol, 46,* 531–537.

Wilson, R.J., & Jonah, B.A. (1986, September). *Impaired drivers and high-risk drivers: Are they chips from the same block?* Paper presented at the Tenth International Conference on Alcohol, Drugs and Traffic Safety, Amsterdam, the Netherlands.

Wilson, R.J., & Jonah, B.A. (1988). The application of problem behavior theory to the understanding of risky driving, *Alcohol, Drugs and Driving,* 4 (3–4), 173–192.

Wilson, R.J., & Jonah, B.A. (1989, October). *The overlap and composition of the DWI and high risk driver populations.* Paper presented at the International Conference on Alcohol, Drugs and Traffic Safety, Chicago, IL.

Yoder, R.D. (1975). Prearrest behavior of persons convicted of driving while intoxicated. *Journal of Studies on Alcohol, 36,* 1573–1577.

Zelhart, P.F., Schurr, B.C., & Brown, P.A. (1975). The drinking driver: Identification of high-risk alcoholics. In S. Israelstam & S. Lambert (Eds.), *Alcohol, drugs and traffic safety: Proceedings of the Sixth International Conference on Alcohol, Drugs and Traffic Safety* (pp. 181–198). Toronto: Addiction Research Foundation of Ontario.

Zylman, R. (1975). Mass arrests for impaired driving may not prevent traffic deaths. In S. Israelstam & S. Lambert (Eds.), *Alcohol, drugs and traffic safety: Proceedings of the Sixth International Conference on Alcohol, Drugs and Traffic Safety* (pp. 225–237). Toronto: Addiction Research Foundation of Ontario.

3

ADOLESCENTS, DRINKING, AND DRIVING: WHO DOES IT AND WHY?

KNUT-INGE KLEPP
CHERYL L. PERRY

In spite of decades of research and educational and legislative efforts to prevent drinking and driving (DD), a large proportion of the population, including young people, continue to drive after drinking. Data from self-reported DD and from roadside surveys suggest that DD among youth is at epidemic proportions (Palmer & Tix, 1986; Williams, Lund, & Preusser, 1986). This practice is more common among males than females, it increases with increasing age (in the age group 15 to 24), and it increases with increasing alcohol consumption. A relatively large proportion of underaged, unlicensed drivers also report engaging in DD. Furthermore, riding with a drinking driver, drinking when riding in someone else's car, and drinking in a parked car seem to be highly prevalent by the time students enter high school (Atkin, Neuendorf, & McDermott, 1983; Wechsler, Rohman, Kotch, & Idelson, 1984).

Thus DD remains an important area of research, and one natural target group for this research is adolescents. Adolescents are overrepresented in alcohol-involved crashes, with associated morbidity and mortality. Adolescents are also in a developmental stage in which DD and related behaviors are initiated and solidified. It is therefore with this group that primary prevention and intervention can be focused. The most notable characteristic of adolescence is change. Whether one contrasts this time to the previous state of childhood or with that associated with entry to adult status, change in adolescence tends to be pervasive across multiple domains of personal and social development and to occur much more rapidly than in most other stages of

42

life. Thus change in adolescents is seen in the area of physical growth as well as in the cognitive processes, with the attainment of formal operational thinking. Change is also seen in social growth, when an adolescent shifts primary affiliations from parents and family toward peers, dating, and the establishment of a personal identity (Erikson, 1963; Havighurst, 1972).

Alcohol consumption, driving a motor vehicle, and driving after drinking are all behaviors that for the majority of people are initially explored and learned during adolescence. Furthermore, many of the psychosocial attributes believed to regulate the occurrence of DD—those associated with personal and environmental attributes such as values, attitudes, beliefs, self-concepts, norms, and expectations—are evident, acquired, or solidified during adolescence. While the hallmark of adolescence is change, the predictability and stability of this change should not be disregarded. It is on these more enduring and predictable characteristics of adolescence that prevention efforts regarding DD involvement can be based.

Despite the cost of DD in terms of morbidity and mortality among adolescents, an understanding of how this behavior is initiated and developed in adolescence is limited. With few exceptions (Beck, 1981), studies to identify factors associated with, or predictive of, DD lack a theoretical guidance and have not taken adolescent developmental stages into account (Klepp, Perry, & Jacobs, 1987). Psychosocial research on adolescent drug use has over the past decades shifted its focus from high-risk youth to drug use and its correlates in normal populations. A large number of factors have been identified as antecedents of the onset and development of drug use, factors that have been synthesized into etiological models that again have provided important guidance for prevention research (Bachman & O'Malley, 1984; Baumrind, 1985; Braucht, 1985; Flay, d'Avernas, Best, Kersell, & Ryan, 1983; Hawkins, Lishner, & Catalano, 1985; Huba & Bentler, 1980; Jessor & Jessor, 1977; Kandel & Yamaguchi, 1985; Perry & Murray, 1985).

In an attempt to extend this research approach to DD, a study was designed to investigate what factors predict DD among adolescents who are about to begin driving or who have recently begun to drive. Employing a theoretical framework modeled from problem behavior theory (Jessor & Jessor, 1977), this study assumed that both automobile driving and alcohol consumption are functional, meaningful, and purposeful behaviors for this population. Environmental (particularly perceived socioenvironmental), personality, and behavioral factors were explored in this study for their association with and predictability of DD. Specifically, the following hypothesis was tested: *Environmental, personality, and behavioral factors extrapolated from problem behavior theory predict DD, or the transition to DD behavior, among driving adolescents.*

In order to test this hypothesis, students from three senior high schools located in different suburban communities in the Minneapolis–St. Paul metropolitan area were asked to participate. Since the legal minimum driving age in Minnesota is 16, students in the transition years of age 15 to 17 were targeted. The opportunities for DD as well as the cultural norms and acceptance of DD in these primarily white, middle-class communities were assessed through an analysis of current legislation, media influences, and interviews with local police, teachers, and chemical-dependency counselors. Students' perceptions of traffic injuries and of DD were assessed through a series of focus groups before two larger questionnaire surveys were conducted with a cohort of students from the three high schools. The purpose of this chapter is to present the major findings of this study and to discuss their potential implications for future efforts in preventing DD among adolescents. Results from the questionnaire survey with high school students have previously been presented in more detail elsewhere (Klepp, 1987; Klepp et al., 1987).

ADOLESCENCE, ALCOHOL, AND THE AUTOMOBILE

When adolescent DD is analyzed as a public health problem, as was the perspective of this study, it is important to keep in mind that today's adolescents are socialized into a society with a relatively unrestricted opportunity structure for driving, drinking, and DD. Furthermore, American society conveys specific norms and values regarding these behaviors, factors that are important to analyze in order to understand why a large proportion of today's youth choose to drink and drive.

The importance of privately owned cars as a mean of transportation for the public, as well as the important economic role cars play in industrialized countries, is evident. In 1985 the private and commercial automobiles per capita ratio was 0.55 in the United States (Minnesota has one of the highest ratios in the country: 0.62) (U.S. Department of Transportation, 1986). However, from the very beginning, the car took on a symbolic value besides the practical one of providing transportation. This symbolic value served by the car is not only reflected in advertising but also in popular cultural expressions such as pop/rock music and movies. Over the decades, these media have generated many powerful images regarding youth and the automobile. In her paper "The Automobile as a Rite of Passage," Amo (1983) analyzes current pop/rock lyrics in terms of how cars, for many young males, are used as a symbol of: (1) acts of romance, love, and sexuality, (2) acts of courage and bravery, including confrontation with mortality, and (3) achievement of personal status. All three being motives which define the rites of passage, she concludes that "as a rite of passage, the modern car has no competition in modern America. Its importance is reflected everywhere" (p. 26).

In a 1959 report to the Minnesota legislature ("Safer Driving by Juveniles in Minnesota") the car was seen as a weapon of rebellion for young people—a reality not unlike the one portrayed in the movie "Rebel without a Cause" (1955), starring James Dean, who himself died in a car crash prior to the release of the movie.

> Undoubtedly many of the young drivers today who roar by in their "souped-up" jalopies, drag race down major highway, . . . play "chicken" in which two cars race towards each other head on until the nerve of one fails and he pulls aside, or drive with their backs to the wheel— many of these are seeking thrills. No doubt also many of them are reacting to the poverty of their emotional lives, to their sense of insecurity, unimportance, and inadequacy. For these youngsters the car is a weapon of rebellion. (Minnesota Commission on Juvenile Delinquency, Adult Crime and Corrections, 1959, p. 29).

In a recent review of the literature regarding driving, lifestyle, and youth, Rothe (1986) found that: (1) cars are a symbol of independence for teenagers, (2) cars are teenagers' symbol of equality with adults, and (3) cars represent increased status in relation to the opposite sex and are often an avenue for sexual experimentation.

Like the automobile, alcohol consumption has also provoked strong feelings (Moore & Gerstein, 1981). These are clearly reflected in the changing availability of alcohol, ranging from a period during which alcohol was easily available and drinking and drunkenness widely accepted as normal (dominating the 150-year colonial era of American history) to the era of Prohibition earlier this century (Moore & Gerstein, 1981). Today, alcohol consumption is well embedded in our culture and is often associated with positive and attractive events, such as parties, sport events, and other leisure-time activities. Even though society at large attempts to restrict alcohol consumption among underaged adolescents (minimum legal drinking ages currently range from 19 to 21 years in the United States), more than 90 percent of high school graduates report drinking alcohol at least once, and 50 to 60 percent have done so by ninth grade (Johnston, O'Malley, & Bachman, 1987).

The alcohol beverage industry is a multibillion dollar industry that, in the United States alone, spends approximately $2 billion a year on marketing (Mosher, 1986). A considerable amount of this advertising associates drinking with fun and games, sex, and popularity. There are overt connections of alcohol with manliness and "macho" sports heroes when targeting men (Malfetti, 1985), and with health and fitness when targeting women (Leiber, 1987). Alcohol advertising is now featured on youth-oriented rock TV stations (such as MTV), and alcohol companies regularly sponsor rock concerts and other events that have a high percentage of youth in their audiences (Mosher, 1986). Popular role models from sports and rock music are featured in advertisements for new types of alcohol products that are lighter and sweeter (e.g., wine coolers) and actively marketed as competitors in the soft-drink market (Mosher, 1986).

Not surprisingly then, alcohol use has been found to serve specific, important functions, which makes it attractive to adolescents. These functions include (1) acting as a mode for gaining independence from parental control, (2) creating a means of expressing opposition to adult authority and to conventional norms and values, (3) acting as a coping mechanism for dealing with personal problems, (4) creating a way of gaining acceptance from peers, (5) creating a means of expressing valued personal characteristics, such as being "experienced" or "cool," and, finally, (6) symbolizing maturity or adulthood (Jessor, 1984; Maddox & McCall, 1964).

Without attempting to give a complete analysis of the role and function of cars and alcohol in today's society, the above discussion suggests and exemplifies how cars and alcohol take on certain specific and similarly attractive functions. Furthermore, these functions are often conveyed in powerful images by popular role models within sports, rock/pop music groups, and movies. And finally, strong economic interest groups in today's society, such as the automobile and alcohol industries, have a vested interest in maintaining and reinforcing these images.

In spite of the functional similarities that alcohol consumption and driving hold for the adolescent, society perceives and approves of them in very different manners. While at 16 years of age most adolescents can legally drive in the United States, one must be 21 years of age to legally purchase and consume alcohol in most states. Even though adolescents report drinking some alcohol at home, most alcohol used by adolescents is being consumed without parental or adult control, supervision, or approval (Harford & Spiegler, 1982). This is where the car plays a large role, providing one of the few opportunities for adolescents to create their own private sphere where alcohol can be consumed without interference from adults. Adolescents report today, as they did 25 years ago, that the automobile is one of the places where alcohol is frequently consumed (Atkin et al., 1983; Maddox & McCall, 1964).

Thus, society at large strongly disapproves of DD among adolescents (as reflected in current legislation and health education campaigns). At the same time, the culture includes social–environmental factors that ascribe more positive functions to drinking and driving as well as DD. These functions may be perceived as highly valuable to adolescents. In order to better understand how adolescents themselves perceive the problem of DD and traffic crashes, it was decided to conduct a series of focus group discussions with high school students as part of this study.

STUDENTS' PERCEPTIONS OF DRINKING AND DRIVING

In order to obtain insights into adolescent's perceptions, beliefs, and language regarding DD and related behaviors, a series of focus group discussions were conducted with 9th- and 12th-graders ($N = 93$), at a fourth high school in the Minneapolis-St. Paul area, prior to the construction of the questionnaire used in the written survey.

The discussions were focused on the following questions: (1) To what extent do adolescents perceive DD as a problem in their community? (2) What are the reasons adolescents drink and drive? (3) In what situational context is DD most likely to occur? Attention was also given to the functional meaning ascribed to cars (driving and owning a car) and to which preventive measures the students perceived to be effective deterrents to DD.

Based on these focus group discussions, it seemed that cars, DD, and traffic crashes were topics that clearly engaged high school students. The younger students, who did not drive themselves, saw DD as normative behavior among older students (as did the older students themselves), and most of the 9th-graders reported having ridden with drunk drivers. The reasons given by students for DD varied from those that expressed a very positive viewpoint, such as seeing it as "cool, fun, or exciting to drink and drive," to very negative viewpoints portraying DD as a result of peer pressure, personal problems, lack of brains, and poor self-image. Another category of responses saw DD merely as a result of someone's needing to get home with no alternative transportation available. Finally, the discussions pointed out that students see parents and older siblings engaging in DD.

Situations in which students reported they drink and drive clustered around parties, weekends, and times when parents are away. Further, students reported a large variety of measures as effective deterrents of adolescent DD. These included most traditional (including punitive) and educational approaches already employed.

The focus group discussions strongly indicated that DD is a salient topic among high school students. Students who had not yet begun driving highly valued their future ability to drive and own a car. At the same time, these younger students had expectations concerning when and why older students did drink and drive, and they perceived that the majority of high school seniors did drive after drinking. Thus students in this age group who are not yet old enough to receive a driver's license seem an important target group for intervention programs designed to deter DD.

PREDICTING THE ONSET OF DRINKING AND DRIVING

In order to test whether the above psychosocial factors alluded to by school staff and students—as well as factors derived from previous theoretical work—actually were predictive of the onset of DD among adolescents, a questionnaire study was conducted with 10th- and 11th-graders at the three participating high schools. A baseline survey took place in spring of 1986 (April–May), and a follow-up survey was conducted 5 to 6 months later (September–October).

Problem behavior theory (Jessor & Jessor, 1977) was selected for this investigation because of its comprehensiveness and repeated predictability of adolescent behavior, especially behaviors such as alcohol and drug use, which are directly associated with DD (Donovan & Jessor, 1985; Donovan, Jessor, & Jessor, 1983; Hays, Stacy, & Dimatteo, 1987; Jessor & Jessor, 1977; Maron et al., 1986). Furthermore, the implications of problem behavior theory for use in preventive efforts are well demonstrated (Jessor, 1982, 1985; Perry & Jessor, 1985).

Theoretical Model

The model employed in this study was derived from the findings from the community analysis and focus group interviews presented above, as well as from problem behavior theory. Although a number of the theoretical factors included here were taken directly from the Jessors' work (Jessor & Jessor, 1977), none of the structures presented in this work are identical with those originally presented by problem behavior theory. The study presented here focuses primarily on factors proximal to DD. All factors included are presented in Figure 3.1. Distal factors included in the personality system take into consideration value placed on academic achievement (importance of doing well in school and of being perceived as a good student by teachers and peers) and on religion (importance of being able to attend religious services/programs and belief in God). Value placed on independence (importance of making independent decisions with respect to leisure-time activities, personal clothing, spending money, and planning for the future) refers primarily to independence from adult regulation and control. Tolerance of deviance (such as stealing, lying, doing damage to property, hitting another person, or staying out all night without permission) is an attitudinal variable, concerned with how "wrong" a person thinks each of these behaviors are. Finally, a measure of self-esteem (how well do you handle day-to-day problems in your life, important decisions, pressure to do things you don't want to do, and having to learn new required skills) was part of the distal personality structure.

The corresponding proximal DD factors included the value of driving and owning a car, tolerance of driving after drinking, and tolerance of riding with a driver who had been drinking. In both cases DD refers to driving after having at least three drinks of alcohol. Perceived risk of negative consequences from DD (ranging from getting caught by parents or police to causing a major accident) is a measure of outcome expectations. Self-efficacy variables included self-confidence with respect to avoiding driving home after too much to drink, self-confidence in preventing a drunk friend from driving, and perceived ability to drive after drinking (i.e., how many drinks you can have and still be a good driver). Finally, perceived functions of DD were included: risk-taking (people drink and drive because it is exciting, it impresses other people, it is fun, and they enjoy taking the

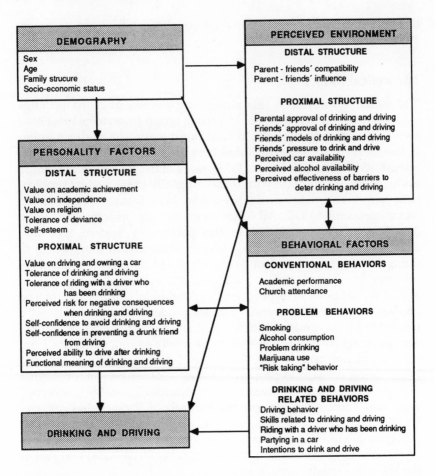

FIGURE 3.1. Factors influencing drinking and driving among adolescents.

risk), risk denial (people drink and drive because they think alcohol won't affect their driving, they think the chance of getting stopped by police is small, and they have poor judgment), and transportation (people drink and drive because it is the only way to get home and it is easier to drive than to find alternative transportation). Persons ascribing positive functions to DD were believed to exercise less control over engaging in it than those ascribing more negative functions to the behavior.

The variables in the distal structure of the environmental system included two factors: parent–friend compatibility (Are friends and parents in agreement with respect to things one personally thinks are important, about what kind of person one should become, and with respect to what one should get out of school?) and parent–friend influence (Whose opinion would a student value the most if he/she had a serious decision to make regarding what to do with one's health, or with regard to what is important to become or to do in life: that of his/her parents or of his/her friends?).

DD-specific factors included friends' approval and modeling of DD, as well as direct pressure from friends to drive after drinking. Similarly, parental approval or disapproval of DD were included. Finally, the opportunity structure and perceived barriers for DD were included. Car availability, alcohol availability, and whether or not parents – or friends' parents – provided alcohol at parties made up the opportunity structure for DD. Barriers included perceived effectiveness of punitive measures to deter DD (effectiveness of mandatory jail terms for drunk driving, tougher enforcement of laws, and suspension of driver's licenses of drunk drivers), perceived effectiveness of measures to reduce car and alcohol availability for adolescents (increased drinking age, higher tax on alcohol, and reduced sales hours, as well as increased driving age), and, finally, perceived effectiveness of "educational and alternative" approaches to deter DD (including educational programs, designated-driver programs, student–parent contracts, nonalcoholic alternatives at entertainment establishments, and improved public transportation).

According to problem behavior theory, behavioral factors can be organized into a conventional behavior structure, represented in this study by church attendance and grade-point average, and a problem behavior structure (behaviors considered by the larger society as inappropriate or undesirable for adolescents). The problem behavior structure in this study consists of alcohol consumption, smoking, and marijuana use, as well as a measure of "risk-taking" behavior (doing something dangerous just for the thrill of it or taking risks when driving in traffic because it makes driving more fun).

DD-related behaviors, including length of time students had had driver's licenses (driving experience), mileage and days driven in the past month, seat belt use, and number of traffic violation tickets were included. Behavioral skills related to avoiding DD situations consisted of identifying appropriate coping skills when a driver was drunk, deciding not to drive because of having had too much to drink, or asking someone else not to drive after drinking. Behavioral intentions to drink and drive in the future (next 6 months), riding with a drinking driver, "partying" in a car, driving after smoking marijuana, and being stopped by the police or arrested for DD were also included in the behavioral structure.

Finally, the following demographic factors were included as background factors: student's age and sex, socioeconomic status (parent's education and job category), and family structure (one- vs. two-parent families and siblings).

The dependent variable, DD, used in this study was a combined scale ranging from 1 for no DD to 6 for those who reported frequent DD. This scale, as well as all the independent variables included in the study, has been presented in detail elsewhere, along with the design and methods employed in this study (Klepp et al., 1987).

Results

Baseline Survey

A total of 1,700 students participated in the baseline survey in the spring of 1986. Eighty-three percent of these students reported driving a motor vehicle in the previous 3 months. Among these drivers, the prevalence of DD was 28%. Eighteen percent reported driving after having had at least two drinks several times in the previous 3 months. Among drivers who reported usually drinking two or more drinks on any one occasion, 45% reported DD at least once in the previous 3 months, and 13% reported driving several times after having had five drinks. Males reported drinking alcohol prior to driving more often than did females. Furthermore, on average, males had driven more days in the past month, reported drinking alcohol more frequently and in larger quantities, and were more likely to have partied in a car and to have driven after smoking marijuana than were females. Males and females did not differ with respect to riding with a drinking driver, having friends who did drink and drive, or reported marijuana use. Older students (17 year olds) reported more DD than did younger students (15 and 16 year olds).

In order to investigate what psychosocial factors were associated with reported DD in the cross-sectional baseline sample, a series of multiple linear regression analyses were conducted. Initially, variables within each theoretical construct with particularly high inter-correlations (> 0.40) were identified, and the variable pool was reduced in order to avoid synonymous variables. Furthermore, variables that highly correlated with and conceptually overlapped the dependent measure of DD were not used in the regression analysis (this included driving exposure, alcohol consumption, driving after smoking marijuana, and intentions to drink and drive in the near future). Results are presented in Table 3.1 for each structure; for the combination of personality and perceived environmental factors; and for the combined set, including variables from all the theoretical structures. Each regression model presented in this table refers to a theoretical structure presented in Figure 3.1. Only factors significantly (p < .05) associated with DD are presented. The regression models were developed using all drivers surveyed, including alcohol users and nonusers. As can be seen from the table, three factors from the personality structure—the perceived ability to drive after drinking alcohol, tolerance for riding with a driver who has been drinking, and lack of confidence in one's ability to decide whether or not to drive after having had too much to drink—were all highly associated with reported DD. These factors remained strongly and significantly associated with DD when controlling for perceived environmental, behavioral, and demographic factors.

Friends' influence on reported DD was expressed through friends' modeling, pressure for, and approval of DD, all factors significantly associated with DD within the perceived environment. In addition, perceived car and alcohol availability, perceived barriers to DD (punitive measures to deter DD), and parents' provision of alcohol at parties were factors associated with DD within the perceived environmental structure. When controlling for personality, behavioral, and demographic factors, perceived car availability and friends' modeling of DD significantly contributed to the explained variance of reported DD.

Factors in the behavioral structure were initially analyzed separately for conventional and problem behaviors and for DD-related behaviors. None of the conventional behaviors remained significant after controlling for marijuana use, risk-taking behavior, problem drinking, and money spent per week. Marijuana use, problem drinking, and risk-taking behavior remained significant when controlling for DD-related behaviors, and both marijuana use and problem drinking were included in the final combined regression model.

Of the factors directly related to DD, that of riding with a drinking driver was most strongly associated with reported DD. In addition, traffic tickets, seat belt use, deciding not to drive because of having had too much to drink, speeding, and identification of strategies to avoid DD were associated with DD. Riding with a drinking driver, traffic violation tickets, deciding not to drive because of too much to

TABLE 3.1. Multiple Regression of Demographic, Personality, Perceived Environment, and Behavioral Factors as Predictors of Drinking and Driving at Baseline

	B	SE B	R^2
Personality Factors			
Perceived ability to drive after drinking	.443****	.024	.32
Tolerance of riding with a driver who has been drinking	.200****	.025	.35
Self-confidence to avoid drinking and driving	−.109****	.023	.37
Perceived Environment			
Friends' modeling of drinking and driving	.195****	.028	.11
Friends' pressure to drink and drive	.144****	.026	.14
Perceived car availability	.184****	.025	.18
Punitive measures to deter drinking and driving	.147****	.026	.21
Friends' approval of drinking and driving	.129****	.027	.22
Parent providing alcohol at party	.089***	.026	.23
Alcohol availability	.082**	.027	.24
Personality and perceived environment factors combined			
Perceived ability to drive after drinking	.394****	.025	.33
Tolerance of riding with a driver who has been drinking	.165****	.025	.37
Friends' modeling of drinking and driving	.102****	.022	.41
Perceived car availability	.145****	.022	.41
Self-confidence to avoid drinking and driving	.098****	.023	.42
Friends' pressure to drink and drive	.077***	.022	.43
Parent providing alcohol at party	.059**	.022	.43
Behavioral Structure			
Conventional and problem behaviors			
Marijuana use	.251****	.027	.15
Risk-taking behavior	.231****	.027	.23
Problem drinking	.153****	.027	.25
Money spent per week	.105****	.026	.26
Drinking-and-driving-related behaviors			
Riding with a drinking driver	.411****	.028	.27
Traffic violation tickets	.133****	.025	.30
Seat belt use	.115****	.027	.32
Deciding not to drive because of too much to drink	.126****	.025	.33
Speeding	.062*	.025	.34
Identify strategies to avoid drinking and driving	.056*	.026	.34

(continued)

TABLE 3.1. *(Continued)*

	B	SE B	R^2
Combined behavioral structure			
Riding with a drinking driver	.311****	.030	.28
Marijuana use	.147****	.028	.31
Traffic violation tickets	.101****	.025	.33
Risk-taking behavior	.127****	.027	.35
Seat belt use	.101****	.026	.36
Problem drinking	.090****	.027	.37
Deciding not to drive because of too much to drink	.074**	.026	.37
Demographic Factors			
Age	.220****	.026	.05
Sex	.143***	.026	.07
Family structure	.097***	.026	.08
Combined Regression Model			
Perceived ability to drive after drinking	.251****	.028	.32
Riding with a drinking driver	.183****	.030	.41
Tolerance of riding with a drinking driver	.135****	.027	.43
Perceived car availability	.107****	.023	.44
Marijuana use	.118****	.026	.46
Age	.094****	.023	.47
Self-confidence in avoiding drinking and driving	−.082***	.025	.47
Deciding not to drive because of too much to drink	.061**	.023	.48
Family structure	.058**	.022	.48
Problems caused by alcohol use	.064**	.025	.49
Sex	.061**	.023	.49
Friends' modeling of drinking and driving	.051*	.025	.49

B = Standardized regression coefficient $^+$
SE B = Standard error of B
R^2 = Multiple R^2 at each step
*$p < 0.05$
**$p < 0.01$
***$p < 0.001$
****$p < 0.0001$
$^+$The standardized regression coefficient is computed by dividing the unstandardized regression coefficient by the ratio of the sample standard deviation of the dependent variable to the sample standard deviation of the regressor.

drink, and seat belt use remained significant within the overall behavioral structure, and the first three of these were included in the final combined regression model.

Finally, three demographic factors—age (older more than younger), sex (males more than females), and family structure (students from single-parent families more than those from two-parent families)— were significantly associated with DD, even when controlling for factors from the other theoretical structures.

Overall, factors from personality, perceived environmental, behavioral, and demographic structures combined to account for a total of 49% of the variance in reported DD among the students surveyed.

The combined regression model was used to calculate a DD psychosocial risk score for each of the driving students (this risk score ranged from 0.1 to 5.3, with a mean value of 1.7 ± 0.9). Ranking these DD risk scores by deciles, our study found more than a fourfold difference in mean reported DD between students in the lower decile and students in the upper decile. Furthermore, when DD was dichotomized into "never DD students" versus "DD students," we found 1% reported DD in the lowest decile and 93% in the highest decile.

The majority of students in the lowest deciles were females from two-parent households, with the average age being 16.5 years and the average grade-point average being at least a B. The majority of these students had not had any alcohol in the past 3 months; felt they could drink less than half a drink and still be a good driver; and agreed that it was very wrong to ride with a driver who had had at least three alcoholic drinks prior to driving. These students felt confident that they would not drive after drinking too much, and most of them knew only one or two other students who would drive after drinking. They were able to identify appropriate strategies to avoid DD, and they did not intend to drink and drive in the future. However, the majority of them thought it would be fairly easy to get alcohol if they wanted to; had access to cars; and, on the average, had driven about every other day in the previous month. Two-thirds of this group reported "nearly always" using seat belts when driving.

The students in the top decile differed strongly with respect to all variables. The majority were males, average age in the group was 17.0 years, almost 40% lived in families headed by a single parent, and the mean grade-point average in this group was low. This group had a high alcohol consumption rate (98% reported drinking at least five drinks on a single occasion), and half reported having experienced problems with parents, teachers, or friends as a result of drinking. A large majority in this group reported that they could be good drivers even after drinking at least four alcoholic drinks prior to driving. These students reported frequently riding with a drunk driver—which they did not perceive as being wrong—and they were accustomed to "partying in cars." They had low confidence in their own abilities to decide whether or not to drive after drinking, and the majority could not identify an appropriate strategy for avoiding DD. This group reported frequent use of marijuana, and the majority had driven after smoking marijuana in the past 6 months. Students in this group also reported knowing at least several students their own age who drove after drinking, and they thought it likely that they themselves would again drive after drinking. Finally, more than 40% of these students owned their own cars, and they had driven almost every day in the previous month.

Cohort Data

After conducting a follow-up survey, a cohort of 1,482 students was established. The baseline combined regression model was applied to the cohort sample both at baseline and at follow-up cross-sectionally (Klepp, 1987). In order to test the extent to which the developed psychosocial regression model was able to *predict* the onset of DD, the model was tested prospectively on a sample of 1,359 students who at follow-up reported that they had been driving a car during the past three months. Of the 12 factors included in this model, five (tolerance of riding with a drinking driver, friends' modeling of DD, deciding not to drive because of having had too much to drink, problem drinking, and family structure) were nonsignificant. The remaining seven variables accounted for 37% of the variance of DD at follow-up.

Intentions to drink and drive was excluded from the original baseline regression model (Table 3.1) because of its conceptual overlap with the dependent DD measure. However, for the purpose of investigating the onset of DD, it was decided to include this factor. The combined regression model for the cohort baseline sample, including intentions to drink and drive but excluding "deciding not to drive because of too much to drink" and "friends' modeling of DD" (both non-significant), is presented in Table 3.2. The regression function from this model (Table 3.2) was used to investigate onset of DD in the following section.

Calculating a baseline DD psychosocial risk score based on this combined cohort regression model (Table 3.2), this study found a mean reported DD at follow-up ranging from 1.0 in the lowest decile

TABLE 3.2. Baseline Combined Regression Model, Including Behavioral Intentions, Applied to Baseline Cohort Drivers

Combined regression model	B	SE B	R^2
Intentions to drink and drive	.208****	.027	.33
Perceived ability to drink and drive	.252****	.026	.44
Riding with a drinking driver	.100***	.027	.46
Perceived car availability	.221*	.023	.47
Tolerance of riding with a drinking driver	.072**	.024	.48
Age	.108****	.023	.49
Marijuana use	.075**	.024	.49
Sex	.067**	.022	.50
Problem drinking	.067**	.023	.50
Family structure	.045*	.021	.50
Self-confidence in avoiding drinking and driving	−.044*	.024	.51

B = Standardized regression coefficient [+]
SE B = Standard error of B
R^2 = Multiple R^2 at each step
*$p < 0.05$
**$p < 0.01$
***$p < 0.001$
****$p < 0.0001$
[+]The standardized regression coefficient is computed by dividing the unstandardized regression coefficient by the ratio of the sample standard deviation of the dependent variable to the sample standard deviation of the regressor.

of predicted DD to 3.9 in the upper decile. Furthermore, when dicothomizing DD into "never DD" versus "DD," only 3% reported DD in the lowest decile compared to 87% in the highest decile.

In order to investigate what factors predicted onset of DD, this study focussed on students who did not drive a car at baseline and on students who drove but reported no DD at baseline. Of the 1,350 driving students with complete data at follow-up, 150 did not drive at baseline and 884 reported no DD at baseline. Incidence rate of DD (i.e., new cases of DD) between baseline and follow-up was 13% among baseline nondrivers and 19% among non-DD drivers at baseline. When these students who reported no DD at baseline were ranked by decile, only 6% of those ranked in one of the four lowest deciles at baseline had been DD at follow-up. In contrast, 89% of those ranked in the highest decile had started to drink and drive. Twenty-seven percent of the students ranked in deciles 5–8 and 51% of the students ranked in decile 9 at baseline reported DD at follow-up. This indicates that the relative risk to begin DD for a student who at baseline classified in decile 10 is 14 times higher than that of a student classified in one of the four lowest deciles. As a large majority of the students were ranked in the lower deciles, it is of interest to note that the relative risk for students who at baseline classified in decile 5–8 were 4.5 times higher than for students classified in one of the four lowest deciles. (For a more detailed presentation and discussion of the results from this cohort-analysis, see Klepp, 1987.)

DISCUSSION

The reported study was designed to investigate factors predictive of DD among adolescents who had recently begun driving. It was hypothesized that environmental, personality, and behavioral factors extrapolated from problem behavior theory would be predictive of DD and of the transition to DD among driving adolescents.

The prevalence rate of DD among the students who drove at baseline was 28%. Males reported DD more frequently than did females, older students more frequently than younger students. Also, students who reported drinking more alcohol per drinking occasion drove more frequently after drinking. These findings are consistent with other prevalence estimates obtained from more representative samples of adolescents in the United States (Williams et al., 1986). Fourteen hundred and eighty-two students took part in both the baseline and the follow-up survey. The incidence rate of DD was 13% among the students who did not drive at baseline and 19% among the driving but non-DD students at baseline.

As predicted by problem behavior theory, perceived environmental, personality, and behavioral factors were able to account for a large proportion of the observed variance in reported DD. The combined psychosocial regression model developed for the 1,416 students driving at baseline accounted for approximately 50% of the variance in reported DD. This regression model (including intentions to drink and drive in the next 6 months) was able to predict the onset of DD among baseline non-DD students. Six percent of the baseline non-DD students in the lowest four deciles of the baseline DD psychosocial risk score actually reported DD at follow-up. In contrast, 27%, 51%, and 89% of the students who did not drink and drive at baseline, but who had a baseline DD psychosocial risk score in decile 5–8, decile 9, and in the top decile, respectively, reported DD at follow-up. The result of this prospective analysis of baseline non-DD students strongly indicates that the identified psychosocial variables precede, and are predictive of, the subsequent onset of DD.

The behavioral variables that were predictive of reported DD included (1) intentions to drink and drive, (2) experiences riding with a drinking driver, (3) having decided not to drive because of having had too much to drink, (4) marijuana use, and (5) having experienced problems with parents, friends, or schools because of drinking. Intentions to drink and drive have also previously been found to be a strong predictor of DD (Beck, 1981). Riding with a drinking driver shows direct experience in observance of the behavior in question. "Partying in a car" was highly correlated with riding with a drinking driver and was, for this reason, excluded from the multiple regression analyses. Both behaviors were highly prevalent among the young nondriving students at baseline, particularly among students who subsequently had begun DD. Since the actual probability of being in a traffic accident is fairly low, the observation of DD—either by friends or parents—without negative outcome may serve to reinforce the normative acceptance of DD. Deciding not to drive because of having had too much to drink was seen as an indicator of possessing skills to avoid DD. Therefore, it was predicted that a positive response to this factor would be associated with less DD. The opposite proved true, showing that students who drink and drive probably have the opportunity to do so frequently and, on some of the occasions, others will intervene and try to prevent DD. Little is known about when (in what situations and after how many drinks) other adolescents will intervene. We also do not know at what level of intoxication, if any, young drivers may decide not to drive because of having had too much to drink.

Students who experienced problems caused by alcohol and who used marijuana most frequently reported more DD. Driving after smoking marijuana was, as mentioned, highly associated with DD, but it was excluded from the multiple regression analyses because of its conceptual overlap with DD. Together, these factors form a picture of a behavioral syndrome in which students who drink more alcohol, smoke more marijuana, party in cars, and ride with drivers who have been drinking are those who are most prone to drink and drive as well as to drive after smoking marijuana. This syndrome has, to a large extent, developed prior to the students' reaching minimum driving age or obtaining a driver's license.

In the perceived environmental structure, car availability, friends' modeling, and pressure to drink and drive emerged as the most significant factors. While having access to automobiles is a necessary condition for enacting the behavior of DD, results from this study are consistent with previous findings showing that students who own a car are most likely to drink and drive (Williams et al., 1986). Friends' modeling of DD was strongly associated with male DD, but not with female DD. For females, it was direct pressure from friends that appeared as a factor associated with increased DD. More than 75% of all students in this study reported having at least one to two friends who drove after drinking. These friends provide powerful role models for DD, even among younger adolescents.

Because of the sensitive nature of the issue, we did not include questions regarding parental DD in this study. However, as seen from the focus group discussions, students see parents modeling DD. Parental modeling has proved to be strongly associated with other driving and health-related behaviors, such as seat belt use (Maron et al., 1986). Parents' and friends' approval of DD were both associated with DD, but not very strongly. These factors had low reliability, indicating that students do not really know what their friends and parents think about DD.

In the personality structure, the perceived ability to be a good driver after drinking, tolerance of riding with a drunk driver, and lack of self-confidence (efficacy) in avoiding DD situations emerged as powerful predictors of DD. Tolerance of DD, tolerance of driving after smoking marijuana, and estimated time of waiting before driving after having five drinks were not included in the regression analyses because of their high correlation with tolerance of DD and perceived ability to drive after drinking. All of these variables were strongly correlated with DD. Perceived ability to drive after drinking appears to be a particularly strong predictor of the onset of DD. These factors form a picture of an adolescent who is not only tolerant of DD but who thinks he/she could drive after drinking without serious consequences and rates his/her skills at avoiding DD as low. This adolescent is one who does not seem to acknowledge the risk associated with his/her DD and seems to be unable to avoid potential danger.

The functional meanings of DD as expressed through the focus group discussions were not seen as strong predictors of DD. This could be due to assessment problems, or it could indicate that DD itself does not represent important values or serve functions adolescents are pursuing. DD might be a "byproduct" of pursuing values represented both by alcohol and by owning and driving a car. If the latter is true, this would suggest that active risk taking is not the main reason that adolescents engage in DD. The fact that females feel pressured to drink and drive might suggest that their DD is a result of wanting to reduce risk: driving the drunk male home. Perceived risk associated with DD was associated with less DD involvement, but it did not emerge as a strong predictor.

Consistent with findings from previous research, we found that males reported more DD than did females. However, DD is not a male-only activity. The incidence data from the cohort actually show that more females than males began DD between baseline and follow-up (males who do drink and drive report to do so more frequently and after consuming more alcohol than females). Finally, family structure (single-parent versus two-parent families) was also predictive of DD, primarily among males, while socioeconomic status was not significantly associated with DD in this homogeneous student population.

Overall, students participating in the questionnaire surveys reported alcohol to be easily available, and those with driver's licenses reported easy access to cars, thus reducing the predictive power of these variables. In spite of this, car availability remained a strong predictor of DD, emphasizing the importance of parent–child contracts with respect to the use of cars. Regulating driving and car availability for young people through legislation might be both an effective measure in reducing adolescents' involvement in traffic crashes (Preusser, Williams, Zador, & Blomberg, 1984; Williams, Karpf, & Zador, 1983) and an acceptable measure to both parents and adolescents (Williams & Lund, 1986; Williams, Preusser, & Lund, 1984).

Recent literature reviews have demonstrated that current educational programs targeted at preventing DD among adolescents have not proven very successful (Grant & Plant, 1985; Mann, Vingilis, Leigh, Anglin, & Blefgen, 1986). By pointing to theoretical factors predictive of DD, the data from this study have several implications for strengthening such educational efforts to prevent DD among adolescents. First, in order to reduce the risk of traffic crashes, prevention efforts need to target the entire adolescent population. Although students in the upper two deciles of the DD psychosocial risk score account for most of the DD in this age group, DD, riding with a driver who has been drinking, and drinking in cars seem to be normative behavior in a large proportion of the adolescent population. Also, most adolescents are exposed to opportunities to drink and drive, and the prevalence of DD appears to increase rapidly with increasing age.

Second, it seems important to tailor traffic safety and drug-abuse prevention programs to students before they reach the legal driving age. By the time students can legally drive, they have already been exposed to DD through riding with drivers who have been drinking or by actually drinking in automobiles. Thus inappropriate and health-compromising behaviors are modeled and expectations for one's own behavior have already been created, as is indicated by the predictive power of intentions to drink and drive among nondrivers at baseline. The increase in the DD psychosocial risk score from baseline to follow-up, as well as the high incidence rate of DD over this time period, points to the need for intervention prior to driving onset. Since schools provide a natural setting for reaching adolescents in both high- and low-risk groups prior to the onset of the behavior, they should be widely utilized in prevention efforts.

Third, the personality attributes of those who are most prone to drink and drive seem to cluster around students' perceived ability to drive after drinking, tolerance of DD, and lack of self-efficacy with respect to avoidance of DD situations. This suggests that in prevention efforts, this perceived ability to drink and drive, as well as tolerance of DD, needs to be discouraged through emphasis on the consequences of DD – not only for the individual who may or may not be directly involved, but for society at large. Methods to alter the normative acceptance of DD should be considered. Alternative health-enhancing behaviors that help prevent the possibility of accidents, and that are practical and possible within the adolescent lifestyle, need to be constructed and reinforced.

Fourth, educational efforts should focus on providing skills that can help adolescents identify and avoid DD situations both as a driver and as a passenger. Such efforts should utilize peer influence to promote sober driving and model appropriate alternatives to both DD and to riding with a drunk driver. While males are most likely to drink and drive, females appear to face substantial pressure to drive after drinking and to ride with a drunk driver. It seems particularly critical that intervention methods provide females with skills they can use to be assertive in situations where they feel pressured to drive or ride after they or their friends have been drinking. It is important, however, that this training focus on young women's own need for self-protection rather than on creating the expectation that they are responsible for the behavior of young males. Both males and females should be taught skills to prevent friends from DD. In school-based, drug-abuse prevention programs, peer leaders have successfully been used as a major part of a strategy for teaching students social skills to resist the pressure to use drugs and to be assertive nonsmokers (Klepp, Halper & Perry, 1986). This strategy should also be explored in DD prevention programs.

Finally, any educational program designed to prevent DD needs to take into account the opportunities for and barriers to DD outside the immediate social environment, that is, in the society at large. Available transportation (including car availability for adolescents), alcohol availability, mass media (including movies, popular music lyrics, and advertising), and access to appropriate, legal places for young people to socialize and drink (or not drink) are all environmental factors affecting DD. Educational programs should help young people to identify these factors as well as to develop strategies to change the environment in order to enhance traffic safety and reduce the cost of DD. Environmental changes, such as the introduction of new legislation regarding alcohol availability, should be utilized as an opportunity to focus on how society at large provides an environmental setting that clearly has an impact on one's own behavior, including DD.

SUMMARY AND CONCLUSIONS

The findings from this study confirm that problem behavior theory provides a theoretical framework useful for organizing and identifying factors predictive of DD among adolescents. Personality, perceived environmental, behavioral, and demographic factors accounted for approximately 50% of the reported variance in DD at baseline among the students participating in this study. Based on the baseline data, this study was able to predict which students would begin to drink and drive within the following 5 months (relative risk of 14). DD appears to be part of a larger syndrome of DD-related behaviors, such as driving after smoking marijuana, riding with a drinking driver, and drinking in cars, as well as other "problem behaviors," such as alcohol and drug use.

Based on these data, it is recommended that school-based, peer-led educational prevention programs be designed that will target young adolescents prior to the age at which a driver's license is obtained. Furthermore, it is recommended that the programs be broad-based and consider DD within the larger context of DD-related behaviors (including use of other drugs and riding with drinking drivers) and traffic safety in general. A multifaceted approach that modifies the predictive factors identified in this study may not only reduce the prevalence of DD but may also enable adolescents to cope with other, related problem behaviors.

REFERENCES

Amo, P. (1983). The automobile as a rite of passage. Unpublished manuscript, University of Minnesota, Minneapolis.

Atkin, C.K., Nuendorf, K.B., & McDermott, S. (1983). The role of alcohol advertising in excessive and hazardous drinking. *Journal of Drug Education, 13*, 313–325.

Bachman, J.G., & O'Malley, P.M. (1984). The youth in transition project. In S.A. Mednick, M. Harway, & K.M. Finello (Eds.), *Handbook of longitudinal research: Vol. 2. Teenage and adult cohorts* (pp. 121–140). New York: Praeger.

Baumrind, D. (1985). Familial antecedents of adolescent drug use: A developmental perspective. In C.L. Jones & R.J. Battjes (Eds.), *Etiology of drug abuse: Implications for prevention* (Research Monograph No. 56) (pp. 13–44). Washington, DC: National Institute of Drug Abuse.

Beck, K.H. (1981). Driving while under the influence of alcohol: Relationship to attitudes and beliefs in a college population. *American Journal of Drug and Alcohol Abuse, 8*, 377–388.

Braucht, G.N. (1985). Problem drinking among adolescents: A review and analysis of psychosocial research. In *Special population issues (Alcohol and Health Monograph No. 4) (pp. 143–164). Washington, DC: National Institute of Drug Abuse.*

Donovan, J.E., & Jessor, R. (1985). Structure of problem behavior in adolescence and young adulthood. *Journal of Consulting and Clinical Psychology, 53*, 890–904.

Donovan, J.E., Jessor, R., & Jessor, S.L. (1983). Problem drinking in adolescence and young adulthood. A follow-up study. *Journal of Studies on Alcohol, 44*, 109–137.

Erikson, E.H. (1963). *Childhood and society* (rev. ed.). New York: Norton.

Flay, B.R., d'Avernas, J.R., Best, J.A., Kersell, M.W., & Ryan K.B. (1983). Cigarette smoking: Why young people do it and ways of preventing it. In P. McGrath & P. Firestone (Eds.), *Pediatric and adolescent behavioral medicine* (pp. 132–182). New York: Springer-Verlag.

Grant, M., & Plant, M. (1985). Alcohol, youth and traffic safety: Public policy—An international perspective. *Alcohol, Drugs, and Driving, 1*, 97–106.

Harford, T.C., & Spiegler, D.L. (1982). Environmental influences in adolescent drinking. In *Special populations issues (Alcohol and Health Monograph No. 4)* (pp. 167–193). Washington, DC: National Institute of Drug Abuse.

Havighurst, R.J. (1972). *Developmental tasks and education* (3rd ed.). New York: McKay.

Hawkins, J.D., Lishner, D., & Catalano, R.F. (1985). Childhood predictors and the prevention of adolescent substance abuse. In C.L. Jones & R.J. Battjes (Eds.), *Etiology of drug abuse: Implications for prevention* (Research Monograph No. 56) (pp. 75–126). Washington, DC: National Institute of Drug Abuse.

Hays, R.D., Stacy, A.W., & Dimatteo, M.R. (1987). Problem behavior theory and adolescent alcohol use. *Addictive Behaviors, 12*, 189–193.

Huba, G.J., & Bentler, P.M. (1980). The role of peer and adult models for drug taking at different stages in adolescence. *Journal of Youth and Adolescence, 9*, 449–465.

Jessor, R. (1982). Critical issues in research on adolescent health promotion. In T.J. Coates, A.C. Petersen, & C.L. Perry (Eds.), *Promoting adolescent health: A dialog on research and practice* (pp. 447–465). New York: Academic Press.

Jessor, R. (1984). Adolescent development and behavioral health. In J.D. Matarazzo, S.M. Weiss, J.A. Herd, N.E. Miller, & S.M. Weiss (Eds.), *Behavioral health: A handbook of health enhancement and disease prevention* (pp. 69–90). New York: Wiley.

Jessor, R. (1985). Bridging etiology and prevention in drug abuse research. In C.L. Jones & R.J. Battjes (Eds.), *Etiology of drug abuse: Implications for prevention* (Research Monograph No. 56) (pp. 257–269). Washington, DC: National Institute of Drug Abuse.

Jessor, R., & Jessor, S.L. (1977). *Problem behavior and psychosocial development: A longitudinal study of youth.* New York: Academic Press.

Johnston, L.D., O'Malley, P.M., & Bachman, J.G. (1987). National trends in drug use and related factors among American high school students and young adults, 1975–1986. Washington, DC: National Institute of Drug Abuse.

Kandel, D.B., & Yamaguchi, K. (1985). Developmental patterns of the use of legal, illegal, and medically prescribed psychotropic drugs from adolescence to young adulthood. In C.L. Jones & R.J. Battjes (Eds.), *Etiology of drug abuse: Implications for prevention* (Research Monograph No. 56) (pp. 193–235). Washington, DC: National Institute of Drug Abuse.

Klepp, K-I. (1987). *Onset and development of drinking and driving among adolescents.* Unpublished doctoral dissertation, University of Minnesota, Minneapolis.

Klepp, K.I., Halper, A., & Perry, C.L. (1986). The efficacy of peer leaders in drug abuse prevention. *Journal of School Health, 56,* 407–411.

Klepp, K.I. Perry, C.L., & Jacobs, D.R., Jr. (1987). Onset, development, and prevention of drinking and driving among adolescents. *European Journal of Psychology of Education, 2,* 421–441.

Leiber, L. (1987). She can have it all: Alcohol promotion targets women. *Bulletin on Alcohol Policy, 6,* 5–8.

Maddox, G.L., & McCall, B.C. (1964). *Drinking among teen-agers* (Monograph of the Rutgers Center of Alcohol Studies, No. 4). CT: College and University Press.

Malfetti, J.L. (1985). Public information and education sections of the report of the presidential commission on drunk driving: A critique and a discussion of research implications. *Accident Analysis and Prevention, 17,* 347–353.

Mann, R.E., Vingilis, E.R., Leigh, G., Anglin, L., & Blefgen, H. (1986). School-based programs for the prevention of DD: Issues and results. *Accident Analysis and Prevention, 18,* 325–337.

Maron, D.J., Telch, M.J., Killen, J.D., Vranizan, K.M., Saylor, K.E., & Robinson, T.N. (1986). Correlates of seat-belt use by adolescents: Implications for health promotion. *Preventive Medicine, 15,* 614–623.

Minnesota Commission on Juvenile Delinquency, Adult Crime and Corrections. (1959). Safer driving by juveniles in Minnesota. Report to the 1959 Legislature, St. Paul, Minnesota.

Moore, M.H., & Gerstein, D.R. (Eds). (1981). *Alcohol and public policy: Beyond the shadow of prohibition.* Washington, DC: National Academic Press.

Mosher, J.F. (1986). Alcohol policy: Focus on youth. *Bulletin on Alcohol Policy, 5,* 6–7.

Palmer, J.W., & Tix, P.E. (1986). Minnesota alcohol roadside survey. Results from 1986. St. Cloud, MN. St. Cloud State University.

Perry, C.L., & Jessor, R. (1985). The concept of health promotion and the prevention of adolescent drug abuse. *Health Education Quarterly, 12,* 169–184.

Perry, C.L., & Murray, D.M. (1985). The prevention of adolescent drug abuse: Implications from etiological, developmental, behavioral, and environmental models. *Journal of Primary Prevention, 6,* 31–52.

Preusser, D.F., Williams, A.F., Zador, P.L., & Blomberg, R.D. (1984). The effect of curfew laws on motor vehicle crashes. *Law and Policy, 6,* 115–128.

Rothe, J.P. (1986). British Columbia secondary students: Lifestyle and driving survey. North Vancouver, British Columbia, Canada. Traffic Safety Planning and Research Department, Insurance Corporation of British Columbia.

U.S. Department of Transportation, Federal Highway Administration. (1986). *Highway statistics 1985: 40th anniversary edition: 1945–85.* Washington, DC: Author.

Wechsler, H., Rohman, M., Kotch, J.B., & Idelson, R.K. (1984). Alcohol and other drug use and automobile safety: A survey of Boston-area teenagers. *Journal of School Health, 54,* 201–203.

Williams, A.F., Karpf, R.S., & Zador, P.L. (1983). Variations in minimum licensing age and fatal motor vehicle crashes. *American Journal of Public Health, 73,* 1401–1402.

Williams, A.F., & Lund, A.K. (1986). Adults' views of laws that limit teenagers' driving and access to alcohol. *Journal of Public Health Policy, 7,* 191–197.

Williams, A.F., Lund, A.K., & Preusser, D.F. (1986). Drinking and driving among high school students. *The International Journal of the Addictions, 21,* 643–655.

Williams, A.F., Preusser, D.F., & Lund, A.K. (1984). High school students' views of laws restricting teenage driving. *Journal of Public Health Policy, 5,* 387–395.

4

ALCOHOLISM, PROBLEM DRINKING, AND DRIVING WHILE IMPAIRED

BRENDA A. MILLER
MICHAEL WINDLE

This chapter reviews and discusses selected research related to the prevalence, correlates, and consequences of problem drinking and alcoholism among DWI offenders. Estimates of serious alcohol problems among drinking drivers vary widely, ranging from 4% to 87% (Bell, Warheit, Bell, & Sanders, 1978; Mozdzierz, Macchitelli, Planek, & Lottman, 1975; Vingilis, 1983). One of the reasons it is difficult to obtain an accurate estimate of the proportion of drinking drivers who have serious alcohol problems is that the definitions of alcoholism vary. The terms *alcoholism, alcohol dependence,* and *alcohol abuse* have all been used to identify serious alcohol problems that interfere with individuals' ability to interact within their personal and social environments. Most typically, these serious alcohol problems manifest themselves in the form of some combination of family, social interaction, legal, health, financial, and/or job problems.

Another reason that comparisons between studies are difficult is that there is great variation in the samples represented by the various studies. Samples have been drawn from roadside surveys and general driver populations, from crash and fatality victims, from arrested and convicted drinking drivers, and from alcoholic populations. Each of the samples may have different rates of serious alcohol problems. The influence of selection effects (e.g., biases associated with specific subsamples of a population) on prevalence estimates of problem drinking and alcoholism among these subsamples is unknown. Thus our estimates of serious alcohol problems within the drinking driving population are most often based on targeted populations that can be considered high-risk groups and, as such, represent a liberal estimate of the prevalence (Vingilis, 1983).

For example, using an alcohol impairment index based on quantity and frequency measures of alcohol consumption and behavioral measures of alcohol use with a sample of first-time DWI offenders, Fine, Scoles, and Mulligan (1975a) found that 50% of first-time offenders could be classified as beginning problematic drinkers, while 8% were considered to have serious drinking problems. Scoles, Fine, and Steer (1984) found that almost 50% of a sample of high-risk drivers (i.e., prior traffic violations and/or reckless driving charges) had alcohol problems. In a longitudinal study of drinking drivers, approximately half of the sample were found to be alcoholics on follow-up (McCord, 1984).

In addition to these concerns with the nonequivalent measurement of alcoholism across studies and sample variation, there are several other salient issues that merit careful attention when evaluating the prevalence of problem drinking and alcoholism among DWI samples. First, the drinking-and-driving population is a dynamic one, with new members continuously being added, some "old" members dropping out (e.g., through altered drinking patterns, altered drinking-and-driving behavior, injury, or death), and a large portion of the membership remaining legally unidentified for most or all of their lives. Thus the representation of DWI offenders in research studies may not be characteristic of the total drinking-and-driving population. Second, the size and characteristics of this population are greatly influenced by a range of social–legal–political events (e.g., changes in laws, federal funding contingency plans, historical-sociodemographic factors such as the age distribution at a given time period). These social–legal–political events may introduce variability into estimates of prevalence across states, regions, or historical time periods.

Despite these concerns, there are several issues that have been highlighted in the previous research and several areas that have been identified to direct future research efforts. In the first section of this chapter, several of the salient screening measures, categorical measurement approaches (e.g., DSM-III), and biochemical indices are reviewed and evaluated with respect to their diverse operationalizations of alcoholism and their relative differential sensitivity. In the second section, a review and evaluation of selective studies of antecedents and correlates of DWI behavior that are considered particularly relevant to the drinking driver with serious alcohol problems are provided. Specifically, research pertaining to personality characteristics and mental health indices among DWI offenders is considered. In the third section, public policy questions that need to be addressed with further research on the drinking driver with serious alcohol problems are identified. A recognition of the number of problem drinkers and alcoholics in DWI samples, and their associated personality characteristics and psychiatric conditions, may facilitate more heterogeneous etiological theories of drinking-and-driving behavior and may offer assistance in choosing from among the current diversified intervention strategies available, including educationally based approaches, alcoholism treatment, and/ or responses by the criminal justice system.

DETECTING SERIOUS ALCOHOL PROBLEMS IN A DRINKING-AND-DRIVING POPULATION

Screening and Diagnostic Instruments for Drinking Drivers

One of the most widely used screening instruments is the Michigan Alcoholism Screening Test (MAST), which was designed by Selzer (1971) to provide a consistent, quantifiable, structured interview instrument to detect alcoholism.[1] The instrument is easy to administer and relatively easy to score, although positive responses to some questions are differentially weighted. A score of 5 or more on the MAST is considered to be highly likely to indicate alcoholism. A score of 4 is considered borderline. This instrument is well known and has been used in a variety of different studies.

The validity of the MAST has been substantiated by comparisons with record data and other diagnostic tests (Selzer, 1971), and internal validity has been demonstrated, with most items adequately discriminating between problem and nonproblem drinkers (Zung & Charalampous, 1975). Additional studies have suggested that the MAST is both reliable and valid (Hedlund & Vieweg, 1984; Skinner & Sheu, 1982; Zung, 1979).[2] However, there is some concern that the MAST produces a high false positive rate of alcoholism (Brady, Foulks, Childress, & Pertschuk, 1982; Gibbs, 1983; Jacobson, 1983). To counter this concern, MAST scores that are higher than the current cutoff of 5 have been proposed. For example, scores in the range of 6 to 12 have been proposed as borderline scores (Jacobson, 1983).

However, most studies continue to use a score of 5 or more as an indicator of serious alcohol problems.

Studies that have used the MAST have reported a sizable percentage of drinking drivers scoring in the alcoholic range. For example, a study of drinking drivers convicted during the early 1970s in California revealed that nearly three-fourths (74%) scored in the alcoholic range of the MAST (Yoder & Moore, 1973). Assessing the percentage of problem drinkers referred for pretrial evaluation of possible alcohol problems in two samples, Zung and Charalampous (1975) reported 68% and 56% scoring as problem drinkers. More recently, a study of drinking drivers convicted in Washington state revealed that approximately half (48%) scored 5 or more on the MAST (Mischke & Venneri, 1987).

Another instrument that has been used to detect serious alcohol problems among drinking drivers is the Mortimer–Filkins (Court Procedures for Identifying Problem Drinkers Questionnaire and Interview), which distinguishes among social drinkers, presumptive problem drinkers, and problem drinkers (Kerlan, Mortimer, Mudge, & Filkins, 1971; Lower, Mortimer, & Filkins, 1971; Mortimer et al., 1971; Mudge, Kerlan, Post, Mortimer, & Filkins, 1971). The Mortimer–Filkins is a 58-item instrument that includes both an interview and a self-administered questionnaire. The instrument was empirically derived and contains questions that are relatively less transparent than those of the MAST. Questions are asked about drinking patterns and problems as well as areas that are not obviously related to drinking, such as health, occupation, family, and financial problems. The Mortimer–Filkins contains a drinking-problem scale score that is weighted positively and a neuroticism scale score that is weighted negatively in order to adjust for a tendency of individuals to endorse items indicative of maladjustment. Cutoff scores were lowered from the original cutoff scores to improve the discriminatory ability of the Mortimer–Filkins for drinking drivers as follows: 39 or less, social drinker; 40–49, presumptive evidence of problem drinker; 50 or more, problem drinker (Filkins, Mortimer, Post, & Chapman, 1973).[3]

The instrument has demonstrated an ability to provide reliable and valid data that distinguish between social drinkers and problem drinkers (Filkins et al., 1973; Mortimer, Filkins, & Lower, 1971). However, more recent studies have suggested slightly lower levels of reliability and validity than reported by the original authors (Mischke & Venneri, 1987).

Fewer studies have used the Mortimer–Filkins to assess the per-

centage of serious alcohol problems in a drinking-and-driving population. Using only the questionnaire component of the Mortimer–
Filkins (which is not recommended by the original authors), Mischke
and Venneri (1987) reported 41% of their sample of drinking drivers
were identified as within the categories of presumptive problem
drinkers or problem drinkers.

A major disadvantage of the Mortimer–Filkins is its length and
difficulty in scoring. Despite these practical limitations, we found that
the Mortimer–Filkins can be a fairly reliable predictor of a clinician's
decision to recommend treatment (Miller, Whitney, & Washousky,
1984), especially when used with other indicators, such as blood
alcohol concentration at the time of arrest and history of previous
drinking-and-driving offenses. However, the Mortimer–Filkins score
alone was most accurate at predicting the clinician's decisions when
the scores were clearly high (clearly in the problem drinker category).
When scores were in the mid to lower ranges, the Mortimer–Filkins
score was less predictive and of limited value in determining the
clinician's decision to recommend treatment. These borderline cases
are also the ones in which it is difficult to determine whether serious
alcohol problems exist with other screening instruments, such as the
MAST.

A comparison of the MAST and of the Mortimer–Filkins with
clinical assessments by alcoholism counselors suggests that the
MAST more closely mirrors the alcoholism counselors' assessments
regarding client involvement with alcohol (Mischke & Venneri, 1987).
In this study the MAST correlated better with the counselor decision
($r = 0.65$) than did the Mortimer–Filkins ($r = 0.46$). Further, for those
cases identified by the counselors as having significant alcohol
problems, the MAST identified 85% of the cases as compared to 65%
identified by the Mortimer–Filkins.

For cases that are determined to be positive on the MAST or
Mortimer–Filkins, clinical assessments of the seriousness of the
alcohol problems can be conducted to determine whether alcoholism
treatment is warranted. One of the more comprehensive assessments
that can be utilized by clinicians for this purpose is the DSM-III
(American Psychiatric Association, 1980) and the more recently
derived DSM-III-R (American Psychiatric Association, 1987). The
DSM classification system determines whether serious alcohol problems exist and will distinguish between alcohol dependence and
alcohol abuse. The DSM-III identifies four critical components for
determining alcohol abuse and alcohol dependence: pathological use,
impaired functioning, signs of tolerance, and signs of physical

dependence. Examples of pathological use include such behaviors as inability to cut down on drinking, binge drinking, blackouts, and drinking despite medical conditions that are known to be affected by drinking. Examples of impaired functioning include loss of job, legal difficulties, and arguments/difficulties with family due to drinking. Signs of tolerance are considered to be a need for larger quantities of alcohol to achieve the same effects or diminished effects experienced with the same amount of alcohol. Examples of signs of withdrawal include morning shakes relieved by drinking and delirium tremens due to cessation or reduction in drinking. Under DSM-III, Alcohol Abuse is determined by a pattern of pathological use and impaired functioning for at least 1 month and Alcohol Dependence is characterized by a pattern of either pathological use or impaired functioning coupled with signs of withdrawal or tolerance for at least 1 month.

In contrast, the DSM-III-R provides a diagnosis of Alcohol Dependence if at least three of the following nine criteria are present for at least 1 month (or recurrently): substance taken in larger amounts or longer than intended; persistent attempts to control use; much time spent obtaining, using, and recovering from use; frequent intoxication or withdrawal when either hazardous or during social/occupational obligations; activities given up or reduced due to use; continued use despite recurrent problems; marked tolerance; withdrawal symptoms; and use to relieve/avoid withdrawal (American Psychiatric Association, 1987). The DSM-III-R Alcohol Abuse diagnosis is a residual category for those who do not meet dependency criteria but exhibit symptoms based on the diagnostic criteria.

In our previous research, we have used the DSM-III diagnostic criteria to identify serious alcohol problems for a sample of 461 drinking drivers referred to an alcoholism treatment center for evaluation of their alcohol problems. We found that 90% reported at least one symptom of impaired functioning, 80% reported at least one symptom of pathological use, and 19% reported a symptom of alcohol withdrawal (Miller, Whitney, & Washousky, 1986). (Tolerance was not assessed in the study due to the difficulty in obtaining appropriate measures of tolerance.) Using these three essential features to determine a diagnosis according to the DSM-III, we determined that 54% of the sample could be diagnosed in the Alcohol Abuse category and 19% could be diagnosed in the Alcohol Dependence category (Miller, Whitney, & Washousky, 1986). Because measures of tolerance were not assessed, this represented a conservative estimate of Alcohol Dependence. However, the sample was drawn from individuals referred for additional evaluation, and, therefore, they represented a portion of the drinking-and-driving population that was more likely to have serious alcohol problems. In addition, approximately two-thirds of the sample had a prior arrest, indicating serious involvement in drinking-and-driving behavior. When this same sample was examined using the DSM-III-R criteria for Alcohol Abuse and Alcohol Dependence, half (51%) of the sample was diagnosed in the Alcohol Dependence category and nearly half (46%) was diagnosed in the Alcohol Abuse category (Wieczorek, Nochajski, Miller, & Whitney, 1989). Only 4% did not have a diagnosis of Alcohol Abuse or Alcohol Dependence. This suggests that the DSM-III-R categorizes individuals more frequently in the most severe category, Alcohol Dependence.

Quantity–Frequency Measures for Drinking Drivers

There is no specific quantity of alcohol that must be consumed in order for an individual to be identified as suffering from serious alcohol problems.[4] Heavy alcohol consumption is often an element of an alcoholism screening test, but the average daily consumption level alone does not provide sufficient information. There is a correlation between average daily consumption levels and development of serious alcohol problems. Typical alcohol consumption patterns of individuals admitted to inpatient facilities reveal high average daily consumption patterns prior to admission to treatment. A study of New York State alcoholism program inpatients revealed an average intake of approximately 11 ounces of absolute alcohol per day in the 30 days prior to treatment (Welte, Hynes, Sokolow, & Lyons, 1979). Drinking drivers have been found to be heavy consumers of alcohol not only at the time of the arrest but also over sustained periods of time (McCord, 1984; Miller et al., 1986; Wilson & Jonah, 1985). Quantity–frequency measures of alcohol consumption have also been found to correlate well with the specific behaviors relevant to studies on drinking and driving. Nationwide survey data revealed that males who have more than 120 drinks per month report social consequences of drinking, such as contacts with police, auto accidents, or other accidents involving injuries or property damage, 20 times more frequently than males who have two to ten drinks per month (Clark & Midanik, 1982).

Alcohol consumption levels are also correlated with diagnostic categories of the DSM-III and DSM-III-R. From our study of 461 drinking drivers assessed for alcoholism treatment, we found that the following three measures of alcohol consumption differed significantly for the Alcohol Dependence and Alcohol Abuse groups and those undiagnosed by the DSM-III: average ounces of alcohol consumed per drinking occasion, average ounces of alcohol consumed per day, and ounces of alcohol consumed at the time of arrest (Miller et al., 1986). For all three measures, the Alcohol Dependence group had the highest consumption levels, followed by the Alcohol Abuse group. The lowest consumption levels were reported by the undiagnosed group.

The use of quantity–frequency measures for assessing alcohol problems among drinking drivers has serious limitations. While level of intake is correlated with alcohol problems, it is not a good indicator by itself. Conceptually there is a problem with trying to use amount of alcohol to assess drinking problems. No single alcohol consumption level establishes a boundary between the social drinker and the drinker with serious alcohol problems. Some individuals, for instance, consume large quantities of alcohol on a regular basis but do not develop serious alcohol problems. In contrast, some individuals who consume moderate levels of alcohol have serious alcohol problems necessitating treatment. Further, there are concerns about underreporting of alcohol consumption with the use of self-reports (Fuller, Lee, & Gordis, 1988).

Despite these limitations, the use of quantity–frequency measures can contribute to our ability to distinguish among drinking drivers and provide a useful categorization of drinking drivers for analytical purposes. Quantity–frequency measures provide useful ways of grouping drinking drivers with serious problems and of characterizing drinking patterns that are useful in treatment approaches. For example, using a group of first-time drinking-and-driving offenders in Philadelphia, Fine, Scoles, and Mulligan (1975b) found three groups of drinking drivers based on drinking styles. Group one drank one or two times per week, imbibing less than six shots of whiskey or the equivalent in wine or beer. They drank in social settings with others and rarely alone. Drinking in excess occurred one or two times per month. This group constituted 46% of the drinking-and-driving population. Group two, which constituted 48% of the first-time offenders, drank two to six times weekly, imbibing a minimum of two pints of liquor or the equivalent in wine or beer. At least one of the following problem behaviors was noted: "high" up to ten times a month; long periods of continuous drinking (more than 6 hours); drinking upon awakening; blackouts; "nervous" disorders; missing meals; drinking during work; alcohol-related arrest not involving driving. The third group, which accounted for 6% of the first-time drinking-and-driving offenders, drank daily, imbibing three or more pints of liquor or the equivalent in wine or beer, and had one or more of the following alcohol-related problems: "high" ten or more times a month; drinking sessions of 12 hours or longer; many blackouts, many missed meals; tremors, agitation, and confusion; excessive perspiration; delirium tremens. These categories facilitate the development of a more comprehensive understanding of drinking drivers as a heterogeneous group. These different typologies of drinking drivers may facilitate development of different treatment modalities and allow matching of clients with treatment (see Wells-Parker, Landrum, and Topping, Chapter 11, this volume).

A recent study conducted with a sample drawn randomly from households in Canada revealed that individuals who reported drinking and driving when ability was impaired were also more likely to report higher consumption levels during their last drinking occasion (Wilson & Jonah, 1985). Further, the number of drinks in the past 7 days was one of the best predictors of frequency of driving after drinking during the past 30 days. Another good reason for assessing drinking drivers' quantity and frequency of alcohol use is the ability to compare their consumption levels with general population studies.

Compared to general populations, convicted drinking drivers are heavy drinkers. For example, Cahalan (1970) found that 12% of the adult population of the United States are classified as "heavy drinkers," defined as persons who consume as much as five or more drinks nearly every day. In contrast, Fine et al. (1975b) reported that 54% of the convicted drinking drivers in their sample can be classified as heavy drinkers. These studies help to distinguish the problem drinker from the social drinker arrested for drinking-and-driving for both the public and policy makers.

Self-Reports of Alcoholism Problems versus Objective Measures

Virtually all of the screening and diagnostic measures rely on the accuracy of individual self-reporting. Self-report questions that ask individuals whether they consider themselves to have a problem with alcohol that warrants treatment differ from self-reports of whether different types of alcohol problems exist for an individual. The latter form the basis of both screening and diagnostic tests for alcohol problems. Simply asking individuals whether they think they have alcohol problems warranting treatment is probably the least reliable method of ascertaining the problem, since admission of problems beyond the drinking-and-driving arrest incident will probably result in additional licensing consequences. Further, alcoholic denial is considered a prominent part of the alcoholic's disorder and is frequently addressed in treatment. An even larger problem can exist in the differing definitions as to what constitutes having a problem with alcohol.

Despite the tendency for individuals to downplay the severity of their drinking problems, there is evidence that a proportion of drinking drivers will report problems sufficient to characterize themselves as having an alcohol problem. In one study of male drinking drivers who attended an alcohol education program, one quarter stated that they thought they had an alcohol problem (Donovan & Marlatt, 1982). Some studies have also made comparisons by asking DWI offenders whether they think they have a drinking problem and comparing the problem rate with those derived from a standardized measure such as the MAST. Yoder and Moore (1973) reported that 26% of first-time offenders thought they had a drinking problem as opposed to the 69% whose MAST scores indicated a drinking problem. A similar increase in detection of drinking problems occurs for repeat DWI offenders; 87% of them scored on the MAST as having a drinking problem compared to the 48% who thought they had a drinking problem (Yoder & Moore, 1973).

Due to the underreporting of alcohol consumption and the problems with screening questions that are transparent, there has been increasing interest in the use of biochemical markers. If a single test or group of tests could be found to identify heavy alcohol consumption, there would be outside validation of self-report consumption measures. Another rationale for the development of biochemical blood markers is that they may facilitate positive treatment outcomes. The physical evidence that drinking affects one's health may result in an increased incentive for individuals to address their alcohol problems.

To date, the biochemical markers most widely investigated are blood tests that screen for liver, nutritional, and other blood abnormalities that are possibly due to heavy alcohol use (Chan, 1990; Eichner & Hellman, 1971; Skude & Wadstein, 1977; Wu, Chanarin, & Levi, 1974). Multiple biochemical tests used to form multivariate composite indices have been proposed to increase the discriminatory ability of blood parameters as a screening device (Dolinsky & Schnitt, 1988; Ryback, Eckardt, Felsher, & Rawlings, 1982; Ryback, Eckardt, Rawlings, & Rosenthal, 1982). To date, most studies on biochemical markers have not focused on drinking drivers. However, in our study of 461 drinking drivers referred to an alcoholism clinic, we found significant differences in some blood tests (i.e., blood urea nitrogen, SGOT, and SGPT) between drinking drivers recommended for treatment and those not recommended for treatment (Miller et al., 1984). Further work needs to be completed to determine how sensitive biochemical markers are for identifying drinking patterns that may characterize the drinking driver with serious alcohol problems. For instance, does heavy consumption of alcohol on weekends (a pattern of consumption typical among drinking drivers) produce significant changes in blood parameters, or is heavy daily consumption necessary to produce changes in the blood biochemistry?

There have been numerous attempts to use blood alcohol concentration (BAC) as a means of determining the extent of the alcohol problems for drinking drivers (National Council on Alcoholism Criteria Committee, 1972). For example, the Grand Rapids study revealed that the BAC was related to both drinking problems and patterns of consumption (Borkenstein, Crowther, Shumate, Ziel, & Zylman, 1974). Fine, Steer, and Scoles (1978) also found BAC correlated with self-reported alcohol problems. Our studies have indicated that the BAC levels for individuals recommended for alcoholism treatment by clinicians are significantly higher as compared to those not recommended for treatment (0.204% vs. 0.177%) (Miller et al., 1984). These results no doubt reflect the use of BAC levels by clinicians in making decisions about who needs alcoholism treatment. Other researchers have indicated that BAC levels on arrest have not correlated well with other assessment measures of drinking problems and should be considered as only one piece of evidence (Forman & Florenzano, 1978–1979; McGuire, 1980).

To summarize, screening and diagnostic tests have been developed that identify serious alcohol problems in drinking drivers. Questions on these instruments include obvious indicators of alcohol problems. Efforts have been made to develop tests that measure physical indicators of serious alcohol problems, such as blood tests indicating liver abnormalities. These tests are more expensive and more difficult to administer than screening and diagnostic tests. Further, even if a blood test could be developed that would adequately screen for serious alcohol problems, there would still be a need for interview and/or questionnaire instruments that could provide more extensive information about these serious alcohol problems. Such information would allow more appropriate matching of clients to treatment modalities. In addition, self-report information is needed to develop a better perspective on the heterogeneity among drinking drivers with serious alcohol problems.

SIMILARITIES BETWEEN PERSONALITY AND MENTAL HEALTH CHARACTERISTICS OF DWI OFFENDERS AND ALCOHOL ABUSERS

Sociodemographic characteristics and psychosocial attributes have been found to differentiate DWI offenders from the general population (e.g., Filkins, 1970; Mozdzierz et al., 1975; Selzer, Vinokur, & Wilson, 1977). The personality and mental health characteristics of drinking-and-driving offenders are of importance in our attempt to understand the dynamics of how serious alcohol problems emerge in this population. Prior research with samples of DWI offenders and alcoholics has found significant associations between personality and mental health functioning and serious alcohol problems (e.g., Donovan, Marlatt, & Salzberg, 1983; Mozdzierz et al., 1975). Our focus is limited to two domains of personality and mental health, namely criminal and deviant behaviors and depressed affect. These two domains currently are the most widely researched within the DWI literature and therefore provide the most adequate database for evaluating influences on, and relationships with, serious alcohol problems.

Prior to discussing research related to personality and mental health characteristics of DWI offenders, it may be useful to consider briefly the ways in which these characteristics may be influential in the drinking-and-driving behavioral cycle. It is widely recognized that not all individuals who drink and drive, do so dangerously. Personality attributes and mental health status often have been viewed as predisposing factors that may moderate the relationship between drinking and hazardous, or dangerous, driving (e.g., Donovan & Marlatt, 1982; Noyes, 1985). We propose that personality attributes and mental health characteristics may influence drinking-and-driving behavior in four ways (though these ways are not exhaustive). First, some personality characteristics (e.g., sensation seeking, poor inhibitory control, deviance proneness) may influence unsafe driving practices whether the driver is drinking or not; drinking behavior may exacerbate the expression of these response tendencies while driving. Second, some personality characteristics (e.g., sensation seeking) may influence drinking locations (e.g., bars) and time of day of drinking and driving, which may, in turn, influence consumption patterns and peak hours of risk for automobile accidents. Third, some personality characteristics (e.g., poor inhibitory control, impulsivity) may influence features of drinking behavior, such as knowing when to quit drinking or when to seek help with driving because of excess consumption. Fourth, some personality characteristics (e.g., aggression, hostility) may be influential in the occurrence of stressful life events (e.g., fights, arguments with spouse or family members), which may, in turn, be associated with escalated drinking and reckless driving (e.g., Noyes, 1985; Selzer, Rogers, & Kern, 1968; Selzer & Vinokur, 1974). As the subsequent research is discussed, it is of importance to bear in mind the four ways enumerated here that may influence drinking and dangerous driving behaviors.

Criminal and Deviant Behaviors among DWI Offenders

A number of research studies have provided converging evidence that features of antisocial behavior, such as aggression, hostility, impulsivity, behavioral deviance, and recklessness, characterize many DWI offenders (e.g., Clay, 1972; Donovan, 1980; Filkins, 1970; McGuire, 1976; Mozdzierz et al., 1975). In a comparison of DWI offenders, registered drivers, and high-risk drivers (i.e., drivers with prior traffic violations but no DWI offenses), Donovan (1980) reported that DWI offenders and high-risk drivers differed significantly from registered drivers and were similar to each other in levels of assaultiveness, verbal hostility, covert hostility, and overt hostility. Selzer and colleagues (1977) found that alcoholics scored more aggressively on aggressive-hostility scales than either DWI offenders or registered drivers. However, DWI offenders scored higher than the general drivers. Mozdzierz and colleagues (1975) investigated differences in personality functioning between alcoholics with a high rate of traffic accidents and violations and those with a low rate. On the basis of the Guilford–Zimmerman Temperament Survey and the Minnesota Multiphasic Personality Inventory (MMPI), Mozdzierz et al. concluded that the group with high rates of traffic accidents and violations were more impulsive, reckless, irresponsible, manipulative, and controlling of others. Sutker, Brantley, and Allain (1980) also used the MMPI to study personality profiles of 500 males arrested for DWI. One of the two primary profiles was characterized by elevated social deviance among a group of heavy drinkers; a second primary profile of heavy drinkers was characterized by elevations in pessimism and depressed affect.

Comparative studies between drinking drivers and alcoholics suggest that the drinking drivers fall between social drinkers, who have few if any problems while drinking, and alcoholics in treatment, who report many drinking-related problems. In a comparative study of drinking drivers and alcoholics, drinking drivers were less likely to report job threatened due to their drinking (2% vs. 14%), spouse threatened to leave due to drinking in past year (4% vs. 26%), attempts to quit drinking (30% vs. 70%), attending Alcoholics Anonymous (5% vs. 56%), defining self as problem drinker (22% vs 82%), or warned by physician that drinking was harming health (2% vs 22%) (Bell et al., 1978).

In one of the few longitudinal studies related to childhood and adolescent antecedents of adult DWI offenders, McCord (1984) investigated differences in aggression and antisocial behavior between men eventually convicted of DWI offenses and men from the same neighborhood who did not become DWI offenders. The fact that both samples were from the same neighborhood excluded, or minimized to some extent, alternative explanations (e.g., socioeconomic status) for observed differences between the two groups. The sample included 36 convicted DWI male offenders and 430 men not convicted of DWI. Results indicated that the convicted DWI offenders were more likely than the nonoffenders to (1) have been convicted for serious crimes against persons and property; (2) be alcoholic; (3) have had greater exposure to parental conflict and aggression; and (4) have gotten into trouble in adulthood through drinking and the physical expression of anger. Thus the findings of this longitudinal study of men suggest distinctly different developmental pathways for eventually convicted DWI offender and nonoffender groups, with DWI offenders manifesting a history of exposure to and engagement in aggressive and more severe antisocial behaviors and higher rates of alcoholism and alcohol-related problems.

Using the psychiatric diagnostic criteria of DSM-II, Finch and Smith (1970) reported that 24% of a sample of drivers involved in fatal accidents exhibited antisocial personality disorders. In addition, a large portion of these persons with antisocial personality disorders were problem drinkers or alcoholics. In a separate study, Argeriou, McCarty, and Blacker (1985) analyzed the criminal records of 1,406 randomly selected DWI offenders in Massachusetts. Consistent with other research (e.g., Waller, 1967; Yoder & Moore, 1973; Zelhart, Schurr, & Brown, 1975), previous criminal arrests were highly characteristic of the DWI offenders. More than 75% of these 1,406 DWI offenders had been arraigned for one or more criminal offenses, and more than 50% had been arraigned for criminal offenses other than or in addition to DWI and traffic offenses. Further, among DWI recidivists, 68% had prior criminal arrests.

Other psychological indicators found to be more prevalent in DWI populations as compared to general driving populations include higher sensation seeking; poorer emotional adjustment; external locus of control; lower self-esteem; and higher levels of depression, suicide, and paranoia (e.g., Donovan, 1980; Selzer & Barton, 1977). Whether there is an accident at the time of the drinking-and-driving arrest may be related to the negative affect of the individual at the time. Steer, Fine, and Scoles (1979) reported that the combination of depression plus hostility plus high BAC is associated with higher rates of automobile accidents.

Evidence is thus accumulating that suggests that a spectrum of impulsive, aggressive, hostile personality attributes, high levels of antisocial behaviors, and multiple criminal acts characterize a significant segment of both the DWI offender population and alcoholics. Problem drinking and alcoholism are quite common among these DWI offenders, and heavy alcohol consumption is frequently involved in transgressions against persons and property. Additionally, as noted previously, these response dispositions and behavioral styles, exacerbated by heavy drinking, are likely to foster negative interactional cycles with significant others (e.g., spouse) and legal authorities, increase stress levels, and reduce social supports. In turn, fostering of this negative feedback may contribute to escalating levels of aggression, hostility, and drinking and driving.

Depressed Affect among DWI Offenders

In addition to the more externalizing behaviors evinced by some DWI offenders, internalizing behaviors (e.g., low self-esteem, depression, alienation) have also been reported to be elevated among some DWI offenders (e.g., Donovan & Marlatt, 1982; Donovan, Queisser, Umlauf, & Salzberg, 1986; Meck & Baither, 1980; Selzer et al., 1977). Many studies also report similar problems among alcoholics (e.g., Mozdzierz et al., 1975; Selzer et al., 1977). Several researchers have proposed that drinking and driving often reflects a depressive reaction to, or an attempt to cope with, stressful life events (e.g., Donovan, 1980; Finch & Smith, 1970; Fine et al., 1975b; Selzer et al., 1977). Selzer and colleagues (1968) reported that 20% of a sample of 96 drivers involved in fatal accidents had been engaged in some sort of stressful experience (e.g., interpersonal, vocational, or financial conflict) within the 6 hours preceding the fatal accident. A large number of these drivers were problem drinkers or alcoholics. Selzer and Vinokur (1974) examined the interrelations between traffic accidents and stressful life events for samples of general population and alcoholic drivers. There were significant correlations between number of traffic accidents and stressful life events for both samples, but the magnitude of the interrelations was stronger for the alcoholic driver sample. More specifically, number of traffic accidents for the alcoholic driver sample was significantly correlated with serious disturbances with wife or with parents and/or in-laws, serious disturbance at work or school, and serious disturbance about finances.

The studies relating more transitory drinking and depression episodes in reaction to stressful life events are complemented by research indicating that depression may be a more pervasive feature of the personality makeup of some DWI offenders (e.g., Mozdzierz et al., 1975; Selzer et al., 1968; Sutker et al., 1980). Selzer and colleagues (1968) reported that 21% of a sample of 96 drivers were clinically depressed. Mozdzierz and colleagues (1975) found a consistent profile among a subset of alcoholics whose driving records revealed one or two accidents. Based on the MMPI and the Guilford–Zimmerman Temperament Survey, these alcoholics manifested a profile of elevated depression and low mania, indicative of a behavioral style of low energy and internalization of conflicts. This group profile contrasted sharply with a more antisocial behavioral style of a group of high-rate traffic offenders. Sutker and colleagues (1980) also used the MMPI with a large sample of male DWI offenders and found that one personality profile among heavy drinkers was characterized by depressed affect and pessimistic mentation. In a comparison of DWI offenders, alcoholics, and a control sample, Selzer and colleagues (1977) reported that DWI offenders manifested higher levels of depressed affect than the control group, but not as high as the levels seen in the alcoholic group.

In two studies that we conducted with convicted DWI offenders referred for alcoholism evaluation, significant associations were found between serious alcohol problems and depressive symptomatology (hereafter referred to as depression). The first study (Windle & Miller, 1989) was based on the first of three interviews conducted over a year and a half. The study examined differences in depression for convicted DWI offenders classified according to DSM-III criteria as alcohol dependent, alcohol abusers, or undiagnosed problem. The highest rate of depression was reported by alcohol-dependent DWI offenders, and the findings were robust for both males and females.

Thus depression among convicted DWI offenders was associated with severity of serious alcohol problems. The second study (Windle & Miller, 1990) used data from all three occasions of measurement to analyze cross-temporal relationships between depression and problem drinking. Covariance structure modeling techniques were used to evaluate alternative "causal" models underlying the multivariate structure of the observed data. The results indicated that between occasion one and occasion two, decreases in depression were significantly associated with decreases in problem drinking; conversely, decreases in problem drinking were significantly associated with decreases in depression. However, between occasion two and occasion three, a reversal in the direction of effects was indicated; that is, between occasions two and three, increases in depression were significantly associated with increases in problem drinking, and conversely, increases in problem drinking were significantly associated with increases in depression.

Windle and Miller (1990) interpret the longitudinal findings regarding depression and problem drinking among DWI offenders as reflecting a biphasic process. Approximately 9 months separated occasions of measurement, and a large percentage of DWI offenders received group intervention designed to educate about alcoholism between the first and second occasions of measurement. The combination of the stressfulness of being convicted of a DWI offense and the intervention may have contributed to a reduction in problem drinking and depression. However, there was no intervention between occasions two and three, and the stressfulness of the conviction may have been considerably attenuated. As such, individuals may more readily return to cycles of problem drinking and depression, which may, over time, result in another DWI arrest or some other problematic outcome (e.g., loss of job, family discord). These longitudinal results thus suggest that depression and problem drinking among DWI offenders reflect a negative cycle that perpetuates drinking-and-driving behavior as well as other destructive acts.

Research with variables reflecting features of depressed affect (e.g., low self-esteem) have also suggested significant differences between DWI offenders and the general population. The results of Selzer and colleagues (1977) indicated that DWI offenders had lower self-esteem than a control group, but not as low as a group of alcoholics.

Several researchers have suggested a model that depicts drinking and driving as resulting from an attempt to cope with stressful situations (e.g., Donovan, 1980; Fine et al., 1975a, 1975b; Selzer et al., 1977). Donovan (1980) observed that there are consistent interrelationships among drinking behavior, personality traits, acute emotional stress, driving-related attitudes, and the availability of appropriate coping skills.

Reasons for drinking for DWI offenders have been analyzed by Donovan (1980) in his study of convicted offenders. Three separate factors have been identified: drinking in response to negative feelings, primarily of an interpersonal nature (e.g., out of anger, resentment, frustration); drinking in response to boredom or loneliness; drinking for social reasons (e.g., to be part of the "in" crowd, to be lively or funny). There is some indication that drinking drivers fall between alcoholics and social drinkers in their description of drinking for tension relief or social relaxation (Selzer et al., 1977). Drinking drivers have also reported drinking to relieve stress more frequently than college students (Beck & Summons, 1985).

In general, drinking drivers drink more frequently and heavily, experience more negative effects from drinking, and often drink to reduce tension. They are more depressed, have lower levels of self-esteem, and more overt and covert hostility (Donovan, 1980, Selzer & Barton, 1977, Selzer et al., 1977).

To summarize, research related to the influences of criminal and deviant behaviors and depressed affect among DWI offenders has indicated an association with serious alcohol problems. It is proposed that these personality and mental health influences are of importance in identifying alternative subtypes of drinking drivers with serious alcohol problems (e.g., Donovan & Marlatt, 1982; Donovan et al., 1986). For example, stressful life events or chronic depressed affect may precipitate heavy alcohol consumption as a coping mechanism (i.e., self-medication). The heavy drinking may: (1) contribute to increases in the frequency of drinking and driving and (2) decrease levels of concentration and psychomotor functioning that will increase the probability of unsafe driving. This drinking-and-driving pattern may be characteristic of only a subset of DWI offenders. A second subtype may be characterized by DWI offenders who are hostile and aggressive and who consistently engage in antisocial activities. Drinking and driving may be a component of a more generalized behavior style rather than a response to a stressful life event or to depressed affect.

The use of typologies has been proposed in the alcoholism literature (e.g., Penick et al., 1984; Zucker, 1987) as a method of identifying alternative etiological pathways with implications for enhancing the efficacy of interventions through treatment matching. A similar approach may be of use in the DWI literature to accommodate the heterogeneous groups manifest in the DWI population (Wells-Parker et al., Chapter 11, this volume).

PUBLIC POLICY FOR THE DRINKING DRIVER WITH SERIOUS ALCOHOL PROBLEMS

Three questions that should be of particular concern to public policy makers regarding the drinking driver with serious alcohol problems are: (1) Is the incidence of crashes for drinking drivers with serious alcohol problems greater than for other drinking drivers? (2) Is the probability of arrest among drinking drivers with serious alcohol problems greater than for other drinking drivers? (3) Is the rate of recidivism for drinking drivers with serious alcohol problems greater than for other drinking drivers?

These questions have not been substantially addressed in the existing literature on drinking drivers. In part that is due to the initial efforts in the drinking-and-driving research to address more general issues, such as deterrence. Serious alcohol problems were also not the focus of citizen groups such as Mothers against Drunk Driving (MADD) and Remove Intoxicated Drivers (RID). These groups successfully focused public attention on the problems of drinking and driving and mobilized legal changes to create stiffer penalties for drinking and driving. They were not, however, designed to examine the offender and why he/she may be involved in such behaviors. Despite the need for more research on these questions, there are a few studies that provide some perspectives on these issues.

Is the incidence of crashes for drinking drivers with serious alcohol problems greater than for other drinking drivers?

Measuring the relationship between serious alcohol problems and crashes has been difficult because of both the varying definitions of what constitutes serious alcohol problems and the lack of behavioral studies of impairment of driving performance of alcoholics/problem drinkers as compared to others who drink and drive (Jones & Joscelyn, 1978). For instance, fatty changes in the liver have been studied to determine whether persons with higher blood alcohol contents were more likely to have serious liver problems and the relationship of these factors to crash victims. As Jones and Joscelyn (1978) note, while fatty livers have been the focus of some investigation, the indicator does not stand alone in its ability to determine the relationships between serious alcohol problems and crashes. Thus this avenue of investigation seems of limited value. What is needed are studies that measure serious alcohol problems more directly.

One approach to this more direct measurement is to ask respondents whether they drink and drive. This approach is especially useful with samples who do not suffer serious consequences by telling the truth, such as in random household samples. In such a study conducted in Canada, Wilson and Jonah (1985) found that persons who reported drinking and driving on one or more occasions when they thought they may have been legally impaired (DWI) were more likely to have had traffic safety violations than either persons who never drove after drinking (NDD) and persons who drove after drinking but did not perceive themselves as legally impaired (DD). Accident rates were also marginally ($p = .05$) higher for the DWI as compared to the DD groups. This type of study has the added advantage of providing data on drinking drivers, regardless of whether or not they are apprehended. The disadvantage of such an approach is that individuals must decide whether they have been driving after drinking to the point of legal impairment.

Research studies pertaining to alcohol-related traffic accidents have suggested that problem-drinking and alcoholic drivers have accident rates twice as high as nonalcoholic drivers and are involved in a disproportionate number of fatal accidents, with some estimates approaching 70% of fatal accidents being associated with problem drinkers or alcoholics (Brown, Bohnert, Finch, Pokorny, & Smith, 1968; Mozdzierz et al., 1975; Schmidt & Smart, 1959; Waller, 1965). In a study of alcoholics admitted to treatment for alcoholism, clients with a history of motor vehicle accidents were likely to have initiated regular drinking and heavy drinking at an earlier age (Yates, Noyes, Petty, Brown, & O'Gorman, 1987). In addition, a greater percentage of clients who had been in accidents reported specific signs of pathological use and impaired functioning as compared to clients who had not been in accidents. For example, the accident group had a mean number of 8.2 criteria for alcohol abuse as compared to 6.4 from the nonaccident group. However, the amount of alcohol consumed at a sitting did not differ for the two groups. One possible reason for this connection is that alcoholics who are drinking heavily at an earlier age are drinking heavily at years when driving risk is greatest. The late teens and early 20s are years when the risk of crashes is greater because of inexperience and more impulsive behavior. This study also linked antisocial alcoholics to an increased risk of alcohol-related motor vehicle accidents.

Studies are needed that not only examine the extent of involvement alcoholics have with accidents but also the extent to which drinking drivers and drinking drivers involved in accidents are alcoholic. While we discussed some earlier studies that have measured the extent of alcohol problems in the drinking-and-driving population, there is a need to continue this line of research with screening instruments that will help us identify different types of drinking drivers with serious alcohol problems. Such studies will contribute to the development of interventions that will be effective in reducing the incidence of further drinking and driving in this population.

There is also a need to examine the use of legal sanctions, such as jail sentences and probation, with drinking drivers who have serious alcohol problems. Negative consequences (e.g., loss of jobs, loss of family) are common among alcoholics in treatment. However, these negative consequences do not necessarily, by themselves, produce change in drinking behavior. Even if the drinking driver with serious alcohol problems is affected by legal sanctions, legal sanctions alone may not be sufficient to produce long-lasting change in drinking behavior. There may well be a need to combine the negative consequences with constructive treatment alternatives. For instance, the combination of a probation sentence with a mandate to alcoholism treatment could be implemented. However, such strategies only provide meaningful intervention if alcoholism treatment specific to the needs of the drinking driver is available.

Is the probability of arrest among drinking drivers with serious alcohol problems greater than for other drinking drivers?

Drinking patterns may also influence the rate of arrest. For example, the number of drinks per occasion has been found to be related to risk of DWI arrest (Damkot, 1982; Donovan, 1980). There is some disagreement as to whether the frequency of drinking events leads to a higher risk of driving and drinking or a higher rate of being apprehended. Related to this issue is the observation that the highest probability of arrest (1 in 50) occurs for persons with BACs of 0.20–0.24%, while the likelihood of arrest for driving while intoxicated has been estimated to be 1 in 200 events for all drivers with a BAC of 0.10% or greater (Beitel, Sharp, & Glauz, 1975). Duration of the drinking pattern may also place some drivers at risk. For instance, one study reports that drinking drivers in classes or treatment in Philadelphia averaged 9.4 years in the current drinking pattern prior to their current arrest (Fine et al., 1978).

Finally, there is some indication that the arrestee population represents the drinking drivers most heavily engaged in drinking-and-driving behavior. For example, in comparison to high-risk drivers and registered drivers, Donovan (1980) found that DWI offenders had a higher probability of driving after drinking, a greater number of days in the month in which they drive after drinking, and that their drinking was more problematic when they drank.

Research that examines the probability of arrest for drinking drivers with serious alcohol problems should also consider whether or not this population has similar drinking-and-driving patterns (e.g., drives the same streets, drives during the same time of day) as those without serious alcohol problems. Some drinking drivers with serious alcohol problems may be less apparent to the police. For example, when tolerance to the effects of alcohol is established, persons with serious alcohol problems may appear less affected at the same BAC than other persons without serious alcohol problems.

Is the rate of recidivism for the drinking driver with serious alcohol problems greater than for other drinking drivers?

In a study of drinking drivers convicted during the early 1970s in California, Yoder and Moore (1973) reported that offenders who had had prior arrests for drinking and driving were significantly more likely to score on the MAST in the alcoholic range than were first-time offenders. A larger percent of repeat offenders (87%) as compared to first-time offenders (69%) scored in the alcoholic range of the test, suggesting that there is a relationship between more serious alcohol problems and recidivism for drinking and driving (Yoder & Moore, 1973). Unfortunately, there is little information available on the relationship between an individual's score on an alcoholism screening test and the subsequent outcome (i.e., did they recidivate?).

Related to the issue of whether drinking drivers recidivate with another drinking-and-driving arrest is the evidence that there are a number of drinking drivers with other criminality problems. These criminality problems include offenses that are obviously related to drinking (e.g., drunkenness) and criminal offenses that may or may not be related to drinking (e.g., assault). For example, for a group of drinking drivers who were referred for alcoholism evaluation, the average number of previous drunkenness arrests was 2.7 and the average number of previous arrests (excluding vehicle traffic law) was 1.9 (Argeriou & Manohar, 1977). Thus studies that propose to evaluate the recidivism of drinking drivers need to consider other illegal activities that may reflect equally serious problems.

NOTES

1. The original version of the MAST consisted of 25 items; one item was not used in scoring, however. Items measure drinking patterns; social, occupational, and health consequences related to drinking; and previous alcoholism treatment experiences. Shortened versions of the MAST have emerged in the literature. However, the majority of attention in the drinking-and-driving research has focused on the original version. For further information on the shortened versions, see Selzer, Vinokur, and van Rooijen (1975); and Zung (1979).

2. While developed for a male population, this screening test has been found to assess adequately alcohol problems among women (Selzer, Gomberg, & Nordhoff, 1979).

3. The original cutoff scores were as follows: less than 60, social drinker; 60–85, excessive drinker; and 85 or more, problem drinker.

4. Quantity–frequency measures typically provide an average daily consumption level of absolute alcohol. For example, a 30-day window may be used to determine the total number of days for which beer, wine, and/or liquor are consumed and the typical number of drinks consumed in a day. The typical amount is then multiplied by the amount of absolute alcohol in the drink (i.e., beer, wine, liquor), multiplying this total by the number of days this particular beverage was consumed. Beer, wine, and liquor are then totaled and divided by 30 days to achieve the average ounces of alcohol consumed per day. By dividing the same total by the total number of drinking days (as opposed to total number of days in the window), the average amount of alcohol consumed per drinking day is determined. In some measures of quantity–frequency, a more sophisticated version is used that also accounts for heavy drinking days. Individuals are asked the usual drinking amount and also asked the number of days that they consume larger quantities. In this manner, the usual quantity–frequency consumption can be adjusted for high-volume days. For further information, see Armor and Polich (1982).

REFERENCES

American Psychiatric Association. (1980). *Diagnostic and statistical manual of mental disorders* (3rd ed.). Washington, DC: Author.

American Psychiatric Association. (1987). *Diagnostic and statistical manual of mental disorders* (3rd ed., rev.). Washington, DC: Author.

Argeriou, M., & Manohar, V. (1977). Treating the problem drinking driver: Some notes on the time required to achieve impact. *British Journal of the Addictions, 72,* 331–338.

Argeriou, M., McCarty, D., & Blacker, E. (1985). Criminality among individ uals arraigned for drinking and driving in Massachusetts. *Journal of Studies on Alcohol, 46,* 525–529.

Armor, D.J., & Polich, J.M. (1982). Measurement of alcohol consumption. In E.M. Pattison & E. Kaufman (Eds.), *Encyclopedic handbook of alcoholism.* New York: Gardner.

Beck, K.H., & Summons, T.G. (1985). Social context of drinking: DWI offenders and college students. In S. Kaye & G.W. Meier (Eds.), *Alcohol drugs and traffic Safety: Proceedings of the Ninth International Conference on Alcohol, Drugs and Traffic Safety — San Juan, Puerto Rico, 1983* (pp. 141–153). Washington, DC: National Highway Traffic Safety Administration, U.S. Department of Transportation.

Beitel, G., Sharp, M., & Glauz, W. (1975). Probability of arrest while driving under the influence of alcohol. *Journal of Studies on Alcohol, 36,* 237–256.

Bell, R.A., Warheit, G.J., Bell, R.A., & Sanders, G. (1978). An analytic comparison of persons arrested for driving while intoxicated and alcohol detoxification patients. *Alcoholism: Clinical and Experimental Research, 2,* 241.

Borkenstein, R.F., Crowther, R.F., Shumate, R.P., Ziel, W.B., & Zylman, R. (1974). The role of the drinking driver in traffic accidents: The Grand Rapids study. *Blutalkohol, 11* (Suppl. 1), 1–132.

Brady, J.P., Foulks, E.T., Childress, A.R., & Pertschuk, M. (1982). The Michigan Alcoholism Screening Test as a survey instrument. *Journal of Operational Psychiatry, 13,* 27–31.

Brown, S.L., Bohnert, P.J., Finch, J.R., Pokorny, A.D., & Smith, J.P. (1968). *Alcohol safety study; drivers who die.* Houston, TX: Baylor University College of Medicine.

Cahalan, D. (1970). *Problem drinkers.* San Francisco: Jossey-Bass.

Cameron, T. (1979). The impact of drinking-driving countermeasures: A review and evaluation. *Contemporary Drug Problems, 8,* 495–565.

Chan, A.K. (1990). Biochemical markers for alcoholism. In M. Windle & J. S. Searles (Eds.), *Children of alcoholics: Critical perspectives* (pp. 39–72). New York: Guilford.

Clark, W.B., & Midanik, L. (1982). Alcohol use and alcohol problems among US adults: Results of the 1979 national survey. In National Institute on Alcohol Abuse and Alcoholism (Ed.), *Alcohol consumption and related problems* (Alcohol and Health Monograph No. 1) (DHHS Publication No. ADM 82-1190). Washington, DC: U.S. Government Printing Office.

Clay, M.L. (1972). Which drunks should we dodge? In *Selected papers of the Twenty-Third Annual Meeting of the Alcohol and Drug Problems Association of North America.* Washington, DC: Alcohol and Drug Problems Association of North America.

Damkot, D.K. (1982). Alcohol incidence in rural drivers: Characteristics of a population and clues for countermeasures. *Drug and Alcohol Dependence, 9,* 305–324.

Dolinsky, Z.S., & Schnitt, J.M. (1988). Discriminant function analysis of clinical laboratory data use in alcohol research. In M. Galanter (Ed.), *Recent developments in alcoholism* (Vol. 6). New York: Plenum.

Donovan, D.M. (1980). *Drinking behavior, personality factors and high-risk driving.* Unpublished doctoral dissertation, University of Washington, Seattle.

Donovan, D.M., & Marlatt, A.G. (1982). Personality subtypes among driving-while-intoxicated offenders: Relationship to drinking behavior and driving risk. *Journal of Consulting and Clinical Psychology, 50,* 241–249.

Donovan, D.M., Marlatt, G.A., & Salzberg, P.M. (1983). Drinking behavior, personality factors and high-risk driving: A review and theoretical formulation. *Journal of Studies on Alcohol, 44,* 395–428.

Donovan, D.M., Queisser, H.R., Umlauf, R.L., & Salzberg, P.M. (1986). Personality subtypes among driving-while-intoxicated offenders: Follow-up of subsequent driving records. *Journal of Consulting and Clinical Psychology, 54,* 563–565.

Eichner, E.R., & Hellman, R.S. (1971). The evolution of anemia in alcoholic patients. *American Journal of Medicine, 50,* 218.

Filkins, L.D. (1970). Research perspectives. In L.D. Filkins & N.K. Gellers (Eds.), *Community response to alcoholism and highway crashes* (pp. 111–116). Ann Arbor: Highway Safety Research Institute, University of Michigan.

Filkins, L.D., Mortimer, R.G., Post, D.V., & Chapman, M.W. (1973). *Field evaluation of court procedures for identifying problem drinkers: Final report.* Ann Arbor: Highway Safety Research Institute, University of Michigan.

Finch, J.R., & Smith, J.P. (1970). *Psychiatric and legal aspects of automobile fatalities.* Springfield, IL: Thomas.

Fine, E.W., Scoles, P., & Mulligan, M.J. (1975a). Alcohol abuse in first offenders arrested for DWI. In S. Israelstam & S. Lambert (Eds.), *Alcohol, drugs, and traffic safety* (pp. 169–174). Toronto: Addiction Research Foundation.

Fine, E.W., Scoles, P., & Mulligan, M.J. (1975b). Under the influence: Characteristics and drinking practices of persons arrested the first time for drunk driving, with treatment implications. *Public Health Reports, 90,* 424–429.

Fine, E.W., Steer, R.A., & Scoles, P.E. (1978). Relationship between blood alcohol concentration and self-reported drinking behavior. *Journal of Studies on Alcohol, 39,* 466–472.

Forman, B.D., & Florenzano, R.U. (1978–1979). Blood alcohol concentration on arrest as an indicator of problem drinking in driving under the influence. *The Psychiatric Forum, 9,* 47–50.

Fuller, R.K., Lee, K.K., & Gordis, E. (1988). Validity of self-report in alcoholism research: Results of a Veterans Administration cooperative study. *Alcoholism: Clinical and Experimental Research, 12,* 201–205.

Gibbs, L.E. (1983). Validity and reliability of the Michigan Alcoholism Screening Test: A review. *Drug and Alcohol Dependence, 12,* 279–285.

Hedlund, J.L., & Vieweg, B.W. (1984). The Michigan Alcoholism Screening Test (MAST): A comprehensive review. *Journal of Operational Psychiatry, 15,* 55–64.

Jacobson, G.R. (1983). Detection, assessment, and diagnosis of alcoholism:

Current techniques. In M. Galanter (Ed.), *Recent developments in alcoholism*. New York: Plenum.

Jones, R.K., & Joscelyn, K.B. (1978). *Alcohol and highway safety: A review of the state of knowledge* (Technical Report No. DOT-HS-803 714). Washington, DC: National Highway Traffic Safety Administration, U.S. Department of Transportation.

Kerlan, M.W., Mortimer, R.G., Mudge, B., & Filkins, L.D. (1971). *Court procedures for identifying problem drinkers: Vol. 1. Manual*. Ann Arbor: Highway Safety Research Institute, University of Michigan.

Lower, J.S., Mortimer, R.G., & Filkins, L.D. (1971). *Court procedures for identifying problem drinkers: Volume 3. Scoring keys*. Ann Arbor: Highway Safety Research Institute, University of Michigan.

McCord, J. (1984). Drunken drivers in longitudinal perspective. *Journal of Studies on Alcohol, 45*, 316–320.

McGuire, F.L. (1976). Personality factors in highway accidents. *Human Factors, 18*, 433–441.

McGuire, F.L. (1980). "Heavy" and "light" drinking-drivers as separate target groups for treatment. *American Journal of Drug and Alcohol Abuse, 7*, 101–107.

Meck, D., & Baither, R. (1980). The relation of age to personality adjustment among DWI offenders. *Journal of Clinical Psychology, 36*, 342–345.

Miller, B.A., Whitney, R., & Washousky, R. (1984). The decision to recommend alcoholism treatment for DWI offenders. *American Journal of Drug and Alcohol Abuse, 10*, 447–459.

Miller, B.A., Whitney, R., & Washousky, R. (1986). Alcoholism diagnoses for convicted drinking drivers referred for alcoholism evaluation. *Alcoholism: Clinical and Experimental Research, 10*, 651–656.

Mischke, H.D., & Venneri, R.L. (1987). Reliability and validity of the MAST, Mortimer–Filkins questionnaire and CAGE in DWI assessment. *Journal of Studies on Alcohol, 48*, 492–501.

Mortimer, R.G., Filkins, L.D., & Lower, J.S. (1971). *Development of court procedures for identifying problem drinkers: Final report*. Ann Arbor: Highway Safety Research Institute, University of Michigan.

Mortimer, R.G., Filkins, L.D., Lower, J.S., Kerlan, M.W., Post, D., Mudge, B., & Rosenblatt, C.A. (1971). *Development of court procedures for identifying problem drinkers: Report on phase I*. Ann Arbor: Highway Safety Research Institute, University of Michigan.

Mozdzierz, G.J., Macchitelli, F.J., Planek, T.W., & Lottman, T.J. (1975). Personality and temperament differences between alcoholics with high and low records of traffic accidents and violations. *Journal of Studies on Alcohol, 36*, 395–399.

Mudge, B., Kerlan, M.W., Post, D.V., Mortimer, R.G., & Filkins, L.D. (1971). *Court procedures for identifying problem drinkers: Volume 2. Supplementary readings*. Ann Arbor: Highway Safety Research Institute, University of Michigan.

National Council on Alcoholism Criteria Committee. (1972). Criteria for the diagnosis of alcoholism. *American Journal of Psychiatry, 129,* 127.

Noyes, R., Jr. (1985). Motor vehicle accidents related to psychiatric impairment. *Psychosomatics, 26,* 569–580.

Penick, E.C., Powell, B.J., Othmer, E., Bingham, S.F., Rice, A.S., & Liese, B.S. (1984). Subtyping alcoholics by coexisting psychiatric syndromes: Course, family history, outcome. In D.W. Goodwin, R.T. Van Dusen, & S.A. Mednick (Eds.), *Longitudinal research in alcoholism.* Hingham, MA: Kluwer-Nijhoff.

Ryback, R.S., Eckardt, M.J., Felsher, B., & Rawlings, R.R. (1982). Biochemical and hematologic correlates of alcoholism and liver disease. *Journal of the American Medical Association, 248,* 2261–2265.

Ryback, R.S., Eckardt, M.J., Rawlings, K.R., & Rosenthal, L.S. (1982). Quadratic discriminant analysis as an aid to interpretive reporting of clinical laboratory tests. *Journal of the American Medical Association, 248*(18), 2342–2345.

Schmidt, W., & Smart, R.G. (1959). Alcoholics, drinking and traffic accidents. *Quarterly Journal of Studies on Alcohol, 20,* 631.

Scoles, P., Fine, E.W., & Steer, R.A., (1984). Personality characteristics and drinking patterns of high-risk drivers never apprehended for driving while intoxicated. *Journal of Studies on Alcohol, 45,* 411–416.

Selzer, M.L. (1971). The Michigan Alcoholism Screening Test: The quest for a new diagnostic instrument. *American Journal of Psychiatry, 127,* 1653–1658.

Selzer, M.L., & Barton, E. (1977). The drunken driver: A psychosocial study. *Drug and Alcohol Dependence, 2,* 239–253.

Selzer, M.L., Gomberg, E.S., & Nordhoff, J.A. (1979). Men's and women's responses to the Michigan Alcoholism Screening Test. *Journal of Studies on Alcohol, 40,* 502–504.

Selzer, M.L., Rogers, J.E., & Kern, S. (1968). Fatal accidents: The role of psychopathology, social stress, and acute disturbance. *American Journal of Psychiatry, 124,* 46–54.

Selzer, M.L., & Vinokur, A. (1974). Life events, subjective stress, and traffic accidents. *American Journal of Psychiatry, 131,* 903–906.

Selzer, M.L., Vinokur, A., & van Rooijen, L. (1975). A self-administered Short Michigan Alcoholism Screening Test (SMAST). *Journal of Studies on Alcohol, 36*(1), 117–126.

Selzer, M.L., Vinokur, A., & Wilson, T.D. (1977). A psychosocial comparison of drunk drivers and alcoholics. *Journal of Studies on Alcohol, 38,* 1294–1312.

Skinner, H.A., & Sheu, W.J. (1982). Reliability of alcohol use indices: The lifetime drinking history and the MAST. *Journal of Studies on Alcohol, 43,* 1157–1170.

Skude, G., & Wadstein, J. (1977). Amylase, hepatic enzymes and bilirubin in serum of chronic alcoholics. *Acta Medica Scandinavica, 201,* 53.

Steer, R.A., Fine, E.W., & Scoles, P.E. (1979). Classification of men arrested for driving while intoxicated, and treatment implications: A cluster-analytic study. *Journal of Studies on Alcohol, 40,* 222–229.

Sutker, P.B., Brantley, P.J., & Allain, A.N. (1980). MMPI response patterns and alcohol consumption in DUI offenders. *Journal of Consulting and Clinical Psychology, 48,* 350–355.

Vingilis, E. (1983). Drinking drivers and alcoholics: Are they from the same population? In R.G. Smart, F. E. Glaser, Y. Israel, H. Kalant, R. E. Popham, & W. Schmidt, (Eds.), *Research advances in alcohol and drug problems* (Vol. 7) (pp. 299–342). New York: Plenum.

Waller, J.A. (1965). Chronic medical conditions and traffic safety, review of the California experience. *New England Journal of Medicine, 273,* 1413–1420.

Waller, J.A. (1967). Identification of problem drinking among drunken drivers. *Journal of the American Medical Association, 200,* 114–120.

Welte, J., Hynes, G., Sokolow, L., & Lyons, J. (1979). *Outcome study of alcoholism rehabilitation units.* Albany, NY: Division of Alcoholism and Alcohol Abuse.

Wieczorek, W.F., Nochajski, T.H., Miller, B.A., & Whitney, R. (1989, August). DSM-III *and* DSM-III-R *alcohol diagnoses for problem-drinker drivers.* Paper accepted for presentation at the 97th Annual Convention of the American Psychological Association, New Orleans, LA.

Wilson, R.J., & Jonah, B.A. (1985). Identifying impaired drivers among the general driving population. *Journal of Studies on Alcohol, 46,* 531–537.

Windle, M., & Miller, B.A. (1989). Alcoholism and depressive symptomatology among convicted DWI men and women. *Journal of Studies on Alcohol, 50,* 406–413.

Windle, M., & Miller, B.A. (1990). Problem drinking and depression among DWI offenders: A three-wave longitudinal study. *Journal of Consulting and Clinical Psychology, 58,* 166–174.

Wu, A., Chanarin, I., & Levi, A.J. (1974). Macrocytosis of chronic alcoholism. *Lancet, 1,* 829.

Yates, W.R., Noyes, R., Jr., Petty, F., Brown, K., & O'Gorman, T. (1987). Factors associated with motor vehicle accidents among male alcoholics. *Journal of Studies on Alcohol, 48,* 586–590.

Yoder, R.D., & Moore, R.A. (1973). Characteristics of convicted drunken drivers. *Quarterly Journal of Studies on Alcohol, 34,* 927–936.

Zelhart, P.F., Schurr, B.C., & Brown, P.A. (1975). The drinking driver: Identification of high-risk alcoholics. In S. Israelstam & S. Lambert (Eds.), *Alcohol, drugs, and traffic safety.* Toronto: Addiction Research Foundation.

Zucker, R.A. (1987). The four alcoholisms: A developmental account of the etiologic process. In P.C. Rivers (Ed.), *Nebraska Symposium on Motivation. 1986: Vol. 34. Alcohol and addictive behaviors.* Lincoln: University of Nebraska Press.

Zung, B.J. (1979). Psychometric properties of the MAST and two briefer versions. *Journal of Studies on Alcohol, 40,* 845–859.

Zung, B.J., & Charalampous, K.D. (1975). Item analysis of the Michigan Alcoholism Screening Test. *Journal of Studies on Alcohol, 36,* 127–132.

PART II

DETERRENCE AND THE DRINKING–DRIVING PROBLEM

5

A NEW LOOK AT DETERRENCE

EVELYN R. VINGILIS

The predominant approach to the drinking–driving problem has been based on legal deterrence through the criminal justice system. Most deterrence research in the arena of alcohol and traffic safety has been limited to one simple question: Is impaired driving reduced under conditions of greater severity and/or certainty of punishment? However useful the question, it is predicated on a model of social control that is exceptionally simplistic. The deterrence model is taken from the so-called classical school of criminology in which individuals were seen as fundamentally hedonistic and therefore deterrable from a crime by swift, sure, and severe punishment. Yet as Meier and Johnson (1977) and Williams (1985) write, the deterrence doctrine is noticeably atheoretical in both its philosophical origins and its historic inattention to developments in the social sciences. The philosophical origins of the deterrence doctrine seem to have discouraged social science scrutiny of the concept's ontological status. The postulated deterrent effect evolved not from systematic observations of the relationship between legal sanctions and behavior, but from a realm of social thought that introduced the concept of deterrence to justify a new legal order (Meier & Johnson, 1977). Thus, although deterrence doctrine assumes certain human motivations, these assumptions were introduced to justify legal reform, not to represent behavior. Until recently, deterrence has reflected a jurisprudential orientation under the direction of legal scholars such as Andenaes (1952, 1966, 1975). In the past two decades, however, social scientists have expanded the deterrence doctrine to encompass other social-control variables and have stepped beyond the assessment of the relationship between severity/celerity/certainty of punishment and official crime indices (Anderson, Chiricos, & Waldo, 1977; Grasmick & Bryjak, 1980; Waldo & Chiricos, 1971). Unfortunately, much of the reconceptualized thinking on deterrence has not yet reached the shores of drinking–driving research. This chapter reexamines deterrence theory in light of the more recent social science literature and introduces a social-control framework better able to represent current research findings in the alcohol and traffic safety field.

Research on the control of drinking–driving has been limited primarily to simple deterrence, defined as the short-term, immediate component of general deterrence. Although Andenaes (1975) and others use general prevention instead of general deterrence to reflect both the fear of punishment and the moral components in this social-control method, typically the literature of English-speaking countries uses general deterrence to signify compliance produced by the existence and administration of the criminal law rather than some other source. Thus the attainment of general deterrence is viewed by Ross (1982) as a "function of the adequacy and persistence of the short-term threat, which thus becomes a prior concern" (p. 9).

THE CLASSICAL DETERRENCE MODEL

Components

The deterrence model posits that the effectiveness of the legal threat is a function of the perceived certainty, severity, and celerity of punishment in the situation of an offense. The greater the likelihood of arrest, prosecution, conviction, and punishment, the more severe the eventual penalty; and the more quickly it is administered, the greater will be the effect of the legal threat (Grasmick & Green, 1980; Ross, 1982). To date, certainty and severity have been investigated to a limited extent in drinking–driving research, while very little information is available on celerity.

As early as 1808, Sir Samuel Romilly stated, "The chief deterrent to crime is not barbarity of punishment but certainty of conviction. The former only results in decreasing the latter and is therefore futile" (quoted in Fattah, 1977 p. 28). Drinking–driving research supports this early statement.

Evidence indicates the positive effect of increments in perceived certainty of punishment due to the introduction of Scandinavian-type laws and as a consequence of enforcement campaigns. Publicized interventions devised to increase the actual probabilities of punishment for drinking and driving seem nearly always to have been accompanied by a reduction in the variables measuring drinking–driving behaviors. However, over time, these reductions have returned to preintervention levels, because, as the prevailing hypothesis suggests, the public became aware that the newly publicized certainty of arrest was greatly exaggerated (Ross, 1982). However, if the enforcement intensity was maintained, deterrence could continue. The introduction of strict enforcement procedures of random breath testing in New South Wales in 1982 appears to have resulted in a long suppression of crash rates (Homel, 1986; Homel, Chapter 7, this volume).

Research on severity of punishment has produced mixed results. Votey's (1978, 1982) and Votey and Shapiro's (1983) statistical analyses lend support to the hypothesis that control efforts work in Sweden to reduce the number of accidents below what it might otherwise have been. They showed that the combination of apprehension and a jail sentence seems to be effective in reducing serious injury accidents, which represent close to 80% of all serious accidents, whereas jail sentences appear to be less effective than fines in reducing the number of fatal accidents. Also, license withdrawal was found to have a uniformly positive effect in reducing accidents. Furthermore, reanalysis of the famous British Road Safety Act of 1967 by Phillips, Ray, and Votey (1984) questions the previous assumption that deterrence effects are short term (Ross, 1982). Phillips and colleagues (1984) constructed a dynamic model relating monthly road casualties to road traffic, rainfall, and alcohol consumption, controlling for the seasonality of the data. Although their analyses confirmed Ross's earlier conclusion that the Road Safety Act significantly reduced casualties, the act was found to account for 2.7% of the variance in road casualties, while miles driven and rainfall accounted for 48.8% and alcohol consumption rates explained 4.2%. Moreover, their analyses showed that the intervention effect, although small, persisted.

However, research on increased severity in the United States has found little evidence of a deterrent effect (Block, 1983; Ross, 1982). The enforcement/adjudication system that carries out the laws passed by legislators is often likely to make its own decisions with regard to the imposition of penalties, based on the individual offender. Informal, sometimes "off-the-record" decisions to impose less stringent penalties than are called for by statute sometimes inhibit the ultimate goal of deterrence and behavior modification. The overall result of such "informal" decisions is sometimes the nullification of the intended effect of the law. Generally, severe sanction approaches in North America have resulted in increased opposition by the courts, the defendants, and defense attorneys; increased plea bargaining; and increased court backlogs, leading to decreased conviction rates (Ross, 1982). That is, increased severity of penalty reduced the certainty of penalty, thereby reducing its deterrent impact.

The final component of the deterrence theory has not been adequately investigated. The effect of celerity of punishment is relatively unknown. Vingilis, Blefgen, Lei, Sykora, and Mann (1988) evaluated the deterrent impact of Ontario's 12-hour license suspension law, a law intended to mete out swift punishment. The results suggested that laws to increase the celerity and certainty of punishment had little short-term deterrent impact without enforcement and publicity of the new laws. That is, perceived certainty seemed more important than celerity.

Thus deterrence research suggests that certainty, celerity, and severity of punishment do not seem to have major long-term impacts. This narrowly conscribed view of deterrence is the essence of why legal threats have had limited impact on drinking driving behavior.

Assumptions

Deterrence is based on a number of assumptions. Some of these assumptions are more valid and verifiable than others.

1. *We are rational beings.*

Because deterrence theory assumes human rationality, it consequently ignores the fact that many offenses are irrational or unintentional in nature (Webb, 1980). Rational decision making, based on the calculation of the expected utility of the impaired driving trip versus the perceived risk of the trip, is far too simple a model to adequately explain impaired driving behavior. Impaired driving, like any other behavior, deviant or otherwise, is more realistically described as emanating from the interaction of "person" factors, including cognitive and other psychological processes both rational and irrational, and "situation" factors, including opportunity and formal and informal sanctions (Vingilis & Mann, 1986).

2. *We are hedonistic beings.*

This assumption refers to basic goals of ordinary human motivation. According to this assumption, habits are developed and conduct is oriented, in fair part at least, by the search for pleasure and the avoidance of pain. Given this premise, the promised pleasure of a criminal act can be countered by the threat of pain that is a basic ingredient in any punishment (Fattah, 1977).

The assumption of pain avoidance cannot, however, be applied generally. A large body of psychological evidence supports the view that some persons may commit crimes because they want to be punished, and in these cases one wonders whether a deterrent would mean the withholding of punishment (Wilkins, 1969).

In some cases the challenge of punishment can be motivation to crime. Some criminals are motivated by a certain desire to feel superior to the law enforcement machinery, to "beat the system" or to commit the "perfect crime" (Fattah, 1977). For example, Snortum (1988) suggests that offenders "may gain special satisfaction in finding ways to 'beat the system,' for example, by acquiring multiple licenses or by sharing 'intelligence' on the likely times and places of sobriety checkpoints" (p. 196).

Hedonistic considerations are only one component involved in the behavior. As Schur (1968) writes, "concentration on hedonistic calculation does justice to neither the unconscious nor the situational and subcultural learning processes that may be involved in crime" (p. 131). Therefore, in addition to the classical deterrence conditions of certainty, celerity, and severity of punishment, a number of other factors specific both to the individual psychological dimensions and the social context must be considered.

3. *We are free to choose.*

As Fattah (1977) states:

> The doctrine of deterrence assumes that individuals are totally or at least partially free to choose between alternatives of behaviour. It implies that criminal behaviour is indeterministic. In Schafer's (1968) words:
> The idea of official punishment itself indicated the lawmaker's assumption that the criminal has freedom of choice. Criminal law assumes that man is free and able to form a "more or less impartial judgement of the alternative actions" and can act "in accordance with that judgement."
>
> The assumption of "freedom of choice," which is basic to the doctrine of moral responsibility and the doctrine of deterrence, has been the subject of fierce attacks over the decades from the sources ranging from the Italian positivistic school to the modern behaviouristic school. The latter school suggests that crime is a product of forces not entirely within the control of the offender. External forces can be considered to affect one's behaviour. This behavioural position indicates that free will is not an accurate conceptualization of human conduct (p. 11).

4. *We are able to control our behavior.*

Related to the assumption of free will or the freedom of choice is the assumption that individuals are capable of controlling their behavior. The ability to control behavior varies widely from one person to another and according to the type of behavior (Fattah, 1977).

As Webb (1980) states, "the motivation of the offender is crucial to understanding the deviant act for he either complies with or violates the law depending, largely, upon his personal and situational motivations" (p. 25). Motivations can be expressive or instrumental. Instrumental motivation is a disposition to engage in behavior in order to attain some specific goal, such as driving after drinking in order to get home from a late-night party, whereas expressive motivation is a disposition to engage in behavior for the pleasure or gratification it provides, such as driving after drinking in order to reduce stress. Furthermore, it has been argued that since instrumental acts are rationally motivated they may be responsive to certain deterrent measures, while expressive acts, being impulsive and less rational, are less likely to be responsive to legal sanction (Webb, 1980). A final motivation, which may fall somewhere between the two, is compulsion. Compulsions irresistibly drive individuals toward some irrational behavior. The classic example, of course, is alcohol addiction in some drinking–driving offenders. This characterization is somewhat oversimplified in that the deviant acts can result from any combination of all three motivations; but if we retain deterrence theory's original emphasis on rational calculation, by definition the impulsive and compulsive acts would be virtually nondeterrable. Indeed, there is evidence that among the drinking–driving population, all three subgroups exist. Vingilis (1983, 1988), in reviewing studies that examine the relationship between drinking–driving and alcoholism, estimated that 25–50% of high-risk drinking drivers, that is, those who have been involved in drinking–driving crashes or arrests, can be viewed as problem drinkers. These drivers could fall into the compulsive drinking–driving offenders category.

There is also research suggesting a young risky driving subgroup characterized as thrill seeking and aggressive (Barnes & Welte, 1988; Wilson & Jonah, 1988). As Barnes and Welte write, "alcohol may have an effect on dangerous driving by releasing aggressive impulses among selected groups of individuals" (1988, p. 382). As Snortum (1988) states, "DUI offenders tend to manifest a host of problems in impulse control and they have strong lifestyle commitments to social activities involving heavy drinking. Therefore, it is to be expected that deterrence gains will be hard won with this group" (p. 196).

It is also questionable whether certain categories of abnormal offenders, such as sociopaths, are able to exercise the necessary control over their own behavior.

5. *We know in every case what is harmful to us.*

Fattah (1977), citing Von Hentig, suggests that there are three suppositions related to harm that form the basis of deterrence: (1) individuals know what is harmful to them, (2) individuals are frightened by the potential of being harmed, and (3) individuals realize in every case the correct steps to avoid harm. Furthermore, these three suppositions assume the behavior of the average person in average life situations. In many instances these suppositions are not realized. The exceptions may be classified into "psychological or normal stages of nondeterrability, and pathological stages of fearlessness" (Fattah, 1977, p. 11). Again, the thrill-seeking and risk-taking driving behavior of so many youth suggests that this assumption of individuals' knowing what is harmful to them is not true for many (Barnes & Welte, 1988; Farrow, 1987).

6. *We can be deterred by fear.*

The concept of deterrence is also based on the assumption that individuals can be deterred by fear. Behaviorists usually do not agree that the fear of punishment is the best and most effective way of controlling or curbing certain types of behavior, because many individuals attempt only to avoid being caught, not to change their behavior. Behaviorists generally consider positive reinforcement to be a superior alternative to punishment (Fattah, 1977). Wilde (1982), for example, has described a West German incentive program for accident-free driving in which, over a 26-year period, the total accident rate dropped by 75%. However, the use of rewards in the traffic safety field has shown generally mixed results (Friedland, Trebilcock, & Roach, 1987).

Furthermore, compliance has always been treated as if it reflects a fear of consequences. However, recent research (e.g., Pestello, 1984) suggests that compliance to the rules may be a phenomenon independent from fear. Individuals may view elements of the sanctioning system as threatening but still be disposed to violate the rules for a number of reasons. As Pestello (1984) suggests, maintaining a good image in the eyes of one's friends, for example, may overshadow any abstract, uncertain fears about committing an offense. The loss of status in one's peer group, when weighed against uncertain sanctions, may make the commission of an offense the most desirable alternative in certain situations. The failure to be deterred from the commission of an offense in the face of certain severe and/or swift sanctions can be a reflection of individual differences. As Pestello (1984) writes, individual characteristics clearly impact on both behavior and attitudes. Homel (1986) found in his survey that deterrence was "dynamic and unstable." He states, "The predictive power of arrest certainty was comparable with the predictive power of informal sanctions, although informal pressures usually prevailed over fear of arrest when perceived group pressures to drink were very strong" (p. 137).

Furthermore, the literature suggests that fear and compliance, the symbolic and behavioral dimensions of deterrence, vary according to type of offender (Chambliss, 1967). The demographic factors of age and sex have shown mixed results of differential deterrability. Tittle and Rowe (1973) found in their experimental study that females were more likely to be deterred, while Silberman (1976) found evidence of the reverse. Jensen, Erickson, and Gibbs (1978) found no sex differences in their sample of high school students, as did Tittle (1980). The drinking-driving literature, however, tends to confirm that females are more deterred than males (Vingilis, Adlaf, & Chung 1982).

In addition, researchers contend that older people are more deterred by sanctions, because they want to maintain their respectability (Pestello, 1984). Again, the drinking-driving research tends to support this finding (Interministerial Committee on Drinking-Driving, 1988).

7. We are knowledgeable of laws and sanctions.

Deterrence theory assumes that the public knows about acts prohibited by the law and about the penalties prescribed for such acts. Knowledge of the law is usually assumed to be a necessary but not sufficient condition for compliance. Research on general deterrence consistently demonstrates that legal sanctions have a greater chance of impact if public education accompanies them (Jonah & Wilson, 1983; Vingilis et al., 1988). Also, Norway and Sweden show somewhat lower rates of alcohol impairment among fatally injured drivers and much lower rates of impairment in roadside breath testing (Snortum, 1984). Furthermore, compared to North American drivers, Norwegian drivers showed greater knowledge of local drinking-driving laws (Snortum, Hauge, & Berger, 1986). However, the degree of knowledge necessary is debatable. A review by Vingilis (1984) found that knowledge about laws was greatest among those who had the greatest need to know, that is, those who were already in conflict with them.

A correct assessment by the public of the risk involved in certain behavior is not, however, necessary for the purposes of deterrence. People may be deterred (or more deterred) because they overestimate the risk of punishment involved. This was indeed the case in the evaluation of the RIDE. (Reduce Impaired Driving in Etobicoke) spotcheck enforcement campaign. After the implementation of the program, subjective perception of detection increased significantly and was overestimated in relation to the objective risk of detection (Vingilis & Salutin, 1980).

In addition, there are other limitations on deterrence theory. The threat of punishment is generally irrelevant in preventing a large part of society from engaging in serious criminal behavior such as impaired driving (Andenaes, 1975; Fattah, 1977; Grasmick & McLaughlin 1978; Webb, 1980).

For many individuals, it is the prescriptions and proscriptions for conduct that are internalized in the socialization process, not the written laws or sanctions that prevent law-breaking. Thus only "inadequately" or "abnormally" socialized individuals fit the classical deterrence model. Deterrent threats and punishments are viewed as relevant only to the criminal groups and those individuals in the marginal category, whereas the remainder of the population will be relatively unaffected by legal deterrents (Webb, 1980).

Deterrence may not be as effective in certain acts of an impulsive or compulsive nature, acts in which high emotions or strong motivations are involved, or for certain types of offenders who are impulsive, compulsive, insane, sociopathic, masochistic, and so forth (Fattah, 1977). Only the instrumental offenders can be viewed as theoretically responsive to legal sanctions. Indeed, drinking–driving research seems to bear out the differential deterrability of drinking drivers who act out of impulsiveness, compulsiveness, and instrumentality. For example, Donovan and Marlatt (1982) found in their subtypes of DWIs that the three groups with the highest number of yearly convictions and accidents had profiles highly suggestive of impulsiveness, such as high levels of driving-related aggression, sensation seeking, irritability, driving for tension reduction, and low levels of driving caution when upset. Additionally, these three groups seemed to be the heaviest drinkers, suggesting that some of them may have had alcohol dependencies. Similarly, Barnes and Welte (1988), Farrow (1987), and Wilson and Jonah (1988) found certain behavioral indices (such as illicit drug use and other delinquencies), personality indices (such as aggression, thrill seeking, and restless intent), and environmental indices (such as peer influence) were predictive of drinking–driving behavior. Furthermore, research by Ross, Klette, and McCleary (1984) on the laws regarding impaired driving in Scandinavia also concluded that the criminal law approach seemed to deter the "less dangerous, moderate drinkers" but not "the more deadly alcoholic." Ontario roadside surveys (Interministerial Committee on Drinking–Driving, 1988) also found greater reductions in 1986 compared to 1979 for the 51–80 mg% category of drinking drivers than for the over 80 mg% category. They go on to suggest:

> With regard to changes in the 51 to 80 mg% category from 1979, those in this category may have been moderate drinkers, and responded to the increased awareness in drinking and driving by moderating their drinking/driving behavior; while the drivers with the higher B.A.C.'s may have been heavier drinkers and found it much more difficult to control their drinking and driving behavior. In support of this hypothesis; there was a significant positive relationship between roadside B.A.C. and the self-report of the number of alcohol drinks consumed in the 7 days prior to being stopped ($r = .22$, $p < .005$) (p. 21).

Homel (1986) found in his surveys of the general population to assess the impact of the introduction of random breath testing (RBT) in New South Wales, Australia, that the greater the respondents' alcohol consumption, and the greater the perceived pressure to drink, the more ways they reported modifying both their drinking habits and travel arrangements. However, Homel also found that among heavy drinkers the contradictory pressures of peer pressure and fear of arrest resulted in *"a psychologically unstable situation, making the deterrent impact of RBT in many cases rather short-lived"* (p 127; emphasis added). (See also Homel, Chapter 7, this volume). Thus at this point all we can safely say is that impaired driving sanctions apparently have some deterrent effect on some individuals under some circumstances.

A SOCIAL-CONTROL MODEL

An alternative conceptualization of deterrence was introduced in the 1970s by social scientists (e.g., Anderson et al., 1977) and more recently embraced by alcohol and traffic safety researchers (e.g., Snortum, 1984). This new conceptualization anchors deterrence in a large context of social control, wherein legal threats constitute but one mechanism that may result in conformity. The other mechanisms are usually called extralegal factors or informal sanctions. Common extralegal factors from criminological literature (e.g., Webb, 1980; Gibbs, 1975) include the following:

1. *Criminal self-image* reflects the degree to which the offender or potential offender perceives himself as a criminal. The degree of criminal self-image can affect the level of criminal activity.
2. *Criminal life organization* describes the extent to which the person's life is organized around his offending behavior. If the organization is high, then there are likely few alternatives, since the offending activities are encompassed in his lifestyle. Habituation, a closely related concept, refers to the offending behavior's becoming habitual and thus harder to break.
3. *Group support* describes the degree to which the offender is supported by his reference group. If a support network is operating, the offending behavior will be reinforced.
4. *Differential association* reflects the learning of skills and rationalizations from criminal referent groups to support further criminal activities.
5. *Moral commitment* describes a person's moral commitment to the law and is a good predictor of criminal activities.

At least two other factors are salient in contributing to criminal activities (Webb, 1980). The first factor is opportunity for and ease of crime commission. This factor is highly relevant to drinking–driving because of the easy availability of alcohol and necessity of vehicles. Vingilis and De Genova's (1984) review of the impact of the legal drinking age in North America found that generally availability of alcohol vis-à-vis the legal drinking age laws was positively correlated with rates of various types of alcohol-related crashes of youth.

A second factor is social stigma and the labeling process. Many individuals may not engage in criminal acts because of the stigma associated with being identified as a criminal. Certainly the thrust of many drinking–driving countermeasure programs is to make drinking–driving "socially unacceptable," with the hope that the stigma attached to being considered a drinking–driving offender will cause many to refrain from the act (Premier's Interministry Task Force on Drinking and Driving, 1983).

In fact, when the statistical contributions of formal and informal sanctions have been directly compared using multivariate analyses, informal sanctions have always shown greater predictive power (e.g., Meier & Johnson, 1977). Norström (1978, 1981), using a multivariate approach to survey data from Swedish drinking drivers, included variables of demographic characteristics, knowledge of the law, moral agreement with the law, perceived risk of accident or arrest, and two "opportunity" variables of estimates of annual driving distance and alcohol consumption. Using path analyses in the first study and the LISREL statistical program in the second, alcohol consumption and moral agreement were the two strongest predictors, while legal knowledge and perceived risk did not contribute to either model.

Using path analysis on American driver survey data, Berger and Snortum (1986) also found an influence for alcohol consumption and moral agreement and no effect for arrest risk and legal knowledge. Two other predictors, preference for beer over other alcoholic beverages and moral attitudes of one's friends, also made independent contributions to the model.

At this point it seems useful to look at the nature of a drinking–driving offender in relation to some of the dimensions of social control just outlined. Tables 5.1, offered for heuristic purposes only, presents a typology of nature of offense on the horizontal axis and some social-control dimensions on the vertical axis. As the table suggests, both impulsive and compulsive drinking–driving offenders seem less likely to be deterred by the conditions of certainty, celerity, and severity of punishment. The extralegal factors are hypothesized to have varying influences on the three motivational types of drinking–driving offenders. From research we would speculate that

TABLE 5.1. Nature of Drinking–Driving Offense and Legal and Extralegal Dimensions Influencing Their Differential Deterrability

Legal and extralegal factors	Impulsive drinking–driving offense	Compulsive drinking–driving offense	Instrumental drinking–driving offense
	Legal sanctions		
Severity	Low	Low	Moderate
Celerity	Low	Low	Moderate?
Certainty	Low	Low	High
	Extralegal sanctions		
Criminal self-image	Low	Low	Low
Criminal life organization	High	High	Low
Group support	High	Moderate	Low
Differential association	High	High	Low
Moral commitment to the law	Low	Low	Moderate

criminal self-image would be low for all three groups. Although research suggests that the general public views drinking and driving as an offensive act (e.g., Goldfarb Consultants, 1983), drinking drivers are least likely to have attitudes and beliefs that drinking and driving is a serious criminal offense (e.g., Wilson, 1984). Criminal life organization and differential association would most likely be low for instrumental drinking–driving offenders, but high for impulsives and compulsives. Recent work on problem behavior theory (e.g., Jessor, 1987; Wilson & Jonah, 1988) suggests that among younger drinking drivers there is a constellation of behavioral and environmental factors indicating a deviant (and rather impulsive) lifestyle. That is, frequent drinking–driving behavior does not seem to represent isolated incidents in otherwise nondeviant young people.

For the compulsive group, the drinking behavior, of course, has become very habitual and thus is harder to break. Group support could be low for the instrumental group. For the compulsives, although research suggests that the problem drinkers and alcoholics seem to support each other's habits (Kotarba, 1977), it seems fair to assume that a great deal of drinking and consequential drinking–driving would occur without group support. For the impulsive drinking–driving offenders, group support could be moderate to high. For example, youthful drinking drivers often joyride and race in the company of their peers, suggesting some group support dynamics. Homel (1986; Chapter 7, this volume) finds peer pressure and collegial pub drinking to be important extralegal factors. Moral commitment to the law would most likely be low for both the impulsive and compulsive offenders and moderate for the instrumental offender. Most research (e.g., Vingilis, 1984; Wilson, 1984) suggests that drinking drivers are least likely to have negative attitudes toward drinking–driving behavior, enforcement, laws, and so forth. These influences are still only hypothetical, but it is obvious that an understanding of the legal and extralegal factors and their relative impact on criminal activities of various types of drinking–driving offenders is fundamental to the development of good countermeasures.

SUMMARY AND CONCLUSIONS

In conclusion, it is important to view the prevention of drinking–driving behavior from a broader context of social control. Simple deterrence is only one component of general deterrence, and informal sanctions are as important as the threat of formal sanctions. Granted, simple deterrence lends itself most easily to being researched. But for the sake of methodologically pure research, we have not asked the broader questions. This in turn has prevented us from understanding the interplay between formal and informal sanctions and consequently has limited our ability to develop effective countermeasures.

In a summary, we need to ask a more complex series of questions, addressing the variability of conditions and circumstances in which drinking-driving does and does not occur. This need has been affirmed at a conceptual level (e.g., Snortum, 1984) but is rarely addressed in the empirical work of alcohol and traffic safety researchers. Research is needed on what person factors are relevent, what situation factors are conducive to deterrence, and, in turn, what the interactions are of the person and situation factors. Homel (1986) summed it up very nicely by stating that deterrence is "a dynamic and unstable situation with a constantly changing mix of those deterred" (p. 136). Clearly, we have been somewhat remiss in our deterrence research, although it is heartening to see new research unfold to encompass the broader realm of the legal and extralegal factors that produce and deter drinking-driving behavior.

REFERENCES

Andenaes, J. (1952). General prevention—Illusion or reality? *Journal of Criminal Law, Criminology and Police Science, 43,* 176–198.

Andenaes, J. (1966). The general preventive effects of punishment. *University of Pennsylvania Law Review, 114,* 949–983.

Andenaes, J. (1975). Criminology, general prevention revisited: Research and policy implications. *The Journal of Criminal Law and Criminology, 66,* 338–365.

Anderson, L.S., Chiricos, T.G., & Waldo, G.P. (1977). Formal and informal sanctions: A comparison of deterrent effects. *Social Problems, 25,* 103–114.

Barnes, G.M., & Welte, J.W. (1988). Predictors of driving while intoxicated among teenagers. *The Journal of Drug Issues, 18*(3), 367–384.

Berger, D.E., & Snortum, J.R. (1986). A structural model of drinking and driving: Alcohol consumption, social norms, and moral commitments. *Criminology, 24,* 139–153.

Block, S.A. (1983). One year later: A preliminary assessment of effectiveness of California's new drinking driving laws. *Abstract and Reviews in Alcohol and Driving, 4,* 9–20.

Chambliss, W.J. (1967). Types of deviance and the effectiveness of legal sanctions. *Wisconsin Law Review, 6,* 703–717.

Donovan, D.M., & Marlatt, G.A. (1982). Personality subtypes among driving-while-intoxicated offenders: Relationship to drinking behavior and

driving risk. *Journal of Consulting and Clinical Psychology, 50,* 241–249.
Farrow, J.A. (1987). Young drivers risk taking: A description of dangerous driving situations among 16- to 19-year-old drivers. *The International Journal of the Addictions, 22*(12), 1255–1267.
Fattah, E.A. (1977). Deterrence. A review of the literature. *Canadian Journal of Criminology, 19*(2), 1–119.
Friedland, M., Trebilcock, M., & Roach, K. (1987). *Regulating traffic safety: A survey of control strategies* (Law and Economics Workshop Series). Toronto: Faculty of Law, University of Toronto.
Gibbs, J.P. (1975). *Crime, punishment and deterrence.* New York: Elsevier.
Goldfarb Consultants. (1983). *Drinking and driving in Canada.* Toronto, Ontario, Canada: Insurance Bureau of Canada.
Grasmick, H.G., & Bryjak, G.J. (1980). The deterrent effect of perceived severity of punishment. *Social Forces, 59*(2), 471–491.
Grasmick, H.G., & Green, D.E. (1980). Legal punishment, social disapproval and internationalization as inhibitors of illegal behavior. *Journal of Criminal Law and Criminology, 71,* 325–335.
Grasmick, H.G., & McLaughlin, S.D. (1978). Deterrence and social control. *American Sociological Review, 43,* 272–278.
Homel, R. (1986). Policing the drinking driver, random breath testing and the process of deterrence. *Macquarie University and the Office of Road Safety.*
Interministerial Committee on Drinking–Driving (1988). *The 1986 Ontario survey of nighttime drivers—Summary report.* Toronto: Ministry of Transportation, Province of Ontario.
Jensen, G.F., Erickson, M.L., & Gibbs, J.P. (1978). Perceived risk of punishment and self-reported delinquency. *Social Forces, 57,* 57–58.
Jessor, R. (1987). Risky driving and adolescent problem behavior: An extension of problem behavior theory. *Alcohol, Drugs and Driving, 3,* 1–11.
Jonah, B.A., & Wilson, R.J. (1983). Improving the effectiveness of drinking driving enforcement through increased efficiency. *Accident Analysis and Prevention, 15,* 463–482.
Kotarba, J.A. (1977, September). *The serious nature of tavern sociability.* Paper presented at the annual meeting of the Society for the Study of Social Problems, Chicago.
Meier, R.F., & Johnson, W.T. (1977). Deterrence as social control: The legal and extralegal production of conformity. *American Sociological Review, 42,* 292–304.
Norström, T. (1978). Drunken driving: A tentative causal model. *Scandinavian Studies in Criminology, 6,* 69–78.
Norström, T. (1981). *Studies in the causation and prevention of traffic crime.* Stockholm: Almqvist and Wiksell.
Pestello, H.G. (1984). Deterrence: A reconceptualization. *Crime and Delinquency, 30*(4), 593–609.
Phillips, L., Ray, S., & Votey, H. (1984). Forecasting highway casualties: The British Road Safety Act and a sense of déjà vu. *Journal of Criminal Justice, 12,* 101–114.

Premier's Interministry Task Force on Drinking and Driving. (1983). *Drinking and driving: A discussion of countermeasures and consequences.* Toronto, Ontario, Canada.

Ross, H.L. (1982). *Deterring the drinking-driver: Legal policy and social control.* Lexington, MA: Lexington Books.

Ross, H.L., Klette, H., & McCleary R. (1984). Liberalization and rationalization of drunk-driving laws in Scandinavia. *Accident Analysis and Prevention, 16*(5–6), 471–487.

Schur, E.M. (1968). *Law and society.* New York: Random House.

Silberman, M. (1976). Towards a theory of criminal deterrence. *American Sociological Review, 41,* 442–461.

Snortum, J.R. (1984). Alcohol-impaired driving in Norway and Sweden: Another look at "the Scandinavian myth" [Special issue]. *Law and Policy, 6*(1), 5–37.

Snortum, J.R. (1988). Deterrence of alcohol-impaired driving: An effect in search of a cause. In M.D. Laurence, J.R. Snortum, & F.E. Zimring (Eds.), *Social control of the drinking driver* (pp. 189–226). Chicago: University of Chicago Press.

Snortum, J.R., Hauge, R., & Berger, D.E. (1986). Deterring alcohol-impaired driving: A comparative analysis of compliance in Norway and the United States. *Justice Quarterly, 3,* 139–65.

Tittle, C.R. (1980). *Sanctions and social deviance: The question of deterrence.* New York: Praeger.

Tittle, C.R., & Rowe, A.R. (1973). Moral appeal, sanction, threat and deviance: An experimental test. *Social Problems, 20,* 488–498.

Vingilis, E. (1983). Drinking drivers and alcoholics: Are they from the same population? In R.G. Smart, F. Glaser, Y. Israel, H. Kalant, R. Popham, & W. Schmidt (Eds.), *Research Advances in Alcohol and Drug Problems* (Vol. 7) (pp. 299–342). New York: Plenum.

Vingilis, E. (1984). Alcohol, young drivers and traffic accidents. *Accident Analysis and Prevention, 16*(5–6), 489–490.

Vingilis, E. (1988, November). *Are drinking-drivers alcoholics? A review of the literature.* Paper presented at the conference on High Alcohol Consumers and Traffic, Paris, France.

Vingilis, E., Adlaf, E., & Chung, L. (1982). Comparison of age and sex characteristics of police-suspected impaired drivers and roadside-surveyed impaired drivers. *Accident Analysis and Prevention, 14,* 425–430.

Vingilis, E., Blefgen, H., Lei, H., Sykora, K., & Mann, R. (1988). An evaluation of the deterrent impact of Ontario's 12-hour licence suspension law. *Accident Analysis and Prevention, 20,* 9–17.

Vingilis, E., & De Genova, K. (1984). Youth and the forbidden fruit: Experiences with changes in legal drinking age in North America. *Journal of Criminal Justice, 12,* 161–172.

Vingilis, E., & Mann, R.E. (1986). Towards an interactionist approach to drinking–driving behaviour: Implications for prevention and research. *Health Education Research, 1,* 273–288.

Vingilis, E., & Salutin, L. (1980). A preventative program for drinking and driving. *Accident Analysis and Prevention, 12,* 267–274.

Votey, H.L., Jr. (1978). The deterrence of drunken driving in Norway and Sweden: An econometric analysis of existing policies. In R. Hauge (Ed.), *Scandinavian studies in criminology: Drinking and driving in Scandinavia* (pp. 79–99). Oslo, Norway: Universiteforlaget Oslo.

Votey. H.L., Jr. (1982). Scandinavian drinking–driving control: Myth or intuition? *Journal of Legal Studies, 11,* 93–116.

Votey, H.L. Jr., & Shapiro, P. (1983). Highway accidents in Sweden. *Accident Analysis and Prevention, 15,* 523–533.

Waldo, G.P., & Chiricos, T.G. (1971). Perceived penal sanction and self-reported criminality: A neglected approach to deterrence research. *Social Problems, 19,* 522–540.

Webb, S.D. (1980). Deterrence theory: A reconceptualization. *Canadian Journal of Criminology, 22,* 23–35.

Wilde, G.J.S. (1982). Critical issues in risk homeostasis theory. *Risk Analysis,* 2(4), 249–258.

Wilkins, L. (1969). *Evaluation of penal measures.* New York: Random House.

Williams, F.P. III (1985). Deterrence and social control: Rethinking the relationship. *Journal of Criminal Justice, 13,* 141–151.

Wilson, R.J. (1984). A national household survey on drinking and driving: Knowledge, attitudes and behavior of Canadian Drivers. Transport Canada, Road Safety, TP5865. Ottawa, Ontario, Canada.

Wilson, R.J., & Jonah, B.A. (1988). The application of problem behavior theory to the understanding of risky driving. *Alcohol, Drugs and Driving,* 4(3–4), 173–191.

6

DRUNK DRIVING ENFORCEMENT, ADJUDICATION, AND SANCTIONS IN THE UNITED STATES

ROBERT B. VOAS
JOHN H. LACEY

In the year of our best enforcement effort, 1983, 1.9 million drivers were arrested for driving while impaired (DWI) in the United States. Although this number has fallen off slightly since that time, approximately 1% of the nation's total licensed drivers are arrested for DWI per year. This is a significant increase over the 1970s, when only about one-half of 1% of licensed drivers were arrested for DWI each year. In 1975 Borkenstein noted that:

> Roadside surveys of the occurrence of alcohol in the driving public have shown that when enforcement is at the current level of 2 arrests per officer per year, and with automobile density what it is in the average congested city today, there are about 2,000 violations for each arrest. A "violation" is a trip from one point to another with a blood alcohol concentration of .10% or higher; thus, in a typical community of 1 million population, with 1,000 patrol officers making two arrests per man per year, there will be 2,000 arrests and 4 million violations. (p. 660)

Since this report the number of licensed drivers arrested for DWI has doubled, and so the ratio of violations to arrests may now be down to 1,000 to 1. Indeed, two studies suggest that where intensive enforcement is applied, the violation-to-arrest ratio can be reduced to approximately 300 to one (Beitel, Sharp, & Glauz, 1975; Hause, Voas, & Chavez, 1982). These higher arrest rates, which are not typical of

116

the enforcement level of the country as a whole, have been shown to produce small reductions in alcohol-related accidents (Voas & Hause, 1987).

There was a significant rise in DWI arrests nationally from 1979 to 1983, which preceded a 10–15% drop in the proportion of highway fatalities that were alcohol-related from 1982 to 1986. The extent to which this increase in arrests contributed to the subsequent decrease in alcohol-related fatalities is difficult to determine. It is probable that the increase contributed as one element in a larger complex of factors, which included citizen activist programs, new alcohol legislation, and increased public interest in health and safety (Howland, 1988). Regardless, it is clear that a doubling of the total number of arrests has had, at best, a modest effect on the alcohol-related casualty rate.

This chapter describes the evolution of the current drunk driving enforcement system in the United States and the principal factors that have shaped the adjudication and sanctioning of DWI offenders.

DWI ENFORCEMENT IN THE UNITED STATES

The drunk driving problem was first recognized in scientific literature in 1904 (NSC, 1976), approximately five years after the first highway safety fatality in the United States. Soon thereafter, the United States and Norway were among the first industrialized nations to make impaired driving a criminal offense. In 1910 New York adopted an impaired driving law, and in 1911 the State of California followed suit. This early criminalization of the drunk driving offense set it apart from other traffic infractions. Higher penalties were provided for this offense, including incarceration and substantial periods of license suspension. In 1924 the State of Connecticut jailed 254 drivers for the DWI offense. Thus, from the early years of this century, the United States treated this offense as seriously as any nation in the world (Voas, 1982b).

The Behavioral-Based Enforcement System

The system of enforcement that has emerged in the United States can be described by the four-step process outlined in Figure 6.1.

The first step in this process is to identify vehicles in the traffic flow which are being driven by impaired operators. This is done based either on the vehicle being involved in a crash, or on the officer on patrol observing unusual, aberrant, or illegal behavior. Once the

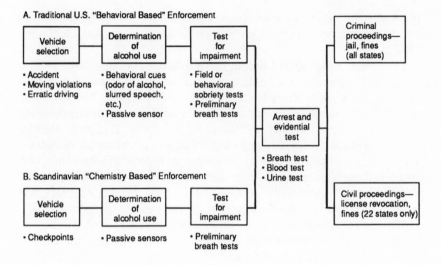

FIGURE 6.1. Stages in the DWI Enforcement Process.

vehicle has been stopped, the second step is performed. The driver is interviewed to determine whether he or she has been drinking and/or shows signs of intoxication (e.g., blood-shot eyes, flushed appearance, slurred speech, odor of alcohol). If this initial interview indicates that the individual may be impaired, the officer normally takes a third step, which is to invite the driver out of the vehicle to perform a set of sobriety tests (walking a straight line, touching the nose with eyes closed, etc.). These, along with the aberrant driving, become the bases of the officer's testimony to support the charge of "driving while intoxicated" (DWI).

The term "drunk driving" presented considerable problems in adjudicating the DWI offense because of its lack of an objective definition. The popular conception of a drunk individual involved highly aberrant behavior (staggering gait, incoherence, etc.). It soon became evident, though, that individuals could be at increased risk of crash involvement without displaying such gross signs of intoxication. Efforts were made to strengthen initial legislation by substituting such terms as "under the influence of alcohol" and, more recently, "impaired by alcohol." However, since there was no objective measure of driving skill available for testing individuals charged with drunk driving, much was left to the often sympathetic interpretation of the jury.

Just before the Second World War a third factor was added to the enforcement process. It involved the use of chemical tests for alcohol to determine impairment. Initially these test results were added to the total evidence presented to support the testimony of the police officer, but once the courts began to accept this new scientific evidence, state legislatures moved to enact laws which specifically provided for chemical testing. In 1939 Indiana became the first state to provide for a chemical test. Maine, New York, and Oregon soon followed Indiana's lead.

This legislation established that chemical test data provided competent evidence of impairment. In addition, these laws established specific alcohol concentrations as presumptive evidence of intoxication. Establishing such a presumption required the defense to provide other competent evidence to rebut the chemical test data or lose its case. The initially prescribed levels followed the recommendations of the American Medical Association (AMA) which proposed that a blood alcohol content (BAC)* of 0.15 or greater produced the presumption that the individual was "under the influence," while a BAC between 0.05 and 0.15 was competent evidence of impairment when supported by other verbal testimony. Finally, the AMA recommendation held that a BAC below 0.05 was presumptive evidence that the individual was not "under the influence." Since the Second World War, most states have lowered this presumptive level to 0.10 and several states have lowered it to 0.08. Recently, the National Safety Council Committee on Alcohol and Drugs has recommended that the presumption that an individual is not impaired when the BAC is below 0.05 be stricken from DWI legislation, since evidence now indicates that performance is impaired at BAC's below 0.05 (Moskowitz & Robinson, 1988).

Thus, with the passage of these laws, a fourth step was added to the enforcement system illustrated in Figure 6.1. Once the police officer obtains sufficient evidence from sobriety tests to convince him that the individual is impaired under a state's DWI law, he will charge the driver with the offense, take the individual into custody, and transport him to the police station for a chemical test. Robert Borkenstein's development of an inexpensive breath-test device, the *Breathalyzer*™, provided a means for police departments to rapidly test individuals for their alcoholic consumption. The use of breath testing in the United States avoided many of the problems experi-

---

*BAC is used in this chapter to denote alcohol content in an appropriate body fluid including blood and breath measurement.

enced in other countries which continued to rely on blood tests and therefore required the services of a police surgeon to come to the station and draw blood. The Borkenstein *Breathalyzer*™ and those breath-test instruments that succeeded it have provided a reliable means of collecting highly accurate breath-test data. States have established control systems for approving and calibrating these units and for training and supervising breath-test operators in each police department.

The success of the chemical test in achieving convictions for impaired driving raised the issue of whether the state could require drivers to submit to this test. In a landmark decision, the Supreme Court decided in the case of *Schmerber vs. California* that the police had the authority to take a blood sample forcibly, under limited circumstances. The Court held, with respect to the Fifth Amendment, that this did not constitute self-incrimination since the evidence gathered was not testimonial but physical in character. Secondly, the Court determined that the forcible taking of a blood sample (in this case from an unconscious driver) did not violate the Fourth Amendment prohibition against unreasonable searches and seizures since there was full probable cause to suspect the driver of driving under the influence. (See Laurence, 1988, for a discussion of the constitutional issues related to DWI enforcement and adjudication.)

This decision opened the way for states to pass laws providing for the forcible taking of blood samples from arrested drivers. However, neither the police departments nor the legislatures wanted to undertake a system in which people would be held down and have needles inserted into their arms as part of the arrest process. Therefore, a compromise was developed under which the state passed legislation providing that any individual operating a vehicle upon the state's highways had provided "implied consent" to giving a sample for a chemical test in the event of a DWI arrest. If the driver, having been arrested, refused to provide a test, then the Motor Vehicle Administrator was empowered to suspend the driver's permit for a varying period of time.

It required almost two decades for all of the states to adopt this implied-consent procedure. To achieve the adoption by the final holdout states it was necessary to increase the safeguards in the breath-testing process. As the breath test became a more important element in the drunk driving litigation process, and as implied-consent statutes gave less opportunity for the driver to refuse testing, states added legislation to require that breath-test devices be more fully automated and equipped with safeguards which would prevent the operator from making errors in the testing process. As a result, automated units were developed which facilitated the process of calibrating and checking the instrument and collecting breath samples. These units also provided a printout, thereby minimizing the possibility of error.

The four-step process shown in Figure 6.1 provides a reasonably effective enforcement system. However, the seriousness of the drunk driving offense, with its potential for a jail sentence and a lengthy driving suspension, provoked great resistance from those charged with the offense. These individuals hired lawyers to argue their cases. The result was that the procedural paperwork for the police officer was increased. The bureaucratic procedures became onerous and frequently required two to four hours for each arrest. This discouraged DWI enforcement activity.

The traditional behavioral enforcement system provides wide discretion to the individual officer in determining which vehicles to stop and, once the vehicle is stopped, whether to proceed with the investigation of the DWI offense. Thus, the officers' attitudes, detection skills, and motivation are extremely important to effective enforcement. In studies of police officers' attitudes toward DWI enforcement most admitted that there were occasions when they did not pursue investigations where they were fairly sure the individual driver was impaired (Oates, 1974; Arthur Young & Co., 1974; Meyers, Heeren, & Hingson, 1987). One of the primary reasons given for such failures to follow through was the length and bureaucratic nature of the paperwork involved.

Arrests were less likely to be made towards the end of an officer's daily tour because completing the arrest would require staying overtime. Officers were also likely to compare the significance of drunk driving with the fairness of the penalties for this offense in making their arrest decision. Where they believed the penalties were inappropriately severe they were prone not to pursue arrests of marginally impaired drivers. Arrests were frequently avoided by allowing a passenger to take over the driving or, in the case of teenaged drivers, driving the individual home (Oates, 1974).

Finally, enforcement activity was often discouraged by the failure of both the police department itself (Mastrofski, Ritti, & Hoffmaster, 1987) and other branches of the criminal justice system to perform effectively. Because of the serious penalties many offenders insisted upon full legal recourse, and court dockets frequently became overloaded. Significant backlogs were created, particularly when defendants demanded jury trials. Where this was the case, the court and the prosecution were motivated to seek plea bargains in which individuals charged with DWI pleaded guilty to a lesser offense in return for having the drunk driving charge dropped. When police have seen this occur they have sometimes been discouraged from making DWI arrests (Oates, 1974).

With the founding of the Department of Transportation, the new Highway Safety Bureau (soon to be the National Highway Traffic Safety Administration) attempted to overcome some of these problems by establishing 35 demonstration programs called Alcohol Safety Action Projects (ASAPs) in the 1970s. These projects were designed to provide for an integrated approach to the drinking–driving problem (NHTSA, 1979). The courts, prosecutors, and police received additional funds and participated in a coordinated program to increase DWI arrests by simplifying police paperwork and by increasing the speed of prosecution and adjudication.

These projects generally succeeded in increasing (and often doubling) the number of arrests for DWI (Levy et al., 1977). The arrest increases were primarily achieved through the employment of special DWI emphasis patrols which operated on weekend evenings. These patrols normally made as many arrests in a year, on the two or three weekend evenings on which they were active, as the full police force had made annually prior to the establishment of the ASAP program. While the ASAP programs came to an end by 1975, this dedicated patrol procedure has continued to be a feature of most communities in which DWI enforcement is emphasized.

Aside from sponsoring the ASAP demonstrations, the federal government attempted to assist DWI law enforcement by developing more scientific and objective procedures for identifying drunk drivers. A program to determine which vehicle maneuvers were most likely to indicate a driver was intoxicated was funded by the NHTSA and resulted in a set of driving "symptoms" which graded the probability that the driver would be at 0.10 BAC or greater (Harris, Howlett, & Ridgeway, 1979). A second research effort was directed at developing a standardized set of field sobriety tests for use by police officers. The sobriety tests commonly in use up until the last decade were highly influenced by individual officers' preferences. The NHTSA sponsored a review of the literature and the development of a standardized set of three tests: lateral gaze nystagmus, body sway, and divided attention. Availability of these tests, particularly the gaze nystagmus test, has increased the capability of the police officer to estimate the probable blood alcohol content of the suspected driver (Tharp, Burns, & Moskowitz, 1981). This research has recently been extended into the area of drug detection (Anderson, 1985; Bigelow et al., 1985). By the latter part of the 1970s the traditional behavioral system for detecting and apprehending drunk drivers had been significantly improved, and close to one million drivers were being arrested each year for this offense.

The Chemistry-Based Enforcement System

The behavioral system of enforcement just described, which developed in the United States, was fairly typical of most industrialized nations. The U.S. system had an advantage in that it was based on breath rather than blood alcohol measurement. This simplified the enforcement process by not requiring the presence of a physician to collect blood. While this system was developing and maturing in the United States, the Scandinavian countries developed a significantly different approach to the enforcement of DWI laws.

In 1936 Norway passed legislation which provided that being in charge of a vehicle and having a BAC in excess of 0.05 was an offense. This was the first of the so-called "illegal per se" laws. Similar laws were later adopted by the other Scandinavian countries. The significance of the "illegal per se" approach is that it circumvents the issue of behavioral interpretation, since the offense has only two relevant criteria—being in charge of a vehicle and having a BAC over a given limit. Once these laws were in place, the police departments in the Scandinavian countries began to use preliminary breath-test (PBT) devices at the roadside. These legal and chemical test changes, when combined with the traditionally severe sanctions provided in Scandinavian laws, became known as the "Scandinavian Model" (Ross, 1975; Andenaes, 1988).

The British Government implemented elements of this "Scandinavian Model" in the Road Safety Act of 1967. Because of the wide publicity elicited from the British press during the period when this new legislation was being debated, the implementation of the program produced one of the most dramatic examples of a change in drinking–driving behavior resulting from DWI legislation (Ross, 1973, 1984). The success of the British Road Safety Act stimulated other nations to attempt somewhat similar programs.

In the United States the implementation of roadside testing was held back because of a challenge to the accuracy of the tube type testers (Prouty & O'Neill, 1971), and due to concerns about whether a roadside breath test could be administered without probable cause to believe that a DWI offense had been committed. The first problem was overcome through the development of miniature, electronic, PBT devices using fuel cell or semiconductor sensors. By the mid-1970s a small fuel cell test device (the "Alco-Sensor"/T) was available, which permitted roadside breath tests to have substantially the same accuracy as could be obtained with the evidential breath-test devices in the police station.

The distribution of PBT equipment to police departments appeared to increase the number of arrests. For example, in the beginning of 1980 a large purchase of roadside breath testers was made by the state of Minnesota and distributed to state and local police departments. A time-series analysis performed by Cleary & Rodgers (1986) suggested that this distribution produced a permanent increase in arrests by Minnesota police agencies. Moreover, Saffer and Chaloupka (in press) compared states with and without "Pre-arrest Breath Test" laws using econometric analysis and found that the states with such laws had lower nighttime fatality rates.

Despite this and other evidence of the utility of roadside breath testing, the use of these devices in the United States has been limited. This is due in part to the uncertainty regarding the amount of evidence of impairment the officer must have before he may require a PBT. This issue has not been resolved by the federal courts. In the absence of a federal court decision, most police departments make use of PBTs only after the field investigation has been completed. In these cases the officer has decided that the driver is impaired and is therefore about to charge him with the DWI offense. The field test device is used at this point to verify the officer's decision and to avoid transporting an individual who later turns out to be below the legal limit to the police station for the evidential test.

Rarely, if at all, are these devices used during the second step of the investigation process shown in Figure 6.1. This is the step where the officer attempts to determine if the individual has been drinking heavily. Because these devices are not used earlier in the arrest process many impaired drivers avoid detection because they fail to give the signs typically observed by police. Field studies (Taubenslag & Taubenslag, 1975; Vingilis, Adlaf, & Chung, 1982; Jones & Lund, 1985) have demonstrated that police officers miss at least half of the impaired drivers with whom they come in contact.

Voas (1982a,b) has distinguished between the "Scandinavian Model" as applied in the British Road Safety Act of 1967 and the full "chemistry-based" system as in the random breath test (RBT) program in New South Wales, Australia (see Homel, Chapter 7, this volume).

This chemistry-based enforcement system is in sharp contrast to the more behavioral approach used in America. Rather than selecting vehicles from the traffic only on the basis of aberrant or illegal behavior, this "chemistry-based" system makes extensive use of random stops at checkpoints. A breath test is conducted on every driver stopped. This systematic stopping of all drivers puts at risk over-the-limit drivers who might otherwise avoid arrest by driving in a manner that avoids detection by the police. Once the field test for alcohol indicates that the driver has an illegal BAC, the individual is charged and taken to the police station for an evidential test.

However, because of the elaborate requirements placed on the use of sobriety checkpoints by the federal courts it is unlikely that the RBT system could be applied in the United States. While under current court decisions a checkpoint operated by a single officer would not be permitted, the significant success of the RBT program as reported by Homel (Chapter 7, this volume) suggests that the more limited sobriety test procedure utilized in the United States could have an impact if used more frequently. He notes that where a checkpoint procedure similar to that of the United States has been applied in Australia the results have been much less dramatic than for the RBT program in New South Wales and Tasmania.

A series of federal court decisions (Ifft, 1983) have established a "balancing" procedure which permits the police to conduct checkpoints under certain highly controlled procedures where the state can demonstrate that this technique is required in order to protect citizens against the hazards posed by the drunk driver. The procedures required by the court are somewhat limiting. Survey sites must be preselected on the basis of drunk driving incidents and inspected for safety. A plan must be developed in advance and approved by highest authority in the police department. Checkpoints must be manned by a number of police officers with their vehicles to provide a significant "show of force" to reassure the drivers that they are not being singled out for investigation. The procedure for selecting vehicles from the traffic flow must limit individual officer discretion in order to insure that arbitrary or biased selection procedures are avoided.

Because of these rather elaborate requirements, checkpoints in the United States have been relatively expensive operations. Considerable controversy has arisen as to whether they are cost effective. This question has, in fact, become the central issue in a key case being reviewed by the U.S. Supreme Court (Voas, 1989). In part, this controversy depends on the objectives of checkpoints. Some police departments hold that deterrence is accomplished by simply stopping and interviewing a large number of motorists, regardless of the number of arrests made. Other departments stress making DWI arrests in checkpoint operations.

Those departments which emphasize driver contacts and the creation of deterrence as the principal roles of checkpoints generally employ very brief interviews (10–15 seconds) and only rarely make use of PBTs. Such brief interviews make it unlikely that the officer can detect any but the most highly impaired drivers. Other departments conduct somewhat longer interviews (resulting in fewer drivers contacted), but make greater use of PBT devices, with a resulting higher arrest rate. Voas, Rhodenizer, and Lynn (1985) demonstrated that a checkpoint can produce more DWI arrests per hour than traditional patrol procedures.

The use of PBTs at checkpoints has been limited by the issue of whether a test can be required without "probable cause," or at least a "reason to believe" that the driver is impaired by alcohol. (Since all vehicles are stopped without regard to driver behavior the officer usually has no evidence of impairment.) In an effort to overcome this limitation, passive sensors have been developed (Voas, 1983; Jones, 1986; Jones & Lund, 1985). These hand-held units pump mixed environmental and expired air from in front of the driver's face into the tester and can be made sufficiently sensitive that they will reliably detect those individuals who are over the legal limit (Jones & Lund, 1985).

Legal analysis of these devices (Fields & Henricko, 1986) suggests that their use does not constitute a "search" under the provisions of the Fourth Amendment. They can therefore be used without establishing probable cause that an offense has been committed. This should make it possible for police to use such devices at sobriety checkpoints. When this is done, a drunk driver can be detected in 10–15 seconds (Voas & Layfield, 1983). Passive sensors are currently being tested by a number of police departments but their constitutionality has not yet been tested in the courts.

Current Status of DWI Enforcement

In 1980 a new element entered the DWI enforcement picture. This was the emergence of citizen activist groups, such as Mothers Against Drunk Driving (MADD) and Remove Intoxicated Drivers (RID) (McCarthy and Harvey, 1988; Ungerleider & Bloch, 1988). These groups succeeded in calling public attention to the drunk driving problem and in motivating legislators to pass new DWI legislation. Most of this legislation has dealt with increasing the penalties for DWI and making them mandatory, or with prohibiting plea bargaining. The general effect of this type of legislation, with respect to enforcement, was to increase the efforts of defendants to avoid conviction, thereby putting increased stress on the quality of the evidence provided by the police officer in court. This increased pressure on the police investigation was counterbalanced somewhat by the adoption of illegal per se laws in 45 states.

In theory, an illegal per se law reduces the requirement on the police officer to present evidence of impairment, however in practice it does not eliminate it entirely. It is still necessary to show probable cause for stopping a vehicle. In addition, despite the per se law, many courts continue to allow defense arguments regarding the behavior of the defendant.

A second significant element in the new wave of legislation was the passage of "administrative per se" laws, which empowered the motor vehicle departments to suspend the licenses of drivers not only for failure to take a chemical test but also for failing such a test. Many of these laws permit the police officer to seize the driving permit at the time of arrest and substitute a notice of hearing which serves as a temporary license. The license is then forwarded to the state department of motor vehicles. The suspension takes place unless the hearing determines that the police officer did not have probable cause to require a chemical test or that the chemical test procedure was faulty. Administrative per se laws provide additional incentives for the police to make arrests by ensuring that arrests for drunk driving will have immediate consequences and that their efforts will not be invalidated by plea bargaining or some other limitation in the judicial procedures. At the same time, such laws add somewhat to the paperwork required at the time of arrest.

This wave of legislation also produced an increase in the number of states that specifically provided for the use of pre-arrest breath tests at the roadside by police officers. However, most police forces continue to use these devices as they had before—only at the end of the investigation.

Perhaps the most significant effect of this wave of legislation and the public attention given to drunk driving was the fact that it reminded police departments and individual police officers of the extent of public support for rigorous DWI enforcement. This public support also resulted in additional funds for many police departments for DWI enforcement and political support to pursue drunk driving arrests more rigorously.

Evaluation of Enforcement Programs

While considerable effort has gone into the enforcement of drunk driving laws in the United States and significant sums have been employed in purchasing equipment and in paying overtime to special DWI patrols, relatively little rigorous scientific evaluation of these efforts has occurred (Jonah & Wilson, 1983). Several factors mitigate against such evaluations. First, most enforcement efforts are implemented as part of a package of new DWI laws, with the result that it is difficult to separate the effect of the increased enforcement effort from other changes in the DWI control system.

Secondly, the public and many policy makers accept relatively superficial evaluations, and so there is little appreciation of the need for rigorous scientific evaluation. For example, many enforcement programs are evaluated on the basis of a change in the number of DWI arrests. This is a completely inadequate basis for such evaluations since changes in the arrest rate are subject to differing interpretations. Increases in arrests are often cited as evidence that intensified enforcement is working. However, decreases in arrests are also cited as evidence that the enforcement process is achieving its goal, because (so the reasoning goes) there are decreasing numbers of drunk drivers on the road. Thus, this measure of enforcement effectiveness is generally useless, although it may be somewhat useful as an intervening variable to help explain reductions in alcohol-related crashes.

The alcohol-related crash criterion presents difficulties because BAC data are principally obtained from fatally injured drivers. BAC data are otherwise available only for that small proportion of less severe crashes in which a DWI arrest is made, which clearly makes these biased statistics. To obtain a more objective measure of enforcement impact, crash series, such as single vehicle crashes occurring late at night, are frequently used. Such crashes are more likely to involve a drunk driver than multivehicle crashes occurring during daylight hours. However, in many communities, relevant crash records are either too poorly kept or the numbers of crashes are too few to provide a good basis for evaluating enforcement programs. A better but much more costly measure is to make use of roadside surveys in which drivers are asked to volunteer a breath sample for research purposes. These surveys provide a measure of the number of drivers who are impaired during those times when most drinking and driving occurs, and can provide an important measure of the impact of an enforcement program.

Two studies have shown changes in the average BAC of drivers using the roadways as a result of enforcement programs. The first of these (Levy et al., 1977) evaluated changes in roadside survey results at 19 of the 35 Alcohol Safety Action Projects. The researchers found a statistically significant reduction in the number of drivers with illegal BACs in roadside surveys conducted after the projects were initiated, compared with results obtained before program implementation. These results, however, were undoubtedly influenced by elements of the ASAP projects other than the increase in enforcement of DWI laws.

A demonstration of impact more specifically traceable to increased enforcement was reported by Voas and Hause (1987) in a study of a three-year special enforcement program in the city of Stockton, California. Over a three-year period they reported a drop of as much as one-third in the number of drivers above the .10 legal limit. This drop in impaired drivers was accompanied by a significant reduction in night time crashes when compared to four other similar cities in the central valley of California. The reduced level of alcohol-related crashes was maintained during the three years of enforcement activity, but tended to disappear when the special enforcement project came to an end.

The Stockton study reported by Voas and Hause provided a good illustration of the typical three-phase interaction between enforcement activity and publicity (Figure 6.2). The Stockton Study began on January 1, 1976 and continued to the end of June 1979. At the end of 1975 and in early 1976, when the program was initiated, its novelty provoked considerable television and newspaper coverage. The number of Saturday night accidents fell throughout this first year (the publicity phase). During the second year, after the publicity dropped off, the public was left to test its expectation of a higher probability of apprehension from contacts with the increased numbers of police officers on the road (the reality testing phase). This period showed an increase in fatal accidents. During the last 18 months of the program, however, accidents leveled off at a rate below the baseline rate (the adjustment phase). Once the program came to an end the accident rate remained at the adjustment level for only about six months and then began to climb very rapidly, surpassing the 74–75 baseline rate within a year of the end of the special program.

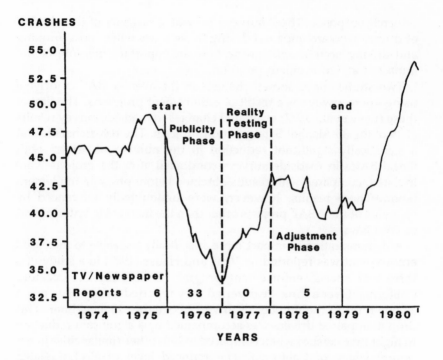

FIGURE 6.2. Phases of impact of a special DWI enforcement program: Stockton data for Friday and Saturday night accidents (8PM–4AM). From "Increased DUI Enforcement Program, Stockton, California" (Technical Report DOTHS-802-205) by J.M. Hause, D. Mattheson, R. Hannon, and E. Chavez, 1977, Washington, D.C.: National Highway Safety Administration.

This three-phase reaction to publicized enforcement programs is reasonably typical of those efforts which have demonstrated at least a temporary impact upon the alcohol-related accident level. Ross (1984) has pointed to these relatively short-term impacts of increased enforcement to suggest that deterrence is not effective in the long run. In the case of Stockton, California, however, the long-term application of the deterrence theory was not really tested, since the intervention has to be maintained permanently, for permanent results. Deterrence theory requires that if the intervention is short term, the deterrent effect is transitory. Several other scientific evaluations of enforcement programs which have found positive results are available in the literature (e.g., Klein, 1982; Lacey et al., 1986; Levy, Shae, & Asch, 1989; Voas, Rhodenizer, & Lynn, 1985).

Overall, the results of traditional enforcement programs in the United States have tended to be similar to those covered in the Ross (1984) international review of DWI programs. Short-term reductions in drinking–driving crashes were obtained in some cases, particularly where enforcement was accompanied by considerable publicity, but the changes tend to be transitory. The transitory nature of enforcement impact may be because the police fail to utilize fully the powers provided to them by the law (as in the case of the British Road Safety Act) or because, after an initial intensification, enforcement efforts return to previous levels (as in Stockton). Finally, as Borkenstein (1975) has hypothesized, it may be necessary to keep changing enforcement procedures in order to make them "new" and newsworthy and thereby attract the attention of the public.

There have been few scientific evaluations of the chemistry-based checkpoint system in the United States. Voas, Rhodenizer, and Lynn (1985) reported on a year-long enforcement program in which checkpoints were implemented every weekend within the city of Charlottesville, Virginia. Their evaluation indicated that the police apprehended approximately 1% of the drivers stopped at the checkpoint. In addition, another 1% of the drivers were arrested for driving without a license. Random digit dialing surveys indicated that approximately one-fourth of the nighttime drivers in Charlottesville came into direct contact with a checkpoint and that over 90% of all drivers were aware of the checkpoint program. Comparison of the nighttime and alcohol-related crash rates in Charlottesville with those of a similar community which did not employ checkpoints indicated that this procedure reduced such crashes by approximately 15%. A similar reduction was apparent when crash rates for Charlottesville were compared with those for the State of Virginia as a whole.

Levy, Shea, and Asch (1989) have reported on an evaluation of a "strikeforce" program in the State of New Jersey which conducted checkpoints during the 1983–1985 period. They evaluated the effect of this checkpoint program independently from two other DWI enforcement efforts occurring during the same period by the use of time series and covariance analysis. They found that the strikeforce program, of which the checkpoints were the major component, was associated with a drop of 10–15% in the single vehicle nighttime crash rate and that this effect was relatively stable over a three-year period. Their analysis indicated that this checkpoint effect was greater than the effects of the other concomitant programs, one of which emphasized public information, while the other emphasized traditional enforcement.

Additional evidence for the impact of checkpoint procedures was obtained by Williams and Lund (1984), who conducted a random digit dialing survey in communities in which checkpoint enforcement procedures were used and compared the attitude and knowledge of the driving public in those communities with those in communities that did not make use of checkpoints. They found that drivers in communities in which checkpoints were used reported higher levels of deterrence of drinking and driving than citizens of counties where checkpoints were not used. Lacey et al. (1986) found evidence for the impact of a special DWI enforcement program on crashes in Clearwater, Florida, although checkpoints were only one among several elements in this program. These studies provide some evidence of the effectiveness of the chemistry-based enforcement system. However, this system will have to receive wider application in the United States before sufficient data can be collected to determine its effectiveness relative to traditional behavioral enforcement and public information programs.

Whether or not this extended use of the checkpoint system will be possible in the United States is uncertain. The procedure has been successfully challenged in the State of Michigan (*Sitz vs. Michigan State Police*), and the U.S. Supreme Court has accepted this case for review. If the Supreme Court upholds the Appellate Court decision, the use of checkpoints will be banned on the basis that they violate the Fourth Amendment to the U.S. Constitution which protects individuals against unreasonable searches and seizures. A review of the evidence presented in this litigation by Voas (1989) suggests that the trial court record inadequately covered existing research. It remains to be determined, however, what the Supreme Court decision will be.

DWI ADJUDICATION IN THE UNITED STATES

Federal vs. State Role

Except in national parks and other federal lands, the full responsibility for dealing with the drunk driving problem lies with the states and localities. The federal government can provide funds and technical assistance to the states to assist in their enforcement efforts and can even apply considerable pressure to persuade states to pass drunk driving legislation. But, in the final analysis, it is the states, not the federal government, that determine the content of drunk driving laws which apply to U.S. drivers.

Early in this century it became obvious that at least a minimum of uniformity would be required among the state vehicle codes in a highly mobile society if commerce and transportation were to be encouraged. In 1926 The National Committee on Uniform Traffic Laws and Ordinances (NCUTLO, 1987) was formed, and the first version of the Uniform Vehicle Code was published in a effort to guide states in their developmental highway legislation. The Uniform Vehicle Code, which is reviewed and revised regularly, remains a significant factor in the development of drunk driving legislation in the states.

In 1966, with the passage of the Highway Safety Act and the formation of the U.S. Department of Transportation, the federal government threw its weight behind uniform vehicle codes by issuing a standard on "Codes and Laws." Despite these efforts to promote uniformity, new laws tend to be adopted over an extended period of time, with one or two states initially accepting a new element, the rest of the states following slowly, and a few holding out perhaps for as long as a decade.

To speed the adoption of laws which the Department of Transportation sees as particularly significant to the drunk driving problem, the U.S. Congress has passed legislation which provides incentive funds to the states which adopt the desired laws. These federal laws (Section 408 and Section 410 of the Highway Safety Act) also provide incentive grants to states to promote more rapid administrative processing of cases so as to decrease the time between arrest and the application of a penalty such as license revocation.

The major weapon available to the federal government to persuade states to pass desired legislation is the threat to withhold funds available to a particular state out of the Federal Highway Trust Fund for road construction and maintenance. This persuasive measure has been used only once in the drinking–driving field, but with great success. This was in the campaign to require states to pass age-21 drinking laws.

Despite the efforts of the federal government and of citizen activist groups (as discussed earlier), significant variations in drunk driving laws still exist between states. For example, only 26 of the states have laws providing for preliminary breath tests, and only 23 states and the District of Columbia have administrative per se laws. Even in the case of such a basic law as the establishment of a per se BAC limit there are still five holdout states which have not enacted this legislation (NHTSA, 1989a).

Local Court Resources

The differences between state laws are not the only barriers to standardizing DWI adjudication in the United States. Most DWI adjudication occurs in local municipal courts which, under the American doctrine of separation of powers, are completely independent of the executive and legislative branches. Most local judges are elected. They can operate independently, not only from the local city and county governments, but also from the other judges within the same court system. Because of the large amount of discretion given to the court, each judge can apply his or her idiosyncratic view of the seriousness of the drinking-driving offense and the characteristics of the offender to the cases that come before him or her. Therefore, there is often considerable variation between judges, and these differences can be magnified by the natural tendency of defense counsels to "judge shop" in an effort to have their cases heard before the most lenient tribunal.

The drinking-driving offense is the most frequent misdemeanor adjudicated in the lower courts of the United States. Because of the large number of cases, efficient handling procedures are important in order to avoid significant case backlogs. It is important to avoid jury trials, when possible, because of the length of time and expense involved in the use of juries. In fact, it is desirable to avoid trials entirely and use plea bargains to clear the cases as expeditiously as possible. This conserves the limited resources of the lower courts in the face of heavy DWI case loads. These courts are vulnerable to pressures that increase backlogs. Both prosecutors and judges are motivated to accept charge reductions and/or sentence modifications in return for pleas which avoid extended trials.

This lack of resources with which to deal with the overcrowding of the lower court system has left these agencies vulnerable to pressures to reduce caseloads. This has been responsible, at least in part, for the practical nullification of some drunk driving legislation. Voas (1975) and Ross (1976) have both pointed to the problems which local courts frequently have in imposing what are viewed as severe sanctions. Laws such as those providing a jail sentence for first-time DWI offenders have frequently been "neutralized" by defendants and their lawyers who, to avoid the possibility of such penalties, enter more not-guilty pleas and make more requests for jury trials. The resulting accommodation by the courts produces an increase in plea bargains and/or a decrease in conviction rates.

Efforts to evaluate the effect of sanctions have often been compromised by the failure of the lower courts to impose such sanctions uniformly because of limitations in their resources. A typical example is provided by Voas (1975) who described the implementation of a new law in the state of Arizona which required a one-day jail sentence upon conviction of driving while impaired by alcohol. Following the passage of this law the Phoenix court system saw a rise from 54% to 85% in the number of requests for a jury trial and a rise from 27% to 74% in not-guilty pleas. At the same time the proportion of individuals convicted of DWI fell from 74% to 57% and the number of cases dismissed rose from 20% to 38%. Thus the legislative attempt to impose a more severe penalty for DWI was at least partially neutralized by forces operating within the lower court system.

The difficulty of obtaining a consensus even within a court system is demonstrated by the study by Robertson, Rich, and Ross (1973) of a court-initiated program in the city of Chicago to impose a mandatory 7-day jail sentence for driving while intoxicated. The program was announced and implemented by the Supervising Judge who directed magistrates in Chicago's traffic courts to sentence persons convicted of driving while intoxicated to 7 days in jail and to recommend to the Motor Vehicle Department that their driver's licenses be suspended for 1 year. Despite this order from the senior judge, only 557 of nearly 6600 drivers arrested in Chicago during the program were actually sentenced to 7 days in jail.

Use of Reduced Penalties

There is extensive evidence that a large portion of the individuals convicted of drinking and driving can be classified as problem drinkers (Nichols et al., 1978), although the full extent of the relationship between traditional alcoholism and drunk driving behavior has yet to be determined (Vingilis, 1983). Despite the lack of unanimity among experts as to whether arrested drivers are problem drinkers, the courts have accepted the concept that a significant portion of those who come before them charged with drunk driving are likely problem drinkers (see Chapter 4, this volume), and have provided for pre-sentence investigations to determine whether there is evidence of problem drinking. Alternative sanctioning programs providing for treatment of those determined to have a drinking problem have also been provided. While the criminal statutes give the court extensive authority under probation to require treatment, most courts attempt to motivate DWI offenders to accept treatment by reducing other penalties such as the fine or the length of the driver's license suspension.

The distinction between the problem and social drinker leads to the issue of the relative utility of punishment as compared to treatment and/or educational measures for dealing with the drunk driver. If drunk driving is principally a social behavior problem, then traditional punitive measures would appear to be the most appropriate sanctions available to the court. On the other hand, if drunk driving is principally a health problem, then court actions need to result in education and treatment programs leading to rehabilitation and recovery. Traditionally, most judges dealing with the drunk driving problem were likely to see the issue as a simple matter of the application of appropriate punitive measures. Despite this tendency, over the last twenty years most courts have been persuaded that it is necessary to provide for the treatment of drunk drivers because of the evidence marshalled by the "experts" that a large portion of those charged with this offense have a drinking problem.

Faced with the need to provide for this treatment option judges have tended to be willing to shorten or eliminate license suspension penalties and to reduce fines to assist the offenders in paying for a requisite treatment or education program. Most courts have developed some semiprofessional capability to identify problem drinkers among the offenders through a simplified presentence assessment procedure applied by court staff using interviews and self-report measures such as the Michigan Alcohol Safety Test (MAST) (Selzer, 1971) and the Mortimer–Filkins Interview and Questionnaire (Filkins, Mortimer, Post & Chapman, 1973). These assessment devices have recently been reviewed by Popkin et al. (1988) and found to be generally inadequate for treatment program definition.

Alternatives to the courts having the responsibility to identify problem drinkers include the use of local alcohol treatment providers and the establishment of local government agencies such as the Alcohol Safety Action Program treatment management agencies. These agencies, which were originally founded during the federal government's ASAP program in the early 1970s, have continued to provide diagnostic and referral services for the courts since the original ASAP programs came to a close. In addition to the provision for diagnostic services most courts have at least two levels of treatment providers; those who conduct a 10–12 hour educational program designed for "social drinkers" and those who conduct more intensive, longer-lasting inpatient and outpatient programs for problem drinkers.

Toward the end of the 1970s the typical lower court in the United States had established a system where most DWI offenders pleaded guilty to the DWI offense, thus avoiding the need for a trial, and in return received a minimum set of sanctions which normally included a fine and a short license suspension. Both the fine and the license suspension could be reduced by attendance at education or treatment programs.

Impact of Citizen Activism

The advent of the citizen activist movement challenged this relatively lenient treatment of the drunk driver. The activist movement of the 1980s, which was powered by the victims of drunk driving accidents, demanded more severe sanctions for this offense (McCarthy & Harvey, 1988; Ungerleider & Bloch, 1988). The movement quickly came to see the judges in the lower courts as the principal barriers to achieving more stringent handling of drunk drivers. An early activity of these organizations was to establish "court watch" programs to pressure judges to impose more severe sentences in DWI cases. They accompanied victims to the court to demand harsher treatment of DWI offenders who had been in accidents causing injuries to others.

Mandatory Penalty Laws

The efforts of MADD, RID, and other activist groups were not limited to the courts. They were even more successful in state legislatures where a large number of laws were enacted in an effort to produce more severe sanctions for the drunk driving offense (Ungerleider & Bloch, 1988). The activists began by demanding legislation establishing more severe penalties for drunk driving. Special interest was shown in jail sentences for first and particularly multiple offenders.

When these laws failed to be fully implemented by the courts the activist organizations took up the cry for "mandatory" penalties, which judges would have to impose. As of 1989, 28 states had laws providing for a mandatory 90-day license suspension for the first DWI offense, and 27 states had laws providing for a mandatory jail sentence for driving while suspended (NHTSA, 1989a). However, in many areas these mandatory penalties were strongly resisted by the offenders and their defense counsels who threatened to extend court backlogs by demanding full trials and even jury trials. Some courts avoided mandatory penalties by allowing pleas to a lesser charge. This led to a third step which was to back mandatory penalties with the addition of "no-plea-bargaining" laws.

Anti-Plea Bargain Laws

While individual judges and/or prosecutors had from time to time adopted policies against plea bargains, the failure in many cases of the courts to impose the sanctions that were supposedly mandatory resulted in the legislatures themselves passing laws which banned plea bargaining. These laws required judges or prosecutors to give specific written reasons for not prosecuting a DWI charge. As of 1989, only 11 states had enacted such laws (NHTSA, 1989a), but initial evaluations of the anti-plea-bargain legislation have indicated that it does have some potential for reducing the number of plea-bargained cases. Figure 6.3, for example, shows the change in the proportion of

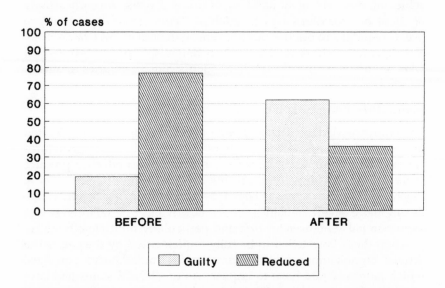

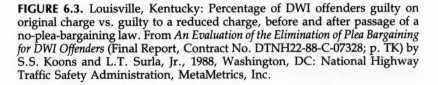

FIGURE 6.3. Louisville, Kentucky: Percentage of DWI offenders guilty on original charge vs. guilty to a reduced charge, before and after passage of a no-plea-bargaining law. From *An Evaluation of the Elimination of Plea Bargaining for DWI Offenders* (Final Report, Contract No. DTNH22-88-C-07328; p. TK) by S.S. Koons and L.T. Surla, Jr., 1988, Washington, DC: National Highway Traffic Safety Administration, MetaMetrics, Inc.

DWI cases that resulted in conviction on the original charge as compared to a conviction on a reduced charge before and after the enactment of an anti-plea-bargaining law in the state of Kentucky (Koons & Surla, 1988). In another community (Fort Smith, AR) studied by these investigators, the proportion of DWI charges reduced to "reckless driving" changed from 42% before, to 7% after, the passage of an anti-plea-bargaining law.

The increased pressure of the citizen activist groups on the courts through court monitoring programs, the enactment of legislation prohibiting plea bargaining, and the adoption of anti-plea-bargaining policies by the judiciary did result in the imposition of penalties such as short jail sentences for first offenders on a more routine basis. These sentences would not have been possible a decade earlier. Over all, the levels of fines were also increased. Where incarceration was not employed, offenders were frequently sentenced to community service programs. The length of license suspensions was generally extended and loss of license became a more uniform result of DWI conviction. Despite this general trend, the penalties for drinking and driving in the United States remain less than those typically imposed in Europe, particularly in relation to loss of license.

Administrative Diversion

The failure of traffic courts to impose license suspension regularly became a particular issue because of research (see below) that demonstrated that this was an effective special deterrent to drunk driving. The desire to increase the use of license suspension as a sanction for drunk driving led to a fourth step to overcome the limitations of the lower courts in adjudicating DWI cases. This was the adoption of administrative per se laws. These laws were built upon the existing implied-consent legislation which was enacted in all states. Under this law a license could be withdrawn by the motor vehicle department if the individual refused to take a breath test. Administrative per se laws, which as of 1989 had been enacted by 27 states (NHTSA, 1989a), added to this the provision that if the individual took the test and was over the state per se limit the license would also be withdrawn.

In this way the complete power to withdraw the license was taken from the courts and placed in the hands of the motor vehicle department. An administrative hearing was required before the license could be withdrawn. The only issues at this hearing were whether the police officer had probable cause to make a stop and require a breath test and whether the breath test was accurate. Unless the offender could successfully challenge these two findings the license was automatically withdrawn for a stated period of time (Reeder, 1981).

This law provided for a two-track process. Whether or not the individual lost his or her license as a result of the administrative per se law, he or she was still subject to being charged with drunk driving and, if convicted in court, subject to the normal penalties. In practice, if the individual lost his or her license under the administrative per se law and was then convicted in court, which would normally result in a second period of suspension, only a single period of suspension would actually be imposed. However, the other court sanctions such as fines and jail time were normally imposed quite independent of the administrative per se process.

The first state to adopt administrative per se was Minnesota in 1983. Currently 24 states have administrative per se laws and several studies have demonstrated that these laws appear to be effective in reducing alcohol-related fatalities in those states that have this legislation (Zador et al., 1988; Klein, 1989).

Overall, the trend in adjudication of drunk driving offenses during the 1980s has been toward the imposition of more severe penalties on a more universal basis than was typical of the adjudication process in earlier periods. However, the adjudication process continues to vary from locality to locality, principally because of the limitations in resources available to the courts.

Limitations in Correction Facilities

Not only are the resources of the court limited, but the resources available to correction departments and local health departments for handling DWI offenders are also inadequate. A recent study by Ross and Voas (1989) illustrates the problem presented to the court by the lack of supporting corrections facilities. A judge, James O'Farrell of the New Philadelphia, OH, Municipal Court, routinely sentenced first-time DWI offenders to 15 days in jail. However, when these offenders were tracked through the corrections system, it became apparent that the county jail was overcrowded and under court order to limit the admission of new inmates. As a result, few of those sentenced to 15 days actually served their time. They were scheduled for admission to the correction facility at a time several months in the future but when the time came for them to report, the institution

was often still over crowded. Eventually they were excused from serving their terms.

An effective adjudication system requires not only reasonable funding for its own processing activities, but also the availability of appropriate sanctioning alternatives. The very large numbers of DWI offenders apprehended each year in the United States, when added to those that result from other significant social problems (such as the control of illicit drugs), have led to a straining of all of the criminal justice facilities and imposed significant limitations upon court action.

DWI SANCTIONING IN THE UNITED STATES

The effectiveness of various sanctions for the drunk driving offense has attracted considerable study in the United States (Voas, 1986 a,b; Nichols & Ross, 1989). However, many of these studies have been handicapped by a lack of agreement on the appropriate criteria for measuring effectiveness. Part of the confusion comes from the multiple purposes that differing sanctions are designed to meet, and part from the conflicting goals of the partisans who promote alternative sanctioning proposals.

It is important, then, when considering the effectiveness of various sanctions used in the American criminal justice system, to understand the perceived purposes and theoretical backgrounds of the most commonly applied sanctions in order to be able to develop reasonable measures of their effectiveness. Overall, sanctions for DWI offenses can be seen as having eight purposes, four of them principally related to the individual offender and four related to broader community and society goals.

Control of Individual Behavior

Punishment

The purpose most generally recognized by the public for sanctions is to punish: that is, to produce sufficiently painful negative consequences that the individual will be deterred from repeating the prohibited behavior. Behavioral scientists have devoted considerable attention to the role of punishment in learning. Unfortunately, little of this theory has been translated to the DWI sanctioning process or its evaluation. The concept of deterrence does recognize both the element of penalty severity and the significance of the time between the offense (the negative behavior to be controlled) and the application of the sanction, based on learning theory research (Ross, 1984).

The usual sanctioning procedures in the lower courts would be expected to be less than fully effective because trial delays are frequently long and the penalties are typically mild (at least in relationship to legislative intent). Thus, the application of sanctions is frequently delayed for some months after the offense has been committed. As Ross (1984) points out, however, there has been little research on the effect of delayed punishment on deterrence.

It is also clear that it is the offenders' perception of the pain produced by the sanction, not the public evaluation of the sanction, which is instrumental in producing behavioral change. It is quite possible, for example, that upper middle-class legislators and citizen activists overestimate the painfulness of a jail term to the offenders who actually receive this sanction, many of whom may have experienced jail previously for other offenses.

Education

The ubiquitous response to DWI offenders in the United States has been the imposition of one or more types of education programs in an attempt to reform their drunk driving behavior through the presentation of information. In the early 1970s the American Automobile Association sponsored the development of an educational program for convicted drunk drivers in Phoenix, Arizona, which became a model for short-term (10–12 hour) programs around the nation. These programs were often sponsored by the American Automobile Association and funded through offenders fees. Offenders were referred by the courts to the programs. Frequently, offenders were motivated to attend by a reduction in the fine or in the length of driving suspension (Stewart & Malfetti, 1970).

A somewhat more sophisticated process was developed as a part of the federally sponsored ASAP which provided for the separation of "problem" from "social" drinkers among those convicted of drunk driving. Short term education programs were used principally with the social drinkers since research conducted as part of the ASAP Program (Nichols, Weinstein, Ellingstad, & Struckman-Johnson, 1978) suggested that the recidivism of problem drinkers was not improved by education programs, while social drinkers who received an educational program demonstrated a small (10%) reduction in recidivism. Evaluation of these education programs in Albuquerque by Swenson and Clay (1977) and in Sacramento by Reis (1982a,b) demonstrated that in certain cases the provision of home study materials was as effective as requiring attendance at lecture courses.

Clearly the use of education as a remedial procedure for dealing with the drunk driver, which assumes that offenders drink and drive out of a lack of information, is a dubious proposition. However, it is well established that most drivers have little understanding of blood alcohol concentration and its relationship to the amount and type of alcohol consumed. It is also possible that they have given little thought to alternatives to drinking and driving such as the "designated-driver" concept. Research by Beirness (1987) suggests that individuals who underestimate their BAC are more likely to drive over the limit.

While a number of education programs for convicted drunk drivers have been evaluated using the recidivism criteria (Mann et al., 1983), none have provided the type of detailed evaluation which relates changes in specific knowledge areas to reductions in drinking and driving. Thus the true benefit of educational procedures continues to be uncertain, particularly since offenders are frequently motivated to take such courses by a reduction of the period of license suspension. Studies of the relative benefits, in terms of accident reduction and recidivism, of license suspension compared with education programs suggest that license suspension is the more effective sanction (Peck, Sadler, & Perrine, 1985). Moreover, there may be a hidden issue in providing information on breath tests and enforcement procedures in general. This training may produce an individual more able to avoid arrest but no less accident involved.

Rehabilitation

The use of rehabilitation programs in the United States was relatively infrequent until the establishment of the Department of Transportation and the issuance of the 1968 Alcohol and Highway Safety Report. That report focused on the role of the problem drinker in alcohol-related crashes and resulted in the development of the ASAP program which, while taking a systematic approach to the strengthening of all community agencies related to the drunk driving problem, emphasized the role of the problem drinker and the development of treatment programs for handling this type of DWI offender. Evaluation of the rehabilitation efforts initiated in the 35 communities which implemented a federally supported ASAP program indicated that most of the rehabilitation efforts applied to problem drinkers were ineffective. Perhaps this was principally because they were relatively short-term efforts. They generally involved from 3 to a maximum of 6 months (Nichols et al., 1978).

Based on this experience the National Highway Traffic Safety Administration funded a three-year treatment demonstration program in the city of Sacramento, California, in which an intensive year-long therapy program was instituted for individuals convicted of driving while impaired. This longer, more intensive, program was possible due to California legislation which allowed multiple offenders to maintain their driving privilege, providing they agreed to participate in a year-long treatment program which involved not only group therapy and attendance at A.A., but also biweekly meetings with probation counselors.

In the Sacramento program a considerable effort was made to separate the "problem" and the "social" drinker groups, with the social drinkers receiving a standard 12-hour education program, while the problem drinkers entered a year-long treatment program. The project provided for the evaluation of two approaches to therapy, a traditional group therapy approach and a novel "skills training" program, against a control group of problem drinkers who received no treatment. The results indicated that the problem drinker rehabilitation program had a slight benefit over no treatment. However, the significance of this finding was reduced by the fact that a group of offenders who received only biweekly counseling sessions had recidivism rates not significantly different from those treated (Reis, 1982a).

The use of rehabilitation as a sanction for the DWI offense assumes that DWI offenders have a health problem and that the way to change their behavior is to deal with their drinking problem. This approach tends to have the further assumption that individuals who have become addicted to alcohol, or who have at least made alcohol central to their lifestyles, cannot change their behavior other than through treatment. Negative reinforcement (punishment) or educational programs will be ineffective in changing their drinking–driving behavior. As noted above, the evidence for the proposition that a large portion of the DWI offenders are problem drinkers is strong, but the relationship of the drinking symptoms demonstrated by this group to the drinking problems manifested by individuals entering traditional alcohol rehabilitation programs or meeting the definition of "alcoholic" has yet to be clearly established (Vingilis, 1983). Nevertheless, the use of treatment for offenders judged to have a drinking problem is a well-established element of the DWI sanctioning process in the United States, and there is some evidence for its effectiveness (Mann et al., 1983; Nichols, 1989).

Incapacitation

A fourth objective of the sanctions directed at the individual offender is the use of incapacitation or physical restraint to prevent the unwanted behavior. This is best illustrated by the jail sentence in which the offender is separated from society under conditions which assure that he cannot repeat the offense. Except in the case of multiple offenders or DWI offenders with other serious crimes, jail sentences for drunk driving have been too short to provide any significant limitation on driving. The use of jail sentences has principally been supported by citizen activists and legislators for their punishment value rather than for their incapacitation effect. There is little evidence that jail sentences have any specific deterrent effect (Voas, 1986a).

The principal application of the incapacitation concept in DWI sanctioning is the suspension/revocation of the license to drive. This penalty is widely applied and apparently widely feared by offenders, who expend considerable effort to avoid a conviction that will result in license suspension. If convicted, they are generally willing to attend relatively lengthy treatment programs in order to avoid suspension.

A significant limitation on the use of license suspension as a method of incapacitating the convicted DWI is the well-documented tendency of offenders to drive despite suspension (Hagen, McConnell, & Williams 1980b; Sadler & Perrine, 1984; Ross & Gonzales, 1988). However, studies have indicated that despite this tendency to continue driving, offenders under suspension drive less and perhaps more carefully (Hagen, McConnell, & Williams 1980a,b; Ross & Gonzales, 1988) and therefore have fewer accidents than convicted offenders who are not suspended.

The National Highway Traffic Safety Administration has funded studies to develop methods for enforcing the driver's license suspension more effectively. However, cost-effective methods of supervising the suspended driver in urban areas have yet to be developed. Further, some difficulty has occurred in prosecuting those offenders who are occasionally caught operating a vehicle while suspended. Many individuals who are stopped and ticketed for offenses while suspended are not charged with the driving-while-suspended offense. Many of those who are charged are not prosecuted, apparently due to administrative and/or communication problems between the Motor Vehicle Department and the courts or to the judicial requirements placed on the court itself. In Virginia, for example, suspension notices are sent out through the mail. Offenders caught driving while suspended generally claim that they did not receive the mail notice. The court, lacking evidence of acceptable legal service, is forced to drop the case.

The tendency of violators to drive while suspended has led to the passage of laws which permit the impounding of the vehicle or the vehicle license tag in 19 states (NHTSA, 1989a). In some of these states (Ohio and Minnesota, for example) the vehicle tag can be replaced by a special tag which will call the attention of the police to the fact that the vehicle is owned by a suspended driver. The effectiveness of these laws has yet to be evaluated.

Another approach to attempting to apprehend more driving while suspended offenders has been the use of computerized terminals in police patrol cars which permit the rapid entry of the vehicle tag number and the interrogation of a special file of vehicles owned by suspended drivers (Miller, 1978). If the system comes up with a match the police patrol car can then stop the vehicle and check the driver for a valid license. While this type of technology provides an opportunity to significantly decrease the number of suspended drivers who are operating illegally, this capability is not widely available.

Community Considerations in Sanctioning

In addition to the four features of sanctions directed at changing individual behavior, there are four factors which are frequently considered in the establishment of sanctions which relate to community goals rather than the intention to reform individual behavior.

General Deterrence

Perhaps the most utilized rationale for sanctions is to create general deterrence—that is, fear of punishment—among all drivers and especially among those drinking drivers who are not apprehended, in order to deter impaired driving. It is the general deterrence value of various penalty alternatives which is most frequently evaluated. Perhaps the largest amount of evaluation literature in general deterrence concerns the impact of license suspension and jail sentences. Surveys of the driving public generally indicate that the license suspension penalty is the best understood and the most feared of the drunk driving sanctions. Two recent studies (Zador et al., 1988; Klein, 1989) have demonstrated that administrative per se suspension laws are effective in reducing alcohol-related accidents in those states which have enacted these laws.

The evidence for the effectiveness of the jail sentence for drunk drivers is less clear. This literature has recently been reviewed by Voas (1986a) and by Nichols and Ross (1989). The principal evidence for the general deterrent effect of jail sentences comes from a study of a judicial policy in Minneapolis, Minnesota, to sentence all first-time DWI offenders to 48 hours in jail. That program was evaluated by Falkowski (1984) and by Cleary and Rodgers (1986) through time-series analysis and found to produce a 20% reduction in nighttime fatal crashes after the policy had been in effect for two months. There was, however, also a concomitant increase in the number of arrests in Hennepin County and the rest of the state of Minnesota concurrent with this policy. It is possible that some of the measured effect was due to this increase in arrests. In the neighboring control Ramsey County, for example, which did not implement the jail policy, there was an increase in arrests and a smaller decrease in nighttime fatalities.

Cleary and Rogers (1986) also found a reduction in fatal crashes in Hennepin County during the period in which the 2-day jail sentence policy was in effect which was greater (25%) than in the remainder of the state (16%). Jones et al. (1987) evaluated a law which provided for a 2-day jail sentence for DWI in the state of Tennessee. Prior to the implementation of this law, nighttime single vehicle fatal crashes were rising in Tennessee, but following its implementation there was a decline in such crashes for the next 2 years. Daytime crashes, however, continued to increase. They concluded that the jail sentence legislation may have contributed to a reduction in alcohol-related crashes of up to 15%.

On a broader national basis, Zador et al. (1988) reported that states with laws requiring jail or community service for first-time DWI offenders demonstrated an estimated 6% reduction in nighttime fatal crashes. However, Klein (1989) repeated their work and did not support their results.

The evidence for the effectiveness of severe sanctions in creating deterrence to drunk driving is sufficiently limited that some investigators, notably Ross (1984), argue that they do not produce deterrence. He suggests that deterrence is primarily a function of the perceived level of enforcement rather than the severity of penalties. While there are few studies to support the significance of penalties in creating general deterrence, it is not clear whether this is because the penalties themselves are ineffective or because the U.S. judicial system has difficulty in applying severe sanctions.

The previously mentioned study by Ross and Voas (1989) of the 15-day jail sanction imposed by the judge in New Philadelphia, Ohio, made use of a questionnaire survey of nighttime drivers to determine the deterrent effect of this sanctioning policy. They found that New Philadelphia drivers were more aware of the sanctions, and rated those sanctions as more severe than did nighttime drivers in a nearby community where jail was rarely used. Thus the basic requirement for deterrence, the perceived severity of the sanction, was present in the New Philadelphia community.

It was not possible for these investigators, however, to determine whether this in turn reduced the amount of drinking and driving because an adequate sample of breath measurements on motorists using the road was not obtained, and the accident data for that small community was too limited to provide reasonable power for a test of the impact of the jail penalty. It seems probable, however, that severe penalties are relatively ineffective in creating deterrence, both because they are irregularly applied and because, in any case, the probability of apprehension in the United States is low. Most U.S. motorists do not expect to be arrested and, therefore, are less concerned about sanctions.

Program Financing

A second community-related factor in DWI sanctioning policy is the collection of funds to offset the cost to the criminal justice system of handling drunk driving cases. While government tax revenues limit funding for court programs in most nations and, as a result, limit resources that can be applied to the drunk driving problem, a unique feature of the American criminal justice system may be the extent to which an attempt is made to collect funds from the offender to offset these costs. A system generally known as "Self-Sufficiency" (NHTSA, 1983) grew out of the experience with the Alcohol Safety Action Projects where it was found that, at least for some communities, the costs of the ASAP could have been financed entirely from offender revenues. In some cases, in fact, communities could have earned a profit on their ASAP investment (Hawkins et al., 1976). While for some years the fines collected by U.S. courts had been used to meet the expenses of the court, the "systems approach" implemented during the ASAP program emphasized the significance of collections from the offender, which were used to provide for the overall needs of the DWI enforcement, adjudication, and sanctioning systems.

The ability to use penalties to raise funds has a significant impact on the type of penalties assessed in the U.S. criminal justice system. Nearly all treatment and education programs for DWI offenders are supported through offender fees. Because it has been possible to collect such fees, the use of treatment as one element of the sanctioning system is essentially ubiquitous throughout the nation. On the other hand, the use of fees to reimburse the corrections department for the costs of incarceration is rare. Partly as a result, the availability of correction facilities for DWI offenders is very limited and few of these offenders are sentenced to jail.

It is likely that in the United States the use of fees, fines, and assessments to help support the DWI criminal justice system will continue. It is also probable that the penalties imposed will tend to favor those programs for which the sponsoring agencies can most easily recover their costs from the offender.

Community Service

A third community-related function of the sanctions used in American courts is the provision of restitution service, either to the community as a whole, or to specific victims of crime. Since drunk driving tends to be a victim-less offense, most DWI restitution programs have been designed to provide general service to the community through such activities as cleaning up public parks and roadways. Some private organizations attempt to provide programs more tailored to the particular skills of the offender. For example, physicians may provide free service in a public hospital, or lawyers may provide free legal services to indigent clients.

The Department of Transportation's National Highway Traffic Safety Administration has attempted to collate information on community restitution programs across the nation (NHTSA, 1985). This survey demonstrated that the use of community service is widespread and involves thousands of convicted DWIs. The cost of managing such community service programs is relatively low compared to alternative sanctions such as incarceration. However, little information is available on the impact of such programs on offender recidivism, though Zador et al. (1988) found that states with laws providing for mandatory jail sentences or *community service in lieu of a jail sentence* had lower alcohol-related fatality rates. Whether or not recidivism is reduced, of course, the use of community service provides a clear benefit to the community as compared to simply incapacitating the offender in jail where costs are experienced by the state and no benefit accrues to the community.

Of some interest are the volunteer organizations that attempt to bring the offender who has, through accident involvement, caused an injury together with the victim to work out a specific restitution program helpful to the injured party. Directors of such programs argue that individualized restitution not only provides whatever financial and service benefit the offender can provide to the victim, but also provides a psychological benefit to the offender, in that the offender can feel more specifically reconciled with society, and this can contribute to rehabilitation. Evidence that such reconciliation leads to a reduction in recidivism is lacking, but it is an intriguing concept which merits evaluation.

Retribution/Education

Ross (1984) notes that retribution is one historic function of sanctions. He argues elsewhere (Ross & Hughes, 1986) that the principal goal of citizen activist groups in seeking legislation to strengthen sanctions is retribution since these groups were organized by the victims of drunk drivers. He suggests that this purpose of sanctions is inappropriate in the instance of impaired driving since the injuries caused through crashes are almost entirely accidental and therefore do not result from a purposeful act which justifies retribution.

The concept of retribution is related to society's standards of behavior. To "deserve" punishment one must break an important rule. The role that the law plays in establishing those principles that educate citizens to the social standards of their society has been highlighted by Andeneas (1988) among others. This is a more subtle role served by severe penalties which has rarely been the subject of scientific discussion. By illustrating the standard of behavior that society expects, the sanction may contribute to interiorization by the public of social goals. This may result in an avoidance of antisocial behavior, not because of deterrence, but because of conformance to perceived social norms.

The United States provides an example of this effect in action. Prior to 1980, despite drunk driving laws which provided for heavy penalties (which, however, were rarely imposed), drinking and driving was generally considered to be socially acceptable behavior. The development in the late 1970s and early 1980s of the citizen activist groups, and the pressure that these groups brought on legislatures to increase the severity of penalties, particularly the use of jail, appears to have had some effect on the societal view of the drunk driving offense. Confinement is generally associated, in the U.S. mind, with criminal behavior. Thus, when this penalty is applied to law breaking it can influence public attitudes. In any case, the attention that MADD and RID brought to the drunk driving problem resulted in such a sufficient change that, by 1985, the National Commission Against Drunk Driving was able to announce support for the goal of making drunk driving "socially unacceptable in the U.S." (NCADD, 1985).

It appears likely that the simple lack of resources and incarceration facilities will ultimately frustrate the efforts of groups such as MADD to pass legislation mandating jail sentences for all DWI offenders. However, it is quite possible that this effort will have a major impact on the public view of this offense and lead to less casual treatment of the individual who drives after drinking.

SUMMARY

The United States has the lowest traffic death rate per vehicle mile in the world. On the other hand, it has the largest number of highway deaths. Within this context, the proportion of those deaths which are related to alcohol is probably as high as in any industrialized nation. This may have more to do with the relative availability and low cost of alcohol, on the one hand, and the relative unavailability and high cost of public transportation, on the other, than with the status of drunk driving enforcement programs. It is clear that the U.S. public and its government will have to deal with these availability issues in a significant and serious fashion if highway deaths and injuries due to alcohol are to be radically reduced. Nevertheless, the United States has succeeded in producing a modest reduction (approximately 15%) in the proportion of fatalities which are alcohol-related during the early 1980's (Fell & Nash, 1989; Williams, 1989). Moreover, as shown in Figure 6.4, the United States has been successful in maintaining this reduction in the face of a rising non-alcohol-related highway death rate.

While it is clear that the drinking–driving problem in the United States cannot be solved solely by the criminal justice system or associated public information and education programs, this system does appear to provide a substrata on which public attitudes may

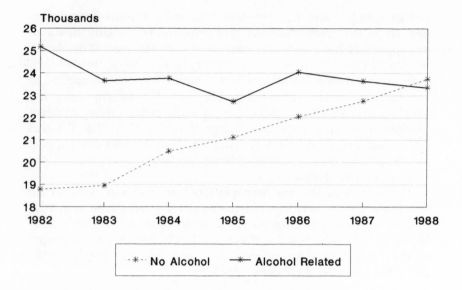

FIGURE 6.4. Six-year trend in alcohol (involving a driver or pedestrian with BAC at or above .01%) and non-alcohol-related traffic fatalities in the United States. From NHTSA (1989b).

work to change lifestyles. These changes can produce significant reductions in the public health problem presented by alcohol-related traumatic injury on the highway. While the research community has treated the drunk driving problem as a public health concern for some years, the public has only recently begun to place this problem within a health context. With the recent trend of popularizing "healthy lifestyles" in the United States, the association of drunk driving and health programs may be useful in combatting this problem.

Meanwhile, the field of traffic safety itself remains at a crossroads. The "Scandinavian" or "chemistry-based" system has been written into the laws of most states through per se legislation. Breathtesting is a consistent feature in all enforcement programs. Nevertheless, both enforcement and judicial programs continue to operate principally on the basis of the traditional behavioral model of enforcement, in which the appearance and conduct of the driver is the central consideration at trial. It remains to be seen whether this process can be streamlined by the adoption of procedures, such as the random breathtest program in Australia (see Chapter 7, this volume) or the widespread use of tests permitted under the 1967 Road Safety Act in Britain (Ross, 1973), or whether enforcement will continue to include chemical testing only as the final step in the arrest process. Much may depend on the extent to which the citizen activist groups are able to both continue to engage the attention of the public and pressure legislators to pass new laws that increase the efficiency of both police departments and the courts.

REFERENCES

Andenaes, J. (1988). The Scandinavian experience. In M.D. Laurence, J.R. Snortum, & F.E. Zimring (Eds.), *Social control of the drinking driver* (pp. 43–63). Chicago: University of Chicago Press.

Anderson, T.E. (1985). Laboratory evaluation of the Los Angeles police department's drugged driver detection procedures. In *NHTSA, Research Notes, May*. Washington, DC: National Highway Traffic Safety Administration

Arthur Young & Company. (1974). *Factors influencing alcohol safety action project police officers' DWI arrests* (Final Report). Washington, DC: National Highway Traffic Safety Administration.

Beirness, D. J. (1987). Self estimates of blood alcohol concentrations in drinking-driving context. *Drug and alcohol dependence, 79–90*.

Beitel, G.A., Sharp, M.C., & Glauz, W.D. (1975). Probability of arrest while driving under the influence of alcohol. *Journal of Studies on Alcohol, 36*, 109–115.

Bigelow, G.E., Bickel, W.E., Roache, J.D., Liebson, I.A., & Nowowieski, P. (1985). *Identifying types of drug intoxication: Laboratory evaluation of a subject-examination procedure* (NHTSA Report No. DOT HS 806 753). Washington, DC: U.S. Department of Transportation.

Borkenstein, R.F. (1975). Problems of enforcement, adjudication and sanctioning. In S. Israelstam & S. Lambert (Eds.), *Alcohol drugs and traffic safety* (pp. 655–662). Toronto, Ontario: Addiction Research Foundation of Ontario.

Cleary, J., & Rodgers, A. (1986). *Analysis of the effects of recent changes in Minnesota's DWI laws: Part III longitudinal analysis of policy impacts*. St. Paul, MN: Research Department, Minnesota House of Representatives.

Falkowski, C.L. (1984). *The impact of two-day jail sentences for drunk drivers in Hennipen County, Minnesota* (Final Report on Contract DTNH22-82-05110). Washington DC: National Highway Traffic Safety Administration.

Fell, J.C., & Nash, C.E. (1989). The nature of the alcohol problem in U.S. fatal crashes. *Health Education Quarterly, 16*, 335–344.

Fields, M., & Henricko, A.R. (1986). Passive alcohol sensors—constitutional implications. *The Prosecutor, 20*, 45–40.

Filkins, L.D. (1983). *The relationship between drivers in alcohol-related accidents and convicted drunk drivers* (Contract MTR-83-001A[5]). Lansing, MI: Michigan Office of Highway Safety Planning.

Filkins, L.D., Mortimer, R.G., Post, D.V., & Chapman, M.M. (1973). *Field evaluation of court procedures for identifying problem drinkers* (Technical Report DOT HS-031-2-303). National Highway Traffic Safety Administration.

Hagen, R.E., Williams, R.L., & McConnell, E.J. (1980a). The traffic safety impact of alcohol abuse treatment as an alternative to mandated licensing controls. *Accident Analysis and Prevention, 11*, 275–291.

Hagen, R.W., McConnell, E.J., & Williams, R.L. (1980b). *Suspension and revocation effects on the DUI offender* (Report #75, CAL-DMV-RSS-80-75). Sacramento, CA: Department of Motor Vehicles, Research and Development Section, Business and Transportation Agency.

Harris, D.H., Howlett, J.G., & Ridgeway, R.G. (1979). *Visual detection of driving while intoxicated. Project interim report: Identification of visual cues and development of detection methods* (NHTSA Report No. DOT HS 805-051). Washington, DC: National Highway Traffic Safety Administration.

Hause, J., Voas, R., & Chavez, E. (1982). Conducting voluntary roadside surveys: The Stockton experience. In M.R. Valverius (Ed.), *Proceedings of the Satellite Conference to the 8th International Conference on Alcohol, Drug, and Traffic Safety* (pp. 104–113). Stockholm: The Swedish Council for Information on Alcohol and Other Drugs.

Hawkins, T.E., Scrimgeor, G., Krenek, R.F., & Dreyer, C.B. (1976). *Summary of ASAP results for application to state and local programs: Vol. II, ASAP costs* (NHTSA Report No. DOT-801-964). Washington, DC: National Highway Traffic Safety Administration.

Howland, J. (1988). Social norms and drunk driving countermeasures. In Graham (Ed.), *Preventing automobile injury: New findings from evaluation research* (pp. 163–180). Dover, MA: Auburn House.

Ifft, R.A. (1983). Curbing the drunk driver under the Fourth Amendment: The constitutionality of roadblock seizures. *Georgetown Law Journal, 71*, 1457–1486.

Jonah, B.A., & Wilson, R.J. (1983). Improving the effectiveness of drinking-driving enforcement through increased efficiency. *Accident Analysis and Prevention, 15*, 463–482.

Jones, I.S. (1986). *The development and evaluation of a passive alcohol sensor.* Washington, DC: Insurance Institute for Highway Safety.

Jones, R., Joksch, H., Lacey, J., & Schmidt, H. (1987). *Field evaluation of jail sanctions for DWI* (Final Report). Washington, DC: National Highway Traffic Safety Administration, Mid-America Research Institute.

Jones, I.S., & Lund, A.K. (1985). Detection of alcohol-impaired drivers using passive alcohol sensor. *Journal of Police Science and Administration, 145*, 153–160.

Klein, T. (1982). *The effect of changes in DWI legislation in the state of Maryland.* Washington, DC: National Highway Traffic Safety Administration.

Klein, T. (1989). *Changes in alcohol-involved fatal crashes associated with tougher state alcohol legislation* (Final Report on NHTSA Contract No. DTNH22-88-C–7-45). Washington, DC: National Highway Traffic Safety Administration.

Koons, S.S. & Surla, L.T., Jr. (1988). *An evaluation of the elimination of plea bargaining for DWI offenders* (Final Report, Contract No. DTNH22-88-C-07328). Washington, DC: National Highway Traffic Safety Administration, MetaMetrics, Inc.

Lacey, J.H., Steward, J.R., Marchetti, L.M., Popkin, C.L, Murphy, P.V., Lucke, R.E., & Jones R.K. (1986). *Enforcement and public information strategies for DWI general deterrence: Arrest drunk driving—The Clearwater and Largo, Florida experiences.* Washington, DC: National Highway Traffic Safety Administration.

Laurence, M.D. (1988). The legal context in the United States. In M.D. Laurence, J.R. Snortum, & F.E. Zimring (Eds.) *Social control of the drinking driver* (pp. 136-168). Chicago: University of Chicago Press.

Levy, D., Shae, D., & Asch, P. (1989). Traffic safety effects of sobriety checkpoints and other local DWI programs in New Jersey. *American Journal of Public Health, 79,* 291-293.

Levy, P., Voas, R.B., Johnson, P., & Klein T. (1977). Evaluation of the ASAPs. *Journal of Safety Research, 10,* 162-176.

Mann, R.E., Leigh, G., Vingilis, E.R., & deGenova, K. (1983). A critical review on the effectiveness of drinking-driving rehabilitation programs. *Accident Analysis and Prevention, 15,* 441-461.

Mastrofski, S.D., Ritti, R.R., & Hoffmaster, D. (1987). Organisational determinants of police discretion: The case of drinking-driving. *Journal of Criminal Justice, 15,* 387-402.

McCarthy, J.D., & Harvey, D.S. (1988). Independent citizen advocacy: The past and the prospects. In, *Surgeon General's workshop on drunk driving: Background papers* (pp. 247-260). Washington DC: U.S. Department of Health and Human Services, Public Health Service, Office of the Surgeon General.

Meyers, A., Heeren, T., & Hingson, R. (1987). Cops and drivers: Police discretion and the enforcement of Maine's 1981 OUI law. *Journal of Criminal Justice, 15,* 361-368.

Miller, G. (1978). *Summary report on project TAGS—An experiment in mass screening of license plates to identify motor vehicle law violators.* Washington, DC: Insurance Institute for Highway Safety.

Moskowitz, H., & Robinson, C. (1988). *Effects of low doses of alcohol on driving related skills: A review of the evidence.* Washington, DC: National Highway Traffic Safety Administration.

National Commission Against Drunk Driving. (1985). *A progress report on the implementation of recommendations by the Presidential Commission on Drunk Driving.* Washington, DC: Author.

National Committee on Uniform Traffic Laws and Ordinances. (1987). *Uniform vehicle code and model traffic ordinance 1987.* Evanston, IL: Author.

National Highway Traffic Safety Administration. (1979). *Summary of national alcohol safety action projects* Washington, DC: Author.

National Highway Traffic Safety Administration. (1983). *A guide to self-sufficient funding of alcohol traffic safety programs* (Contract HS 806 432). Washington, DC: Author.

National Highway Traffic Safety Administration. (1985). *Community service restitution programs for alcohol related traffic offenders: The 5 As of community service* (Vols. 1–3; Contract No. DOT HS 806 767). Washington, DC: Author.

National Highway Traffic Safety Administration. (1987). *Assessment of citizen group court monitoring programs* (Final Report DOT HS 807 113). Washington, DC: Author.

National Highway Traffic Safety Administration. (1989a) *Digest of alcohol– highway safety related legislation* (7th ed.; Report No. DOT HS 807 359). Washington, DC: Author.

National Highway Traffic Safety Administration. (1989b). *Fatal accident reporting system 1988: A review of information on fatal traffic crashes in the United States in 1988* (DOT HS 807 507). Washington, DC: Author.

National Safety Council. (1976). *Alcohol and the impaired driver.* Chicago, IL: Author.

Nichols, J.L. (1989). *DWI education and other treatment programs in the U.S.: Their potential and their effectiveness.* Paper presented at the 11th International Congress on Alcohol, Drugs, and Traffic Safety, Chicago, IL.

Nichols, J.L., & Ross, H.L. (1989). The effectiveness of legal sanctions in dealing with drinking drivers. In, *Surgeon General's Workshop on Drunk Driving: Background papers* (pp. 93–112). Washington, DC: U.S. Department of Health and Human Services, Public Health Service, Office of the Surgeon General.

Nichols, J.L., Weinstein, E.B., Ellingstad, V.S., & Struckman-Johnson, D.L. (1978). The specific deterrent effect of ASAP education and rehabilitation programs. *Journal of Safety Research, 10,* 177–187.

Oates, J.F., Jr. (1974). *Factors influencing arrests for alcohol-related traffic violations.* Washington, DC: National Highway Traffic Safety Administration.

Peck, R.C., Sadler, D.D., & Perrine, M.W. (1985). The comparative effectiveness of alcohol rehabilitation and licensing control actions for drunk driving offenders: A review of the literature. *Alcohol, Drugs, and Driving; Abstracts and Reviews, 1,* 15–40.

Popkin, C.L., Kannenberg, C.H., Lacey, J.H., & Waller, P.F. (1988). *Assessment of classification instruments designed to detect alcohol abuse* (Contract No. DTNH22-87-R-07328). Washington, DC: National Highway Traffic Safety Administration.

Prouty, R.W., & O'Neill, B. (1971). *An evaluation of some quantitative breath screening tests for alcohol.* Washington, DC: Insurance Institute for Highway Safety.

Reeder, R.H. (1981). *Analytical study of the legal and operational aspects of the Minnesota law entitled "Chemical test for intoxication."* Washington, DC: National Highway Traffic Safety Administration.

Reis, R.E. (1982a). *The traffic safety effectiveness of educational counseling programs for multiple offense drunk drivers* (Final Report. Contract No. DOT HS-6-01414). Washington, DC: National Highway Traffic Safety Administration.

Reis, R.E. (1982b). *The traffic safety effectiveness of education programs for first offense drunk drivers*. Final Report. Contract No. DOT HS-6-01414. Washington, DC: National Highway Traffic Safety Administration.

Robertston, L., Rich, R., & Ross, H. (1973). Jail sentences for driving while intoxicated in Chicago: A judicial policy that failed. *Law and Society Review, 8*, 55–67.

Ross, H.L. (1973). Law, science and accidents: The British Road Safety Act of 1967. *The Journal of Legal Studies, 2*, 1–78.

Ross, H.L. (1975). The Scandinavian myth: The effectiveness of drinking-and-driving legislation in Sweden and Norway. *The Journal of Legal Studies, 4*, 285–310.

Ross, H.L. (1976). The neutralization of severe penalties: Some traffic laws studies. *Law and Society Review, 10*, 403–413.

Ross, H.L. (1984). *Deterring the drinking driver: Legal policy and social control.* Lexington, MA: Lexington Books.

Ross, H., & Gonzales, P. (1988). The effect of license revocation on drunk-driving offenders. *Accident Analysis and Prevention, 20*, 379–391.

Ross, H.L., & Hughes, G. (1986). Getting MADD in vain—drunk driving: What not to do. *The Nation, 13*, 663–664.

Ross, H.L., & Voas, R.B. (1989). *The new Philadelphia story: The effects of severe penalties for drunk driving.* Washington, DC: AAA Foundation for Traffic Safety.

Sadler, D.D., & Perrine, M.W. (1984). *An evaluation of the California drunk driving countermeasure system* (Vol. 2). Sacramento, CA: California Department of Motor Vehicles.

Saffer, H., & Chaloupka, F. (in press). *Breath testing and highway fatality rates.* Paper supported by Grant No. 1 R01 AA07593 from the National Institute on Alcohol Abuse and Alcoholism to the National Bureau of Economic Research.

Selzer, M.L. (1971). The Michigan alcoholism screening test: The quest for a new diagnostic instrument. *American Journal of Psychiatry, 127*, 1653–1658.

Stewart, E.I., & Malfetti, J.L. (1970). *Rehabilitation of the drunken driver.* New York: Teachers College Press.

Swenson, P.R., & Clay, T.R. (1977). *An analysis of drinker diagnosis, referral and rehabilitation activity, ASAP Phoenix, Arizona* (NHTSA Report No. DOT-HS-0521-068). Washington, DC: National Highway Traffic Safety Administration.

Taubenslag, W.N., & Taubenslag, M.J. (1975). *Selective traffic enforcement program (STEP): Fort Lauderdale, Pasco Services, Inc.* (Final Report). Washington, DC: National Highway Traffic Safety Administration.

Tharp, V., Burns, M., & Moskowitz, H. (1981). *Development and field test of psychophysical tests for DWI arrest.* NHTSA Report No. DOT-HS-805-864, p. 88. Available from NTIS, Springfield, VA 22151.

Ungerleider, S., & Bloch, S.A. (1988). Perceived effectiveness of drinking-driving countermeasures: An evaluation of MADD. *Journal of Studies on Alcohol, 49*, 191–195.

Vingilis, E. (1983). Drinking drivers and alcoholics: Are they from the same populations? *Research Advances in Alcohol and Drug Problems, 7,* 299–342.

Vingilis, E.R, Adlaf, E.M., & Chung, L. (1982). Comparison of age and sex characteristics of police-suspected impaired drivers and roadside- surveyed impaired drivers. *Accident Analysis and Prevention, 14,* 425–430.

Voas, R.B. (1975). A systems approach to the development and evaluation of countermeasure programs for the drinking driver. In M.E. Chafez (Ed.), *Research treatment and prevention: Proceedings of the Fourth Annual Alcoholism Conference of the National Institute of Alcohol Abuse and Alcoholism, June 1974.* (DHEW Publication No. (ADM) 76-284). Washington, DC: U.S. Government Printing Office.

Voas, R.B. (1982a). Selective enforcement during prime-time drinking-driving hours: A proposal for increasing deterrence without increasing enforcement costs. *Abstracts and Reviews in Alcohol and Driving, 4,* 3–21.

Voas, R.B. (1982b). *Drinking and driving: Scandanavian laws, tough penalties and United States alternatives* (Final Report on NHTSA Contract DTNH-22-82-P-05079). Washington, DC: NHTSA.

Voas, R.B. (1983). Laboratory and field tests of a passive alcohol sensing system. *Abstracts and Reviews in Alcohol and Driving, 4,* 3–21.

Voas, R.B. (1986a). Evaluation of jail as a penalty for drunken driving. *Alcohol, Drugs and Driving: Abstracts and Reviews, 2,* 47–70.

Voas, R.B. (1986b). Special preventive measures. In *Proceedings of the 10th International Conference on Alcohol, Drugs, and Traffic Safety, Amsterdam* (pp. 131–138). Amsterdam: Elsevier.

Voas, R.B. (1989). *Sobriety check points, an evaluation.* Paper presented at the 11th Triannual meeting of the International Committee on Alcohol, Drugs and Traffic Safety, Chicago, IL.

Voas, R.B., & Hause, J.M. (1987). Deterring the drunken driver: The Stockton experience. *Accident Analysis and Prevention, 19,* 81–90.

Voas, R.B., & Layfield, W.A. (1983). Creating general deterrence: Can passive sensing help? *The Police Chief, 50,* 56–61.

Voas, R.B., Rhodenizer, A.E., & Lynn, C. (1985). *Evaluation of Charlottesville checkpoint operations.* Washington, DC: NHTSA.

Williams, A.F. (1989). *Changes in alcohol-impaired driving and crashes involving alcohol in the 1970s and 1980s.* Paper presented at the 11th International Meetings on Alcohol, Drugs, and Traffic Safety, Chicago, IL.

Williams, A.F., & Lund, A.K. (1984). Deterrent effect of roadblocks on drinking and driving. *Traffic Safety Evaluation Research Review, 3,* 7–18.

Zador, P.K., Lund, A.K., Field, M., & Weinberg, K. (1988). *Alcohol-impaired driving laws and fatal crash involvement.* Washington, DC: Insurance Institute for Highway Safety.

7

RANDOM BREATH TESTING AND RANDOM STOPPING PROGRAMS IN AUSTRALIA

ROSS HOMEL

About the worst insult you can hurl at an Australian man is to accuse him of being a "wowser." Associated historically with the temperance movement, and allied with the interests of evangelical Protestants (the Methodists, Presbyterians, and Salvation Army in particular), wowsers attacked "drinking, gambling, smoking, divorce, women's fashions, sport on Sundays, modern verse, contemporary novels, living in flats, working mothers, and lipstick" (Horne, 1971, p. 64).

Over the past hundred years, major battles between the wowsers and the libertines have been fought over access to alcohol, with the forces of temperance achieving perhaps their greatest victory with the 6:00 P.M. closing of pubs during the First World War. They failed, however, to achieve their ultimate goal of prohibition. Since the early 1930s, and particularly since the Second World War, wowsers have been almost completely defeated by their antipuritanical enemies (a "slow, disorderly retreat," as Horne puts it), so much so that drinking now permeates nearly every aspect of daily life. By the mid-1970s alcohol consumption in Australia had climbed to the same levels as in the gold rush days of the 1850s, but at the cost of increases in alcohol-related diseases, violent crime, and road deaths (Room, 1985; Wallace, 1985).

The Australian conscience, although liberated, is somewhat troubled by these health and social indicators. Although the old temperance agenda of a higher drinking age, fewer alcohol outlets, shorter hours, and weaker liquor is not actually being resurrected, a loose

159

alliance of health workers, academics, government officials, and politicians is working to at least "hold the line" on availability and to relate taxation to alcohol content. Because "the caricature of the 'wowser' as a thin, hawk-nosed puritan, dressed in black and bearing a rolled umbrella . . . has left an indelible image on the Australian consciousness" (Room, 1985, p. 176), to be acceptable this "neotemperance" response to alcohol-related problems must be couched in the language of the laboratory rather than that of the pulpit. The image of the white-coated scientist must replace that of the black-coated puritan.

More than that, however, problems and solutions must be selected with care. Alcohol-impaired driving is a good target for neotemperance activity, since there is widespread agreement in the community that something firm needs to be done (Homel, 1988; Loxley, Blaze-Temple, Binns, & Saunders, 1988), but socially acceptable solutions to the problem are more difficult. Although the temperance movement was not, of course, unique to Australia, what was perhaps unique was the vehemence of the rejection of the wowser vision of the world (Room, 1985). This has created a contemporary climate in which alcoholic beverages are not only made ever more freely available, but suggestions that drinking–driving casualties, a major and undesirable consequence of the Australian love affair with ethyl alcohol, could be reduced by restrictions on alcohol availability are greeted with skepticism, even derision. For example, in a recent survey in Western Australia, Loxley and colleagues (1988) found that promoting low-alcohol products and increasing the cost of alcohol were perceived as the least effective ways of tackling drinking and driving. On the other side of the continent, the New South Wales (NSW) Minister for Police felt compelled to dissociate himself publicly from a report produced by his own department that recommended, among other things, that the legal drinking age be raised from 18 to 21 (Commissioner of Police for New South Wales, 1988). More dramatically, in August 1989 the NSW government confirmed its commitment to *increased* alcohol availability, especially in "designated tourist areas," by passing legislation that largely deregulated hotel opening hours.

Drinking–driving countermeasures must therefore be developed scientifically; but more than that, they must be based on approaches around which there is a high degree of consensus in the community. At the present time, measures that are believed to focus on the deterrence or education of individuals are much more likely to receive support than measures designed explicitly to reduce alcohol consumption through social interventions.

Again, this emphasis on the deterrence and education of the individual is by no means unique to Australia (Mosher, 1985). But what is truly surprising about recent antipodean developments is the wholehearted manner in which the deterrence doctrine has been translated into rigorous and effective action, at least in some jurisdictions. Roadblocks as a drinking–driving countermeasure have been employed in a number of countries, including Norway, Sweden, France, New Zealand, and the United States, but in none of these countries has the mass breath testing of motorists, selected at random, become the centerpiece of social policy (Homel, 1988). Random breath testing, Australian-style, represents a distinctive approach to the problem posed by the alcohol-impaired driver, and as such merits special treatment.

In general, random breath testing (RBT) involves arbitrarily selected checkpoints, often on main roads, that are varied from day to day and from week to week and that are not announced publicly prior to the RBT operation. Motorists passing a checkpoint, which is designed to be highly visible, are pulled over for a preliminary roadside breath test in a more or less haphazard manner, and all drivers pulled over are asked to take a test, regardless of the type of vehicle or their manner of driving. No attempt is made to detect symptoms of alcohol use, no record checks are run (although in some jurisdictions licenses are checked), and no equipment checks are conducted. Drivers returning a negative breath test result are not detained, and they usually drive away after a delay of about a minute. Drivers who are positive on the screening test are detained for an evidential breath test, with 50 mg % being the per se limit in most states.

As an enforcement tool, RBT stands in marked contrast to roadblocks or random stopping programs, which prior to 1989 were used in Queensland and Western Australia as a general deterrent to drinking and driving. The critical difference is that in roadblocks only motorists who were judged by police to have been drinking were asked to take a breath test. In practice, very few drivers were breath tested in roadblocks. For example, in Queensland fewer than 1 driver in 100 pulled over, ostensibly for a license and equipment check, was subjected to a roadside breath test (Queensland Transport Policy Planning Unit, 1987). At the psychological level this exercise of police discretion in roadblocks may undermine their purpose, since a major argument for RBT is that motorists know they can be tested even if they believe they are very good at concealing the fact that they have been drinking.

The purpose of this chapter is to review the use and effectiveness of random breath testing and random stopping programs across Australia, using as a theoretical framework a model of the relationship between legal interventions and traffic offenses. Because RBT is a very "pure" expression of the deterrence doctrine, a "causal chain" depicting the deterrence process constitutes the heart of the model. However, the model provides more than an account of how legal interventions like RBT may be translated into behavior change via fear of legal punishments. Research summarized later in this chapter suggests that the impact of RBT on informal sanctions operating in the drinking situation was a major ingredient in its success in New South Wales. Thus informal sanctions and other nonlegal sanctions are incorporated in the model, together with aspects of the physical and social environments that could be affected by new laws or enforcement programs. The "environmental aspects" of the model are an attempt to encompass some of the concerns of the neotemperance movement and to indicate how direct deterrent measures may interrelate with other types of legal interventions.

In reviewing the impact of RBT and roadblocks across Australia, it is demonstrated that RBT *as implemented* is not uniformly successful; its effects depend critically on its manner of enforcement. In particular, RBT must be publicized and enforced in the New South Wales and Tasmanian manner in order to achieve "maximum" potential (one breath test for every three licensed drivers each year, yielding a permanent reduction of about one-third in alcohol-related fatalities and serious injuries). In addition, it is demonstrated that not every potential offender reacts in the same way to the legal threat embodied in RBT legislation and enforcement. Consistent with deterrence theory, evidence will be presented from two states that those with a previous conviction for drinking and driving, which includes many heavy drinkers, are *more* responsive to the legal threat than those without previous experience of the law.

The review of RBT and roadblocks will be restricted to the Australian literature, partly because RBT in Australia is of unique importance as an enforcement tool and partly because the U.S. experience with sobriety checkpoints is analysed elsewhere in this volume (Voas & Lacey, Chapter 6). Nevertheless, the review of random stopping programs in Australia forms a useful bridge to the international literature on roadblocks, since these programs have much in common with Australian and overseas approaches to sobriety checkpoints not involving RBT.

The hostility of some U.S. courts to roadblocks (Sutton, Farrar, &

Campbell, 1987; Westling, 1986) demonstrates that a countermeasure that thrives in one culture may not transplant easily to foreign soils. This raises questions of how a successful deterrence-based approach may be adapted and about the relationship between measures like RBT and the broader neotemperance environmental approaches discussed earlier. These questions are considered at the end of this chapter, where it is argued that some of the indirect effects on drinking practices and beliefs that RBT may be beginning to have in New South Wales (particularly through the provision of an excuse to say "no") may be the "entering wedge" for more far-reaching reforms.

A MODEL OF THE RELATIONSHIP BETWEEN LEGAL INTERVENTIONS AND TRAFFIC OFFENSES

In considering the impact of legal interventions such as RBT, it will be useful to clarify briefly the nature of the assumed deterrence process and to consider those aspects of the social and physical environments that may be susceptible to manipulation through legal means. A detailed study of the deterrence of drinking–driving may be found in Homel (1988), and the model presented here builds on that work (see also Homel & Wilson, 1988). A key feature of the model, which is set out diagrammatically in Figure 7.1, is that it incorporates nonlegal sanctions (such as the financial cost or inconvenience of *not* committing an offense), which it is assumed can be influenced by various forms of legal interventions.

The classical deterrence process, in which a legal intervention influences criminal behavior via perceptions and fears of legal sanctions, is represented by the central path in the figure. The physical and social environments are shown at the top and bottom of the figure to emphasize that sanctions and any behavioral responses operate within an overall opportunity structure determined by environmental factors. It is assumed that these environmental factors can themselves be manipulated through legal means.

Simply stated, the model depicts a causal chain linking the commission (or noncommission) of traffic offenses with legal interventions. The links in the chain are *exposure* of the population to enforcement and/or publicity about the law, *evaluations* of the significance of this exposure by the affected individuals (depicted by the symbol "e" in the diagram), *perceptions* of the properties of both legal and nonlegal sanctions (e.g., the perceived likelihood of apprehen-

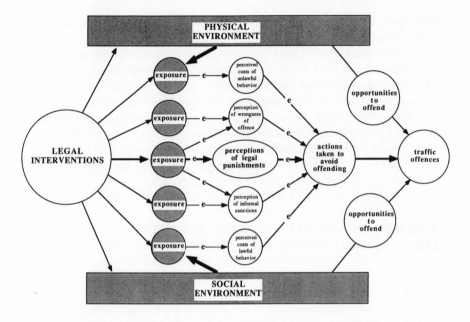

FIGURE 7.1. Model of the relationship between legal interventions and traffic offenses. From "Law and Road Safety: Strategies for Modifying the Social Environment, with Particular Reference to Alcohol Control Policies" by R. Homel and P. Wilson, 1988, *Australian and New Zealand Journal of Criminology, 21,* p. 107. Reprinted by permission of the author.

sion by police or the perceived inconvenience involved in not committing the offence), *evaluations* of the personal significance of these perceptions (e.g., not all individuals with a given perception of the likelihood of arrest attach the same weight to the perception), and *actions taken* to avoid committing the offense as a result of evaluations of the perceptions of legal and nonlegal sanctions.

An individual is assumed to be subject to several social-control mechanisms: guilt feelings resulting from the internalization of norms, the threat of social stigma resulting from informal sanctions, and the threat of physical and/or material deprivation. One source of material deprivation is formal, legal punishments (loss of license, etc.), but other sources include the costs and inconveniences involved in not committing an offense (e.g., paying for a taxi home after a party) as well as the nonlegal material costs entailed in committing an offense. As examples of the costs entailed in committing an offense, some drivers may refrain from speeding because they are conscious of fuel costs or the potential of speed humps to damage their vehicles. Other major material costs are entailed in having an accident. Fear of crashing, and particularly the fear of damaging their own vehicle, presumably restrains many a driver from foolhardy and illegal driving behaviors, including alcohol-impaired driving.

The point is that the fear of legal punishments competes with all these other threatened sanctions. In order to decrease unlawful driving, one could use legal means to enhance the direct legal threat, or one could use legal means to manipulate these other nonlegal sanctions. This accounts for the multiple forms of exposure depicted in Figure 7.1. It may be that increasing the legal threat will of itself influence the nonlegal sanctions, as indicated in Figure 7.1. For example, punishment or the threat of punishment for drinking and driving may actually make someone more aware of the risks and feel more guilty about future violations (not simply more wary of being caught). Alternatively, legal actions may be aimed directly at manipulating the internalization of norms or at informal punishments imposed by peers and others. For example, the use of warning letters to errant drivers may strengthen internal control mechanisms (Rothengatter, 1982). Again, licensing laws may be devised to require bartenders to intervene if a patron has had too much to drink (Simpson, Beirness, Mayhew, & Donelson, 1985). Such interventions may have a marked effect on the informal group processes that frequently encourage drinking to excess.

Because the sanctions depicted in Figure 7.1 do not all operate in the same direction, the model proposes that when individuals who have been drinking or who plan to drink make decisions about transportation they are faced with a *choice among losses* (Homel, 1988). If they drive after drinking, they run the risk of getting caught or of having a crash; they may in addition feel guilty, and they may (just possibly) incur the displeasure of friends, spouse, or mother-in-law. If they avoid driving after drinking, they may be ridiculed by friends (especially likely in the Australian context among young, working-class males) and they will certainly have to make alternative arrangements for transportation. The theoretical importance of this is that they are faced essentially with a choice between a certain loss (the costs and inconveniences of getting home from the party some other way) and a merely possible loss (getting caught or having a crash). Common sense as well as the psychological research into decision making (Carroll & Weaver, 1986; Homel, 1988; Kahneman & Tversky, 1982) suggest that in this situation people will generally act in a risk-seeking fashion; they will cut their losses and drive home impaired—unless, of course, the psychological calculus can be altered, perhaps by making the legal threat more potent.

Differential Deterrability

Everyday experience suggests that some people are more responsive than others to formal and informal sanctions. This is sometimes referred to as "differential deterrability"—all people are not equally deterrable in all situations (see Vingilis, Chapter 5, this volume). This phenomenon is implicit in the model, since individuals differ in their evaluations of what their exposure to legal interventions actually means to them, form individual perceptions of the chances of arrest or of the severity of penalties, and assign different weights to perceptions that may be very similar (the evaluation process again). However, not much is known about the cognitive processes whereby individuals assimilate and interpret such signals as highly visible police roadside breath testing. Moreover, it is likely that there are complex interactions among aspects of the situation and the characteristics and responses of individuals (Vingilis & Mann, 1986).

In literature reviewed by Homel (1988), there is a great deal of controversy about the composition of the drinking–driving population and the possibility of differential deterrability. One problem is that little can be said specifically about the responses of such groups as young drivers or heavy drinkers to legal sanctions unless one augments deterrence theory with insights from other streams of research (Tittle, 1980). For present purposes, it will be sufficient to point to those few aspects of deterrence theory itself which suggest ways in which the deterrent effectiveness of drinking–driving laws may vary across different subgroups of the population. Evidence for these and some other aspects of differential deterrability is included in the review of random breath testing later in this chapter.

The most important prediction arising directly from deterrence theory is that people who have previously suffered legal punishments for drinking and driving (or perhaps for other offenses) will be more responsive to the threat of further punishment than those who have never experienced arrest and conviction (Tittle, 1980). Although those previously convicted may not regard the risk of apprehension as being any higher than those without a conviction (that is, they may not be any more *sensitive* to the legal threat), they will have a greater fear of punishment, having already experienced it, and will therefore make more attempts to comply with the law than someone without a conviction. In the terminology of the model depicted in Figure 7.1, convicted offenders will differ from people without a conviction in their *evaluations* of their perceptions of legal sanctions.

A second prediction of deterrence theory also relates to previous experience with the law: Those who have committed an offense but have escaped punishment will have lower perceptions of the chances of arrest than those who have not committed the offense. This is referred to as the *experiential* effect (Minor & Harry, 1982), and it has considerable empirical support in the deterrence literature.

Modifications to the Environment

In general, legal countermeasures may either be aimed directly at the individual road user or at the user's social or physical environment. Environmental countermeasures may have as their aim the manipulation of sanctions (e.g., increasing the inconvenience entailed in offending), or they may be designed specifically to limit opportunities to offend (e.g., night curfews for young drivers or legal restrictions on hotel opening hours). Manipulation of opportunities to offend through environmental action are shown explicitly in Figure 7.1. The alterations in the physical or social environments implicit in exposure to legal interventions are indicated by the broad arrows from the environmental boxes to the exposure circles and by the shading of the exposure circles in the same way as the environmental boxes.

In summary, deterrence (fear of legal punishments) is the most direct way in which legal actions such as RBT can influence behavior, but legal interventions can also have a great impact through manipulation of the various forms of nonlegal sanctions. In addition, legal actions designed to have a direct deterrent effect may influence behavior by altering these nonlegal sanctions. To a greater or lesser extent, manipulation of all forms of sanctions entails alterations in the social or physical environment, since legal interventions must enter the world of potential offenders before they can affect their behavior. Legal interventions can also have a profound effect by altering the physical or social environment in ways that limit opportunities to commit offenses. Whether any given society is prepared to tolerate the changes in ways of life entailed in such alterations to the environment is, of course, another question, well illustrated by the fading influence of the wowser in Australia and the demise of the "six o'clock swill."

RANDOM STOPPING AND RANDOM BREATH TESTING

In Figure 7.1, "legal interventions" appears as an exogenous variable, with no visible means of support. Moreover, the distinctions between enacting a law, publicizing it, and actually enforcing it are ignored, except by implication through the inclusion of "exposure." In practice, of course, new laws or enforcement programs do not just happen; they have a history and a specific social context, and the connections among enactment, publicity, and enforcement are frequently tenuous and ill defined. This is especially the case for random breath testing in Australia, where variations among states and territories, as well as variations within a single jurisdiction over time, make it impossible to speak of a single intervention called "random breath testing." Consequently, a necessary first step in the review of RBT, Australian-style, is to describe clearly the phenomenon under investigation.

I have argued in earlier work (Homel, 1988) that in Australia there are four major types of RBT or random stopping programs, and that only one type–the "boots and all" New South Wales model with intensive, visible, and continuous enforcement and extensive, continuous publicity–has been unambiguously successful. While still generally true, the typology is in need of some revision, since the perceived success of RBT in New South Wales has stimulated most other jurisdictions to modify their approaches. Effectively, there is in progress a gradual convergence toward the New South Wales model, even in Queensland, where the opposition to mass breath testing using RBT has been most vehement.

Table 7.1 contains an overview of the diverse array of random testing and random stopping programs in Australia, together with the dates the relevant legislation or program was introduced. It also includes a summary of recent developments and an indication of the nature of the impact of enforcement in each jurisdiction. The two non-RBT states, Western Australia and Queensland, are shown separately, although it should be noted that both these states moved from random stopping to full random breath testing late in 1988. Jurisdictions are listed in the order in which RBT legislation was introduced.

It is perhaps significant that New South Wales and Tasmania, the two states that have achieved the greatest success with RBT, were (not counting Western Australia and Queensland) the most recent entrants in the field. To some extent planners in these states learned from the experiences of Victoria and South Australia, although the evidence from the interrupted time-series research that was being compiled by H. Laurence Ross at the time (Ross, 1982) probably played a more important role in the formulation of policy (Staysafe, 1982).

In what follows the experience of each state or territory is described, with a view toward assessing both the deterrent effectiveness of each program and whether it has had any impact on nonlegal sanctions or on the broader social environment. The experiences of New South Wales and Tasmania are described first, since their no-holds-barred, "boots and all" approach has had a significant influence on other Australian jurisdictions. Otherwise, the order of treatment accords with the historical development of RBT, as set out in Table 7.1.

New South Wales and Tasmania: RBT "Boots and All"

New South Wales and Tasmania introduced RBT almost simultaneously and adopted a similar approach from the beginning. The distinctive elements of this approach are: (1) at least one random test for every three licensed drivers is given each year, resulting in high levels of exposure to RBT; (2) extensive formal or informal publicity is focused specifically on RBT; (3) RBT is not only highly visible, it is hard to predict where it will be operating and it is hard to evade once it is in sight, thus increasing the perceived probability of apprehension for drinking and driving; and (4) the enforcement and focused publicity are maintained at high levels permanently, with provision for special additional local or seasonal campaigns. From a theoretical point of view, the significance of this all-out approach is that it represents a very pure and single-minded operationalization of the key concepts of general deterrence, thus providing a perfect opportunity for testing the general deterrence model both as a theory and as a guide to effective action (Homel, 1988).

Tasmania

Much more is known about the implementation and impact of RBT in New South Wales than in Tasmania, but Tasmania, with its small size, has probably achieved an intensity of enforcement unmatched anywhere else in the world. For example, in 1985 more than 200,000 roadside tests were conducted out of a driving population of only

TABLE 7.1. An Overview of Random Breath Testing and Random Stopping in Australian States and Territories

Jurisdiction	Date of introduction	Enforcement approach	Recent developments	Impact
		A hesitant approach to RBT		
Victoria	July 1976	Low-level enforcement of RBT, supplemented by short-term blitzes	Increase in overall testing rate after 1983, but not all RBT	Clear short-term impact of blitzes, overall impact unclear
		RBT with a slow start		
Northern Territory	February 1980	Low-level enforcement of RBT	Not known	Public support, but impact on crashes not known
South Australia	October 1981	Low-level RBT enforcement, preceded by press controversy	More random tests, more publicity, back-street patrols	Slight initial temporary effect; recent evidence of more impact
Australian Capital Territory	December 1982	Low-level enforcement of RBT	No major developments	Initial impact on casualties

RBT "boots and all"

New South Wales	December 1982	Intensive publicity, highly visible and intensive RBT enforcement	Publicity and enforcement levels maintained	Immediate and permanent decline in alcohol-related casualties
Tasmania	January 1983	Very intensive RBT, extensive informal publicity	Intense enforcement maintained	Apparently permanent decline in alcohol-related casualties
RBT by the back door (random stopping programs)				
Western Australia	November 1980	Roadblocks with testing of detected drinking drivers—regular blitzes	RBT legislation introduced October 1988 (18-month trial)	Temporary effect of intensive roadblocks
Queensland	August 1986	(RID = reduce impaired driving) Roadblocks with testing of detected drinking drivers, plus publicity	Decline in RID publicity, possible decline in level of enforcement; introduction of RBT law late 1988	Marked temporary impact of RID, with complete return of alcohol-related fatalities to pre-RID levels

171

268,887 (Sutton et al., 1986). Three mobile breath analysis units are commonly transferred to at least five different sites in a 8-hour shift, where testing can proceed uninterrupted over the shift. Occasional massive operations are undertaken, and only after their completion are public announcements made by the authorities. It is thought that by this method the public will remain convinced that RBT is not an empty threat. Given limited financial resources, publicity through the electronic media is not bought by the government, but extensive free publicity is achieved through newspapers. In addition, a daily list of the names of convicted drinking drivers is published in the papers, which in a small community may have significant effects on public attitudes as well as on the offenders themselves.

Tasmania's small population facilitates intensive enforcement but makes analysis of casualty data difficult, and no survey data are available to complement the analysis of accidents. Nevertheless, there are clear indications that RBT has worked. Although annual data exhibit erratic variations (the proportion of dead drivers with illegal levels of alcohol varied from 19% to 51% in the years 1983 through 1987), when averaged over time, the indicators are positive. Thus alcohol involvement in fatal crashes in the 3-year post-RBT period was 42% less and casualty crashes 29% fewer than for the 6 years prior to RBT (Federal Office of Road Safety, 1986). Given that Tasmanian testing levels are unique, and given the absence of other kinds of data, further fine-grained analyses of the accident data are urgently required.

New South Wales Enforcement and Publicity

To boost enforcement, when RBT was introduced in New South Wales about 200 extra police were recruited for highway patrol work. In the first 12 months of RBT (December 17, 1982, to December 31, 1983), 923,272 preliminary breath tests were conducted, representing approximately one test for every three licensed drivers (Cashmore, 1985). To put this figure into perspective, it should be compared with the 113,985 nonrandom preliminary breath tests conducted in 1982. It should also be compared with the 1 million tests in Sweden, with its population 8.3 million, in the first 3 years of RBT and the 335,000 tests in 18 months in France, with a population 10 times as large as that of New South Wales (Homel, 1988). Since 1983, approximately 1.3 million preliminary tests have been conducted each year, more than 90% of which are due to RBT.

Strategies of enforcement have changed over time. Initially RBT was carried out (as in Tasmania) using special vans and converted buses, but breakdowns and limitations in flexibility led within 12 months to the rule that each highway patrol vehicle should carry out 1 hour of RBT per shift. Following the work of Cashmore (1985), testing was intensified in the early hours of the morning to counter the trend for inebriated drivers to delay their trips home. In 1987 "mobile RBT patrols" were introduced to complement the work of the stationary test sites. The purpose of these patrols was to police side roads within 4 kilometers of the main testing site, in order to deter motorists from attempting to evade RBT. In response to police pressure to allow "random" testing that yielded a higher "hit rate" and reduced police boredom, since 1988 mobile RBT patrols have been freed from restrictions and may essentially "roam free," although the great bulk of random testing is still conducted from highly visible stationary vehicles. Because it is less visible, mobile testing potentially poses a threat to the long-term effectiveness of RBT in New South Wales, although recent data suggest that, despite these misgivings, the deterrent impact has been positive (Superintendent Merv Lane, personal communication, August 1989).

Most of these measures have been supported by professional media publicity as well as by extensive coverage over the years in news media (Cashmore, 1985). The initial publicity campaign had as its theme: "How will you go when you sit for the test, will you be under .05 or under arrest?" Television publicity depicted police carrying out RBT in a friendly and efficient manner, but it also carried the message that RBT could not be evaded by such methods as turning into side roads (a "real nightmare" for drinking drivers, as one of the advertisements put it). No attempt was made to emphasize the penalties—the entire emphasis was on the threat of arrest and on the humiliation entailed for someone who "failed the test." This focus on the operations of RBT and on the threat of arrest for drinking drivers has, on the whole, been maintained.

The proportion of Sydney motorists who have been breath tested has increased steadily, from 25% prior to RBT to 53% in February 1987, with some motorists having been breath tested five or more times. It is interesting to note, therefore, that nearly half of all metropolitan drivers have still not been breath tested, despite the large number of tests annually. On the other hand, in 1987, 83% of a sample of 600 Sydney motorists reported that they had seen RBT in operation in the last 6 months (Homel, Carseldine, & Kearns, 1988). Moreover, those actually tested undoubtedly drive more often at night, when RBT is more likely to be operating, and are therefore the population most at risk for drinking and driving (McLean, Clark, Dorsch, Holubowycz, & McCaul, 1984).

The Impact of RBT in New South Wales

An analysis of weekly accident data was reported by Homel and colleagues (1988). One diagram from this article, showing the cumulative sum (CUSUM) graph for alcohol-related fatalities, is reproduced as Figure 7.2. A CUSUM is a series of numbers that are the cumulative sum of the differences between an observed series and the corresponding expected series (Woodward & Goldsmith, 1964). In Figure 7.2, the expected count was the average of the weekly data on drivers and riders killed with blood alcohol content (BAC) over 50 mg % for 3 years prior to the introduction of RBT. These data were not available before 1980, so the pre-RBT period is restricted to 3 years. The post-RBT period is 4 years.

The key to interpreting Figure 7.2 is to regard the number below the zero line as the "accumulated benefit" due to RBT at any time after its

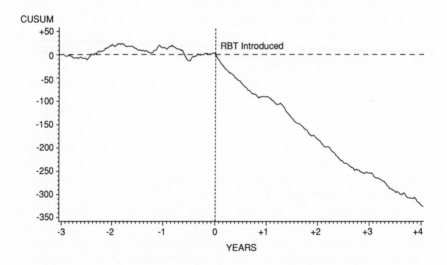

FIGURE 7.2. Cumulative sum graph (CUSUM) of weekly drivers and riders killed with a BAC in excess of 50 mg % for 3 years prior to and 4 years after RBT (New South Wales). From "Drink-Drive Countermeasures in Australia" by R. Homel, D. Carseldine, and I. Kearns, 1988, *Alcohol, Drugs and Driving*, 4 (2), p. 131. Copyright 1988 by *Alcohol, Drugs and Driving*. Reprinted by permission.

introduction. If the CUSUM graph maintains a downward slope (which it generally does in Figure 7.2), a benefit is still being derived from RBT, in comparison with the average accident level that would have prevailed if RBT had not been introduced. If the graph becomes horizontal, a benefit is no longer being accumulated and accidents have reverted to their pre-RBT level. If the slope actually becomes positive, the accumulated benefit of RBT is being eroded by an accident rate higher than the average pre-RBT level.

It is clear from Figure 7.2 that on only a few brief occasions have alcohol-related fatalities approached pre-RBT levels. During the 3 years prior to the introduction of RBT, the average number of automobile drivers and motorcycle operators with a BAC of 50 mg % or more who were killed was 4.36 per week. In the 4 years after RBT this average dropped 36% to 2.81. Other statistical series, notably total fatal crashes and a surrogate for alcohol-related crashes (single-vehicle accidents on a curve at night), show exactly the same pattern, although the decline in total fatal crashes (5 years before to 5 years after RBT) was only 22%, consistent with the expectation that RBT had its major impact on alcohol-related crashes.

Further analyses of NSW crash data are required in order to dispel lingering doubts that factors other than RBT may have contributed to the decline in accidents. In particular, there is a need to update the interrupted time-series analysis reported by Arthurson (1985) and to analyze trends in non-alcohol-related crashes as well as those involving alcohol. Nevertheless, the results are fairly convincing and are supported by survey data collected by the NSW Traffic Authority (Homel et al., 1988).

Self-reports of drinking before driving more often than once a month declined slightly, from around 46% in 1982 to 41% in 1987. There was a more marked decline in the proportions admitting to driving at least once a month over their own self-assessed safe BAC limit, the figures being 16% in 1982 and only 6% in 1984. Corresponding to these declines in self-reported drinking–driving, between 1982 and 1987 there was a steady trend for drinkers to rely more on counting drinks than on checking their feelings and coordination, an increase in the numbers making prior arrangements not to drive home after a celebration, an increase in the perceived probability of apprehension for drinking and driving, and a decline in the proportion of respondents who believed they could do something to avoid RBT. All the survey indicators are consistent with the contention that the decline in alcohol-related casualties depicted in Figure 7.2 is due largely to RBT.

*The Process of General Deterrence and the Impact of
RBT on the Social Environment in New South Wales.*

Based on survey data collected within the first few months of RBT,
Homel (1988) analyzed in detail the central deterrence pathways
depicted in Figure 7.1. This analysis supported the thesis that RBT
had an initial deterrent impact of considerable magnitude, since there
were relationships (in the expected directions) among levels of actual
police testing, exposure of the target population to RBT, perceived
certainty of arrest, and steps taken to avoid drinking and driving. In
other words, the causal chain at the heart of the deterrence process
was supported by the analysis.

However, longitudinal data (based on interviews with 185 motorists 6 weeks apart) demonstrated that the deterrence process was very
unstable. Direct exposure to RBT through being tested or through
driving past an RBT station resulted in an increase in use of strategies
to avoid drinking and driving (such as leaving the car at home or
getting a sober companion to drive), but a lack of exposure to RBT,
strong peer pressure to drink in a group situation, or successful
drinking–driving episodes (the experiential effect) correlated with
declines in measures taken to avoid drinking–driving. Among those
who felt the greatest pressure to drink in a group situation, an *increase*
between interviews in the perceived risk of arrest on any one trip
corresponded to a *decline* in attempts to avoid drinking and driving,
consistent with the predictions of prospect theory that a certain loss
(loss of status) will outweigh a merely possible loss (getting caught).

A most important aspect of the analysis was the finding that 40% of
respondents claimed that RBT made it easier to resist pressure to
drink in a group situation. In fact, this provision of an "exculpatory
defense" (Gusfield, 1981) was as important an influence on behavior
as the direct deterrent impact of RBT. This illustrates how a legal
intervention may influence nonlegal sanctions surrounding the commission of an offense, in the manner depicted in Figure 7.1. More
recent survey data, collected in four Australian states in mid-1988
(Berger, Snortum, Homel, Hauge, & Loxley, 1989; Homel, Berger,
Loxley, Snortum, & Hauge, 1990), suggest that RBT in New South
Wales is continuing to exercise a strong influence on behavior
through the same indirect mechanism. In response to a question on
how often respondents use police breath testing as an excuse to limit
their drinking in a group situation, only 48% of NSW respondents
answered "never," in comparison with 57% in Queensland, 63% in
Victoria, and 67% in Western Australia. Clearly, the impact of police

breath testing is of major importance as an influence on group drinking practices, especially in New South Wales, where the enforcement of RBT has been so intense.

Evidence for an impact of RBT in New South Wales on the broader social environment is less systematic and more equivocal. Initially, proprietors of clubs and pubs complained of greatly reduced patronage, and there is evidence that overall beer consumption, relative to levels in other states, declined for a period (Cashmore, 1985). However, the most marked effects appear to have been a trend away from on-premises drinking, especially draught beer, to buying packaged alcohol and consuming it away from licensed premises. Responses of the liquor industry, in New South Wales and other states, have included the heavy promotion of low-alcohol beers ("breathe easy" is a current advertising slogan) and the development of more up-market drinking establishments that provide good food and entertainment. In addition, patron-operated breathalyzers have proliferated in clubs, pubs, and naval establishments (E. L. Sly, personal communication, November 10, 1988).

Paradoxically, although firm statistics are not available, the very success of RBT in persuading many people to leave their cars at home when they travel to or from pubs is believed by some police and railway officials to have contributed to increased levels of drunkenness and violence on trains, as well as to more violence, street crime, and disorderly conduct in the vicinity of pubs at closing times. Part of the reason for these possible unintended outcomes is the inadequacy of public transport in many areas, especially in the early hours of the morning, and the unwillingness of taxi drivers to pick up drunks.

Despite these possible side effects, a major positive result of the introduction of RBT has been to increase markedly the level of public support for the concept of random testing, a phenomenon also noted in other states (Monk, 1985). While support in New South Wales in 1982 (before the law) was 64%, in 1983 85% thought it should continue. By 1987 the level of support had grown to 97% (Homel et al., 1988). Even more significant, the percentages willing to label a drinking driver who crashes or is stopped by police as "irresponsible, a criminal, or a potential murderer" rose to their highest levels ever in the 1987 government survey (Homel et al., 1988). This is the first piece of quantitative evidence that moral attitudes toward drinking and driving may be changing in New South Wales. Of course, it is difficult to prove that RBT (or any other factor) is the major cause of this change, but since RBT is known to have had a major impact on behavior, it provides a plausible explanation for at least some of the change in attitudes. Perhaps RBT has acted for some people as a "moral eye-opener" (Andenaes, 1983, p. 2).

Victoria: A Hesitant Approach to RBT

The apparent success of RBT in Victoria was a major reason for its introduction in South Australia and New South Wales. Indeed, in the early 1980s RBT in Victoria had assumed something of the status of a local "Scandinavian myth" (Homel, 1988). However, as South (1988) emphasizes, although alcohol involvement in fatal crashes or in casualties admitted to hospital generally declined between 1977 and 1986, it is impossible to attribute this decline to any one factor. RBT is almost certainly part of the explanation, but exactly how much a part is difficult to say. Alternative explanations (which apply across the nation) include general mass media publicity and drinking–driving education, industry initiatives (e.g., free soft drinks for "designated drivers" and the promotion of low-alcohol beers), and increases in the relative price of draught beer.

Victoria was the first jurisdiction in the world to introduce compulsory wearing of seat belts (in 1970) and since then has maintained a reputation for innovative road safety programs (Ross, 1982). In this tradition, the introduction of RBT in July 1976 was a daring initiative, given the beery atmosphere of the mid-1970s, but it seems that most of the daring went into passing the law, with little left over for actual enforcement. In the early months, random testing was conducted for only 10 hours per week and was restricted to the Melbourne metropolitan area (RACV Consulting Services, 1983). In the first full year of operation (1977), 19,006 tests were conducted, compared with nearly 1 million in New South Wales in the first year of RBT in that state.

After the dramatic success of the NSW law in 1983, testing in Victoria was increased from about 60,000 per annum to 314,000 (in 1986), with a concomitant increase in expenditure on drinking–driving and RBT publicity. However, the rate of testing is still far short of the one in three licensed drivers achieved in New South Wales and adopted as a goal by Victorian authorities (South, 1988). It is not entirely clear whether the shortfall in the test rate is due to a lack of political will and a corresponding lack of police resources, or whether it reflects confusion concerning the objectives of mass breath testing. The fact that Victoria is not much smaller in population than New South Wales but is geographically more compact suggests that police could easily achieve NSW testing levels if political pressure were applied.

What has happened recently, instead of an increase in RBT testing levels, is that while RBT has not been neglected, drinking–driving enforcement has been combined with other types of traffic enforcement. For example, over Christmas 1987 police were instructed to increase their vigilance for drinking drivers in the course of their usual traffic duties. This "alcohol check" campaign was supported by television publicity between November 1987 and January 1988. An evaluation of the campaign was carried out, based on a pre–post telephone survey of different samples of 400 men aged 18 to 30 living in Melbourne (Harrison, 1988). In the second survey there was a large increase in the proportion of respondents who believed police would breath test for any reason, even if they did not notice the presence of alcohol, but only a modest decline in self-reported drinking and driving (mainly in the 21–24 age range). Paradoxically, the changed perceptions of the certainty of police breath testing derived from a misunderstanding of the television publicity, since during the campaign police only breath tested motorists pulled over for other traffic matters if the motorists failed a sobriety check (Harrison, 1988). Although beneficial in the short term, this situation is unstable, since the major influence on deterrence is probably drivers' direct experiences of police testing (Homel, 1988). Later campaigns have therefore put more emphasis on routine breath testing (e.g., of all speeding drivers).

Preliminary Breath Testing and Random Breath Testing

Personal observation of the current Victorian approach to drinking–driving law enforcement suggests that in the absence of strong political commitment, police may to some extent have lost sight of the major purpose of RBT, which is general deterrence. The campaigns that involve breath testing some or all of the traffic violators noticed by the police cannot have a major deterrent impact, since most drinking drivers believe (rightly) that they can drive well enough to avoid detection. Legislation passed in March 1987 has given police wide discretionary powers, similar to those relating to mobile RBT in New South Wales, allowing them to request any motorist to submit to a preliminary breath test at any time, regardless of their manner of driving and regardless of whether they have committed an offense or had an accident. While this law extends the net to include motorists other than traffic violators, in practice this form of preliminary breath testing is less visible to the public and is more directed to detecting inebriated drivers than stationary RBT. In other words, the procedure essentially involves a form of "target testing," with the result that many more motorists test over 50 mg % than in stationary RBT.

The worrying thing from the point of view of those concerned with general deterrence is that target-oriented preliminary breath tests now constitute about 40% of all preliminary tests in Victoria. Police have been required to increase the total number of breath tests, and in fact have been allotted monthly quotas, but no instructions have been issued concerning the ratio of RBT to non-RBT preliminary tests. Naturally, police officers prefer a method of enforcement that is more obviously "productive" than RBT, with the result that in many areas RBT appears to have become a residual activity.

Random Breath Testing Blitzes

Despite an apparent current failure to appreciate the full general deterrent potential of RBT, a unique feature of Victorian RBT enforcement was the use, between 1977 and 1983, of intensified periods of random testing in regions of Melbourne selected according to a predetermined experimental design. The main evidence that RBT has had an impact in Victoria comes from evaluations of these six scientifically planned police blitzes (e.g., Cameron & Strang, 1982; Cameron, Strang, & Vulcan, 1980; As an example of the method, during October, November, and December 1978, police each week carried out an average of 100 hours of RBT on Thursday, Friday, and Saturday nights in one of four sectors of Melbourne. Over the period of the experiment, all four sectors were systematically blitzed.

Using nighttime serious casualty accidents as a surrogate for alcohol-involved accidents, Cameron and Strang (1982) evaluated the effects of three periods of intensified enforcement in 1978 and 1979. They reported a 24% reduction in accidents in the areas and weeks of RBT operations, a 23% reduction in the areas of RBT operations during the 2 weeks after operations ceased, and an 11% "contamination effect" in nearby areas (apart from those directly influenced). They also carried out a cost-benefit analysis, concluding that the preventive value of each police labor hour was in the range A $150 to $589 (or more).

The Process of General Deterrence and the Impact of RBT on the Social Environment

Scattered information in Victorian government publications throws some light on the operations of the mechanisms set out in Figure 7.1. In a survey of 401 drivers who had consumed liquor on at least one occasion during the previous 7 days, Hutchinson (1987) reported that

44% had been stopped at some time for a random breath test. This suggests a reasonable level of exposure to the law, although after 10 years one could perhaps have expected a higher figure. Respondents were also asked to assess the risk of being stopped for a random test during a journey of 20–30 minutes. For a journey anytime, 70% rated their chances as at most "not very likely," although this proportion dropped to 19% for a Saturday night journey. Unfortunately, this study did not explore the links between exposure and perceptions of risk, nor between perceptions and behavior.

The evidence for a general preventive effect of RBT, through modifications to the social environment or through attitude change, is indirect and inconclusive. Hutchinson (1987) presents evidence that the great majority of potential drinking drivers in Victoria would be embarrassed to lose their licenses because of a drinking–driving conviction, but it is not clear that the social condemnation of drinking and driving has changed markedly in the past decade (MacLean, Hardy, Lane, & South, 1985), nor that any change is linked directly with legal innovations like RBT. There is perhaps stronger evidence (if only circumstantial) that moves toward "more civilized" patterns of drinking and the promotion of low-alcohol beers (especially the latter) are direct responses of the liquor industry to RBT and other drinking–driving countermeasures, as they have been elsewhere. Moreover, coin-operated breath testers in licensed premises have become commercially viable in the past 2 or 3 years, as they have in New South Wales. Significantly, there is no evidence for a decline in overall alcohol consumption in Victoria since the introduction of RBT (South, 1988).

South Australia and the Territories: RBT with a Slow Start

Between February 1980 and October 1982, the Northern Territory, South Australia, and the Australian Capital Territory (ACT) introduced RBT. In each case, enforcement levels were relatively low to begin with and the impact of the law was slight. There are no published evaluations for the territories, although in the Australian Capital Territory there was a statistically significant reduction in the number of road users hospitalized in the first 3 months (Federal Office of Road Safety, 1986), and in the Northern Territory total road deaths fell by 14.2% in the first year (Bungey & Sutton, 1983).

The Northern Territory is characterized by a low population, long distances, poor roads, extremes of climate, vehicle overcrowding (especially in the vicinity of aboriginal reserves), and other problems that make the enforcement of any traffic law especially difficult. In fact, random testing is carried out at the rate of approximately one test for every seven license holders, which is not a bad level of testing, given the difficulties and the lack of resources. The Northern Territory generally has the highest rate of alcohol involvement in fatal crashes, consistent with the high "hit" rate of between 1% and 2% for RBT. The Road Safety Council of the Northern Territory has recommended an increase in random testing, and there is considerable public support for the law (Federal Office of Road Safety, 1986).

The Introduction of RBT in South Australia

There are several reasons why evaluation of RBT in South Australia is of particular importance. These relate to the controversy surrounding its introduction and to the limited resources devoted initially to its enforcement, as well as to the quality of the data (unique in Australia) obtained through the use of random roadside surveys as an evaluation tool.

As Bungey and Sutton (1983) note, in many respects South Australia's experience with RBT has been unique, since it was opposed not only by specific interest groups but also by one of the two major daily newspapers. The total number of newspaper articles and letters about the issue rose sharply in 1980, after the election of a pro-RBT Liberal government, and peaked in June 1981, when the legislation was proclaimed. *The News* was so strongly opposed to the law that it referred to the first offender apprehended as a "victim" (Bungey & Sutton, p. 28). Nevertheless, the publicity generated by the controversy appeared to have a salutary impact on drinking drivers, since the number of drivers admitted to hospital with an illegal (80 mg %) BAC showed a marked dip in June and July 1981. This decline is noteworthy because it occurred 4 months *before* the police were actually geared up to enforce the law (October 1981). The importance of media publicity (whether positive or negative), independent of actual enforcement, has also been noted by Ross (1973) in his evaluation of the impact of the 1967 British breathalyzer law.

Partly as a result of the media opposition, the initial enforcement of RBT was very low-key, with only two RBT units operating in the Adelaide metropolitan area and only a few country towns having police trained to use evidentiary devices (King, 1988). There was little official publicity.

For their evaluation, McLean and his colleagues (McLean et al.,

1984) conducted three 24-hour roadside surveys involving nearly 30,000 drivers. These surveys were carried out between January and May 1981 (pre-RBT), February and June 1982, and February and June 1983. In the three surveys, the researchers found 2.7%, 2.3%, and 2.7% of drivers over the limit of 80 mg % BAC. The reversion to pre-RBT levels was not quite as complete when the percentages of drivers with *any* alcohol were examined, leading the authors to conclude that initially RBT had an effect on all drinking drivers but that a year later the residual effect was concentrated among light drinkers, some of whom gave up drinking altogether when they were driving. These data are consistent with self-reports of decreased drinking and driving recorded by Fisher and Lewis (1983). McLean and colleagues also reported a short-lived reduction in late-night casualty accidents and a temporary reduction in the involvement of alcohol among drivers admitted to hospital, both outcomes being restricted to the metropolitan area.

The results of the evaluation seem clear: A low-key, unpublicized enforcement campaign caused a slight, temporary reduction in drinking and driving and in alcohol-related casualties. However, a number of points should be kept in mind. First, the pre-RBT survey was completed as the newspaper controversy was reaching a peak, with the result that the impact of RBT may have been understated by the roadside surveys. Second, the roadside survey data, together with data from questionnaires mailed back by breath-tested motorists, indicated that even the minimal level of RBT enforcement achieved in South Australia had a disproportionate impact on drivers with a previous conviction for drinking and driving. This finding is explored later in this chapter, in the context of differential deterrability. Finally, the evaluation demonstrated clearly that many drivers took action to avoid RBT sites, especially by using back roads. This finding was consistent with a 40% increase, in relative terms, in the proportion of accidents occurring on back streets between 10:00 P.M. and 3:00 A.M. on Friday and Saturday nights. Thus the evaluation pointed to some subtle aspects of the impact of RBT and suggested ways in which enforcement could be improved.

Recent Developments in South Australia

Responding to the evaluations, and comparing the results of RBT in South Australia with those in New South Wales, the South Australian government moved late in 1986 to intensify greatly the enforcement of RBT and to support the enforcement with an extensive publicity campaign, emphasizing both the risk of detection and the penalties (Legislative Council of South Australia, 1985). The aim was to match the NSW level and style of enforcement, with an increase in the number of tests so that roughly one-third of motorists were tested each year. In addition, there was a move away from RBT sites that were predictable and able to be seen a long way ahead, steps were taken to prevent drivers from turning off before reaching an RBT site, and "block testing" of eight vehicles at one time was introduced to counter the (correct) belief of some drivers that if they "hung back" in passing traffic they would not be pulled over for a test. A further important development, imported from New South Wales, was the requirement that each traffic patrol car perform 1 hour of RBT per day, during the afternoon shift.

From a scientific point of view, this intensification of RBT enforcement, supported by publicity, is of particular importance, since it affords an opportunity to test whether the weak initial intervention crippled RBT as an effective deterrent. The evaluation reported by King (1988) suggests that this "paper tiger" theory is not correct and that even the late introduction of a "boots and all" approach can yield dividends. A telephone survey of 501 men aged 18–50 revealed that most (72%) were aware of an increase in RBT sites, with about a third of the sample mentioning the use of block testing by the police. Nearly all the sample (97%) had seen an RBT station at some time, and three-quarters had seen one within the previous 3 months. Almost half had been tested personally within the last year. Thus exposure levels comparable to those in New South Wales were achieved during 1987.

Roadside surveys conducted by McLean and colleagues before and after the increase in RBT at 20 sites around Adelaide for 7 days a week between 10:00 P.M. and 3:00 A.M. revealed a decline in actual levels of drinking and driving at all times and among all age groups (King, 1988). The percentage over 80 mg % BAC declined from 4.3% to 2.5% overall, with more marked declines for women, drivers aged 21–29, and those driving between 11:00 P.M. and 1:00 A.M. Fatalities in the 12 months from May 1987 were 13% less than expected on the basis of the previous 5 years, and alcohol involvement in fatal crashes also declined. However, more time is required to evaluate fully the impact on accidents.

The Process of General Deterrence and the Impact of RBT on the Social Environment

The telephone survey (King, 1988) suggested that fear of apprehension was more important than fear of having an accident among drivers who avoided driving over the legal limit. This supports general deterrence as an explanation for the observed declines in drinking and driving. In their earlier work, McLean and colleagues (1984) explored the links between the perceived probability of apprehension, self-reported drinking and driving, and actual BAC levels obtained in the roadside surveys. They found that the perceived probability of apprehension increased between 1981 and 1982, consistent with a deterrence interpretation of the impact of RBT, and did not decline in 1983. For each survey there was a moderate negative relationship between the current perceived probability of apprehension and self-reported drinking and driving over the past year, but in the absence of longitudinal data it is not clear whether this relationship reflects experience (successful drinking–driving episodes cause lower perceptions of the chances of arrest) or deterrence (higher perceived chances of arrest cause less drinking–driving) (Minor & Harry, 1982). More interestingly, there was a statistically significant (but weaker) relationship, in the expected direction, between the perceived probability of apprehension and driving over the legal limit in the roadside survey. Since in this case the behavioral measure reflects *current actual behavior* (rather than self-reported drinking and driving in the past), this relationship furnishes stronger (but not conclusive) evidence for a deterrence interpretation.

Evidence from South Australia for broader environmental impacts of RBT is limited, as it is in other jurisdictions. Bungey and Sutton (1983) report changes in drinking patterns, with lunch time trading up and early evening trading down, more drinking at suburban venues within walking distance, and a drop in bar trade in licensed clubs. In addition, low-alcohol beer gained ground. These changes are generally consistent with trends in other states and are probably at least partly due to RBT. However, consistent with the Victorian experience, McLean and colleagues (1984) found no evidence for a decline in general (self-reported) alcohol consumption. On the contrary, there was evidence for an actual *increase* in the frequency with which respondents drank between 1981 and 1983.

Random Stopping in Western Australia and Queensland: RBT by the Back Door

Until late 1988, when both states introduced RBT legislation, Western Australia (WA) and Queensland utilized random stopping programs, in which only a small proportion of motorists pulled over were breath tested—2% in Perth (Western Australia) and fewer than 1% in Queensland. In addition, fewer motorists were stopped each year than with RBT in New South Wales and Tasmania, with one roadblock check for every six license holders in Perth and one in nine in Queensland (Queensland Transport Policy Planning Unit, 1987; WA Police Department, 1988)

Western Australia

Random stopping began in November 1980 in Western Australia, conducted initially in the form of blitzes. According to the only published evaluation of these operations (Maisey & Saunders, 1981), the Christmas/New Year campaign in 1980–1981 resulted in a reduction in nighttime casualty crashes comparable to that obtained in Victoria using full random testing. This supports the argument that RBT is not an essential ingredient for the success of short-term intensive campaigns (Homel, 1988). In June 1986 random stopping was intensified on a long-term basis, with a claimed reduction of 6% in nighttime casualty crashes (WA Police Department, 1988).

Survey data do not support the contention that random stopping had a major deterrent impact. A police survey (Van Brakel, 1987) indicated that only 38.3% of drivers in Western Australia were aware of any new police method to deal with drinking and driving, including random road checks. A survey of 500 respondents in June 1988, reported by Loxley and Lo (1988), revealed that only 18% had ever been pulled over for a roadside check and that (not surprisingly) 67% thought it unlikely that they would be pulled over for a police breath test in the next month. Thirty-nine percent of drinkers admitted to driving "while slightly intoxicated" during the past year, compared with about 29% in the eastern states (Berger et al., 1989). Loxley and Lo (1988) conclude that "only minimal deterrence from drink-driving as a result of roadblock testing was operating in WA" (p. 80).

In discussions I had with police in Western Australia early in 1988, they made it clear that police officers actually conducting roadblocks did not like them, since they were perceived as an inherently dishonest procedure (a "back-door" approach). While everyone—the police and the public—knew that random breath testing was the real objective, the police were required to perform an elaborate charade involving licenses and equipment, all the time "sniffing the air" for signs of alcohol. It is likely that pressure from police, combined with public support for RBT (80% were in favor in mid-1988; Loxley & Lo, 1988), were factors in the decision to legislate RBT for a trial period of 18 months.

Preliminary analysis of the impact of RBT for the first 3 months of

1989 revealed a 23% reduction in nighttime fatalities and injuries relative to the same period in 1988 and relative to daytime fatalities and injuries (Smith, personal communication, April 1989). However, police data show that while a large number of drivers were stopped (at a high rate of six tests for every ten license holders, on a full-year basis), only about 50% of stopped drivers were tested (WA Police Department, 1989). In addition, drivers were often detained for a full 5 minutes while the legislation was explained and equipment checked. This suggests that police were confusing random stopping and RBT and that, consequently, the long-term deterrent impact of RBT in Western Australia is not assured.

Queensland

In many ways Queensland is the most interesting state in Australia. It is, as Charlton (1987) has observed, more than a geographical entity—it is also a state of mind. Sometimes referred to disparagingly in the south as "the Deep North," Queensland has a higher percentage of its population engaged in rural pursuits or resident in provincial cities than other parts of Australia, and it is characterized by a widespread acceptance of conservative values. Politically dominated by the National party, which has its power base in rural areas, the public service and the police force are heavily politicized.

Both random stopping and full RBT were resisted by the government in Queensland longer than anywhere else in Australia. The introduction of RBT late in 1988 should probably be seen primarily as an attempt by the new National party regime to distance itself from past errors and corruption, which were the subject of a Royal Commission (the Fitzgerald Enquiry). It is probably also a response to the failure of the random-stopping program, RID ("reduce intoxicated driving"). RID began in August 1986, accompanied by intense publicity over Christmas 1986. Despite the low rate of actual testing, there was a 16.1% decline in fatal crashes in the first 12 months, compared with the mean for the previous 3 years. Fatal crashes in which the driver had a BAC in excess of 50 mg % declined by 32.9%, and late-night weekend fatal crashes declined by 28.2% (Queensland Transport Policy Planning Unit, 1987). However, by July 1987 the road toll was at levels similar to those that existed prior to the introduction of RID, and the Queensland Transport Policy Planning Unit (1988) concluded that "any improvements which resulted from the introduction of RID have been lost" (p. 4).

Preliminary data on the operation of RBT revealed a 26% reduction in fatalities for the first 4 months of 1989, relative to the average for the same period over the previous 4 years, suggesting a marked short-term impact of RBT comparable in size with that achieved in Western Australia (R. Maunder, personal communication, May 1989). In addition, while stopping rates were comparable with those in Western Australia (nearly six stops for every ten license holders), as in Western Australia not all drivers stopped were tested. A high 2.4% of tests yielded readings over 50 mg % BAC, indicating that police were mixing target testing and random testing. In combination with poor media publicity and evidence that stationary RBT was not as visible as in New South Wales, the high rate of positive tests suggests that, like their Western Australian counterparts, police in Queensland may fail to achieve a long-term general deterrent effect through RBT.

Differential Deterrability: Evidence from the Enforcement of RBT

Evidence is accumulating from a number of jurisdictions that among those most responsive even to weak interventions are groups often considered "undeterrable." In examining the initial impact of RBT in New South Wales, Homel (1988) found that heavy and moderate drinkers modified both their drinking and their travel arrangements more than light drinkers and that fear of legal punishments was a major reason for their behavior. Using an improved measure of behavior change, Loxley and Lo (1988) report the same result for Western Australia *prior* to the introduction of RBT. Snortum, Hauge, and Berger (1986), in a comparison of compliance with drinking-driving laws in Norway and the United States, found that 85% of Norwegian respondents who usually reach high BACs when they drink claimed total abstention on the last drinking occasion when they had the responsibility of driving home. They comment that "this seems too good to be true" (p. 161). Snortum (1988) also cites evidence from Holland and the United States that "problem" drinkers responded more to drinking-driving countermeasures in those countries than did light drinkers.

These findings are important, since, as Snortum (1988) comments, they jar traditional assumptions about the "hopeless drunk." If confirmed in subsequent research, it will be necessary to rethink aspects of deterrence theory and countermeasure strategies. However, it is possible that part of the explanation for this unexpected finding may be found directly in deterrence theory as it is presently understood. For the reasons set out earlier in this chapter, one group of heavy drinkers who are predicted to respond more than other groups to the threat of legal punishments are those with a previous conviction for drinking and driving. In evaluating the early impact of RBT in New South Wales, Homel (1988) found that although previously convicted drivers (who comprised 7.4% of the sample of drinking motorists) did not rate the chances of apprehension as being any higher than did other motorists, for a given level of arrest certainty they took more steps to avoid drinking and driving than did their nonconvicted counterparts. This result is depicted graphically in Figure 7.3.

Figure 7.3 suggests that because they have suffered arrest followed by the legal punishments for drinking and driving, previously convicted offenders are more deterred by their perceptions of sanctions than those who have not been arrested (Tittle, 1980). However, this interaction was only marginally statistically significant, because convicted offenders were a small minority of the sample and, in addition, some criticisms can be directed at the measure of behavior change (Homel, 1988). It is especially interesting, therefore, that McLean and colleagues (1984), testing large numbers of motorists in roadside surveys in South Australia, also found evidence that previously charged drivers responded much more strongly to RBT than

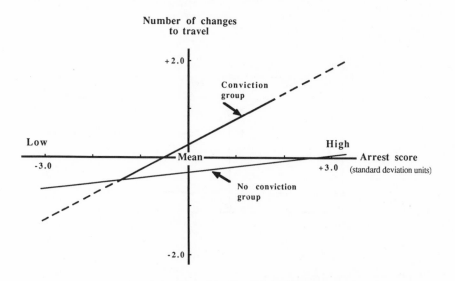

FIGURE 7.3. Number of modifications to travel arrangements: interaction between arrest certainty and a conviction for drinking and driving (unadjusted for other factors). From *Policing and Punishing the Drinking Driver: A Study of General and Specific Deterrence* (p. 177) by R. Homel, 1988, New York: Springer-Verlag. Copyright 1988 by Springer-Verlag. Reprinted by permission.

those not previously charged, even though (as in New South Wales) they did not rate the chances of getting caught as being any higher than drivers without a conviction. Their results are depicted graphically in Figure 7.4.

Figure 7.4 shows that after the introduction of RBT, the rate of driving over the legal limit among previously charged drivers approximately halved, while there was no change among drivers without a charge. (Note that these drinking–driving rates were based not on self-reports but on the actual BAC levels obtained in the roadside surveys.) The lower level of impaired driving persisted for charged drivers, although it still represented a much higher rate of drinking and driving than for drivers without a charge (consistent with my research).

Although the result in Figure 7.4 can in turn be criticized (for example, the data on whether a driver had a charge was based on a 40% response rate, and the analysis needs to be controlled for other variables, including level of drinking), the patterns in Figures 7.3 and 7.4 are remarkably consistent, given the different methods on which they are based. Together they encourage the conclusion that previously convicted drivers are indeed a particularly responsive subgroup

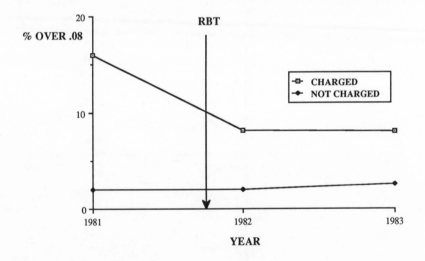

FIGURE 7.4. Percentage of previously charged and not previously charged drivers with over 80 mg % BAC in roadside surveys in Adelaide, South Australia. Data from *Random Breath Testing in South Australia: Effects on Drink-Driving, Accidents and Casualties* (p. 3.52) by A. McLean, M. Clark, M. Dorsch, O. Holubowycz, and K. McCaul, 1984, Adelaide, SA: NH & MRC Road Accident Research Unit, University of Adelaide.

of the target population, even when the legal intervention is as weak, as RBT was initially in South Australia.

CONCLUSIONS: RANDOM BREATH TESTING AND BEYOND

The 1980s were a time of rapid development in Australia in the use of mass breath testing as a primary means of combating drinking and driving. By 1989, it had become clear that random testing "boots and all," using the New South Wales and Tasmanian approach of intensive and continued enforcement and extensive publicity, was perceived as the optimum model for achieving a general deterrent effect, and most states and territories had taken steps to emulate this approach. Even Western Australia and Queensland, those states that had relied hitherto on random stopping rather than RBT, had opted for the New South Wales model, with the goal of annually conducting one breath test for every three licensed drivers.

In this final section, some guidelines for an effective program of random breath testing are distilled from the literature. This is followed by a discussion of the broader and more political issues of how an effective RBT program can be achieved and maintained and an investigation of whether there are better ways of reducing alcohol-related traffic casualties. The chapter concludes with some (fairly pessimistic) speculations on whether "boots and all" RBT can flourish outside Australia.

Effective RBT: Lessons from the Australian Experience

Although Victoria was first into the field with RBT, it has never been clear how much of the decline in alcohol-related casualties recorded in that state was due to RBT, especially since it has never been enforced at anything like the levels obtaining in New South Wales and Tasmania. RBT clearly achieved short-term reductions in casualties when it was enforced through the use of blitzes, but similar effects have been achieved through random stopping in other parts of Australia (Maisey & Saunders, 1981) and through saturated enforcement overseas (e.g., Sykes, 1984). In any case, long-term reduction in accidents is the primary goal of drinking–driving law enforcement.

The experience of South Australia, where a timid introduction was followed some years later by more whole-hearted enforcement and publicity, suggests that the impact of RBT is pretty much a linear function of the resources devoted to it. The same conclusion could be drawn by comparing the performances of New South Wales, Victoria, and the states of Queensland and Western Australia before they introduced RBT. In particular, the experiences of Queensland and Western Australia with random stopping conform closely to the pattern observed by Ross (1982) in his review of the international literature on deterrence—an initial reduction in casualties, followed within a year or so by a return to preintervention accident levels.

Nothing in the Australian literature encourages the belief that roadblocks or sobriety checkpoints, without the use of full random testing, are capable of delivering a substantial and sustained reduction in alcohol-related casualty crashes. In this respect, the Australian literature is consistent with what is known of the effects of sobriety checkpoints in North America (e.g., Williams & Lund, 1984). *In addition, however, the Australian literature suggests equally as strongly that full random testing is also not capable of achieving long-term reductions in casualties unless it is rigorously enforced and extensively advertised.* If visible enforcement and publicity are maintained, the deterrent impact is maintained; if visible enforcement is relaxed, the deterrent impact starts to wane.

The need for continued, intense enforcement of and publicity about RBT rather than random stopping is the central lesson of the Australian experience. Evaluation suggests that the entire NSW program, including media publicity, costs about A $3.5 million per annum. This is estimated conservatively to save 200 lives each year, with total dollar savings to the community of at least A $140 million per annum (Carseldine, 1988). However, this cost-benefit analysis takes no account of the possible side effects of increased violence and disorder due to drinking on trains and in public places. Improvements in public transport, increased security on trains, and the provision of subsidized transport from drinking establishments might reduce somewhat the estimated financial benefits of RBT.

Based on the literature summarized in this chapter, as well as earlier work (Homel, 1988), it is clear that in order to achieve optimum results with RBT certain guidelines, beyond the rather gross and arbitrary "one test for every three license holders," must be observed. Some of these guidelines are listed below.

1. While RBT operations should be visible, the visibility must also be "threatening" (King, 1988). What this means is that drivers should not believe that RBT operations can be easily evaded once they are in sight, and they should not be able to adopt such tactics as hanging

back in a group of cars in order to avoid being pulled over. The actual means of achieving these conditions will vary from jurisdiction to jurisdiction, and even from area to area. They will probably also vary depending on the time of day and the day of the week.

2. The goal of threatening visibility is to increase the perceived chances of apprehension for drinking and driving. Experimentation within each jurisdiction is required in order to determine how much testing should be conducted at times and places of high traffic volume when the incidence of drinking and driving is low, and how much should be conducted when traffic volume is low, but the incidence of drinking–driving (and accidents) is high.

3. Continuous feedback to police on the goals and effectiveness of RBT is required to counter inevitable trends for apprehension-based enforcement policies to displace RBT. Preliminary breath testing in Victoria and mobile random testing in New South Wales are signs of this trend. Media publicity about stationary RBT is helpful in this respect, since it provides a model for police to emulate and encourages them in the knowledge that they have the full support of the government.

4. Media publicity is essential in order to launch RBT "with a bang." Subsequently, visible enforcement is probably more important than publicity, but periodic media blitzes (usually around Christmas) act to boost the visibility of RBT. Publicity should be centered around RBT and should not be simply educational in content.

5. Penalties no more severe than fines of a few hundred dollars and license suspensions of a few months duration are required. Imprisonment is unnecessary, costly, and counterproductive (Homel, 1988).

6. RBT as a preventive policy must be run in parallel with enforcement methods that aim to maximize the apprehension rate. One reason for this is that the overall goal of general deterrence is better achieved if persistent offenders experience for themselves arrest and conviction, since convicted offenders are more responsive to the threat posed by RBT. In addition, it is necessary to target offenders who believe that RBT can be avoided. Thus stationary RBT operations, which are not designed to catch many offenders, can never be the sole mode of drinking–driving law enforcement.

Achieving and Maintaining Deterrence through RBT

While RBT appears to have been successful in New South Wales, it should be recalled that deterrence is an unstable process at the individual level, with peer pressure, lack of exposure to RBT, and successful drinking–driving episodes operating to erode perceptions and behavior patterns built up through earlier exposure to RBT. This is the main reason that enforcement and publicity must be maintained at high levels, at least until drivers start to police their own behavior and informal social controls are strengthened. However, this need for long-term, high-level enforcement creates a number of problems, not the least of which is that over time police and politicians may lose sight of the primary goal of general deterrence. My impression is that strong leadership at the political level is required to ensure that RBT "stays on the rails." In the absence of such leadership, there is a tendency, noted earlier, for police to revert to a more obviously "productive" enforcement approach. On the other hand, the perceived success of a program like RBT to some extent ensures its continuation in pristine form, since any government will tend to back a proven winner.

If strong political leadership is the key, how is it to be found, and indeed how did RBT "boots and all" ever get started? As Snortum (1988) has noted, "a tally of all drinking–driving deterrence studies which were based on vigorous and consistent implementation of legal threat would make a rather short list." (p. 288). Why are wholehearted enforcement programs so rare? While the answer to the general question can be found in Gusfield's (1981) brilliant analysis, my analysis of the NSW experience suggests that the confluence of several social trends, in interaction with some specific political events, were the key factors leading to RBT.

One important factor was public opinion, with support for RBT growing from 37% in 1973 to 79% in 1981, a year before the law was introduced (Homel, 1986). As noted earlier, the 1970s were a time of increased alcohol consumption, and public anxiety about the negative social impact of alcohol use tended to focus on drinking and driving. Despite a variety of government measures to reduce alcohol-related accidents during this period (such as increasing the penalties, reducing the per se BAC level to 50 mg %, and extending preliminary breath testing to nearly all traffic offenders and those involved in accidents), the road toll remained static. By contrast, the road toll in Victoria, and alcohol-related casualties in particular, were declining, and RBT was popularly believed to be the cause. Significantly, although public opinion was strongly in favor of RBT, citizens' groups, U.S.-style, were not in evidence. The importance of this is that such groups tend to favor policies emphasizing detection and punishment (Homel, 1988), and their influence could have diverted political attention from a preventive approach.

The strategy was adopted of forming a bipartisan standing committee on road safety (the "Staysafe Committee"), under the chairmanship of a backbencher with strong ministerial ambitions. The chairman accepted the recommendations of a group of expert advisers (who were influenced by the work of Laurence Ross) that RBT supported by intense visible enforcement and extensive publicity offered the best hope of at least short-term gains (Staysafe, 1982). The government took a political risk, introduced the law, and provided the resources for the media publicity, but perhaps even more significant was the fact that police actually enforced the law in the manner recommended. The centralized structure of the NSW police force was definitely a major reason for the level of enforcement achieved, since all traffic police throughout the state were required to follow orders and had little choice in how or where to conduct RBT.

In summary, RBT "boots and all" in New South Wales happened because RBT was believed to have worked in Victoria, most people believed that alcohol-related road deaths were a major problem, public opinion was strongly in favor of RBT, there was an absence of strong lobby groups (including citizens' groups) who could have diverted resources from a preventive approach, and on the basis of expert opinion the government was prepared to take the political risk. RBT worked because it was supported by extensive publicity and the police force was structured in such a way that the threatened enforcement levels could actually be delivered. RBT continues to work because neither the politicians nor the police have (yet) lost sight of the central goal of general deterrence. However, the long-term success of RBT may possibly be endangered, eventually, by a growth in mobile testing, which is concentrated on apprehending offenders rather than on maintaining, through "threatening visibility," a high perceived probability of apprehension among potential offenders.

Alternatives to Random Breath Testing

Laurence Ross, whose work was so influential when RBT in New South Wales, was being considered, has, paradoxically, been a consistent and severe critic of deterrence-based approaches to the reduction of alcohol-related casualties (e.g., Ross, 1988a, 1988b; Ross & Hughes, 1986). While conceding (Ross, 1988a) that "drink-driving law enforcement that manages to breath-test a third of the driving population every year may exceed the threshold for long-term effectiveness" (p. 75) and conceding the cost-effectiveness of the NSW program, he nevertheless argues that RBT is like "a mass stop and frisk, which cannot clearly be distinguished from, say, stopping all passing pedestrians to be sniffed by dogs for the possession of drugs or to be patted down to see whether they are carrying weapons" (p. 75). He emphasizes, by contrast, such strategies as increasing the cost and diminishing the convenience of alcohol consumption, designing better highways, and removing environmental hazards, such as trees (Ross, 1988b).

There is no doubt that Ross's emphasis on the need for institutional and environmental countermeasures is absolutely correct. The model set out in Figure 7.1 was designed to incorporate precisely these kinds of measures, a number of which have already been implemented in Australia. Contrary to the impression that might be gained from reading this chapter, the reduction of drinking and driving through deterrence has only been a central concern of Australian policy makers for about the last 15 years. Prior to this, and even during this period, many more resources have been devoted to such things as vehicle design rules, compulsory wearing of seat belts, road upgrading, and modifications to the roadside environment than have been devoted to RBT (Homel et al., 1988). Australia was among the first countries in the world to legislate for seat belts and motorcycle helmets and, unlike the United States, has achieved a high level of compliance with these laws.

The crux of the problem is that alcohol-related casualties still occur at a very high rate in Australia, despite seat belts, helmets, and a more forgiving roadside environment—and *despite RBT* (Berger et al., 1989). The removal of roadside hazards has been a priority in Victoria for more than 10 years, but Cunningham (1986) concluded that the results of this program have been "unimpressive" (p. 62). It is hard to avoid the conclusions that Australians drink (and drink and drive) more than is good for them and that modifications to the roadside or vehicle environment, while absolutely necessary, are not going to provide an early or complete solution to the problem.

In this context, Ross's recommendations concerning controls on alcohol availability are attractive. Unfortunately, in view of Australian attitudes and drinking practices, no measures that would potentially achieve anything have any chance of getting off the ground. I have already referred to the history of the temperance movement and to the fate of the wowsers. The wowsers were condemned not only because they were sanctimonious and judgmental but also because the laws they supported did actually have the effect of "increasing the cost and diminishing the convenience of alcohol consumption" (Ross, 1988b, p. 864). Moreover, nothing much has changed.

According to a recent NSW survey (Homel & Flaherty, 1988), although there is very little community support for any form of increase in availability of alcohol through the liberalization of liquor laws, there is also very little support for reductions in availability. Fewer than one-third of the population support reductions in outlets or opening hours or an increase in the legal age for purchasing alcohol. In other words, most people are happy with the status quo. Casswell (1985) and Petersen (1987) have highlighted the very real political difficulties that face Australian governments in implementing "control of consumption" policies, with Petersen emphasizing the disparity between prevention rhetoric and actual policy implementation.

The unique importance of RBT in the Australian context may now be a little clearer to the foreign reader. It is one of the few socially acceptable "alcohol countermeasures" that has achieved a widespread measure of success. In my view, the long-term value of RBT will be not so much the direct reduction in deaths and injuries as the changes in drinking practices and attitudes that it may have helped bring about. Total per capita alcohol consumption has declined 16% from a peak in 1977–1978 of 13.2 liters (Commonwealth Department of Community Services and Health, 1988), and RBT has probably been one factor in this decline. More directly, RBT has dramatized the role of alcohol in road deaths, has perhaps begun to change attitudes toward drinking and driving in New South Wales, and has had a marked impact on the dynamics of drinking in group situations.

In short, RBT may be the "entering wedge" for further countermeasures that do not explicitly target consumption but rather capitalize on the new social climate, particularly on the changing nature of public drinking. Server intervention programs, which directly modify the drinking environment without reducing profits or affecting the enjoyment of patrons (Homel & Wilson, 1987; Saltz, 1987), are an obvious policy priority, both in Australia and overseas.

Can RBT Be Exported?

Civil liberties considerations are at the heart of Ross's objections to RBT and have been a major reason for the limited implementation of roadblocks in North America (Homel, 1988). In this connection, it should be noted that there was quite a vigorous debate concerning civil liberties in New South Wales prior to the introduction of RBT but that the final position of the NSW Council for Civil Liberties was that "a civil liberty might be set aside in the specific instance if it can be demonstrated that the practice of random breath tests achieves the aim of reducing road deaths" (NSW Council for Civil Liberties, 1982, p. 1). I have argued (Homel, 1988) that RBT is more analogous to the random (and intrusive) checks of passengers and personal baggage prior to entering an aircraft than it is to the situations referred to by Ross (1988a). Such checks are widely accepted as a necessary sacrifice in the fight against terrorism.

However the issue of civil liberties is resolved at an individual level, the fact remains that RBT "boots and all" is unlikely to be allowed in the United States, given the constitutional barriers. What is more likely is that more limited forms of random stopping will be allowed in some states and that these will take their place alongside other enforcement strategies. In other words, RBT will never become the cornerstone of enforcement policy as it has in most parts of Australia. This may indeed be an appropriate stance, given that there is more scope in the United States for direct alcohol-control policies, such as raising the legal drinking age. Although the constitutional barriers may be less formidable in other countries, such as Canada and the United Kingdom, my judgment is that in these countries as well, the influence of civil liberties groups, conservative politicians, the liquor industry, and even (as in Britain) sections of the police will combine to prevent a "boots and all" implementation of RBT, although more limited forms of roadblock enforcement will be intensified.

The irony of this situation is that in view of the literature reviewed in this chapter, if RBT is not adopted "boots and all," it may as well not be adopted at all.

ACKNOWLEDGMENTS

Portions of this chapter were presented at the conference on Alcohol and Crime, organized by the Australian Institute of Criminology in Perth, April 1989. I would like to thank David Hawks, Dale Berger, Warren Harrison, and Barry Taylor for their very helpful comments on an earlier draft, and Ross Maunder, Ian Smith, and Gavin Maisey for supplying information on RBT in Queensland and Western Australia.

REFERENCES

Andenaes, J. (1983, November). *Prevention and deterrence—General and special.* Paper presented at the 9th international conference on Alcohol, Drugs and Traffic Safety, San Juan, Puerto Rico.

Arthurson, R. (1985). *Evaluation of random breath testing.* (Research Note RN 10/85). Sydney, NSW: Traffic Authority of New South Wales.

Berger, D., Snortum, J., Homel, R., Hauge, R., & Loxley, W. (1989, October). *Social, cultural, and legal influences on alcohol-impaired driving: Compliance in Australia, the United States and Norway.* Paper presented at the 11th international conference on Alcohol, Drugs and Traffic Safety, Chicago.

Bungey, J., & Sutton, A. (1983). *Random breath tests and the drinking driver: The South Australian experience.* Adelaide, SA: Alcohol and Drug Addicts Treatment Board/Office of Crime Statistics.

Cameron, M.H., & Strang, P.M. (1982). Effect of intensified random breath testing in Melbourne during 1978 and 1979. *Australian Road Research Board Proceedings, 11,* 1–12.

Cameron, M.H., Strang, P.M., & Vulcan, A.P. (1980, June). *Evaluation of random breath testing in Victoria, Australia.* Paper presented at the 8th international conference on Alcohol, Drugs and Traffic Safety, Stockholm, Sweden.

Carroll, J., & Weaver, F. (1986). Shoplifters' perceptions of crime opportunities: A process tracing study. In D.B. Cornish & R.V. Clarke (Eds.), *The reasoning criminal: Rational choice perspectives on offending* (pp. 19–38). New York: Springer-Verlag.

Carseldine, D. (1988, November). *Random breath testing in NSW—Some indicators of continuing success.* Paper presented at the 1988 Conference of Police Personnel Involved in Breath Testing, Penrith, NSW.

Cashmore, J. (1985). *The impact of random breath testing in New South Wales,* Sydney, NSW: Bureau of Crime Statistics and Research.

Casswell, S. (1985). The organisational politics of alcohol control policy. *British Journal of Addiction, 80,* 357–362.

Charlton, P. (1987). *State of mind: Why Queensland is different.* Sydney, NSW: Methuen Haynes.

Commissioner of Police for New South Wales. (1988). *A police strategy to address unlawful consumption and possession of alcohol by juveniles: A proposal submitted to the Minister of Police and Emergency Services by the Commissioner of Police.* Sydney, NSW: Commissioner's Policy Unit, Police Headquarters.

Commonwealth Department of Community Services and Health. (1988). *Statistics on drug abuse in Australia.* Canberra, ACT: Australian Government Publishing Service.

Cunningham, J. (1986). 1977 and beyond—A review of roadside hazard management in Victoria since the 1977 symposium. *Proceedings of the Thirteenth Australian Road Research Board Conference, 13* (9), 54–63.

Federal Office of Road Safety. (1986). *Drinking driving controls in Australia.* Canberra, ACT: Author.

Fischer, A.J. & Lewis, R.D. (1983). *Survey of attitudes towards random breath testing* (Vol. 2). Adelaide, SA: Economics Department, University of Adelaide.

Gusfield, J. (1981). *The culture of public problems: Drinking–driving and the symbolic order,* Chicago: University of Chicago Press.

Harrison, W. (1988). *Evaluation of a drink–drive publicity and enforcement campaign*, Melbourne, VIC: Road Traffic Authority.

Homel, P., & Flaherty, B. (1988). *Attitudes of the NSW public to the relaxation of liquor laws*. Sydney, NSW: Directorate of the Drug Offensive, NSW Department of Health.

Homel, R. (1986). *Policing the drinking driver: Random breath testing and the process of deterrence*. Canberra, ACT: Federal Office of Road Safety.

Homel, R. (1988). *Policing and punishing the drinking driver: A study of general and specific deterrence*. New York: Springer-Verlag.

Homel, R., Berger, D., Loxley, W., Snortum, J., & Hauge, R. (1990). *The general prevention of drinking and driving: A comparative study of complicance with drinking and driving laws in Australia, the United States and Norway* (Report prepared for the Criminology Research Council). Sydney, NSW: Macquarie University, School of Behavioural Sciences.

Homel, R., Carseldine, D., & Kearns, I. (1988). Drink–drive countermeasures in Australia. *Alcohol, Drugs and Driving, 4* (2), 113–144.

Homel, R., & Wilson, P. (1987). *Death and injury on the road: Critical issues for legislative action and law enforcement*. Canberra, ACT: Australian Institute of Criminology.

Homel, R., & Wilson, P. (1988). Law and road safety: Strategies for modifying the social environment, with particular reference to alcohol control policies. *Australian and New Zealand Journal of Criminology, 21,* 104–116.

Horne, D. (1971). *The lucky country* (3rd ed.). Blackburn, VIC: Penguin.

Hutchinson, D. (1987). *Drink driving attitudes and behavior, stage II, quantitative*. Melbourne, VIC: Road Traffic Authority.

Kahneman, D., & Tversky, A. (1982). The psychology of preferences. *Scientific American, 246* (1), 136–142.

King, M. (1988). *Random breath testing operation and effectiveness in 1987*. Adelaide, SA: Road Safety Division, SA Department of Transport.

Legislative Council of South Australia. (1985). *Report of the Select Committee of the Legislative Council on review of the operation of random breath testing in South Australia*. Adelaide, SA: Author.

Loxley, W., Blaze-Temple, D., Binns, C., & Saunders, B. (1988). *Drinking and driving in Western Australia: Knowledge, attitudes and practices* (working draft). Perth, WA: National Centre for Research into the Prevention of Drug Abuse.

Loxley, W., & Lo, S.K. (1988). *By the back door: Experiences and perceptions of road block testing of drink drivers in Western Australia, 1988* (working draft). Perth, WA: National Centre for Research into the Prevention of Drug Abuse.

Maisey, G., & Saunders, C. (1981). *An evaluation of the 1980/81 Christmas/New Year traffic enforcement blitz* (Research and Statistics Report No. 16). Perth, WA: Road Traffic Authority.

McLean, S., Hardy, J., Lane, J. & South, D. (1985). *Survey of drink-driving behaviour, knowledge and attitudes in Victoria, December 1983*. Melbourne, VIC: Road Traffic Authority.

McLean, A., Clark, M., Dorsch, M., Holubowycz, O., & McCaul, K. (1984). *Random breath testing in South Australia: Effects on drink-driving, accidents and casualties.* Adelaide, SA: NH & MRC Road Accident Research Unit, University of Adelaide.

Minor, W.W., & Harry, J. (1982). Deterrent and experiential effects in perceptual deterrence research: A replication and extension. *Journal of Research in Crime and Delinquency, 19,* 190-203.

Monk, K. (1985). *Public attitudes to random breath testing.* Melbourne, VIC: Road Traffic Authority.

Mosher, J. (1985). Alcohol policy and the Presidential Commission on Drunk Driving: The paths not taken. *Accident Analysis and Prevention, 17,* 239-250.

NSW Council for Civil Liberties. (1982). *Random breath testing and civil liberties.* Paper distributed to all members of the NSW ALP Caucus, and available from the Council for Civil Liberties, 149 St. Johns Road, Glebe, NSW, 2037, Australia.

Petersen, A. (1987). Alcohol policy and health promotion: Rhetoric and reality. *Australian Journal of Social Issues, 22,* 333-344.

Queensland Transport Policy Planning Unit. (1987). *Evaluation of the reduce impaired driving (RID) campaign.* Brisbane, QLD: Queensland Department of Transport.

Queensland Transport Policy Planning Unit (1988). *Report on the 1988 road toll as at the end of July.* Brisbane, QLD: Queensland Department of Transport.

RACV Consulting Services. (1983). *Road safety in Victoria: Existing countermeasures and their effects* (Report presented to the Social Development Committee of the Parliament of Victoria). Melbourne, VIC: Author

Room, R. (1985). "An intoxicated society?": Issues then and now in Australia. In J. Cavanagh, F. Clairmonte, & R. Room (Eds.), *The world alcohol industry with special reference to Australia, New Zealand and the Pacific Islands* (pp. 147-216). Sydney, NSW: Transnational Corporations Research Project, University of Sydney.

Ross, H.L. (1973). Law, science and accidents: The British Road Safety Act of 1967. *Journal of Legal Studies, 2,* 1-78.

Ross, H.L. (1982). *Deterring the drinking driver: Legal policy and social control.* Lexington, MA: Lexington Books.

Ross, H.L. (1988a). Deterrence-based policies in Britain, Canada and Australia. In M.D. Laurence, J. R. Snortum, & F.E. Zimring (Eds.), *The social control of drinking and driving* (pp. 64-78). Chicago: University of Chicago Press.

Ross, H.L. (1988b). Editorial: British drink-driving policy. *British Journal of Addiction, 83,* 863-865.

Ross, H.L., & Hughes, G. (1986, December). Getting MADD in vain: Drunk-driving: What not to do. *The Nation,* pp. 663-664.

Rothengatter, T. (1982). The effects of police surveillance and law enforcement on driver behavior. *Current Psychological Reviews, 2,* 349-359.

Saltz, R. (1987). The roles of bars and restaurants in preventing alcohol-impaired driving: An evaluation of server intervention. *Evaluation and Health Professions, 10,* 5–27.

Simpson, H.M., Beirness, D.J., Mayhew, D.R., & Donelson, A.C. (1985). *Alcohol-specific controls: Implications for road safety.* Ottawa, Canada: Traffic Injury Research Foundation.

Snortum, J.R. (1988). On seeing the forest and the trees: The need for contextual analysis in evaluating drunk driving policies. *Evaluation and Program Planning, 11,* 279–294.

Snortum, J.R., Hauge, R., & Berger, D.E. (1986). Deterring alcohol-impaired driving: A comparative analysis of compliance in Norway and the United States. *Justice Quarterly, 3,* 139–165.

South, D. (1988). *Changes in alcohol involvement in accidents in the ten years 1977–1986, and the factors that may have been responsible.* Melbourne, VIC: Road Traffic Authority.

Staysafe (1982). *Alcohol, other drugs and road safety* (First report of the Joint Standing Committee on Road Safety, Parliament of New South Wales). Sydney, NSW: Parliament of New South Wales.

Sutton, L., Farrar, J., & Campbell, W. (1986, September). *The effectiveness of random breath testing: A comparison between the state of Tasmania, Australia, and four states in the eastern United States.* Paper presented at the 10th international conference on Alcohol, Drugs and Traffic Safety, Amsterdam, The Netherlands.

Sykes, G.W. (1984). Saturated enforcement: The efficacy of deterrence and drunk driving. *Journal of Criminal Justice, 12,* 185–197.

Tittle, C.R. (1980). *Sanctions and social deviance: The question of deterrence.* New York: Praeger.

Van Brakel, R. (1987). *A survey of driver attitudes to drink driving and speeding behavior, and various young driver crash countermeasures* (Research and Statistics Report No. 87/4). Perth, WA: Research and Statistics Section, Police Department of Western Australia.

Vingilis, E., & Mann, R.E. (1986). *Towards an interactionist approach to drinking–driving behavior: Implications for prevention and research.* Unpublished manuscript, Addiction Research Foundation, Toronto, Canada.

WA Police Department. (1988, January). *Road safety trends.* Newsletter of the Police Department's Research and Statistics Section, Perth, WA.

WA Police Department (1989, March). *Road safety trends.* Newsletter of the Police Department's Research and Statistics Section, Perth, WA.

Wallace, C. (1985). The Australian brewing and winemaking industries: An outline. In J. Cavanagh, F. Clairmonte, & R. Room (Eds.), *The world alcohol industry with special reference to Australia, New Zealand and the Pacific Islands* (pp. 123–146). Sydney, NSW: Transnational Corporations Research Project, University of Sydney.

Williams, A.F., & Lund, A.K. (1984). Deterrent effects of roadblocks on drinking and driving. *Traffic Safety Evaluation Research Review, 3,* 7–18.

Woodward, R., & Goldsmith, P. (1964). *Cumulative sum techniques* (I.C.I. Monograph No. 3). Edinburgh: Oliver & Boyd.

PART III

OTHER PREVENTIVE MEASURES

8

ALCOHOL AVAILABILITY, PER CAPITA CONSUMPTION, AND THE ALCOHOL-CRASH PROBLEM

ROBERT E. MANN
LISE ANGLIN

Few would argue with the proposition that an individual who consumes less alcohol is at lower risk for alcohol problems than an individual who consumes more alcohol, other factors being equal. If "population" is substituted for "individual" in this proposition, the same logic might still hold. Many studies clearly demonstrate that it does for alcohol-related problems such as cirrhosis rates (Bruun et al., 1975; Popham, Schmidt, & deLint, 1978; Single, 1988). As a result of this and related work, it has become widely accepted in the public health field that control of alcohol availability and average levels of alcohol consumption in a population is the first step in prevention of those problems. This general approach to the prevention of alcohol problems will be referred to as "availability theory" (Single, 1988) in this chapter.

The purpose of this chapter is to assess the applicability of availability theory to the drinking–driving problem. First, some general features of availability theory will be described. Second, evidence linking per capita consumption, alcohol availability, and alcohol-related crashes will be described. Third, some conclusions will be drawn about the place of availability theory in reducing the alcohol–crash problem.

---

*The views expressed in this document are those of the authors and do not necessarily reflect those of the Addiction Research Foundation.

THE AVAILABILITY THEORY APPROACH TO ALCOHOL PROBLEMS

Availability theory evolved from work done in France (Ledermann, 1956, 1964), Canada (e.g., Seeley, 1960), and the Scandinavian countries (e.g., Bruun, Koura, Popham, & Seeley, 1960). Ledermann (1956, 1964) examined the distribution of alcohol consumption in different populations, concluding that there was a relatively invariant relationship between the mean level of alcohol consumption and the dispersion of consumption. He developed specific formulae that permitted the calculation of the proportion of the population drinking at any particular level based on knowledge of the mean level of consumption. At approximately the same time, Canadian and Scandinavian researchers were exploring the relationship between alcohol consumption and alcohol problems in populations (e.g., Bruun et al., 1960; Popham, 1956; Schmidt & Bronetto, 1962). Extending this work to economic concerns, Seeley (1960) observed that relative price of alcohol also correlated very strongly with both alcohol consumption and cirrhosis death rates. These empirical relationships in populations (alcohol availability influences consumption levels, which influence problem levels) form the basis of the availability theory approach to alcohol problems. These relationships have been observed many times, both over time and between populations (e.g., Bruun et al., 1975; Popham et al., 1978; Single, 1988).

An important issue with availability theory is the nature of alcohol problems. In particular, some approaches to these problems suggest that alcoholics and nonalcoholics differ sufficiently from each other so as to constitute separate populations. If this is the case, then factors that influence the alcohol consumption patterns of nonalcoholics, such as availability and price, would not influence the consumption patterns of precisely those groups of individuals whose alcohol consumption is of concern. Ledermann's (1956, 1964) proposition that alcohol consumption in a population can be characterized by a single, log-normal distribution (termed the "single distribution model"; Schmidt & Popham, 1978) provided a basis for proposing that the target group of excessive drinkers within a population could be influenced by availability factors. Skog (1980a, 1980b, 1985) has demonstrated that, while specific predictions based on Ledermann's propositions may differ somewhat from observed data, general predictions are substantially correct. What may be the most important prediction—that is, that heavy or hazardous drinkers are affected by alcohol availability—has been confirmed by research (e.g., Cartwright, Shaw, & Spratley, 1978; Kendell, de Roumanie, & Ritson 1983; Room, 1984).

In any case, Ledermann's proposition is not necessary to the availability theory approach to alcohol problems, since much research has attested to its validity. The bases of availability theory are demonstrable relationships among alcohol availability (defined broadly to include price, legal drinking age, density of outlets, hours of sale, and so forth), alcohol consumption, and alcohol problems; reductions in availability will tend to be followed by reductions in consumption and problem rates, while increases in availability will tend to be followed by increases in consumption and problem rates (for discussions and reviews of the relevant research, see Bruun et al., 1975; Popham et al., 1978; Skog, 1985; Single, 1988). This is not to say that availability control should constitute the only strategy in efforts to reduce alcohol-related problems. However, its demonstrated validity has led to its wide adoption by the public health community as the cornerstone of such efforts (e.g., Moser, 1980).

APPLICABILITY OF AVAILABILITY THEORY TO THE ALCOHOL–CRASH PROBLEM

Although the availability theory approach has been generally accepted by the public health community, its acceptance by workers in the alcohol–crash area is less notable. For example, Hauge (1988) states:

> The hypothesis that there is a connection between overall alcohol consumption and harmful effects also implies that, other things being equal, if alcohol consumption increases in a population, the percentage of motor-vehicle drivers driving under the influence of drinking should increase accordingly. . . . The results of the studies in this review do not, however, seem to support this hypothesis. (p. 185).

Similarly, Noordzij (1987), in a discussion of the provisional state of knowledge, says that "[m]easures designed to cut down the consumption of alcohol in general have not been shown to have any or clear effect on road safety" (p. 8). This contrast between the alcohol–traffic safety field and the general public health field seems surprising. Since this difference may arise in part from methodological issues, these issues will be considered briefly before the research is examined.

Methodological Issues in Measuring the Alcohol–Crash Problem

In addition to the variety of methodological problems that can hinder any research effort, there are two issues that have had a large impact on research in this field. The first is the nature of research designs that can be used to examine links among alcohol availability, per capita consumption, and crashes; the second is the difficulty of assessing whether or not a crash involves alcohol.

With regard to the first issue, studies attempting to link population measures of alcohol consumption, alcohol availability, and alcohol-related crashes have been restricted to quasi-experimental or correlation designs. These designs may range from simple inspection of trend data (e.g., Drew, 1979) to complex time-series or regression approaches (e.g., Votey, 1984). However, none is able to establish causation directly, as true experimental designs are able to do (Campbell & Stanley, 1963); in such situations the accumulation of substantial evidence and the ruling out of various alternative hypotheses are necessary before causal interpretations can be drawn with any assurance (as in the case of the link between smoking and lung cancer). However, the argument can always be made (and it is made where large economic interests are involved) that such research can never prove causation. In addition to having to take into account the inherent interpretive weaknesses of these types of studies, the researcher, being unable to control the relevant variables, has to search for naturally occurring opportunities for data collection. Such opportunities may be limited and so constituted as to minimize the likelihood of observing any effects. For example, Hauge (1988) reported on efforts to examine the effects of reduced availability (a 9-week liquor store strike in Norway) on traffic safety. No appreciable effects were observed; however, the impact of the strike on actual consumption of alcohol could not be determined with any degree of accuracy, since people hoarded wine and spirits before the strike and beer consumption increased during the strike (the sale of beer was not affected by the strike).

The second issue, the problem of determining whether or not a crash is alcohol-related, is complex. It is theoretically possible to obtain blood alcohol content (BACs) on every driver involved in an accident. However, even BACs may underestimate the role of alcohol in accidents, since a delay in obtaining them can produce lower levels due to the metabolism of alcohol. In practice, it has been impossible in any jurisdiction to date to implement BAC testing of all crash-involved drivers; some jurisdictions (e.g., Ontario) have recently succeeded in obtaining BACs on most drivers killed in accidents. Since these data sets are as yet relatively few in number, researchers have turned to other measures of alcohol's impact on road safety. These include police-reported alcohol involvement in crashes and numbers of drinking–driving charges, or surrogate measures such as drivers killed in nighttime or single-vehicle crashes. These and other measures are used because they provide at least some indication of alcohol involvement in road safety problems. For example, Beirness, Haas, Walsh, and Donelson (1985) found that single-vehicle accidents involve drinking drivers more often than multiple-vehicle accidents. Official statistics and surrogate measures have proved useful in evaluating drinking–driving countermeasures (e.g., Ross, 1982). However, many problems may be encountered in their use. For example, according to official statistics, of the 926 road fatalities in 1979 in Sweden (with a per capita consumption of 6.02 liters of absolute alcohol), 124 (or 13.4%) were classified as having been involved in an alcohol-related accident (Adrian, 1985). In Italy (with a per capita consumption of 12.14 liters of absolute alcohol), 25 of 8,318 road fatalities (or .003%) were classified as alcohol-related; however, Ferrara and Rozza (1985) found, in an unselected sample of 2,000 accident-involved drivers in northeast Italy collected between 1978 and 1982, that 52.7% had a positive BAC. This example points out the potential lack of sensitivity and specificity of official statistics and surrogate measures. Noordzij (1983) found potential problems with virtually all surrogate measures. If official statistics and surrogate measures must be relied on, a convergent strategy, which takes into account the extent to which different measures are in agreement, has been recommended (Mann & Anglin, 1988; Noordzij, 1983).

Studies of the Relationship between Per Capita Consumption and Traffic Safety

As noted, an important step in establishing the validity of the availability theory approach to the alcohol–crash problem is to establish whether or not a relationship exists between average consumption levels and crash rates. Studies that consider this question and provide some measure of strength of relationship are summarized in Table 8.1. As can be seen, there is a wide variation in populations examined, time intervals considered, and, to a lesser extent, results obtained.

Several studies have observed no significant relationship between

TABLE 8.1. Studies of the Relationship between Consumption and Various Traffic Safety Measures

Study	Sample	Results and comments
Schmidt & Smart (1963)	U.S. states, number not specified, 1939, 1955	$r = -0.28$ and 0.01 for consumption and proportions of drinking drivers in accidents in the two years, respectively
Room (1974)	48 contiguous U.S. states, c. 1960	(1) $r = -0.42$ for consumption and arrest rate for driving while intoxicated in cities over 10,000 population (39 states) (2) $r = 0.27$ for changes in consumption and changes in arrest rate c. 1940–1960
Smart (1976)	Roadside survey data from France, 1969; U.S., 1971; Maine, 1971; Alberta, 1971; South Dakota, 1971; Netherlands, 1970 & 1971; Norway, 1971	(1) $r = -0.24$ for consumption and mean BAC of nonaccident drivers with alcohol in blood (2) $r = -0.07$ for consumption and % of sample over .10 BAC (3) $r = 0.50$ for consumption and % of sample with some alcohol in blood
Douglass et al. (1980)	Michigan, 1970–1977	Significant correlations among alcohol-related property damage and injury accidents and beer and wine sales (corrected for seasonal fluctuations with ARIMA time series model) at lags of 0 and 1 month (correlations with spirit sales not significant)
Colon & Cutter (1983)	50 U.S. states plus D.C., 1976	Multiple regression analyses (dependent variables = fatal accident and driver fatality rates); beer consumption contributed significantly to both analyses (although not reported, the authors comment that total per capita consumption did not correlate significantly with fatalities)
Votey (1984)	Sweden (cross-sectional and 1954–1977 series); Norway (cross-sectional and 1956–1972 series)	Used econometric techniques to assess impact of several factors, including consumption, on fatal and other accidents; concludes "there is a substantial unanimity . . . that increases in alcohol consumption levels are associated with higher accident levels. . . ." (p. 123)

(continued)

TABLE 8.1. (*cont.*)

Study	Sample	Results and comments
Kendell (1984)	United Kingdom, 1970–1982	$r = 0.70$ for consumption and drinking-driving conviction rate
Simpson et al. (1985)	Canada, 1960–1981	$r = 0.32$ for consumption and traffic fatality rate
Mann et al. (1987)	Ontario, 1957–1984	(1) $r = -0.04$ for consumption and drinking drivers involved in fatal accidents per million kilometers traveled (2) $r = 0.80$ for consumption and drinking drivers involved in fatal accidents per 100,000 population (3) $r = 0.95$ for consumption and the ratio of drinking drivers to nondrinking drivers in fatal accidents
Walsh (1987)	Ireland, 1968–1984	Multiple regression analyses (dependent variables = total fatality rate and proportion of fatalities occurring at night); per capita consumption contributed significantly to both analyses.
Mann & Anglin (1988)	Ontario, 1957–1983	Multiple regression analyses (dependent variables = drinking driver fatality rate, single-vehicle fatality rate, and nighttime fatality rate); per capita consumption contributed significantly to all three analyses.
Smart et al. (1989)	10 Canadian provinces, 1974–1983	Multiple regression analyses (dependent variable = change in rates of drinking–driving charges); changes in per capital consumption contributed significantly and also interacted significantly with changes in AA membership.

per capita consumption and traffic safety measures. In some cases small sample sizes are employed, and in others insensitive measures are used. For example, Simpson, Beirness, Mayhew, and Donelson, (1985) examined the correlation between per capita consumption and total fatalities in Canada between 1960 and 1981. Smart (1976) examined the relationship between per capita consumption and three measures of numbers of drinking drivers on the road for eight countries or states with available roadside survey data. Some of the correlations were in predicted directions, but none were statistically significant. Useful though they may be, such studies do not permit definite conclusions because of methodological limitations.

Larger samples were employed by Schmidt and Smart (1963) and Room (1974). In two of three cases, the relationship was opposite to that predicted, that is, negative. Schmidt and Smart (1963) used "the frequency of drinking violations on the part of drivers in fatal accidents" (p. 28) in 1939 and 1955 as a measure of alcohol involvement in crashes, which ranged from 0% to 25% in the former year and 1% to 50% in the latter. Their results illustrate the difficulty in using official statistics, for example, lack of standardized collection and reporting procedures. Room's (1974) measure was "the rate of arrests for 'driving while intoxicated' in cities over 10,000 population per head of population 15 years and over" (p. 23) in 39 states. Room cautions that this measure (and other problem measures) "may well be . . . as much a measure of state policy as of the conduct of individuals" (p. 22). Mäkelä (1978) and Popham, Schmidt, and Israelstam (1984), in considering studies that found no positive relationship between consumption and traffic safety, suggest that traffic safety measures are influenced by many factors in addition to alcohol consumption.

The remainder of the studies in Table 8.1 report some form of significant positive relationship between consumption and traffic safety measures. In most cases, these studies provide some control for potential limitations or problems observed in the studies just described. Correlations of consumption and traffic safety problems withi n one region over time (Mann & Anglin, 1988) or of changes in these measures over several regions (Room, 1974, Smart, Mann, & Anglin, 1989) may reduce error resulting from differing methods of classification of accidents in different regions. Measures used in other studies provide more direct indices of alcohol-related accidents or statistically control for general road safety trends and other factors influencing accident rates (Colon & Cutter, 1983; Douglass, Wagenaar, & Barkey, 1980; Mann & Anglin, 1988; Mann, Smart, Vingilis, Anglin, & Duncan, 1987; Votey, 1984; Wagenaar, 1984; Walsh, 1987), thus removing some of the confounding influence of factors such as improvements in vehicle design, introduction of seat belt laws, seasonal trends, and so forth.

In a related research field, investigators have attempted to develop models explaining motor vehicle death rates (e.g., Loeb, 1987; Peltzman, 1975); among the factors included in such models has been per capita alcohol consumption. In a recent review of U.S. studies,

Zlatoper (1989) concludes that there is an important relationship between per capita consumption and traffic deaths.

It seems, therefore, that the majority of studies now report some form of positive relationship between per capita consumption of alcohol and traffic safety problems, particularly alcohol-related deaths. Studies that find this positive relationship are methodologically stronger than those that do not, because the latter often do not control for factors that would tend to obscure such a relationship. Thus the applicability of availability theory to the drinking–driving problem is supported by studies of the consumption–traffic safety relationship.

Studies of the Effects of Alcohol Availability on Traffic Safety

Studies of the correlation between alcohol consumption and traffic safety problems in populations can demonstrate whether or not a relationship between these measures exists and what direction it takes. However, the observation of a relationship does not prove that a change in consumption will lead to a change in traffic safety. In order to determine whether or not a cause-and-effect relationship may exist, researchers have studied situations in which changes in alcohol availability have been made, for example, through changes in legal availability of alcohol or strikes affecting its production, or have examined the relationship between problems and availability across areas with differing levels of availability.

Changes to the Legal Drinking Age in North America

In the 1970s and 1980s, legal drinking ages in many North American jurisdictions were first lowered and then (in some cases) raised again. These changes constituted a major natural experiment of the effects of increased and then reduced alcohol availability on the affected age groups. While it is clear that many or most individuals who are within a few years of the legal age consume alcohol (Mann, Vingilis, Adlaf, Kijewski, & DeGenova, 1985), legal availability appears to have an impact on drinking patterns and amounts consumed (e.g., Smart, 1977; Wagenaar, 1982).

Because of the interest in the effects of changes in legal drinking age, in particular with regard to traffic safety, many investigations of this issue have been carried out (e.g., Schmidt & Kornaczewski, 1973; Williams, Zador, Harris, & Karpf, 1983) and substantive reviews of this literature have appeared (U.S. General Accounting Office, 1987; Vingilis & DeGenova, 1984; Wagenaar, 1983; Williams, 1986). Since these researchers have agreed consistently, the individual studies will not be reviewed here. Their conclusions have been that, while there has been some variability in impact, which may be due in part to methodological differences between studies, a decrease in legal drinking age results in increased alcohol-related crashes and fatalities and an increase in legal drinking age results in decreased alcohol-related crashes and fatalities among the affected age groups.

Measures of General Availability — Correlational Studies

Several studies have examined relationships among traffic safety problems and measures of alcohol availability (e.g., numbers of outlets selling alcoholic beverages) over different regions. Watts and Rabow (1983) employed regression analyses to examine the impact of sociodemographic and availability measures (numbers of outlets selling different types of beverages) on felony and misdemeanor drunk-driving arrest rates over 213 California cities in 1977. Numbers of outlets selling on-premises beer only were positively related to both types of arrests, while numbers of outlets selling on-premises beer and wine were positively related to felony arrests.

Somewhat different results were obtained by Colon and Cutter (1983), who employed U.S. state-level data for 1976 to regress traffic fatality rates onto demographic characteristics, levels of beer consumption, and numbers of on-premises outlets. This latter measure of availability was negatively related to accident rates. Subsequently, Colon (1983) observed that states with "dry" counties — that is, counties where the sale of alcohol was prohibited — had significantly higher single-vehicle fatality rates than completely "wet" states. Colon (1983) and Colon & Cutter (1983) interpret these findings as suggesting that when accessibility of alcohol is restricted, people may drive more to obtain and drink it and therefore be involved in more alcohol-related accidents.

Natural Experiments in Increased Availability

In many western jurisdictions in recent years, changes in the laws governing the sale of alcohol have had the effect of making alcohol more accessible. For example, hours of sale for on-premises consumption and for off-premises purchase have been increased, and alcohol can be served on Sundays. These legal changes provide natural experiments on the traffic safety effects of increased availability of alcohol.

A series of studies on the effect of increased hours of sale of alcoholic beverages in Australia have been reported by Smith (for a summary, see Smith, 1987a). The increased hours were due to the introduction of Sunday alcohol sales in the cities of Perth, Brisbane, and Victoria (Smith, 1978, 1987b, 1988a) and in the state of New South Wales (Smith 1987c), the extension of hotel closing hours from 10 P.M. to 11 P.M. in New South Wales (Smith, 1987d), and the introduction of flexible hotel trading hours (which permitted hotels to stay open later than the previous 10 P.M. closing time) in Tasmania (Smith, 1988b). In all of these instances, significant increases in either fatal or injury-producing accidents were observed for the time period in which alcohol became more available in comparison with previous years, control time periods, or control areas where no changes were introduced.

In the United States, several states introduced legislation permitting sale of liquor-by-the-drink (LBD) in the 1960s and 1970s; Blose and Holder (1987) evaluated the effects of this increase in availability in North Carolina. Prior to the introduction of LBD in 1978, restaurant and tavern patrons could purchase beer and wine but could only consume liquor if they brought their own. Comparisons of counties that did and did not introduce LBD demonstrated that introduction of LBD was associated with increased consumption of alcohol (Holder & Blose, 1987) as well as with significant increases in police-reported alcohol-related accidents and in single-vehicle nighttime accidents involving male drivers 21 years of age and older (Blose & Holder, 1987). Consistent with these and the Australian observations, Douglass et al. (1980) found, in their analysis of relationships between measures of alcohol availability and problems in the state of Michigan between 1970 and 1977, significant positive correlations between new Sunday sales permits and traffic mortality.

Other studies, however, have observed differing effects of increased alcohol availability. Smart and Docherty (1976) examined the effects on various types of accidents (alcohol-involved, nighttime, total) of introducing on-premises consumption of alcohol in a small Ontario city. Pre–post comparisons with a control city demonstrated either no effect of introducing on-premises consumption or, for some measures (total accidents, accidents resulting in drinking–driving charges), an effect suggesting that increased alcohol availability improved traffic safety. Smith (1985) examined the traffic safety impact of extended trading hours of licensed premises permitted during the 1982 Commonwealth Games in Brisbane. Comparisons with earlier periods revealed no significant impact of the extended hours, although Smith suggested that the results may have been complicated by a police enforcement campaign mounted during the games. Thus the balance of information suggests that increased availability is associated with increased accidents; however, there may be occasional situations where this relationship is not observed.

Natural Experiments in Decreased Availability

Opportunities to study the impact of decreased availability on alcohol–crash rates have been somewhat limited. The majority of studies have examined the effects of strikes by beverage production or distribution workers. Giesbrecht (1988) has recently reviewed the effects of these strikes on a variety of alcohol-related measures, including traffic safety measures. Therefore, this literature will be summarized but not described in detail.

Significant reductions in Friday accidents were reported by Brown (1978) as a result of a 4-week strike influencing beer, but not other alcohol, availability in Aukland, New Zealand. Weekly accident totals revealed similar but nonsignificant reductions. Reductions of drunk-driving rates have been reported (statistical significance levels not provided) as a result of a 5-week liquor store strike in Finland (Mäkelä, 1980) and a 2-month strike of "supervisors and officials" of the Swedish alcohol monopoly (Andréasson & Bonnichsen, 1966). Smart (1977) described the effects of a 2-month strike affecting sales of liquor and wine in Newfoundland and a 1-month strike affecting sales of all alcoholic beverages in Nova Scotia. No significant effects were observed, although there appeared to be a reduction in highway fatalities of approximately 30% during the period of the strike for both provinces. Hauge and Irgens-Jensen (1981; see also Hauge, 1988) described the effects of a 9-week strike by workers at Norway's state-operated wine and spirits monopoly. No significant impact on total accidents was observed, although there was a decrease of 5.8% when compared to the previous year. Decreases in injury accidents and fatalities were also described; however, no significance tests are reported, and the authors suggest that the effects were minimal and may have been due to longer-term trends in accident patterns.

There are many methodological issues involved in considering these studies (Giesbrecht, 1988). For example, the impact on actual consumption can only be estimated, since there was opportunity to stockpile alcohol, switch to other types of alcohol still available, obtain and consume alcohol in licensed premises, and/or obtain alcohol from nearby unaffected areas during all these strikes. A related issue is the possibility that more consumption may occur outside the home, since individuals may drive more to obtain and consume alcohol. However, in spite of these and other limitations, the data do suggest that reduced drinking–driving and traffic safety problems can sometimes be observed, although the reductions are less marked than those observed for other alcohol-related problems, such as public drunkenness and domestic violence (Giesbrecht, 1988).

Reduced Economic Availability

Two studies have examined the impact of reduced economic availability of alcohol. Smart and Adlaf (1986) examined the effects of banning "happy hours" (sale of alcohol at reduced prices in specified time periods) in Toronto in 1984. No significant changes were observed on the amount of alcohol sold in an observational study of drinking behavior. However, significantly fewer drinking–driving charges were brought by the police during the affected time period after the ban, but not in a control time period. The data suggest a positive traffic safety impact of the ban, but the authors note that numerous factors could account for the results. Cook (1981) examined the impact of increases in liquor taxes on liquor consumption and traffic fatality rates in those U.S. states that raised taxes between 1961 and 1975 (39 instances). He observed significant reductions in both consumption and traffic fatality rates as a result of these tax increases when data from the year following the increases were compared with those from the year preceding the increases. Thus both studies observed traffic safety benefits associated with decreased availability.

SUMMARY OF THE EVIDENCE

The following conclusions are justified by the evidence reviewed here. First, there is a positive relationship between per capita consumption and the drinking–driving problem. In the past this relationship may have been obscured by such factors as lack of consistency in official records and substantial changes in general road safety. When efforts are made to take these factors into account, a consistent and strong relationship emerges. Second, increased and reduced availability of alcohol to specific age groups through changes in legal drinking age results in corresponding increases and decreases in crash involvement. Third, increases in alcohol availability due to extended hours of sale or other measures that increase access tend to result in more crashes and injuries. Fourth, decreases in alcohol availability through strikes or increased relative price tend to result in reduced crashes, injuries, and fatalities. These four points are entirely consistent with the availability theory approach to alcohol-related problems and support its applicability to the drinking–driving problem.

Two observations, though, suggest that changes in alcohol availability may differ in effects on traffic safety measures and other alcohol-related problems in some specific instances. The first observation concerns the nature and location of outlets for alcohol. Colon (1983) and Colon and Cutter (1983) have suggested that an inverse relationship may exist between numbers or density of on-premises outlets and traffic safety, that is, where numbers of outlets are fewer or reduced, people may drive more to obtain and consume alcohol. Some evidence for this suggestion was also presented by Smith (1987a), who observed a trade-off between cirrhosis and accident mortality in adjacent Australian states as a function of types of outlets. While the evidence is not consistent (Watts & Rabow, 1983), this issue is clearly an important one worth further study.

A second concern arises from comparisons of situations in which availability increased because of extended hours of sale (e.g., Smith, 1987a) with situations in which availability decreased because of strikes (e.g., Smart, 1977). In both cases, changes in traffic safety measures were in the direction predicted by availability theory. However, the relevant studies suggest that it may be easier to increase traffic safety problems by increased availability than to decrease them by decreased availability of alcohol. In other words, the effects of increased and decreased availability on traffic safety may not be symmetrical.

These issues may arise because alcohol-involved accidents are more of an acute, rather than a chronic (e.g., cirrhosis), complication of alcohol consumption and because alcohol problems such as cirrhosis and accidents are affected by other factors in addition to alcohol consumption (e.g., Popham et al., 1984; Vingilis & Mann, 1986).

THE PLACE OF AVAILABILITY THEORY IN DRINKING–DRIVING PREVENTION

Approaches based on availability theory appear to have been largely ignored by policy makers in recent efforts to reduce deaths and injuries due to impaired driving, with the exception of changes in the drinking age. Among other reasons for this neglect may be an impression that countermeasures based on availability theory are incompatible with other drinking–driving countermeasures. This impression is not correct.

In the past, there has been pessimism about the ability of specific countermeasures to effect a lasting reduction of the alcohol–crash problem (e.g., Ross, 1982). However, more recent work indicates that drinking–driving countermeasures can have beneficial effects (e.g., Homel, Chapter 7, this volume; Mann, Vingilis, & Stewart, 1988a; Wells-Parker, Landram, & Topping, Chapter 11, this volume). This evidence leads to the perspective that truly effective prevention of the alcohol–crash problem will require implementation of a range of complementary programs and policies acting in a consistent manner (Liban, Vingilis, & Blefgen, 1987; Mann et al. 1988d; Snortum, 1988; Vingilis & Mann, 1986).

From this perspective, availability considerations become fundamental to prevention, since population levels and patterns of alcohol consumption can be strongly influenced by taxes and legislation (e.g., Bruun et al., 1975; Popham et al., 1978; Single, 1988). Thus control measures can influence the drinking behavior of the general population; that portion of the population still at risk for alcohol-related problems, such as drinking and driving, can then be influenced through additional preventive efforts, such as education, deterrence, and rehabilitation. A case in point is the reduction in cirrhosis rates in some parts of the world that has occurred in recent years, following a long period of increase. The available data suggest that this reduction is related most strongly to corresponding changes in per capita consumption levels and to increased resources (treatment for alcohol abuse, Alcoholics Anonymous) for assisting individuals with alcohol problems (Mann, Smart, Anglin, & Adlaf, in press; Mann, Smart, Anglin, & Rush, 1988b; Romelsjo, 1987; Smart & Mann, in press). Smart and Mann (in press) have suggested that the stabilization and slight decline in alcohol consumption that have occurred in recent years, after a long period of escalating consumption, have created conditions in which the effects on population cirrhosis rates of factors other than consumption can be observed. There is evidence that recent reductions in the alcohol–crash problem may be due to a similar situation; that is, the stabilization and decline in per capita consumption that have occurred in Canada, the United States, and some other countries are having the effect of both reducing the alcohol–crash problem itself and permitting the beneficial effects of other countermeasures to be observed (e.g., Fell & Klein, 1986; Mann & Anglin, 1988; Smart et al., 1989; Snortum, 1988).

ACKNOWLEDGMENTS

We wish to express our appreciation to Paola Greco, Eric Single, Evelyn Vingilis, and Jean Wilson for their kind help and valuable comments.

REFERENCES

Adrian, M. (1985). *Statistics on alcohol and drug use in Canada and other countries* (Vol. 1). Toronto: Addiction Research Foundation.

Andréasson, R., & Bonnichsen, R. (1966). The frequency of drunken driving in Sweden during a period when the supply of alcoholic drink was restricted. In R.N. Harger (Ed.), *Alcohol and traffic safety* (pp. 279–284). Bloomington: Indiana University Press.

Beirness, D.J., Hass, G.C., Walsh, P.J., & Donelson, A.C. (1985). *Alcohol and fatal road accidents in Canada: A statistical look at its magnitude and persistence.* Ottawa: Department of Justice.

Blose, J.O., & Holder, H.D. (1987). Liquor-by-the-drink and alcohol-related traffic crashes: A natural experiment using time-series analysis. *Journal of Studies on Alcohol, 48,* 52–60.

Brown, R.A. (1978). Some social consequences of partial prohibition in Auckland, New Zealand. *Drug and Alcohol Dependence, 3,* 377–382.

Bruun, K., Edwards, G., Lumio, M., Mäkelä, K., Pan, L., Popham, R.E., Room, R., Schmidt, W., Skog, O.-J., Sulkunen, P., & Osterberg, E. (1975). *Alcohol control policies in public health perspective.* Helsinki: Finnish Foundation for Alcohol Studies.

Bruun, K., Koura, E., Popham, R.E., & Seeley, J.R. (1960). *Liver cirrhosis as a means to measure the prevalence of alcoholism.* Helsinki: Finnish Foundation for Alcohol Studies.

Campbell, D.T., & Stanley, J.C. (1963). *Experimental and quasi-experimental designs for research.* Chicago: Rand McNally.

Cartwright, A.K.J., Shaw, S.J., & Spratley, T.A. (1978). The relationships between per capita consumption, drinking patterns and alcohol related problems in a population sample, 1965–74. *British Journal of Addiction, 73,* 237–258.

Colon, I. (1983). County-level prohibition and alcohol-related fatal motor vehicle accidents. *Journal of Safety Research, 14,* 101–104.

Colon, I., & Cutter, H.S.G. (1983). The relationship of beer consumption and motor vehicle policies to fatal accidents. *Journal of Safety Research, 14,* 83–89.

Cook, P.J. (1981). The effect of liquor taxes on drinking, cirrhosis and auto fatalities. In M.H. Moore & D. Gerstein (Eds.), *Alcohol and public policy:*

Beyond the shadow of prohibition (pp. 255–285). Washington: National Academy of Sciences.

Douglass, R.L., Wagenaar, A.C., & Barkey, P.M. (1980). The relationship of changing alcohol availability to acute and chronic social and health problems. In M. Galanter (Ed.), *Currents in alcoholism* (Vol. 4) (pp 401–425). New York: Grune & Stratton.

Drew, L.R.H. (1979). Road casualties—Australia 1952 to 1977: A reduced alcohol-related problem. *Australian Journal of Alcohol and Drug Dependence, 5*, 122–123.

Fell, J.C., & Klein, T. (1986). *The nature of the reduction in alcohol in U.S. fatal crashes.* Warrendale, PA: Society of Automotive Engineers.

Ferrara, S.D., & Rozza, M. (1985). Alcohol, drugs and road accidents: Epidemiological study in north-east Italy. In S. Kaye & G.W. Meier (Eds.), *Alcohol, drugs and traffic safety* (pp 469–485). Washington, DC: U.S. Department of Transportation.

Giesbrecht, N. (1988). *Strikes as natural experiments: Their relevance to drinking patterns and complications, and availability and prevention issues.* Toronto: Addiction Research Foundation.

Hauge, R. (1988). The effects of changes in availability of alcoholic beverages. In M.D. Laurence, J.R. Snortum, & F.E. Zimring (Eds.), *Social control of the drinking driver* (pp. 169–187). Chicago: University of Chicago Press.

Hauge, R., & Irgens-Jensen, O. (1981). Road traffic accidents and liquor store strikes: Some Scandinavian experiences. In L. Goldberg (Ed.), *Alcohol, drugs and traffic safety* (Vol. 3) (pp. 1160–1177). Stockholm: Almqvist and Wiksell.

Holder, H.D., & Blose, J.O. (1987). Impact of changes in distilled spirits availability on apparent consumption: A time series analysis of liquor-by-the-drink. *British Journal of Addiction, 82*, 623–631.

Kendell, R.E. (1984). The beneficial consequences of the United Kingdom's declining per capita consumption of alcohol in 1979–82. *Alcohol and Alcoholism, 19*, 271–276.

Kendell, R.E., deRoumanie, M., & Ritson, E.B. (1983). Effects of economic changes on Scottish drinking habits 1978–1982. *British Journal of Addiction, 78*, 365–379.

Ledermann, S. (1956). *Alcool, alcoolisme, alcoolisation.* Paris: Presses Universitaires de France.

Ledermann, S. (1964). *Alcool, alcoolisme, alcoolisation: Mortalité, morbidité, accidents de travail.* Paris: Presses Universitaires de France.

Liban, C.B., Vingilis, E.R., & Blefgen, H. (1987). The Canadian drinking-driving countermeasure experience. *Accident Analysis and Prevention, 19*, 159–181.

Loeb, P.D. (1987). The determinants of automobile fatalities: With special consideration to policy variables. *Journal of Transportation Economics and Policy, 21*, 279–281.

Mäkelä, K. (1978). Level of consumption and social consequences of drinking. In Y. Israel, F.B. Glaser, H. Kalant, R.E. Popham, W. Schmidt, &

R.G. Smart (Eds.), *Research advances in alcohol problems* (Vol. 4) (pp. 303–348). New York: Plenum.

Mäkelä, K. (1980). Differential effects of restricting the supply of alcohol: Studies of a strike in Finnish liquor stores. *Journal of Drug Issues, 10,* 131–144.

Mann, R.E., & Anglin, L. (1988). The relationship between alcohol-related traffic fatalities and per capita consumption of alcohol, Ontario 1957–83. *Accident Analysis and Prevention, 20,* 441–446.

Mann, R.E., Smart, R.G., Anglin, L., & Adlaf, E. (in press). Cirrhosis reductions in the U.S.: Associations with per capita consumption and A.A. membership. *Journal of Studies on Alcohol.*

Mann, R.E., Smart, R.G., Anglin, L., & Rush, B.R. (1988b). Are decreases in liver cirrhosis rates a result of increased treatment for alcoholism? *British Journal of Addiction, 83,* 683–688.

Mann, R.E., Smart, R.G., Vingilis, E.R., Anglin, L., & Duncan, D. (1987). Alcohol-related accident statistics in Ontario between 1957 and 1984–Is the problem increasing or decreasing? In P.C. Noordzij & R. Roszbach (Eds.), *Alcohol, drugs and traffic safety–T86* (pp. 245–249). Amsterdam: Elsevier.

Mann, R.E., Vingilis, E.R., Adlaf, E.M., Kijewski, K., & DeGenova, K. (1985). A comparison of young drinking offenders with other adolescents. *Drug and Alcohol Dependence, 15,* 181–191.

Mann, R.E., Vingilis, E.R., & Stewart, K. (1988a). Programs to change individual behaviour: Education and rehabilitation in the prevention of drinking and driving. In M.D. Laurence, J.R. Snortum, & F.E. Zimring (Eds.), *Social control of the drinking driver* (pp 248–269). Chicago: University of Chicago Press.

Moser, J. (1980). *Prevention of alcohol-related problems: An international review of preventive measures, policies, and programmes.* Toronto: World Health Organization/Addiction Research Foundation.

Noordzij, P.C. (1983). Measuring the extent of the drinking and driving problem. *Accident Analysis and Prevention, 15,* 407–414.

Noordzij, P.C. (1987). Background paper T86. In P.C. Noordzij & R. Rosbach (Eds.), *Alcohol, drugs and traffic safety–T86* (pp. 1–11). Amsterdam: Elsevier.

Peltzman, S. (1975). The effects of automobile safety regulation. *Journal of Political Economy, 83,* 677–725.

Popham, R.E. (1956). The Jellinek alcoholism estimation formula and its application to Canadian data. *Quarterly Journal of Studies on Alcohol, 17,* 559–593.

Popham, R.E., Schmidt, W., & deLint, J. (1978). Government control measures to prevent hazardous drinking. In J. Ewing & B. Rouse (Eds.), *Drinking: Alcohol in American society–Issues and current research* (pp. 239–266). Chicago: Nelson-Hall.

Popham, R.E., Schmidt, W., & Israelstam, S. (1984). Heavy alcohol consumption and physical health problems: A review of the epidemiologic evidence. In R.G. Smart, H.D. Cappell, F.B. Glaser, Y. Israel, H. Kalant, R.E. Popham, W. Schmidt, & E.M. Sellers, (Eds.), *Research advances in alcohol and drug problems* (Vol. 8) (pp. 149–182). New York: Plenum.

Romelsjo, A. (1987). Decline in alcohol-related inpatient care and mortality in Stockholm county. *British Journal of Addiction, 82,* 653–663.

Room, R. (1974). Interrelations of alcohol policies, consumption, and problems in the U.S. States. *Drinking and Drug Practices Surveyor, 9,* 21–31.

Room, R. (1984). Alcohol control and public health. *Annual Review of Public Health, 5,* 393–417.

Ross, H.L. (1982). *Deterring the drinking driver: Legal policy and social control.* Lexington, MA: Lexington Books.

Schmidt, W., & Bronetto, J. (1962). Death from liver cirrhosis and specific alcohol beverage consumption. *American Journal of Public Health, 52,* 1473–1482.

Schmidt, W., & Kornaczewski, A. (1975). The effect of lowering the legal drinking age in Ontario on alcohol-related motor vehicle accidents. In S. Israelstam & S. Lambert (Eds.), *Alcohol, drugs and traffic safety* (pp. 763–770). Toronto: Addiction Research Foundation.

Schmidt, W., & Popham, R.E. (1978). The single distribution theory of alcohol consumption: A rejoinder to the critique of Parker and Harman. *Journal of Studies on Alcohol, 30,* 400–419.

Schmidt, W., & Smart, R.G. (1963). Drinking–driving mortality and mortality and morbidity statistics. In B.H. Fox & J.H. Fox (Eds.), *Alcohol and traffic safety* (pp 27–43). Bethesda, MD: U.S. Department of Health, Education and Welfare.

Seeley, J.R. (1960). Death by liver cirrhosis and the price of beverage alcohol. *Canadian Medical Association Journal, 83,* 1361–1366.

Simpson, H.M., Beirness, D.J., Mayhew, D.R., & Donelson, A.C. (1985). *Alcohol-specific controls: Implications for road safety.* Ottawa: Traffic Injury Research Foundation.

Single, E.W. (1988). The availability theory of alcohol-related problems. In C.D. Chaudron & D.A. Wilkinson (Eds.), *Theories on alcoholism* (pp. 325–351) Toronto: Addiction Research Foundation.

Skog, O.-J. (1980a). Is alcohol consumption lognormally distributed? *British Journal of Addiction, 75,* 169–173.

Skog, O.-J. (1980b). Liver cirrhosis epidemiology: Some methodological problems. *British Journal of Addiction, 75,* 227–243.

Skog, O.-J. (1985). The collectivity of drinking cultures: A theory of the distribution of alcohol consumption. *British Journal of Addiction, 80,* 83–99.

Smart, R.G. (1976). Per capita alcohol consumption, liver cirrhosis death rates, and drinking and driving. *Journal of Safety Research, 8,* 112–115.

Smart, R.G. (1977). Effects of two liquor store strikes on drunkenness, impaired driving and traffic accidents. *Journal of Studies on Alcohol, 38,* 1785–1789.

Smart, R.G., & Adlaf, E.M. (1986). Banning happy hours: The impact on drinking and impaired-driving charges in Ontario, Canada. *Journal of Studies on Alcohol, 47,* 256–258.

Smart, R.G., & Docherty, D. (1976). Effects of the introduction of on-premise drinking on alcohol-related accidents and impaired driving. *Journal of Studies on Alcohol, 37,* 683–686.

Smart, R.G., & Mann, R.E. (in press). Factors in recent reductions in liver cirrhosis deaths. *Journal of Studies on Alcohol.*

Smart, R.G., Mann, R.E., & Anglin, L. (1989). Decreases in alcohol problems and increased Alcoholics Anonymous membership. *British Journal of Addiction, 84,* 507–513.

Smith, D.I. (1978). Impact on traffic safety of the introduction of Sunday alcohol sales in Perth, Western Australia. *Journal of Studies on Alcohol, 39,* 1302–1304.

Smith, D.I. (1985). *Extended trading hours during the 1982 Brisbane Commonwealth Games and traffic accidents.* West Perth: W.A. Alcohol and Drug Authority.

Smith, D.I. (1987a, September). *Australian studies of the effect of increasing the availability of alcoholic beverages.* Paper presented to the Research Conference on Statistical Recording Systems of Alcohol Problems, Helsinki, Finland.

Smith, D.I. (1987b). *Effect on traffic accidents of changing the days and hours of sale of alcoholic beverages in Australia.* West Perth: W.A. Alcohol and Drug Authority.

Smith, D.I. (1987c). Effect on traffic accidents of introducing Sunday hotel sales in New South Wales, Australia. *Contemporary Drug Problems, 14,* 279–294.

Smith, D.I. (1987d). *Effect on traffic accidents of replacing 10 P.M. with 11 P.M. hotel closing in New South Wales, Australia.* West Perth: W.A. Alcohol and Drug Authority.

Smith, D.I. (1988a). Effect on traffic accidents of introducing Sunday alcohol sales in Brisbane, Australia. *International Journal of the Addictions, 23,* 1091–1099.

Smith, D.I. (1988b). Effect on traffic accidents of introducing flexible hotel trading hours in Tasmania, Australia. *British Journal of Addiction, 83,* 219–222.

Snortum, J.R. (1988). On seeing the forest and the trees: The need for contextual analysis in evaluating drunk driving policies. *Evaluation and Program Planning, 11,* 279–294.

U.S. General Accounting Office. (1987). *Drinking-age laws. An evaluation synthesis of their impact on highway safety.* Gaithersburg, MD: Author.

Vingilis, E.R., & DeGenova, K. (1984). Youth and the forbidden fruit: Experiences with changes in legal drinking age in North America. *Journal of Criminal Justice, 12,* 161–172.

Vingilis, E.R., & Mann, R.E. (1986). Towards an interactionist approach to drinking–driving behaviour: Implications for prevention and research. *Health Education Research, 1,* 273–288.

Votey, H.L. (1984). Recent evidence from Scandinavia on deterring alcohol-impaired driving. *Accident Analysis and Prevention, 16,* 123–138.

Wagenaar, A.C. (1982). Aggregate beer and wine consumption: Effects of changes in the minimum legal drinking age and a mandatory beverage container deposit law. *Journal of Studies on alcohol, 43,* 469–487.

Wagenaar, A.C. (1983). *Alcohol, young drivers and traffic accidents.* Lexington, MA: Lexington Books.

Wagenaar, A.C. (1984). Alcohol consumption and the incidence of acute alcohol-related problems. *British Journal of Addiction, 80,* 173–180.

Walsh, B.M. (1987). Do excise taxes save lives? The Irish experience with alcohol taxation. *Accident Analysis and Prevention, 19,* 433–448.

Watts, R.K., & Rabow, J. (1983). Alcohol availability and alcohol-related problems in 213 California cities. *Alcoholism: Clinical and Experimental Research, 7,* 47–58.

Williams, A.F. (1986). Raising the legal purchase age in the United States: Its effects on fatal motor vehicle crashes. *Alcohol, Drugs and Driving, 2,* 1–12.

Williams, A.F., Zador, P.L., Harris, S.S., & Karpf, R.S. (1983). The effect of raising the legal minimum drinking age on involvement in fatal crashes. *Journal of Legal Studies, 12,* 169–179.

Zlatoper, T.J. (1989). Models explaining motor vehicle death rates in the United States. *Accident Analysis and Prevention, 21,* 125–154.

9

YOUTH ANTI-DRINKING–DRIVING PROGRAMS

KATHRYN STEWART
MICHAEL KLITZNER

Traumatic injury causes more deaths among American adolescents and young adults aged 14–24 than all other causes combined (Paulson, 1983), and traffic crashes are the leading cause of traumatic injuries (Lewis, 1988; Robertson, 1981). Traffic crashes have been cited as the cause of about half of all accidental deaths in adolescents and young adults and have also been cited as the cause of half of all spinal-cord injuries (Robertson, 1981). Not only adolescent drivers but also their passengers (who tend to be adolescents) are at significantly increased risk when compared to older age groups (Insurance Institute for Highway Safety, 1984).

The exact contribution of alcohol use to youth traffic crashes has been debated (e.g., Cameron, 1982; Zylman, 1973). However, the conclusion appears inescapable that alcohol is a major causal factor (Cameron, 1982; Lewis, 1987). Young drivers are overrepresented in alcohol-related fatal crashes even when driving exposure is controlled for (Vegega, 1984). Although alcohol-related traffic fatalities among adolescents steadily decreased from 1982 to 1985, they increased again in 1986 to a level just below that of 1983 (U.S. Department of Transportation, 1987). Unpublished Fatal Accident Reporting System data for 1987 suggest another downturn, but overall death-rates still exceed those observed in 1985.

The most compelling evidence for a causal link between alcohol and youthful crash involvement comes from studies of changes in minimum alcohol purchase age (e.g., Fell, 1988; Hingson et al., 1983; Smith et al., 1984; Wagenaar, 1982a, 1982b, 1983). Although results have varied from state to state and from study to study, consistent reductions in youthful crash involvement have been observed following increases in minimum purchase age.

Crash data reflect only a small segment of the youth drinking–driving problem. Overall, youthful drivers are much more likely than their older counterparts to report driving after drinking (Hingson, Howland, Morelock, & Heeren, 1988). Recent survey data gathered from the nation's high school seniors (Bachman, Johnston, & O'Malley, 1987) revealed that approximately one in four seniors had driven after drinking in the 2 weeks predating the survey, and approximately one in six had driven after having had five or more drinks in a row. During the same 2-week period, two in five seniors had ridden with a drinking driver, and one in five believed the driver had consumed five or more drinks. Driving while impaired (DWI) and riding with impaired drivers (RWID) would appear to be a regular occurrence for a significant proportion of American youth.

It is also clear that the youth DWI/RWID problem is not limited to impairment due to alcohol. Data from a 1983 survey of 18- to 24-year-olds (Elliot, 1987) revealed that one in five respondents had driven while high on marijuana and that nearly one in ten had driven while high on other drugs. Moreover, the prevalence rate for DWI was twice as high for multiple-drug users as it was for youth who used only alcohol. Convention (and available research) dictates an emphasis on alcohol-related countermeasures in the discussions that follow. However, countermeasures for youth that deal with other drugs will also be discussed where relevant.

Current knowledge of the causes and correlates of youth DWI/RWID is incomplete. The majority of relevant studies have focused on alcohol consumption and related problems rather than on DWI, and only a very limited number of studies have focused on factors that predispose, reinforce, and enable riding with impaired drivers. In addition, predisposing, reinforcing, and enabling factors have often been studied in isolation, complicating assessments of the relative contribution of different variables or classes of variables to DWI/RWID.

Most studies of the causes and correlates of DWI/RWID have focused on the characteristics of individual youths. These studies suggest that personality factors—such as aggressiveness, intolerance of authority, nonconformity, escapism, immaturity, poor academic performance, greater participation in social activities, and positive attitudes toward drinking and toward drinking and driving per se— are associated with increased drinking and driving (Boyd &

Huffman, 1984; Douglass, 1983; Grey Advertising, 1975; Klitzner, Gruenewald, Rossiter, Bamberger, & Roth, 1987; Klitzner, Vegega, & Gruenewald, 1988; Kraus, Steele, Ghent, & Thompson, 1970; Krohn, Akers, & Radosevich, & Lanze-Kaduce, 1982; Lightsey & Sweeney, 1985; Lowman, 1981; Milgram, 1982; Williams, Lund, & Pruesser, 1986).

A second broad area of correlational research has focused on social influences, especially those associated with the peer group. Numerous studies have reported increased alcohol consumption among youth who associate with peers who drink and/or approve of drinking (Biddle, Biddle, Bank, & Martin, 1980; Krohn et al., 1982; Nusbaumer & Zusman, 1981; Scoles & Fine 1981; Vejnoska, 1982). Jessor (1987) has recently extended problem behavior theory (Jessor & Jessor, 1977) to youthful risky driving, including DWI (see Jonah, Chapter 2, this volume, for a review). Jessor suggests that youth who are more influenced by friends than parents, and whose friends model risky driving behaviors, are more likely to report risky driving. Studies have also assessed the effects of mass media on youth DWI with mixed results (Atkin, Hocking, & Block, 1984; Atkin, Neuendorf, & McDermott, 1983; Strickland, 1983)

Recently, researchers have become interested in the special characteristics of youth drinking and youth driving that lead to elevated risk of crashes. For young drivers, risk of crash involvement begins to increase at very low blood alcohol concentrations (BACs), and studies suggest that any measurable BAC can result in a significantly increased risk for younger drivers (Farris, Malone, & Lilliefors, 1976; Perrine, Waller, & Harris, 1971; Simpson, Mayhew, & Warren, 1982). Thus the gap between risky and illegal BACs for youth in most states is large, and "safe" consumption guidelines publicized for adults may be dangerously misleading when applied to youth. The more rapid impairment of the younger drinker is reflected in the fact that crash-involved adolescents are likely to have lower BACs than their older counterparts (Cameron, 1982) and in the higher risk of fatal crashes for young drivers when compared to adults with comparable BACs (Bergeron & Joly, 1986).

It has been suggested that the simultaneous acquisition of driving skills and drinking experience further increases the likelihood that crashes will occur (Lewis, 1988; O'Day, 1970), and that youth who drive while impaired tend to be riskier drivers in general (Bergeron & Joly, 1986). Näätänen and Summala (1976) have also noted the importance of considering the "extra motives" (beyond simple transportation) that driving may fulfil for youth. These include tension reduction, the need for competition, showing off, and deliberate risk taking. Summala (1987) suggests that these extra motives may be more important than lack of driving skill in contributing to poor youth driving performance.

Research conducted for the National Institute on Alcohol Abuse and Alcoholism (NIAAA) suggests a number of structural and contextual factors that may serve to associate drinking with driving in adolescents (URSA/Pacificon, 1980). These data suggest that, for many youth, the automobile represents the only place where privacy may be relatively certain. Drinking and other negatively sanctioned behaviors may most likely go undetected when undertaken in cars. Consistent with this assumption, data from the 1986 yearly survey of high school seniors (Bachman et al., 1987) revealed that over half of all seniors who drink have done so in cars, and approximately 28% report doing so "some of the times" or "most of the times." It has also been suggested that driving constitutes a social occasion for youth and that the rides to and from a social event constitute a prelude to and continuation of that event (Farrow, 1987). Thus drinking in cars may be a simple extension of other teen drinking.

The NIAAA data suggest that youth are more likely than adults to drink all that they possess at any given time, thereby eliminating problems of storage or hiding of contraband alcohol. Moreover, data reported by Vegega and Klitzner (1989), Farrow (1987), and Bachman et al. (1987) suggest that the great majority of teen drinking occurs outside the home. Thus the structure of teen drinking may lead to the consumption of large quantities of alcohol in settings that subsequently require some sort of transportation home.

In general, it appears that the factors that predispose, reinforce, and enable youth DWI and RWID are similar to those risk factors associated with other adolescent health-risk behavior (Jessor, 1987). Social and normative influences, risk-taking orientation, and individual differences in attitudes toward and beliefs about drinking itself and drinking and driving all appear to contribute to increased or decreased risk.

Of particular import in considering DWI and RWID specifically, however, is the powerful role played by alcohol consumption per se in increasing risk of both DWI and RWID (for which consumption is not a prerequisite). Klitzner and colleagues (1988) present recent survey data suggesting that DWI/RWID risks increase directly and potently as a function of both quantity and frequency of alcohol consumption. Similarly, interviews with youth who have engaged in DWI/RWID (Vegega & Klitzner, 1989) suggest that alcohol is viewed as an inextricable part of the youth culture, and DWI/RWID were viewed as "inevitable" results of the strong association between youth socializing and youth drinking. Thus it seems unlikely that meaningful reductions in youth DWI/RWID can be realized without significant attention to changes in youth drinking practices.

THE NATURE AND EFFECTIVENESS OF COUNTERMEASURES FOR YOUTH

The past two decades have witnessed a rapid expansion in the number and types of programs and strategies employed to prevent youthful DWI and RWID. A review of 133 youth DWI prevention models (Vegega & Klitzner, 1988) revealed enormous diversity of focus, underlying assumptions, and activities. Youth DWI/RWID countermeasures span a spectrum including school curricula, clubs, alternative transportation, alternative (alcohol-free) parties, teen retreats, and youth-focused legislation and regulation.

Current DWI/RWID prevention strategies can be grouped into three major categories—those mainly concerned with the prevention of drinking, those mainly concerned with separating drinking and driving, and those concerned with preventing mortality and morbidity when and if DWI/RWID occur. The differences among these approaches can be illustrated by considering the natural history of DWI and RWID. Figures 9.1 and 9.2 present, in highly simplified flow diagrams, the processes that lead to DWI/RWID and related mortality and morbidity.

These flow diagrams suggest three points at which DWI/RWID strategies and programming can be directed. Point 1 represents strategies that have as their primary objective the prevention of drinking and the establishment of nondrinking lifestyles among youth. Such programs include any of those that either attempt to alter the factors that predispose, reinforce, or enable drinking among individual youth (e.g., school curricula, "say no" organizations,

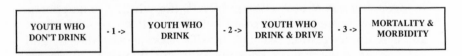

FIGURE 9.1. Natural problem history of youth DWI (assumes youth will drive).

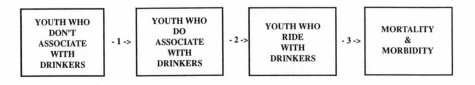

FIGURE 9.2. Natural problem history of youth RWID.

intervention programs for users) or attempt to reduce access to alcohol (e.g., alcohol-free alternative parties, increases in minimum purchase age, server training, limiting outlets, education of retail clerks). Strategies at point 1 would not, of course, address the problem of youth who ride with impaired drivers when parents or other adults are the drivers.[1]

Point 2 represents strategies that attempt to disassociate drinking and driving. Here, although youth alcohol use may still be of concern, the major objective is to address risk factors that lead drinking youth to drive or that lead youth who associate with drinkers to be passengers. Examples of strategies at point 2 include SafeRides, designated drivers, alternative transportation, direct intervention (e.g., taking keys), parent/student transportation "contracts," general and specific deterrence, and a variety of licensing strategies.

Finally, point 3 represents strategies that attempt to limit morbidity and mortality among drinking drivers, their passengers, and those with whom they crash. Examples of these strategies include passive restraints, other vehicle-related technologies, highway design elements such as breakaway sign posts, and so forth.

Point 1 Strategies

Many point 1 strategies (those that attempt to reduce youth drinking) have been extensively studied. In particular, school-based strategies of various types have been the object of intense research scrutiny for almost two decades. Three of the most popular of such approaches are affective education, life-skills approaches, and resistance training. These approaches share many common characteristics, and in practice they are often indistinguishable. However, they represent somewhat different historical trends, and a distinction is often made among them in the literature.

Affective education programs, which have their basis in humanistic psychology, first appeared in the early 1970s, in part as a response to the recognition that "scare tactics" or information alone had little effect on youth behavior. These programs, which remain popular today, vary in emphasis, but they generally include exercises to improve self-concept or build self-confidence and to teach decision-making and communication skills. Many of these programs (especially the earlier versions) include exercises aimed at helping youth to clarify their values concerning alcohol and other drug use. Also included in many affective education programs are techniques for coping with stress, managing shyness, and dealing with social pressures to use drugs and engage in other health-compromising behavior.

In their earliest forms, affective education programs focused on allowing youth to "discover" for themselves how they would deal with alcohol and other drugs, and teachers were cautioned to be nondirective. More recent affective education programs have become more directive, incorporating a nonuse message. However, many affective education programs still emphasize personal choice, leading to ill-defined and sometimes conflicting program objectives (Coulsen, 1987; Moskowitz, 1983).

Schaps and his colleagues (e.g., Moskowitz, Malvin, Shaeffer, Shaps, & Condon, 1983; Moskowitz, Schaps, & Malvin, 1982; Moskowitz, Schaps, Schaeffer, & Malvin, 1984; Schaps, Moskowitz, Condon & Malvin, 1982) conducted a well-designed, multiyear evaluation of affective education strategies—the Napa Experiment. The Napa Experiment studied a number of popular strategies, including cooperative learning, teacher training, "alternatives," and drug education. The cooperative-learning strategies were implemented in the elementary grades by specially trained teachers. These strategies were designed to improve classroom climate, increase self-esteem, and increase bonding to the school. The teacher-training component included skills building in classroom management, positive discipline, and communications skills. The alternatives component was offered as a junior high school elective and involved cross-age tutoring and the operation of a school store. These activities were designed to improve social skills and to provide opportunities to engage in activities that could replace the need for drugs. Finally, two drug education courses were conducted in the 7th and 8th grades by trained specialists. The courses used a values/decision-making model combined with training in assertive techniques to resist social pressures to use drugs. The courses differed in the amount of specific drug information provided.

The results of the Napa Experiment did not support the affective education model. No systematic or consistent changes were found in any of the affective variables (e.g., self-esteem, bonding to school, communication skills) that were measured. In addition, no consistent effects on drug use were observed. In one study, the drug education courses produced an immediate reduction of alcohol and marijuana use among 7th-grade girls, but this effect dissipated at a 1-year follow-up. In a second study, a reduction in cigarette smoking was observed among 7th-grade girls. This reduction was still in evidence at a 1-year follow-up. However, no effects in any study were observed for 7th-grade boys or for 8th-graders of either sex.

Life-skills approaches (e.g., Botvin, 1987; Botvin, Baker, Resnick, Filazzola, & Botvin, 1984; Botvin & Wills, 1985) are highly similar to the affective education programs, although they claim theoretical roots in social-learning theory (Bandura, 1969) as opposed to humanistic psychology. Originally applied to the prevention of cigarette smoking, these approaches have been expanded to address specifically other gateway substances, including alcohol and marijuana.

Typically, life-skills programs last from 12 to 20 sessions and include drug information regarding the short- and long-term effects of drugs, prevalence rates, social acceptability, and the process of drug initiation, values clarification and decision making, relaxation training, and social-skills training, including skills at resisting social influences to use drugs and alcohol. Often the programs are led by specially trained peer leaders, and an often-researched question is whether or not such peer leaders produce superior results to those observed with classroom teachers. Another variation of life-skills programs includes "booster" sessions provided at regular intervals to program participants.

Botvin (1987) conducted a multiyear study of life-skills programs that include in the design comparisons of teacher versus peer instruction and assessments of the effects of booster sessions. In general, the results favored peer-led sessions accompanied by boosters, although none of the reductions in alcohol or marijuana use were dramatic. Moreover, it appeared that the peer-led booster group was superior to the peer-led group without boosters *before* any booster sessions occurred. This puzzling result suggests possible nonequivalencies between the two groups, which may weaken any conclusions drawn from the data. By the second-year follow-up, positive program effects were largely eroded. High rates of attrition and possible differential attrition across groups make interpretation of these findings difficult. In sum, however, the results of this and other studies have failed to demonstrate the ability of life-skills approaches to produce consistent or lasting effects on drug and alcohol use.

Resistance training approaches also claim roots in social-learning theory and, like life-skills approaches, were originally designed to prevent cigarette smoking (e.g., Evans, 1976; Hurd et al., 1980; McAlister, Perry, Killen, Slinkard, & Maccoby, 1980; Perry, Killen, Slinkard, & McAlister, 1980). However, these approaches tend to be more limited in scope, focusing on teaching and rehearsing skills to resist peer and other social pressures to use drugs and alcohol. Sometimes refusal techniques are demonstrated on film, and sometimes they are presented by live models. In general, these programs have demonstrated success in reducing the onset of cigarette smoking. However, success with other substances, including alcohol, has been much more limited (Moskowitz, 1989). One such program focused specifically on alcohol (Shope & Dielman, 1985) failed to find even immediate effects on consumption. In general, the potential of resistance training to reduce alcohol and drug use remains unproven.

Interestingly, most of the students in the Shope and Dielman study already reported having the targeted refusal skills at the pretest (Moskowitz, 1989). Similarly, a recent study of youth DWI (Vegega & Klitzner, 1989) failed to find much evidence that direct peer pressure plays a role in either alcohol use or drinking–driving among youth. Thus the limited success of resistance training in preventing alcohol use might be explained by limited validity for one of its major premises—that it is a lack of refusal skills that leads youth to use alcohol.

Reviews of other popular school-based strategies to prevent alcohol and drug use and abuse (e.g., Goodstadt, 1985; Klitzner, 1987; Moskowitz, 1989; Wittman, 1982) generally concur that evidence in support of such programs is sparse. Although increases in knowledge and changes in attitudes are often reported, effects on behavior have been weak, inconsistent, transient, and sometimes in the wrong direction.

The failure to demonstrate educational program effects has been attributed to failures in program models, to failures in program implementation, and (more optimistically) to weak or inappropriate research designs (Klitzner & Bell, 1987; Moskowitz, 1983). Whatever the causes, there currently is no scientific mandate for adopting any particular educational approach to alcohol and drug use reduction and prevention.

Recent attention has focused on the potential of strong school drug and alcohol policies to reduce student consumption. As discussed by

Moskowitz (1987), there are a number of mechanisms by which such policies may reduce substance use. These include providing a public statement of norms and expectations, facilitating the early identification and remediation of substance-related problems, and limiting the availability of substances, at least on campus.

Moskowitz (1987) surveyed a national sample of public high school administrators concerning their school policies, concluding that "the extent of a school's problems due to student alcohol or drug use . . . is affected by how well the school's overall discipline policy is implemented," although the fact that this research was based on administrator reports (rather than actual measures of substance use and related problems) limits the strength of these conclusions. Moskowitz and Jones (1988) also found that among administrators who reported that student drug and alcohol problems had decreased over the past 5 years, the most common explanation provided was an improvement in the school's discipline policy or its implementation. In addition, most high school administrators saw greater effects coming from discipline policies and their implementation than from school-based prevention or treatment programs.

Several strategies to control youth access to alcohol have been studied with varying results. The uniform 21 purchase age (e.g., Fell, 1988; Hingson et al., 1983; Smith et al., 1984; Wagenaar, 1982a, 1982b, 1983) and increased taxation (Coate & Grossman, 1985; Saffer & Grossman, 1985) have been shown to have an impact on the sequelae of consumption, including youthful crashes, although effects on consumption itself have been difficult to document. Failure to document effects on consumption may have to do with methodological difficulties in measuring such effects, or it may result from the inadequacy of a simple, direct model of the effects of youth access to alcohol on consumption and related problems.

The effects of number of alcohol outlets per capita on consumption have also received some scrutiny, although there have been no studies that have focused directly on youth. The results of these studies have been mixed, with one study demonstrating lower consumption in states with fewer outlets (Ornstein & Hannsens, 1985) and two studies failing to find such effects (Hoadly, Fuchs, & Holder, 1984; Schweitzer, Intriligator, & Salehi, 1983). A fourth study revealed effects of number of outlets on alcohol-related problems, including felony and misdemeanor DWI arrests, in 213 California cities (Watts & Rabow, 1983). This study did not include direct measures of consumption.

Student assistance programs to intervene with alcohol- and drug-using youth (e.g., Chambers & Morehouse, 1983; Morehouse, 1982) have been studied from a process perspective, but rigorous assessments of student drinking outcomes are not available. Other popular approaches (e.g., prevention "clubs," alcohol-free recreation, concerned parent groups) have received minimal research attention.

Point 2 Strategies

Of the available strategies aimed at point 2 (separating drinking from driving), perhaps the most extensively discussed is deterrence. Unfortunately for the current discussion, existing research does not generally address specific effects on youth. Ross (1984, 1985) and Moskowitz (1989) provide extensive reviews of various deterrence-based strategies, including increased penalties, per se laws, enforcement crackdowns, and administrative license revocation. In general, these reviews suggest that enforcement crackdowns, especially when accompanied by extensive media coverage, can have short-term (months to a few years) effects. On the other hand, a study of increased enforcement in France that focused specifically on drivers under 25 (Jayet, 1986) failed to find a deterrent effect.

Recently, concern over the risk of crashes associated with even very low BACs in youth has motivated some states to adopt a lower legal BAC limit for youth than for adults. In most of these states, license revocation is either an automatic or discretionary penalty for violations. Drummond, Cave, and Healy (1987) studied a zero BAC limit for first-year drivers in Australia. Preliminary data suggest that this law reduced nighttime, weekend driving—a peak time period for youth crash involvement (e.g., Farrow, 1987; Robertson, 1980). However, actual crash data concerning the Australian zero BAC law were not available at the time the research report was prepared.

Hingson, Heeren, and Morelock (1986, 1989) studied the effects of a 0.02 BAC limit and administrative license revocation for 1 year on youth in Maine. Initial results (Hingson et al., 1986) revealed that self-reported DWI and self-reported nonfatal crash involvement among drivers aged 19 and under declined significantly when compared to Massachusetts adolescents and Maine adults. Declines were most dramatic for those who were aware of the law. In addition, actual injury and fatal crashes among Maine teenagers increased at a much lower rate than for drivers 20 years of age and over. Follow-up results (Hingson et al., 1989) have generally mirrored the 1986 findings, although differences between Maine and Massachusetts adolescents have declined to a nonsignificant level. This lack of difference appears to be due to a "catching-up" on the part of Massachusetts teenagers, perhaps owing to the high level of antidrug and anti-DWI activity in that state. Hingson and colleagues (1989) also note that enforcement of the 0.02 BAC law is difficult due to problems of detecting low blood alcohol levels. Police appear to arrest juveniles with less regularity than adult offenders.

Several states have experimented with license revocation as a sanction against possession of alcohol and other drugs by young people. In testimony before the National Commission on Drunk Driving (National Commission Against Drunk Driving, 1988), Judge C. Foley of Milwaukee, Wisconsin, credited such a law with significant reductions in youth DWI between 1982 and 1986. However, the existence of a zero BAC law in Wisconsin, increased public awareness of the youth DWI problem, and the lack of comparison data render interpretation of these reductions difficult. At this time, the effects of license revocation as a sanction for youthful alcohol and other drug possession are unproven.

A recently popular strategy for separating drinking from driving is to issue youth restricted licenses that limit the hours during which a vehicle may be operated. Impetus for such a strategy derives from the previously cited observation that youth DWI and fatal crashes are most likely in the evenings, especially weekend evenings. As reported by Williams (1987), at least 18 states have some sort of curfew restrictions. Williams cites a study of restrictions in four states by Preusser, Williams, and Zador (1984) that suggested dramatic reductions in crashes during the restricted hours. He also cites additional data from New York, Louisiana, and Maryland that support the efficacy of restricted driving hours for youth. Despite one study of the Maryland law that did not reveal effects on crash rates (McKnight, Hyle, & Albrecht, 1983), Williams concludes that curfew restrictions can substantially reduce youth crash involvement.

Other licensing approaches to reducing youth crashes include making driver's licenses more difficult to obtain and presenting the license in juvenile court to both the youth and his/her parents. Preliminary data from California (Hagge & Marsh, 1986) suggest positive results from making licenses more difficult to obtain, although, as noted by Williams (1987), the California program has so many facets that it is impossible to determine which elements contribute to the positive results and which do not.

Separation of youth drinking from youth driving has also been attempted through educational strategies. There is little evidence that such programs reduce crash rates (Moskowitz, 1989; Williams, 1987).

One well-conducted Canadian evaluation of a drinking–driving education program (Albert & Simpson, 1985) demonstrated decreased intentions to DWI, but these decreases were realized at the cost of an increase in reported drinking frequency. Some critics of driver education (Robertson, 1981; Robertson & Zador, 1978) have suggested that such programs may actually increase crash rates by increasing the licensure of 16- and 17-year-olds. However, as discussed by Moskowitz (1989), these claims are based on short-term results and may not justify possible long-term negative effects of discontinuing driver education.

Cognizant of the general failure of drinking–driving education programs, the National Highway Traffic Safety Administration (NHTSA) sponsored the development of a peer intervention program (McPherson, McKnight, & Weidman, 1983) aimed at enabling and motivating adolescents to intervene in the drinking-and-driving behavior of their peers. The program provided 8 hours of role playing as well as 1 hour of alcohol and traffic safety information. A true experiment with random assignment compared the peer intervention program to a traditional drinking-and-driving education program (McKnight & McPherson, 1986). Students in the peer intervention program reported statistically significant gains in intervention behavior at follow-up intervals of 1 to 4 months. The actual magnitude of these effects appears small, although the description of the behavioral measure provided by McKnight and McPherson is too sketchy to determine the meaning of the differences reported.

Students Against Driving Drunk (SADD.; Anastas, 1983) represents an attempt to change school and community norms with regard to youth DWI/RWID. Klitzner and colleagues (1987) conducted an evaluation of SADD in two cities in the western United States. This quasi-experimental study failed to find effects of SADD on any drinking or drinking–driving variables. However, weak program implementation in the SADD schools, high subject attrition from the research study, and other design confounds limit the strength of these conclusions.

Alternative transportation (e.g., SafeRides, designated drivers) as a means of separating drinking from driving has not been well evaluated (Klitzner et al., 1988). Klitzner and colleagues (1987) provide preliminary data on parent/student contracting. These data suggest that signing contracts increases the likelihood that youth will call parents for a ride. However, no differences in DWI or RWID as a result of signing the contract were observed. This somewhat puzzling result suggests that although signers are calling home, safer transportation does not result.

Critics of alternative transportation strategies have objected to these approaches on the grounds that they implicitly sanction youth drinking. Klitzner and colleagues (1987) failed to find evidence that signing parent/student contracts had effects on youth drinking or related problems. On the other hand, Klitzner et al. (1988) found that heavier drinkers also report using more transportation alternatives. The meaning of this latter result is unclear. It may, indeed, confirm the fears of critics of alternative transportation strategies, or it may simply reflect the fact that heavier drinkers have more reasons for using and opportunities to use transportation alternatives.

Point 3 Strategies

When interventions at point 1 and point 2 fail, the probability of a crash can still be reduced by improvements in roadway and vehicle design. Young drivers, by virtue of their inexperience and lack of driving skill, are especially vulnerable to engineering flaws—automobile controls that are difficult to use, braking systems that cause skidding, roadways that are poorly marked. Although all drivers and passengers benefit from improvements in roadway and vehicle design, young drivers, especially when they are impaired, would derive particular benefit.

When crashes do occur, the risk of serious injury or death can be substantially reduced through various measures to increase occupant safety. Safety has been improved in recent years by structural changes in automobiles and the removal of hazardous objects in the passenger compartment. However, the proper use of lap–shoulder belts is the most important action that an individual driver or passenger can take. Figures reported by NHTSA indicate that use of safety belts can reduce the risk of serious or fatal injuries by 40–55%. Unfortunately, the very age group most likely to be involved in crashes is the group least likely to use safety belts. The use rate for the nation as a whole is 43%, while only 20% of the 15- to 19-year-old group use belts. Use rates among young drivers who have been drinking is even lower. When young drivers who reported driving after drinking were asked if they had done anything to make driving "safer" on these occasions, 72% reported that they had. Of these, 68% slowed down, 44% watched road signs more carefully, 34% watched for police, and 24% took back roads. By contrast, only 8% fastened their safety belts (Klitzner et al., 1987).

Increasing safety belt use rates among youth make a significant contribution to reducing injury and death. NHTSA's education and outreach program for increasing belt use emphasizes implementing a combination of four approaches—face-to-face education, incentive programs, mandatory use laws, and employer (or in this case, perhaps, school) requirements.

By 1990, all new cars sold in the United States will be required to have either automatic safety belts or air bags. This regulation is an important step forward. But because most young people do not drive new cars, the impact on youthful mortality and morbidity may be limited. Thus continued development of strategies to promote safety belt use and aggressive implementation of those strategies found to be effective should be a priority.

Multicomponent Strategies

One common indictment of many attempts to prevent alcohol- and drug-related problems among youth is too narrow a programmatic focus (Goodstadt, 1986; Huba, Wingard, & Bentler, 1980; Klitzner, 1987; Klitzner & Bell, 1987). That is, communities have tended to focus on one kind of response (e.g., a school curriculum, a SADD club, a police crackdown) to the exclusion of other types of responses.

Recently some communities have attempted to overcome the narrowness and fragmentation of past responses to youth DWI by instituting communitywide, systemic responses that attempt to implement a coordinated and comprehensive package of countermeasures that are mutually reinforcing. Thus a community might institute a strong antialcohol use school policy, work to restrict alcohol sales to minors through increasing alcohol beverage control enforcement, rigorously enforce DWI laws, institute roadblocks, aggressively prosecute and heavily sanction youthful DWI offenders, promote safety belt use, and develop community resources for the treatment of addicted teens. Ten communities that are attempting to implement communitywide responses are described by the Pacific Institute for Research and Evaluation (in press).

The communitywide model has considerable theoretical and conceptual appeal, and many of the strategies communities appear to be using have been shown to be effective in their own right (e.g., increased enforcement, reductions in alcohol availability to youth). To date, however, rigorous evaluations of multicomponent, communitywide anti-DWI programs have been extremely limited.

Perhaps the most relevant research is the Lackland Air Force Base

Experiment (Barmark & Payne, 1961), which effectively reduced DWI among airmen through a variety of normative, informational, and enforcement strategies. It is unclear, however, that strategies shown to be effective in the highly insular and controlled environment of a military installation will also be effective in the less well controlled environments of most American communities.

The communitywide model has shown promise in other health areas, notably the reduction of risk factors associated with cardiovascular disease (Farquhar et al., 1977; Puska et al., 1985). However, the effectiveness and feasibility of systemwide responses to the youth DWI problem await further research.

CONCLUSIONS

Proven technologies exist for reducing the death and disability suffered by youth as a result of drinking and driving. These include restrictions on youth access to alcohol and restrictions on youth driving. The problem is not so much one of finding effective countermeasures as it is of overcoming societal inertia to implement them. Thus far, the uniform 21 alcohol purchase age is the only proven countermeasure to be adopted nationwide. In some states, even the threatened loss of federal highway funds did not guarantee speedy legislative action.

Williams (1987) poses the question of whether society is ready to take the steps necessary to improve the current situation with regard to youth drinking and driving. He responds: "To the extent that legislative restrictions are necessary to rectify the situation, [this] question can at present be answered in the negative" (p. 116). A major item on the nation's public health agenda should be to educate parents, legislators, and other concerned citizens about the regulatory measures that can be taken to realize additional meaningful reductions in youth DWI.

Of course, regulatory responses will only be effective to the extent that they are enforced (Ross, 1984). In general, the quality of enforcement of novel DWI laws decreases over time, an effect observed in Maine's experience with 0.02 BAC legislation enacted in 1982 (Hingson et al., 1989). Public support must be developed for the vigorous and continued enforcement of new laws as well as for their enactment.

It is also clear that regulation alone will never be a complete answer to the youth DWI/RWID problem. Youth will always have access to alcohol and will always have access to cars. Indeed, licensing restrictions will never affect all teenagers, since a significant minority of adolescent drivers are unlicensed (Klitzner et al., 1988; Williams, Lund, & Pruesser, 1985). Moreover, the high crash rates of teenagers continue into the early 20s—an age group to whom purchase age restrictions do not apply. Thus, in addition to regulatory responses, continued efforts should be made to develop prevention programs that affect the drinking and drinking-and-driving choices of individual young people.

Prevention program development and research need to break away from the unsuccessful models of the past. New approaches are needed that are firmly grounded in an understanding of the factors that predispose, reinforce, and enable alcohol use and DWI/RWID among adolescents. Given the current state of knowledge, such an understanding will require a program of additional research into the etiology of drinking and DWI/RWID among adolescents. This is not to imply that the testing of new program models should be delayed until a comprehensive and widely accepted set of etiological models is available. Rather, program research and etiological research should be seen as complementary endeavors, with data from one area of inquiry informing theory development and research activities in the other.

It is clear that significant programmatic attention must be paid to youthful alcohol consumption per se. It is possible, in theory, to separate drinking from driving among adolescents. However, these behaviors are currently so inextricably intertwined that successful DWI/RWID prevention programs may ultimately be those with a heavy emphasis on reducing alcohol consumption.

Finally, continued efforts should be made to change social norms regarding youthful alcohol use and DWI/RWID. It has been argued that changes in social norms and values as a result of two decades of antismoking activities and programs have contributed significantly to the efficacy of smoking cessation and prevention programs (Leventhal & Cleary, 1980; Moskowitz, 1983; Polich, Ellickson, Reuter, & Kahan, 1984). Similar changes in drinking and DWI/RWID norms toward greater intolerance can facilitate the adoption of effective regulatory measures (Moskowitz, 1989) and can also have a direct impact on youth behavior (Klitzner et al., 1988). The communitywide approach discussed earlier is one appealing strategy for effecting normative change, because it attempts to involve all segments of the community in combating the youth drinking–driving problem.

NOTES

1. Some DWI/RWID program developers have labeled point 1 programs as "prevention programs" in order to distinguish them from point 2 programs, which have been labeled as "intervention programs." This distinction seems somewhat artificial, since both types of strategies seek to prevent the occurrence of DWI/RWID.

REFERENCES

Albert, W., & Simpson, R. (1985). Evaluating an educational program for the prevention of impaired driving among grade 11 students. *Journal of Drug Education, 15,* 57–71.

Anastas, R. (1983). *SADD chapter handbook and curriculum guide.* Marlboro, MA: Students Against Driving Drunk.

Atkin, C., Hocking, J., & Block, M. (1984). Teenage drinking: Does advertising make a difference? *Journal of Communications, 34,* 157–167.

Atkin, C., Neuendorf, K., & McDermott, S. (1983). The role of alcohol advertising in excessive and hazardous drinking. *Journal of Drug Education, 13,* 313–326.

Bachman, J., Johnston, L., & O'Malley, P. (1987). *Monitoring the future: Questionnaire responses from the nation's high school seniors.* Ann Arbor: Institute for Social Research, University of Michigan.

Bandura, A. (1969). *Principals of behavior modification.* New York: Holt, Rinehart & Winston.

Barmark, J., & Payne, D. (1961). The Lackland Accident Countermeasures Experiment. In *Proceedings of the 40th Annual Meeting of the Highway Research Board* (pp. 221–232). Washington, DC.

Bergeron, J., & Joly, P. (1986). Young drivers' attitudes and drunk driving habits as a function of their accident involvement and violation record. In T. Benjamin (Ed.), *Young drivers impaired by alcohol and other drugs* (pp. 185–192). London: Royal Society of Medicine Services.

Biddle, B., Biddle, B., Bank, J., & Martin, M. (1980). Social determinants of adolescent drinking. *Journal of Studies on Alcohol, 41,* 215–241.

Botvin, G. (1987). *Factors inhibiting drug use: Teacher and peer effects.* Rockville, MD: National Institute on Drug Abuse.

Botvin, G., Baker, E., Resnick, N., Filazzola, A., & Botvin, E. (1984). A cognitive–behavioral approach to substance abuse prevention. *Addictive Behaviors, 9,* 137–147.

Botvin, G., & Wills, T. (1985). Personal and social skills training: Cognitive behavioral approaches to substance abuse prevention. In C. Bell & B. Battjes (Eds.), *Prevention research: Deterring drug abuse among children and adolescents* (pp. 8–49). Rockville, MD: National Institute on Drug Abuse.

Boyd, N.R., & Huffman, W. (1984). The relationship between adult maturity and drinking–driving involvement among young adults. *Journal of Safety Research, 15,* 1–6.

Cameron, T. (1982). Drinking and driving among American youth: Beliefs and behaviors. *Drug and Alcohol Dependence, 10,* 11–33.

Chambers, J., & Morehouse, E. (1983, January). A cooperative model for preventing drug and alcohol abuse. *National Association of Secondary School Principals Bulletin,* pp. 81–87.

Coate, D., & Grossman, M. (1985). *Effects of alcohol beverage prices and legal drinking ages on youth alcohol use: Results from the second national health and nutrition examination survey.* Unpublished manuscript. National Bureau of Economic Research, New York.

Coulson, W. (1987). *Principled morality vs. consequentialism: Reflections on recent conversations with drug educators.* San Diego: Center for Enterprising Families.

Douglass, R. (1983). Youth, alcohol, and traffic accidents: Current status. *Recent developments in alcoholism* (Vol. 1). New York: Plenum.

Drummond, A., Cave, T., & Healy, D. (1987). The risk of accident involvement by time of week – An assessment of the effect of zero BAC legislation and the potential of driving curfews. In T. Benjamin (Ed.), *Young drivers impaired by alcohol and other drugs* (pp. 385–392). London: Royal Society of Medicine Services.

Elliot, D. (1987). Self-reported driving while under the influence of alcohol/drugs and the risk of alcohol/drug-related accidents. *Alcohol, Drugs, and Driving, 3* (3–4), 31–44.

Evans, R. (1976). Smoking in children: Developing a social psychological strategy to deterrence. *Journal of Preventive Medicine, 5,* 122–127.

Farquhar, J., Maccoby, N., Wood, P., Alexander, J., Breitrose, H., Brown, P., Haskell, W., McAlister, A., Meyer, A., Nash, J., & Stern, M. (1977). Community education for cardiovascular health. *Lancet,* 1192–1195.

Farris, R., Malone, T., & Lilliefors, H. (1976). *A comparison of alcohol-involvement in exposed and injured drivers: Phases I and II* (Report No. DOT-HS-4-00954). Washington, DC: National Highway Traffic Safety Administration, U.S. Department of Transportation.

Farrow, J. (1987). Young driver risk taking: A description of dangerous driving situations among 16- to 19-year-old drivers. *International Journal of the Addictions, 22* (12), 1255–1267.

Fell, J. (1988, July). *Effectiveness of raising the drinking age to 21.* Paper presented at the 14th International Forum on Traffic Records Systems, San Diego.

Goodstadt, M. (1985). Shaping drinking practices through education. In J. von Wartburg, P. Magnenat, R. Muller, & S. Wyss (Eds.), *Currents in alcohol research and the prevention of alcohol problems* (pp. 85–106). Berne, Switzerland: Hans Huber Publishers.

Goodstadt, M. (1986). School-based drug education in North America: What is wrong? what can be done? *Journal of School Health, 56,* 278–281.

Grey Advertising. (1975). *Communications strategies on alcohol and highway safety* (Vol. 2) (Report No. DOT HS-803-714). Washington, DC: U.S. Department of Transportation.

Hagge, R., & Marsh, W. (1986). *The traffic safety impact of provisional licensing.* Sacramento: California Department of Motor Vehicles.

Hetherington, R., Dickinson, J., Cipywnyk, K., & Hay, D. (1979). Attitudes and knowledge about alcohol among Saskatchewan adolescents. *Canadian Journal of Public Health, 70,* 247–259.

Hingson, R., Heeren, T., & Morelock, S. (1986). Preliminary effects of Maine's 1982 0.02 law to reduce teenage driving after drinking. In T. Benjamin (Ed.), *Young drivers impaired by alcohol and other drugs* (pp. 377–384). London: Royal Society of Medicine Services.

Hingson, R., Heeren, T., & Morelock, S. (1989). Effects of Maine's 1983 .02 law to reduce teenage driving after drinking. *Alcohol, Drugs, and Driving, 5,* (1), 25–36.

Hingson, R., Howland, J., Morelock, S., & Heeren, T. (1988). Legal interventions to reduce drunken driving and related fatalities among youthful drivers. *Alcohol, Drugs, and Driving, 4,* 87–98.

Hingson, R., Scotch, N., Mangione, T., Meyers, A., Glantz, L., Heeren, T., Liu, N., Muscatel, M., & Pierce, G. (1983). Impact of legislation raising the legal drinking age in Massachusetts from 18 to 20. *American Journal of Public Health, 73,* 163–170.

Hoadly, J., Fuchs, B., & Holder, H. (1984). The effects of alcohol beverage restrictions on consumption: A 25 year longitudinal analysis. *American Journal of Drug and Alcohol Abuse, 10,* 375–401.

Huba, G., Wingard, J., & Bentler, P. (1980). Applications of a theory of drug use to prevention programs. *Journal of Drug Education, 10,* 25–38.

Hurd, P., Johnson, C., Pechacek, T., Bast, C., Jacobs, D., & Luepker, R. (1980). Prevention of smoking in seventh grade students. *Journal of Behavioral Medicine, 3,* 15–28.

Insurance Institute for Highway Safety. (1984). *Status Report, 19,* 1–3.

Jayet, M. (1986). Penal policy for preventing young drivers from drinking: Scope, limits, and principles. In T. Benjamin (Ed.), *Young drivers impaired by alcohol and other drugs* (pp. 295–300). London: Royal Society of Medicine Services.

Jessor, R. (1987). Risky driving and adolescent problem behavior: An extension of problem behavior theory. *Alcohol, Drugs, and Driving, 3,* 1–12.

Jessor, R., & Jessor, S. (1977). *Problem behavior and psychosocial development: A longitudinal study of youth.* New York: Academic Press.

Klitzner, M. (1987). An assessment of the research on school-based prevention programs. In *Report to Congress on the nature and effectiveness of federal, state, and local drug prevention/education programs.* Washington, DC: U.S. Department of Education.

Klitzner, M., & Bell, C. (1987, October). *Youth drug and alcohol abuse prevention:*

Why we can't answer the question, "what works?" Paper presented at the 115th annual meeting of the American Public Health Association, New Orleans, LA.

Klitzner, M., Gruenewald, P., Rossiter, C., Bamberger, E., & Roth, T. (1987). Students Against Driving Drunk: A national study—Final report. Bethesda, MD: Pacific Institute for Research and Evaluation.

Klitzner, M., Vegega, M., & Gruenewald, P. (1988). An empirical examination of the assumptions underlying youth drinking/driving prevention programs. *Evaluation and Program Planning, 11,* 219–235.

Kraus, A., Steele, R., Ghent, W., & Thompson, M. (1970). Pre-driving identification of young drivers with high risk of accidents. *Journal of Safety Research, 2,* 55–56.

Krohn, M., Akers, R., Radosevich, M., & Lanze-Kaduce, L. (1982, Fall). Norm qualities and adolescent driving and drug behavior. *Journal of Drug Issues,* pp. 349–359.

Leventhal, H., & Cleary, P. (1980). The smoking problem: A review of the research and theory in behavioral risk modification. *Psychological Bulletin, 88,* 370–405.

Lewis, C. (1988). *Preventing traffic casualties among youth: What is our knowledge base? Alcohol, Drugs and Driving, 4(1),* 1–7.

Lightsey, M., & Sweeney, M. (1985). Life problems experienced from drinking: Factors associated with level of problem drinking among youthful DWI offenders. *Journal of Alcohol and Drug Education, 30,* 65–82.

Lowman, C. (1981). Facts for planning, no. 3: U.S. teenage alcohol use in unsupervised social settings. *Alcohol Health and Research World, 6.*

McAlister, A., Perry, C., Killen, J., Slinkard, L., & Maccoby, N. (1980). Pilot study of smoking, alcohol, and drug abuse prevention. *American Journal of Public Health, 70,* 719–721.

McKnight, A., Hyle, P., & Albrecht, L. (1983). *Youth license control demonstration project* (NTIS No. DOT-HS-806-616). Washington, DC: National Highway Traffic Safety Administration, U.S. Department of Transportation.

McKnight, J., & McPherson, K. (1986). Evaluation of peer intervention training for high school alcohol safety education. *Accident Analysis and Prevention, 18,* 339–347.

McPherson, K., McKnight, A., & Weidman, J. (1983). *Supplemental driver safety program development: Final report: Volume 1. Developmental Research and Evaluation.* Washington, DC: National Highway Transportation Safety Administration, U.S. Department of Transportation.

Milgram, G. (1982). Societal attitudes toward youthful drinking. *Journal of Drug Education, 12.*

Morehouse, E. (1982). The student assistance program: An alcohol and drug abuse prevention model. In E. Arnowitz (Ed.), *Prevention strategies in mental health* (pp. 113–125). New York: PRODIST.

Moskowitz, J. (1983). Preventing adolescent substance abuse through drug education. In T. Glynn, C. Leukefeld, & J. Ludford (Eds.), *Preventing adolescent drug abuse: Intervention strategies* (National Institute on Drug Abuse Research Monograph No. 47, DHHS Publication NO. (ADM)83-1280) (pp. 233–249). Washington, DC: U.S. Government Printing Office.

Moskowitz, J. (1987). *School drug and alcohol policy: A preliminary model relating policy implementation to school problems.* Berkeley, CA: Pacific Institute for Research and Evaluation/Prevention Research Center.

Moskowitz, J. (1989). The primary prevention of alcohol problems: A critical review of the research literature. *Journal of Studies on Alcohol, 50,* 54–88.

Moskowitz, J., & Jones, R. (1988). Alcohol and drug problems: Results of a national study of school administrators. *Journal of Studies on Alcohol, 49*(4), 299–305.

Moskowitz, J., Malvin, J., Schaeffer, G., Schaps, E., & Condon, J. (1983). Evaluation of a cooperative learning strategy. *American Educational Research Journal, 20,* 687–696.

Moskowitz, J., Schaps, E., & Malvin, J. (1982). A process and outcome evaluation of a Magic Circle primary prevention program. *Evaluation Review, 6,* 775–788.

Moskowitz, J., Schaps, E., Schaeffer, G., & Malvin, J. (1984). Evaluation of a substance abuse prevention program for junior high school students. *International Journal of the Addictions, 19,* 419–430.

Näätänen, R., & Summala, H. (1976). *Road user behavior and traffic accidents.* Amsterdam and New York: North Holland/American Elsevier.

National Commission Against Drunk Driving. (1988). *Youth driving without impairment: Report on the youth impaired driving public hearings* Washington, DC: Author.

Nusbaumer, M., & Zusman, M. (1981). Autos, alcohol, and adolescents: Forgotten concerns and overlooked linkages. *Journal of Drug Education, 11,* 167–178.

O'Day, J. (1970, October). Drinking involvement and age of young drivers in fatal accidents. *Hit Laboratory Reports,* pp. 13–14.

Ornstein, S., & Hannens, D. (1985). Alcohol control laws and the consumption of distilled spirits and beer. *Journal of Consumer Research, 12,* 200–213.

Pacific Institute for Research and Evaluation. (in press). *The introduction of effective systemwide strategies to combat youth drug and alcohol abuse: Assessment report.* Bethesda, MD: Author.

Paulson, J. (1983). Accidental injuries. In R. Behrman & V. Vaughan (Eds.), *Nelson handbook of pediatrics* (pp. 261–263) Philadelphia: Saunders.

Perrine, M., Waller, J., & Harris, L. (1971). *Alcohol and highway safety: Behavioral and medical aspects.* Burlington: University of Vermont Press.

Perry, C., Killen, J., Slinkard, L., & McAlister, A. (1980). Peer teaching and smoking prevention among junior high school students. *Adolescence, 15,* 277–281.

Polich, J., Ellickson, P., Reuter, P., & Kahan, J. (1984). *Strategies for controlling adolescent drug use.* Santa Monica, CA: Rand Corporation.

Preusser, D., Williams, A., & Zador, P. (1984). The effects of curfew laws on motor vehicle crashes. *Law and Policy, 6,* 115–128.

Puska, P., Nissinen, A., Tuomilehto, J., Salonen, J., Koskela, K., McAlister, A., Kottke, T., Maccoby, N., & Farquhar, J. (1985). The community-based strategy to prevent coronary heart disease: Conclusions from the ten years of the North Karelia Project. *Annual Review of Public Health, 6,* 147–193.

Robertson, L., & Zador, P. (1978). Driver education and fatal crash involvement of teenage drivers. *American Journal of Public Health, 73,* 959–965.

Robertson, L. (1981). Patterns of teenage driver involvement in fatal motor vehicle crashes: Implications for policy choice. *Journal of Health Politics, Policy and Law, 6,* 303–314.

Ross, H. (1984). *Deterring the drinking driver: Legal policy and social control.* Lexington, MA: Lexington Books.

Ross, H. (1985). Deterring drunken driving: An analysis of current efforts. *Journal of Studies on Alcohol,* (Suppl. 10), 122–128.

Saffer, H., & Grossman, M. (1985). *Effects of beer prices and legal drinking ages on youth motor vehicle fatalities.* Unpublished manuscript. National Bureau of Economic Research, New York.

Schaps, E., Moskowitz, J., Condon, J., & Malvin, J. (1982). Process and outcome evaluation of a drug education course. *Journal of Drug Education, 12,* 353–364.

Schweitzer, S., Intriligator, M., & Salehi, H. (1983). Alcoholism, an econometric model of its causes, its effects, and its control. In M. Grant, M. Plant, & A. Williams (Eds.), *Economics and alcohol: Consumption and control.* London: Croom Helm.

Scoles, P., & Fine, E. (1981). Substance abuse patterns among youthful drinking drivers. *Alcoholism: Clinical and Experimental Research, 5.*

Shope, J., & Dielman, T. (1985, October). *An elementary school-based peer resistance program of prevention of adolescent alcohol misuse.* Paper presented at the annual conference of the Illinois Alcoholism and Drug Dependence Association, Ann Arbor, MI.

Simpson, H., Mayhew, D., & Warren, R. (1982). Epidemiology of road accidents involving young adults: Alcohol, drugs, and other factors. *Drug and Alcohol Dependence, 10,* 35–63.

Smith, R., Hingson, R., Morelock, S., Heeren, T., Mucatel, M., Mangione, T., & Scotch, N. (1984). Legislation raising the legal drinking age in Massachusetts from 18 to 20: Effects on 16 and 17 year-olds. *Journal of Studies on Alcohol, 45,* 534–539.

Strickland, D. (1983). Advertising exposure, alcohol consumption, and misuse of alcohol. In M. Grant, M. Plant, & A. Williams (Eds.), *Economics and alcohol: Consumption and controls* (pp. 201–222). London: Croom Helm.

Summala, H. (1987). Young driver accidents: Risk taking or failure of skills.

Alcohol, Drugs, and Driving, 3, 79–91.

URSA/Pacificon. (1980). *Campaign strategy report for the NIAAA public information campaign.* Rockville, MD: National Institute on Alcohol Abuse and Alcoholism.

U.S Department of Transportation. (1987). *Fatal Accident Reporting System: 1986 summary report.* Washington, DC: Author.

Vegega, M. (1984, September). *Deterring drinking–driving among youth: Some research needs.* Paper presented at the annual convention of the American Psychological Association, Toronto.

Vegega, M., & Klitzner, M. (1988). What have we learned about youth anti-drinking–driving programs? *Evaluation and Program Planning, 2*, 203–217.

Vegega, M., & Klitzner, M. (1989). Drinking and driving among youth: A study of situational risk factors. *Health Education Quarterly, 16,*(3), 373–388.

Vejnoska, I. (1982). Putting the brakes on teenage drunk driving. *Police Chief, 49.*

Wagenaar, A. (1982a). Aggregate beer and wine consumption: Effects of changes in the minimum legal drinking age and a mandatory beverage container deposit law in Michigan. *Journal of Alcohol Studies, 43*, 469–488.

Wagenaar, A. (1982b). Preventing highway crashes by raising the legal minimum age for drinking: An empirical confirmation. *Journal of Safety Research, 13*, 57–71.

Wagenaar, A. (1983). *Alcohol, young drivers, and traffic accidents: Effects of minimum age laws.* Lexington, MA: Lexington Books.

Watts, R., & Rabow, J. (1983). Alcohol availability and alcohol-related problems in 213 California cities. *Alcoholism: Clinical and Experimental Research, 7*, 47–58.

Williams, A. (1987). Effective and ineffective policies for reducing injuries associated with youthful drivers. *Alcohol, Drugs, and Driving, 3*, 109–117.

Williams, A., Lund, A., & Preusser, D. (1985). Teenage driver licensing in relation to state laws. *Accident Analysis and Prevention, 17*, 135–145.

Williams, A., Lund, A., & Preusser, D. (1986). Drinking and driving among high school students. *International Journal of the Addictions, 21*, 643–655.

Wittman, F. (1982). Current status of research demonstration programs in the primary prevention of alcohol problems. In *Prevention, intervention, and treatment: Concerns and models* (pp. 3–57). Washington, DC: U.S. Government Printing Office.

Zylman, R. (1973). Youth, alcohol, and collision involvement. *Journal of Safety Research, 5*, 58–72.

10

PROGRAMS FOR THE REHABILITATION AND TREATMENT OF DRINKING–DRIVING MULTIPLE OFFENDERS IN THE FEDERAL REPUBLIC OF GERMANY

WOLF-R. NICKEL

Society in the Federal Republic of Germany (FRG) and other countries in Western Europe has denied for many years (and in many areas still denies) the dangers of alcohol consumption in general as well as the specific risks of drinking and driving. Until recently there has been a widespread tendency to underestimate the effect of alcohol on human performance; the majority of drivers do not know how much alcohol can be consumed before the maximum legal blood alcohol content (BAC), which differs from country to country, is reached. In general, people underestimate the amount of consumption required to reach the legal BAC. The consequence is that many drivers believe they have driven under the influence without having been caught by the police. They pity those drivers with the "bad luck" of having been caught, because they feel it could easily have been themselves. They develop an attitude of false solidarity with those apprehended. This in turn makes it difficult for politicians to support the measure long since proposed by experts: lowering the BAC limits. The discussion about mandating zero BAC when driving has recently arisen again. In the FRG there is a political move toward more security; the dangers of drinking and driving are more and more recognized.

Alcohol causes more damage (death, sickness, injury, and economic loss) than all other forms of addiction combined. In the FRG at least 4,000 fatal accidents a year are related to alcohol (Müller, 1976). Although this is a widely known fact, the integration of alcohol consumption with other aspects of daily living leads to enormous resistance to change. This problem is not peculiar to Germany or Europe but is worldwide.

This chapter deals briefly with rehabilitation attempts in some European countries but focuses mainly on the German experience with education and rehabilitation of the convicted drinking driver. German drinking–driving laws, particularly as they apply to these programs, are described. The development, goals, content, and conditions of administration of one specific German treatment model are presented in detail. This is followed by a summary of the outcome evaluation and a discussion of the reasons for its success and failure.

OVERVIEW OF EXISTING PROGRAMS IN EUROPE

This overview cannot be comprehensive, since there are many European programs that have never been reported on or evaluated. A detailed description of programs in the German-speaking countries has been published by Spoerer, Ruby, and Hess (1987). The programs mentioned all refer to treatment of alcohol-related problems in road traffic.

The European approach has for a long time been (and in most countries still is) more or less punitive as far as individual violations are concerned; preventive measures taken against drinking and driving tend to be very similar across Europe and are almost exclusively directed at the public and the driving population in general. In the FRG after World War II the tradition of driver assessment was continued. In the mid-1950s the federal government passed laws and regulations that required drivers reconvicted of drinking and driving to have their driving ability assessed by medical–psychological experts before relicensing.

Although Winkler (1974) initiated group discussions for reconvicted drinking drivers in the FRG as early as 1971, it was not until the late 1970s and early 1980s that education and rehabilitation alternatives received serious consideration in other European countries. Only within the last decade have there been more systematic attempts, across Europe, to reduce drinking and driving by means of treatment, for example, Cooke and Martin (1988) in the United Kingdom; Lambregts, Soenveld, and Bovens (1987) in the Netherlands; Huguenin and Hess (1982) in Switzerland; Zuzan (1979) and Michalke (1979) in Austria; Hole (1986) in Norway; and Simonnet and Forrestier (1979) in France. A number of international workshops on driver improvement and rehabilitation have been carried out in the German-speaking countries since 1979; their primary purpose is the exchange of experience and the development of new approaches.

Most courses last from 3 to 12 weeks (with an average of about 6 weeks) and a total of 12 to 26 hours in four to ten sessions. The number of participants is typically limited (between 6 and 12). In general, participation is voluntary, but clients must meet certain criteria (e.g., no addictions, no criminal offenses, sufficient knowledge of the language).

Since driving under the influence of alcohol in combination with accident causation is punished with imprisonment in some European countries (e.g., Austria), courses for prisoners have been developed in those countries. Normally, however, courses are directed to the reconvicted drinking driver who does not suffer imprisonment.

In the Federal Republic of Germany three different models for driving while impaired (DWI) recidivists have been developed. Their characteristics differ with respect to the psychological theory on which the program is based. The IFT (Institute fur Therapieforschung) model is based on a moderate behavioristic approach, the IRAK (Individualpsychologische Rehabilitation Alkoholauffalliger Kraftfahrer) model is based on individual psychological theory, and the LEER (named after the town in which it was first carried out) model is embedded in a group dynamic framework. These programs differ not only with respect to the underlying theory but also with respect to the number of sessions and their total duration. The LEER model is the shortest, with 14 hours in six sessions (one per week); the IFT model lasts up to 7 weeks, with a total of 24 hours; and the IRAK model comprises 13 2-hour sessions within 7 weeks (Winkler, Jacobshagen, & Nickel, 1988).

THE LEGAL BASIS FOR REHABILITATION IN THE FRG

The legal provisions applying to DWI offenders are highly complicated and will therefore be presented in a condensed and simplified manner. Roughly speaking, two main groups of offenders are distinguished: those having committed an offense at a BAC of more than 0.08 mg/ml but less than 0.13 mg/ml, and those having been caught with a BAC of more than 0.13 mg/ml. The latter are subject to the penal code and are fined an amount according to average monthly income; the court imposes a license revocation of from 6 months to lifetime (depending on the severity of the violation), with an average of 1 1/2 to 2 years (for repeat offenders). Repeat offenders applying for license renewal after the period of revocation has expired are required to undergo a medical–psychological examination. There are two possible results of the examination: The driver will either be judged fit to operate a car and get his/her license reinstated or be judged unfit to drive. In the latter case the outcome of more refined psychological examination is used to decide on the possibility of the offender's participating in a course. Winkler (1985) found that out of 51,679 drivers who had been examined medically and psychologically in the FRG in 1984, 33% had been judged unfit to operate a car (i.e., their deficiencies could not be corrected by participation in a treatment program). Another 18.5% had been judged eligible to participate in a program, and 48.5% had been judged fit to operate a car without further specific educational measures.

Those drivers judged eligible to participate in a program decide whether or not they want to take part. If they participate, they are required to sign an agreement concerning duties to be fulfilled in order to receive a certificate of participation; this certificate will normally result in being issued a new license by the authority. The duties of the participants include completing assigned homework, participating in group discussion, not disturbing the course, and never appearing under the influence of alcohol.

Participants who do not comply are expelled from the course and do not receive certificates of participation. Their driver's licenses will not be reissued unless they are able to present medical–psychological evidence proving their fitness to drive. Regulations in the FRG prohibit the reissuance of a license to a disqualified driver.

The reissuance of a driver's licence to a person who has been judged unfit to operate an automobile depends on a legal writ issued by the ministries of the federal *Länder* (states); this process may change in the near future, since there are now efforts to incorporate driver rehabilitation programs into federal law.

OBJECTIVES AND CONTENTS OF DWI PROGRAMS FOR REPEAT OFFENDERS

It is not possible to cover the contents of the programs in detail; there are many publications dealing with the objectives, their underlying psychological theory, and the structure and content derived from that theory. To make clear why the programs are effective, however, it is necessary to point out some of the most important factors.

The target of driver improvement is to change attitudes toward drinking and driving, drinking habits, and drinking-and-driving habits. Rehabilitation programs are intended to improve the individual's self-observation and self-control and thus initiate behavioral changes (Hebenstreit et al., 1982).

The LEER model developed by Winkler (1974, 1985), for example, puts much weight on applying group dynamics in group discussions, mutual analyses of drinking behavior, self-observation and self-control exercises, behavior modification techniques, and homework. Information on the physical and mental effects of alcohol, though part of the program, is by no means the central focus. Course leaders are professional psychologists experienced in psychological assessment of drivers and specially trained in behavior modification. It is their task to act as moderators much more than as teachers or instructors.

The total duration of the LEER program is 2 years. The course is composed of a preparatory phase of 2 to 3 weeks, six course sessions (with a maximum of eight to ten participants) of 2 to 3 hours each, and a reinforcement phase after completion of the course sessions and relicensing. Two years after the last course session participants reconvene to exchange their experiences. The contents of the course consist mainly of analysis of drinking–driving behavior, information on alcohol and road traffic, and self-observation and self-control practice.

The analysis of drinking–driving behavior consists of three parts. The first part takes place in the preparatory phase; the participant has to keep a drinking diary in order to collect data on his/her individual drinking pattern. The second part focuses on individual driving habits in connection with typical drinking situations in order to formulate strategies to avoid drinking–driving and prepare alternative behavioral concepts. Finally, the analysis considers the personal development of drinking habits, including their causes and the learning conditions that promote them; this is usually achieved by biographical analysis during one of the course sessions.

Information on the role of alcohol in traffic accidents is given within group discussions whenever appropriate. For example, participants are asked to compute the overall cost of their drinking–driving violations (in order to demonstrate the tremendous amount of money spent) and discuss this aspect with other group members. The course leader also discusses the possibility of further assistance and medical or psychological help outside the course. This is necessary since some individuals, in the course of group discussion and accumulation of knowledge on their drinking habits, increasingly recognize their pathological involvement with alcohol consumption and their need for further professional help. In order to include the participants' environment in the process of rehabilitation, course leaders encourage the continuation of group discussion with friends, spouses, or relatives after hours, with a report on results.

The participants are expected to remain in touch with their course leader after completion of the course. They are offered six to seven pamphlets with additional information, reminders, and homework in order to reinforce specific parts of the program, especially those referring to self-observation and drinking habits.

EVALUATION OF DRIVER IMPROVEMENT PROGRAMS IN THE FRG

Evaluation Conditions and Procedure

Treatment programs have been carried out since 1977 in the FRG by different organizations. The Technischer Überwachungs-Verein Hannover was awarded a research contract by the Federal Highway Research Board (Bundesanstalt für Strassenwesen) to evaluate program effectiveness.

The evaluation could not use a true experimental design (random assignment to experimental or control group) because drivers judged unfit to drive could not get their driving privileges restored for experimental purposes. Therefore the control group consisted of 1,344 reconvicted drivers whose driving privileges had been restored without prior educational measures, after medical–psychological examination. The experimental group consisted of 1,544 reconvicted male drivers who had been judged disqualified to drive without prior treatment but whose driving privileges would be restored immediately after treatment. All participated voluntarily. Figure 10.1 shows the relative position of both groups with respect to the total sample of reconvicted drivers.

It is important to note that this type of selection very much favors the control group, that is, those drivers who had been judged fit to drive without further educational measures and whose reconviction rate had *a priori* been expected to be better than that of drivers judged unfit to drive (experimentals). For program effectiveness to be judged satisfactory, an independent project group required that the recidi-

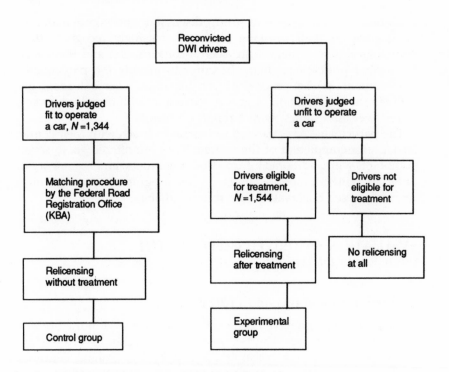

FIGURE 10.1. Selection of experimental and control groups.

vism rate of experimentals (those judged disqualified to drive) should not exceed that of the controls (those judged fit to drive) significantly (Hebenstreit et al., 1982).

Traffic records of both experimentals and control were observed for 36 months after relicensing. A variety of sources of possible influence on the reconviction rate had to be controlled, including intensity of law enforcement by the police, regional drinking habits, observance of selection criteria by examiners, and the course leaders' behavior during treatment.

Individual difference variables were collected from experimentals in order to allow the examination of their impact on selection and recidivism. These included age, previous driving record (including DWI offenses), arrest BAC, education, occupation, marital status, individual drinking habits, intellectual capacity, and symptoms of addiction.

In order to determine the amount of change in knowledge and

attitudes toward drinking and driving, special questionnaires had to be developed and administered before and after treatment.

Program Effects on Knowledge, Attitudes, and Behavior

A highly significant change in knowledge and attitudes after program participation was observed. However, there was no significant association between these variables and recidivism (Nickel, Jacobshagen & Winkler, 1987).

Behavioral changes were measured by the number of DUI offenses registered after relicensing. Whereas 18.3% of the controls were reconvicted within a period of 36 months, a significantly smaller proportion (14.0%) of the experimental group relapsed. Thus those judged fit to drive without attending the program relapsed more often than those whose problems were considered serious enough to require treatment before relicensing.

Individual Difference Factors and Recidivism

Experimentals aged 18–24 relapsed more frequently than older ones, regardless of the treatment model administered. Controls in the 18–24 age group were reconvicted more frequently than older individuals and their peers in the experimental groups (Table 10.1). This is consistent with the finding that the reconviction rate of those having had their first offense before the age of 20 is higher than that of first offenders at a later age (Winkler et al., 1988).

TABLE 10.1. Age Group and Recidivism

| | Relicensing after | | | | |
| | Examination and treatment | | Examination without treatment | | |
Age group	n	Reconviction %	n	Reconviction %	$p < 0.05$
18¾24	193	19.2	271	21.0	n.s.
25¾34	542	15.9	549	18.8	n.s.
35¾49	680	10.7	440	17.3	+
50¾66	116	7.6	84	19.0	+
All	1,531	13.4	1,344	18.8	+

With respect to marital relations, it was found that clients without marital problems had a significantly lower reconviction rate (10.9%) than those with self-reported problems (26.9%). In addition, clients who had begun regular alcohol consumption at an early age showed a significantly higher reconviction rate than those who had started to drink at a later age (Nickel et al., 1987).

Factors Influencing Treatment Outcome

Intensity of Law Enforcement by Police

The intensity of law enforcement by the police has been measured by the number of breath tests taken in all federal *Länder* of the FRG throughout the preevaluation and evaluation period. In order to relate the number of breath tests to mileage in the specific region, it was also necessary to account for the consumption of gasoline as an indicator of exposure. The differences between various regions were highly significant, ranging between 62 breath tests per 500 tons of gasoline in North-Rhine-Westfalia to 10 breath tests per 500 tons in Bavaria. However, a comparison between high- and low-intensity regions (Table 10.2) showed no significant tendency toward higher recidivism rates in high-intensity regions.

Regional Drinking Habits

Drinking habits differ substantially between the north and south of the FRG. The consumption of beer, wine and spirits was obtained from data presented by Persy (1985) and Spiegel (1981). In order to examine the influence of regional drinking habits, a comparison between regions with high versus low consumption rates was carried out. The results (Table 10.3) show that there were no significant differences between recidivism rates in regions with high and low consumption rates.

TABLE 10.2. Reconviction and Intensity of Law Enforcement

Intensity of law enforcement	% Reconviction	
	Experimentals	Controls
high	13.8	18.9
low	12.4	17.7

TABLE 10.3. Regional Drinking Habits and Reconviction Rate

Average regional alcohol consumption	% Reconviction	
	Experimentals	Controls
low	12.7	17.6
high	13.7	18.5

Observance of Selection Criteria by Examiners

The psychologists in charge of the medical–psychological examination were supposed to observe a number of criteria that had been designed to determine an individual's eligibility for treatment. To be included, the prospective client had to have two drinking–driving convictions. Exclusion criteria included excessive drinking or addiction, physical damage by alcohol and/or other drugs, physical disabilities, psychotic symptoms, an IQ below 70, or language problems. The analysis of selection criteria demonstrated that the psychologists did not have difficulties in observing them.

Another measure possibly influencing treatment outcome is that of individual differences between psychologists in determining program eligibility. Therefore, the recidivism rates of drivers assessed by psychologists with high and low rates of rejection were compared. There was a slight but nonsignificant tendency for psychologists who rejected more drivers after medical–psychological examination to "produce" fewer recidivists.

Course Leaders' Behavior during Treatment

The influence of the course leader on participants during treatment may be important but it is difficult to determine. In an attempt to examine this factor, behavioral questionnaires were developed exclusively for this purpose and administered to participants. A factor analysis of the data revealed four main factors, labeled "nondirective behavior", "social-integrative behavior," "tolerance," and "competence."

It was impossible to correlate the individual course leaders' scores to the reconviction rate of participants, because German law requires anonymity in order to protect individual privacy. However, the influence was assessed by comparison of high-score with low-score participants. No differences were found between groups with respect to recidivism.

DETERMINANTS OF PROGRAM EFFECTIVENESS

The task of evaluating different programs did not include the objective of differentially examining and determining the effect of single treatment components. Therefore the following remarks on why the programs work the way they do are more or less speculative. Nevertheless, there are a number of important agents that appear to be common to all three models (IFT, IRAK, and LEER) and seem to contribute to the success of the programs.

The Selection Process

It is unreasonable to expect substantial short-term behavior change in individuals who have lost control of their drinking habits and developed addictive behaviors. Since this course is designed to reduce the frequency and amount of drinking rather than to establish total abstinence (which would be necessary for the addict), no alcohol-dependent or drug-dependent individuals are admitted. Similarly, as previously described, clients with psychopathological disorders, an IQ below 70, insufficient knowledge of the German language, or an extremely high degree of neuroticism and/or psychotic symptoms are not admitted. Clients with one or more of those characteristics need different forms of treatment, in most cases on an individual basis. In many cases medical–psychological examination leads to specific suggestions with respect to other forms of intervention. Our experience shows that creating a largely homogeneous group of drinking–driving offenders with corrigible deficiencies is one of the most important factors determining the success of treatment. Most evaluation studies have shown that neglecting this factor produces nonsignificant differences between treatment and nontreatment groups.

The Role of Course Leaders

Who Is a Good Counselor?

Research on the process of therapy has tried to focus on the primary qualities of counselors. Many researchers (e.g., Coche, 1977; Pierce, Carkhuff & Berenson, 1967) have shown that the "efficient counselor" can be characterized as showing empathy, being competent, and being consistent and reliable. "Showing empathy" is ranked first and "competence," second. Teachers with these qualities have classes with higher academic achievement, less aggressive and more social potential, and higher group coherence.

Emphasizing these qualities in the selection and training of course leaders is an important contribution to the success of group treatment. For example, a course leader who is not competent will either easily be detected as such by the group or will constantly be occupied with hiding it; in either case, lack of competence will reduce the willingness of the group to accept the leading and triggering role of the course leader and will seriously disturb dynamic processes.

Moreover, a lack of empathy demonstrated by the course leader will soon create a climate of distance and lack of personal involvement. Members of the group will feel hesitant to present personal views, and thus the development of cognitive change and behavior control will be inhibited. The course leader with inconsistent behavior lacks leadership attributes and will not be able to prevent the development of fear, insecurity, and disorientation in the group. In addition, course leaders must be aware of the fact that many of those clients who have serious drinking problems or are on the verge of addiction need and want individual guidance.

Training and Supervision of Course Leaders

Course leaders have previous experience with drinking–driving offenders through extended diagnostic work. This experience enables the course leader to detect defense mechanisms and cope with questionable self-reports on drinking behavior. Course leaders are trained in a variety of therapeutic techniques, particularly in how to evoke and handle group dynamics. They take part in special seminars designed to assist them in dealing with difficult situations by feedback and further training. In recent years, an important focus has been on the combination of continuous diagnostic practice with the carrying out of treatment. Finally, it is judged important in the LEER model to have the course leader carry out the final session with participants at 2-year follow-up. All course leaders are continuously supervised; the process of supervision involves such activities as common performance of a complete session by two course leaders, use of videotape feedback, discussion of problems with the supervisor, and reception of feedback on personal impact and efficiency.

Why Are DWI Treatment Models of Different Duration Equally Effective?

The LEER model—as compared to the other two German models that have been evaluated—is by far the shortest in duration (which is the main reason for its comparatively low cost), yet it is equally effective in reducing recidivism. However, this result is not specific to the DWI treatment field.

Therapy research has not been able to demonstrate convincingly the effectiveness of a single psychological treatment method (Eysenck, 1952). Prioleau (1983) claimed that the efficiency of psychotherapy does not depend on its duration or on the skill of the therapist, and Grawe (1987) pointed out that the methods of therapy research in the past have not been adequate. He suggested that there is a need to develop alternative research methods in order to be able to detect "patterns of effectiveness" that may be highly individual.

Behavior modification procedures covering a wide range of techniques are more effective than those that are highly specific (e.g., Bandura, 1977; Karasu, 1986); usually the latter are derived from psychotherapeutic ideologies or schools. Integrated approaches that focus on the specific type of problem have been applied successfully (e.g., Bandura, 1977). The LEER model follows such an integrated approach, because its focus is the specific behavioral attributes and situational variables that result in drinking and driving. This model employs different therapeutic strategies (e.g., affective experiencing, cognitive mastery, behavioral regulation) and educative measures (e.g. videotape feedback, group discussion, role playing, information sessions, homework, *in vivo* practice) that allow the course leader to apply appropriate techniques, dependent on different group settings and the specific problems being dealt with. This model therefore displays a high degree of adaptability to any situation and problem that might arise during treatment. The LEER model also offers clients participation in additional activities during the 2 years following treatment; former participants receive up to six letters signed by the course leader that encourage them to reflect on important topics and join a final session of exchange of experiences.

In summary, at present we can only speculate on the question of why treatment programs work with repeat drinking–driving offenders. However, experimental research into this specific question would be very expensive. The present point of view in the FRG is a highly pragmatic one: Treatment does work, and therefore the time has come to postpone further research and start working with the programs.

Interaction of Factors Influencing Treatment Success

The question of why programs with different theoretical backgrounds and durations do not differ with respect to treatment outcome cannot be answered on the basis of the German program evaluation. Nevertheless, it seems probable that treatment success has to be attributed, with varying degrees of significance, to a wide variety of factors (including those discussed in this chapter). These factors interact with one another, thus forming a system of modification agents. An analysis of the similarities of the different programs, since all appeared equally successful, might suggest what factors are most responsible for success. All German programs are identical in the following characteristics: the use of a group setting in courses, the use of similar media, the prevalence of empathy and competence among leaders, and their relatively high cost. Participants share the following common characteristics: homogeneity with respect to number of DUI convictions and punishments, license withdrawal, and medical–psychological examination before treatment.

Possible Reasons for Failure in Individual Cases

It would be easy to state that the main reasons for failure (which has to be acknowledged in at least 13% of the participants) are the same as those for success, that is, whenever one of the change agents has not been properly applied. It may be instructive to look more closely at the possible reasons.

The evaluation study has demonstrated that the recidivism rate of participants is higher than average in the following cases: drivers between the ages of 18 and 25; drivers with marital problems; and drivers with a combination of DWI, driving without a license, and three or more nonalcohol traffic offenses. These findings have influenced the selection process in that drivers exhibiting several risk factors are no longer admitted. They do have the chance, however, to take part in different programs designed to treat them more individually.

Another reason for failure is the participation of undetected alcohol addicts; diagnostic procedures have to be improved in order to reduce the number of dropouts (e.g., those who fail to comply with the signed agreement not to appear under the influence of alcohol) and addicts receiving a certificate of participation.

Besides problems in the initial psychological assessment, there are a number of factors affecting failure during treatment. These factors can be categorized as those caused by course leader mistakes, lack of group cohesion, and management mistakes.

If the course leader fails to recognize serious personal problems, participants might not manage to relate their personal problems to their drinking habits. If the counselor fails to initiate the process of self-observation at the beginning of treatment and does not control the results of such experience, participants may not be able to develop and maintain the skills to deal with future conflict situations. Counselors who put too much emphasis on providing information and improving clients' knowledge often tend to omit more efficient therapeutic mechanisms. Finally, if the counselor does not succeed in establishing a climate of confidence, some of the group members may not disclose important information about their drinking habits and thus inhibit shaping procedures.

Apart from counselor mistakes, there may be unfavorable conditions in a particular group with respect to homogeneity, thereby affecting group cohesion, which seems to be an important precondition for the uninhibited exchange of information and ideas. Management mistakes (such as accepting too many drivers for a course, failing to inform clients about dates in time, failing to provide sufficient working material, etc.) are rare and therefore do not appear to affect treatment success.

CONCLUSION

The international literature on rehabilitation programs makes clear that it is impossible to compare their success or failure unless the conditions under which they are administered are compared as well. Very frequently, however, the conditions (e.g., the legal system, licensing regulations) are not reported. The German experience in driver rehabilitation has shown that in order to reduce the probability of further drinking and driving, there has to be punishment *and* treatment. There has to be an adequate period of license withdrawal in order to demonstrate to the individual driver the problems caused by his/her behavior and to create a sufficiently stable motivation for change. Only after the driver has overcome these obstacles does treatment (in the sense of driver improvement and rehabilitation) become meaningful and efficient.

Perhaps it would be presumptuous to expect that by continually improving assessment, rehabilitation, and supervisory techniques we could attain the goal of completely eliminating drinking–driving. The individual causes of human behavior and their interactions are sufficiently complicated to make such an expectation utopian. Nevertheless, this is the goal at which we must aim.

REFERENCES

Bandura, A. (1977). Self-efficacy: Toward a unifying theory of behavioral change. *Psychological Review, 84,* 191–215.

Coche, E. (1977). Training of group therapists. In F.W. Kaslow (Ed.), *Supervision, consultation and staff training in the helping professions* (pp. 235–263). San Francisco: Jossey-Bass.

Cooke, J., & Martin, J. (1988). *Don't take the risk! The course for alcohol-impaired drivers.* Hampshire Probation Service.

Eysenck, H.J. (1952). The effects of psychotherapy: An evaluation. *Journal of Consulting Psychology, 16,* 319–324.

Grawe, K. (1987). Die Effekte der Psychotherapie. In Bericht über den 35. *Kongreß der Deutschen Gesellschaft für Psychologie in Heidelberg, 1986, Band 2* (pp. 515–534). Toronto: Hogrefe.

Hebenstreit, B.V., Hundhausen, G., Klebe, W., Kroj, G., Spoerer, E., Walther, R., Winkler, W., & Wuhrer, H. (Dez., 1982). Kurse für auffällige Kraftfahrer. *Schlußbericht der Projektgruppe "Kurse für auffällige Kraftfahrer"* (pp. 19–26). Cologne: Bundesanstalt für Straßenwesen.

Hole, G. (1986). Risikoverringerung durch Verbesserung von Fahrerselektion, Führerscheinausbildung und Lenkerprüfung. In PRI, *Bericht des Weltkongresses "Verkehrssicherheit der Zukunft, sozialer und ökonomischer Effekt".* Vienna: Prevention Routiere Internationale (PRI) Kuratorium für Verrkehrssicherheit (KfV).

Huguenin, R.D., & E. Hess (Eds.). (1982). *Driver Improvement. Rahmenbedingungen und Methoden der Verhaltensbeeinflussung in der Ausbildung, Weiterbildung und Nachschulung von Fahrzeuglenkern. Bericht über den zweiten internationalen Workshop, Mai 1981.* Gwatt, Bern: Schweizerische Beratungsstelle für Unfallverhütung (BfU).

Karasu, T.B. (1986). The specificity versus nonspecificty dilemma: Toward identifying therapeutic change agents. *American Journal of Psychiatry, 143,* 687–695.

Lambregts, E.C.F., Soenveld, A.E., & Bovens, R.H.L.M. (1987). Drink-driving projects inside and outside prison in the Netherlands: Content and effectiveness. In P.C. Noordzij & R. Roszbach (Eds.), *Alcohol, drugs and traffic safety—T86* (International Congress Series, No. 721). Amsterdam: Elsevier.

Michalke, H. (1979). Problemorientiertes Training für alkoholauffällige Kraftfahrer. In W.D. Zuzan (Ed.), *Driver Improvement. Erster Internationaler Workshop: Psychologische Behandlungsmodelle für verkehrsauffällige Kraftfahrer, 9–13 Oktober 1978* (pp. 144–168). Salzburg: Tagungsbericht, Kuratorium für Verkehrssicherheit.

Müller, A. (1976). *Der Trunkenheitstäter im Straßenverkehr, Beiträge zur empirischen Kriminologie.* Frankfurt, Bern.

Nickel, W.R., Jacobshagen, W., & Winkler, W. (1987). Evaluation of the effectiveness of treatment programs for DUI recidivists in the FRG. In

P.C. Noordzij & R. Roszbach (Eds.), *Alcohol, drugs and traffic safety—T 86* (pp. 561–565). Amsterdam: Elsevier.

Persy, A.M. (1985). Untersuchungen zu "Alkohol und Fahren." In *Die Entwicklung des Alkoholkonsums in der Bundersrepublik Deutschland, Band 12, Bericht zum Forschungsprojekt 7612/52* Bergisch-Gladbach: Bundesanstalt für Straßenwesen, Bereich Unfallforschung.

Petry, J. (1985). *Alkoholismustherapie: Vom Einstellungswandel zur kognitiven Therapie.* Munich: Urban und Schwarzenberg.

Pierce, R., Carkhuff, R., & Berenson, B. (1967). The effects of high and low functioning supervisors upon counselors in training. *Journal of Clinical Psychology, 23,* 212–215.

Prioleau, L. (1983). An analysis of psychotherapy versus placebo studies. *The Behavioral and Brain Sciences, 6,* 275–310.

Simonnet, M., & Forrestier, M. (1979). *Après permis et problèmes de postapprentissage—Tranche conditionelle; compte rendu d'activités* (Cahier d'étude No. 7841112). Paris: Onser.

Spiegel (1981). *Dokumentation Prozente (2).* Hamburg: Spiegel-Verlag.

Spoerer, E., Ruby, M., & Hess, E. (Eds.). (1987). *Nachschulung und Rehabilitation verkehrsauffälliger Kraftfahrer* (Dokumentation von Kursen und der Literatur zum Driver Improvement; Faktor Mensch im Verkehr No. 35). Braunschweig: Rot-Gelb-Grün.

Winkler, W. (1974). Gruppengespräche nach wiederholter Trunkenheit am Steuer. *Blutalkohol, 11,* 178–188.

Winkler, W. (1985). Reducing driving under the influence of alcohol by special treatment programs. In M.R. Valverius (Ed.), *Punishment and/or treatment for driving under the influence of alcohol and other drugs* (pp. 12–32). Stockholm.

Winkler, W., Jacobshagen, W., & Nickel, W.R. (1988). *Wirksamkeit von Kursen für wiederholt alkoholauffällige Kraftfahrer.* Unfall- und Sicherheitsforschung Straßenverkehr, Heft 64, Bergisch-Gladbach: Bundesanstalt für Straßenwesen, Bereich Unfallforschung.

Zuzan, W.D. (1979). Einzeltraining mit Mehrfach- und Alkoholtätern. In W.D. Zuzan (Ed.), *Driver Improvement: Erster internationaler Workshop: Psychologische Behandlungsmodelle für verkehrsauffällige Kraftfahrer. 9–13 Oktober 1978* (pp. 169–175). Salzburg: Tagungsbericht.

11

MATCHING THE DWI OFFENDER TO AN EFFECTIVE INTERVENTION STRATEGY: AN EMERGING RESEARCH AGENDA

ELISABETH WELLS-PARKER
JAMES W. LANDRUM
JEFF S. TOPPING

In the United States, the use of remedial interventions, such as rehabilitation, treatment, education, and probation, to alter the behavior of drinking–driving (DWI) offenders was emphasized during the 1970s and early 1980s. Accompanying this trend, state and federal agencies supported large-scale studies to evaluate the effects of these interventions on traffic safety and alcohol outcomes (e.g., Hagen, Williams, & McConnell, 1979; Holden & Stewart, 1981; Landrum et al., 1982; Nichols, Weinstein, Ellingstad, Struckman-Johnson, & Reis, 1981; Popkin, Li, Lacey, Stewart, & Waller, 1983; Reis, 1982a, 1982b; Sadler & Perrine, 1984). Reviewers of the resultant evaluation literature have concluded that remedial interventions have had a small beneficial effect on the drinking and driving behaviors of DWI offenders (Mann, Leigh, Vingilis, & DeGenova, 1983; Peck, Sadler, & Perrine, 1985). On the other hand, reviewers have also emphasized that other sanctions, such as license suspension, could have a stronger impact on various target behaviors, such as accident involvement (Peck et al., 1985; Waller, 1985). The conclusion that remedial programs are only marginally effective has been cited as a reason for U.S. policy makers' deemphasis on rehabilitation in favor of less expensive or more punitive DWI sanctions (McAllister, 1988).

Even so, remedial interventions are unlikely to be abandoned by either the alcohol treatment community or the traffic safety community. In many states in the United States, the DWI conviction is viewed as a unique opportunity for the early identification and remediation of alcohol problems. Also, judges have become hesitant to enforce many of the newer, more punitive laws (Waller, 1985; Wells-Parker & Cosby, 1988), and these new laws have not had the dramatic impact that was envisioned by their supporters (National Highway Traffic Safety Administration, 1986; Ross, 1982). As disappointment with many of the harsher sanctions grows, emphasis has been placed on a multiple strategy approach, which includes remedial intervention in conjunction with measures such as license suspension to alter DWI offenders' behaviors (Surgeon General's Workshop on Drunk Driving: Background Papers, 1988).

Evidence about DWI offenders has led reviewers to reevaluate the conclusions that have been drawn from the remedial intervention research (Mann, 1988; Vingilis & Mann, 1986). Underlying this reevaluation is a consensus among DWI researchers that (1) significant heterogeneity exists among DWI offenders not only with regard to alcohol abuse but also with regard to personality, attitudinal, behavioral (e.g., driving and risk taking), and other dimensions as well and that (2) this heterogeneity is clinically relevant. That is, DWI clients who differ according to these characteristics will show predictably different outcomes to specific interventions; therefore, offenders should be matched to the most effective intervention strategy.

This matching hypothesis not only has established a new research strategy for improving remedial interventions but also has suggested an explanation for the failure to find large, overall intervention effects in most evaluation studies. Conceptually, the client/intervention matching hypothesis has been shown to be an interaction hypothesis (Miller & Hester, 1986). If significant offender intervention interactions exist, then the main effects model that typically has been used to evaluate the intervention is incomplete and misleading. That is, the overall or main effect of intervention would be a mean effect of the intervention across the levels of the offender characteristics with which it interacts; therefore, the main effect term would fail to express the effect of the intervention for the relevant levels of client characteristics. Using this reasoning, if any single intervention is not consistently effective for offenders with differing characteristics, then the overall effect of that intervention within any heterogeneous sample of offenders will often be small (Wells-Parker, Anderson, McMillen, & Landrum, 1989).

Within the general alcohol treatment field, the matching hypothesis has been extensively examined, and relevant research has been reviewed (Miller & Hester, 1986). In this chapter, research that is relevant to the matching hypothesis within the DWI intervention field will be reviewed. DWI interventions can have broad traffic safety objectives, and alcohol treatment is just one component of these interventions. In the DWI intervention area, research on the matching hypothesis is in its early stages of development, and much of the current research, although not directly testing the hypothesis, is germane to specifying testable versions of the hypothesis. A testable version of the hypothesis must include operational definitions of client variables and of intervention variables that should interact. Much of the current research, such as the development of DWI offender typologies, has focused on identifying these relevant variables. Direct tests of the matching hypothesis are rare, and the few research efforts that have attempted a direct test will be discussed. Finally, concerns for future research on the matching hypothesis will be considered, and possibilities for new strategies that would assist in developing knowledge about client intervention matching will be explored.

DEVELOPMENT OF THE MATCHING HYPOTHESIS WITHIN THE DWI INTERVENTION FIELD

Initial distinctions among DWI offenders focused on the identification of levels of drinking problems. Variables such as blood alcohol content (BAC), number of prior DWI and/or alcohol-related offenses, and psychometric or clinical indicators of drinking problems were combined to distinguish groups of offenders that differed according to the severity of alcohol problems. Within this approach, it was reasoned that individuals with more severe alcohol problems would also be higher traffic safety risks, and specific psychometric instruments, such as the Mortimer–Filkins Questionnaire and Interview (Mortimer, Filkins, & Lower, 1971), were devised to identify severity of alcohol problems in a traffic safety context. In the United States, such schemes were widely adopted within DWI intervention programs. Using these assessment schemes, screened "high-problem" (vis-à-vis alcohol) offenders often were diverted out of educative programs and into more intensive treatment programs. This diversion was based on the findings of early short-term intervention studies that alcohol/traffic safety education programs benefited offenders with less severe alcohol problems but not offenders with more severe problems (Mann, 1988; Nichols, Weinstein, Ellingstad, & Struckman-Johnson, 1978). The diversion of screened "high-problem" offenders out of educative programs constituted an acceptance of a simple unidimensional version of the matching hypothesis. Also, the diversion has rendered it impossible to test the differential effectiveness of educational modalities for "low-problem" and for "high-problem" offenders within most of the available evaluation studies (Mann et al., 1983). However, findings summarized across studies lend support to the idea that education programs benefit offenders with lower levels of alcohol problems but that short-term interventions, including education formats, are ineffective or harmful for offenders with more severe alcohol problems when such interventions are administered without additional treatment (Mann, Vingilis, & Stewart, 1988). More intense, longer, and individually oriented programs appear to benefit offenders with more severe alcohol problems (Mann et al., 1988). Assessment and screening issues associated with this unidimensional scheme have been extensively reviewed elsewhere, and problems have been identified (Donovan, Marlatt, & Salzberg, 1983; Mann, 1988; Wendling & Kolody, 1982). In reviewing this approach, Mann and colleagues (1983) concluded

> Offenders, by definition, are individuals who have committed both an alcohol offense and a driving offense. . . . Traditionally, in DWI rehabilitation literature, the assumption has been made that the DWI offender has only an alcohol problem. In fact, the literature supports the contention that the offender has problems in *both* areas. (p. 446)

Suspecting that variables besides alcohol problem indicators were needed to predict future traffic risk among DWI offenders, researchers began to assess DWIs on a variety of personality, attitudinal, behavioral, demographic, and criminal record characteristics in order to improve traffic risk prediction. In this regard, it has been shown that these dimensions are related to high-risk driving behavior, recidivism, and/or accident involvement (Donovan et al., 1983; Perrine, 1975). Refinement of this multidimensional approach to risk prediction is ongoing (Perrine, 1987). Researchers also began to suspect that these dimensions were not only relevant to prediction of traffic risk but were also clinically relevant. That is, they suspected that different intervention approaches were needed not only for offenders who differed on severity of alcohol problems but for offenders who differed along these other dimensions as well. Thus the recognition that the DWI offense was a driving as well as a drinking problem, and the development of multidimensional models of traffic risk prediction, expanded the concept of matching DWI clients to intervention into additional domains.

In addition, researchers were influenced by trends in the alcohol treatment field. As multidimensional models were developing within the DWI intervention area, the matching hypothesis was developing within the general alcohol treatment area (Glaser, 1980; Miller & Hester, 1986), accompanying such trends as the development of multidimensional models of alcoholism (e.g., Wanberg, Horn, & Foster, 1977). Within the framework of the matching hypothesis in the alcohol treatment field, multivariate client typologies were constructed (Skinner, 1982). The purpose of these typologies was to identify subtypes, so that each subtype would have relatively homogeneous treatment needs but different subtypes would require different treatment strategies. Several such multivariate typologies have been developed specifically for DWI offenders (Arstein-Kerslake & Peck, 1986; Donovan & Marlatt, 1982; Mann et al., 1983; Steer, Fine, & Scoles, 1979; Wells-Parker, Cosby, & Landrum, 1986). In order for these typologies to have either practical or heuristic value for improving intervention effectiveness, several requirements must be met. First, relevant offender characteristics must be identified, and reliably distinct subtypes based on those characteristics must be specified. The typology must be replicable within independent samples and externally validated (Skinner, 1982). Ultimately, validation of a typology must focus on whether different interventions vary in effectiveness across subtypes.

DWI OFFENDER TYPOLOGIES

One of the earliest DWI typologies was developed using a sample of 1,500 male offenders in Pennsylvania (Steer et al., 1979). Three alcohol impairment variables—arrest BAC, a quantity/frequency impairment index, and the Stanford Impairment Index (a self-administered alcohol problems questionnaire)—as well as the Psychoneurotic/Stability Scale of the Eysenck Personality Inventory were used to derive seven subtypes. These ranged from a modal subtype with relatively low scores on all scales to a subtype with elevations on all four variables. For external validation, subtypes were compared on variables not used in the cluster analysis. In this validation analysis, subtypes with no elevations on any of the alcohol impairment variables were found to contain more Caucasians than did other subtypes. Also, subtypes with elevations on one or more impairment indices were found to contain individuals who were more likely to have been in previous alcohol treatment. Specific intervention recommendations involving the use of motor vehicle sanctions, additional assessment, alcohol treatment, group or individual counseling, probation, and criminal penalties were made for each subtype. However, the efficacy of the recommended interventions for the specific subtypes has not been evaluated.

Two typologies have been based on Minnesota Multiphasic Personality Inventory (MMPI) profiles. Mulligan, Steer, and Fine (1978) identified several subtypes, including offenders with normal profiles, individuals with profiles indicating certain psychotic features, and individuals with profiles indicating primarily neurotic disturbances. Also, when MMPI scale scores of 500 male offenders in South Carolina were subjected to a linear typal analysis, four distinct profiles emerged (Sutker, Brantley, & Allain, 1980). These profiles involved elevations of the various combinations of subscales 2, 4, and 9 of the MMPI. These scales are indicative of depression, psychopathic deviance, and acting-out behavior, respectively. Profiles that were identified by elevations on scale 2, which indicated depressed affect, were associated with self-reports of heavier drinking as compared to other profiles. Morey and Skinner (1986) have placed these MMPI subtypes of DWI offenders within a three-dimensional model of psychopathology.

Using a different strategy, Donovan and Marlatt (1982) developed a DWI offender typology based on predictors of high-risk driving and accident involvement. After exhaustively reviewing the literature on DWI offender characteristics and high-risk driving predictors, they concluded that there was substantial overlap between DWI arrestees and high-risk drivers generally (Donovan et al., 1983). Measures of 16 personality and attitudinal variables that had been shown to be related to accident risk were administered to a sample of 172 male DWI offenders in Washington state. Responses were subjected to a hierarchical cluster analysis, and five subtypes were derived. These were externally validated using demographics, alcohol use, driving-risk variables, and subsequent driving records (Donovan et al., 1983; Donovan, Queisser, Umlauf, & Salzberg, 1986). One subtype, the modal group, showed high levels of emotional adjustment and low levels of depression, aggression, sensation seeking, and risky driving attitudes (such as hostility, driving for tension reduction, and competitive speed). This subtype was also distinguished by having the highest average social position, fewest accidents and violations, and lowest levels of alcohol consumed per occasion. Another "adjusted" subtype emerged that was characterized by high average assertiveness scores combined with very low levels of risky driving attitudes. In addition, a third subtype appeared that had high scores on resentment and depression along with low scores on perceived personal control over outcomes in general and accidents in particular. This group had moderate scores on other risk-enhancing characteristics.

Preference for speed and driving aggressiveness characterized a fourth subtype that showed high levels of many risk-enhancing characteristics, such as assaultiveness, sensation seeking, and hostility. This "risk-enhancing" subtype was also the youngest group, had the most accidents and violations on record, and reported the highest level of alcohol consumption per occasion. A fifth subtype was also characterized by elevated scores on most of the risk-enhancing characteristics, although elevations were generally not as pronounced as with the fourth subtype. For this fifth subtype, especially high elevations were found on a measure of driving to reduce tension.

It was suggested that the "adjusted" subtypes that had relatively low levels of consumption per occasion could benefit from self-control drinking programs, whereas the "depressive" subtypes could benefit from assertiveness training or depression self-management skills training, while the "risk-enhancing" subtypes, with high hostility levels, could benefit from "cognitive–behavioral anger-management" skills training (Donovan & Marlatt, 1982).

Using identical measures and statistical techniques, Donovan, Umlauf, and Salzberg (1988) have recently derived "risk-enhancing" subtypes and "depressive" subtypes as well as relatively "adjusted" subtypes among high-risk drivers who were identified because of high numbers of driving violations but no recorded DWIs. It was suggested that no single theoretical construct could account for drinking and high-risk driving in either population and that no single intervention was appropriate for either the entire population of DWIs or the entire population of high-risk drivers. However, specific constructs and specific interventions could account for both drinking and high-risk driving for similar subtypes in the different populations. For instance, it was suggested that coping deficit theory (see Donovan et al., 1988) could provide both an explanation for drinking and driving and a theoretical framework for intervention with "depressive" subtypes who tend to exhibit poor coping skills and low perceived personal control. On the other hand, problem behavior theory (Jessor & Jessor, 1977; Wilson & Jonah, 1988), which integrates personality, environmental influences, and behavior systems, would be useful in accounting for drinking and driving within the "risk-enhancing" subtypes (Donovan et al., 1988). In problem behavior theory, each behavior is considered to be part of a broader system of deviant behavior. Viewed from the perspective of problem behavior theory, successful programs for "risk-enhancing" subtypes would have to take into account the broader integrated system of personality, environment, and behavior, rather than focusing only on drinking-and-driving behaviors (Donovan et al., 1988). Finally, drinking and driving could be linked only marginally to personality and attitudes for "adjusted" types (Donovan et al., 1988). Alternative perspectives, such as viewing drinking and driving as a transportation issue, could suggest intervention and prevention techniques for these "adjusted" groups.

Approaching the development of typologies from a different database, Wells-Parker and colleagues (1986) applied a Q mode factor analysis to comprehensive arrest histories of 353 male DWI offenders in Mississippi. Demographic factors, drinker status variables, and accidents were used for external validation. A "low-offense" subtype, the modal group, was characterized by the lowest average number of overall arrests and also contained all offenders with no arrest besides the index DWI arrest. A "mixed-offense" subtype had a higher average number of total arrests than the "low-offense" subtype but no elevation for a single type of arrest. The youngest subtype, the "traffic" subtype, was characterized by high numbers of hazardous moving violations other than DWI. Two small subtypes emerged with the highest number of arrests in the sample. These were also the oldest subtypes. The "public-drunkenness" subtype and the "license-violation" subtype had multiple offenses, including DWI, equipment violations, and disturbance arrests.

Using demographic and drinker status profiles, subtypes derived from the arrest history database were compared to subtypes from studies from other databases. The most deviant "license-violation" and "public-drunkenness" subtypes appeared similar to subtypes that had elevated BAC levels and other alcohol impairment indicators in the typology of Steer et al. (1979). In both studies (Steer et al., 1979; Wells-Parker et al., 1986), these subtypes were relatively small, were the oldest emerging subtypes, had the highest alcohol impairment indicators, and showed an underrepresentation of Caucasians as compared to other subtypes. Both studies also identified a relatively nondeviant modal subtype with relatively low levels of alcohol impairment and few arrests. The "traffic" subtype appeared similar to Donovan and Marlatt's (1982) most extreme "risk-enhancing" subtype in that both subtypes were the youngest and had the highest numbers of hazardous moving violations in each of the respective studies. Although some comparability of subtypes was found across these studies, it was noted that each study identified apparently unique subtypes, suggesting that emerging subtypes are to some extent dependent on the specific variable domains within the database.

Treatment implications with regard to the arrest typology were discussed by Wells-Parker et al. (1986). For example, an integrated intervention program that would deal with such factors as assaultiveness and general deviance, as well as excessive consumption of alcohol, and that would include a lengthy monitoring period was suggested as appropriate for the relatively small "public-drunkenness" and "license-violation" subtypes.

A unique typology study was conducted using a sample of 2,889 DWI offenders in California (Arstein-Kerslake & Peck, 1986). This study offered methodological advantages of a large sample size and cross-validation of derived clusters. Also, two different typologies were derived using the same subject sample. One typology used variables from the psychometric domain, and the second typology used variables from the descriptive domain. This permitted explicit comparisons of typologies derived from different domains. Subsequent treatment compliance as well as 4-year accident and conviction rates were used as external validation variables. For the psychometric typology, 13 factors from the Life Activities Inventory (see Arstein-Kerslake & Peck, 1986), which gives information about life status, current activities, and personality characteristics, were analyzed using a K means cluster algorithm. Factors included extroversion/introversion, compliance/aggressiveness, self-confidence/depression, conservatism/nontraditionalism, paranoid/naive trust, residential stability, alcohol consumption, alcohol problems, physical health problems, treatment receptiveness, financial status, family interactions, and social involvement. A similar statistical analysis was conducted for the descriptive typology, which included demographics, arrests, BAC, intake diagnosis, prior arrest and accident variables, and scores on the Mortimer–Filkins instrument as variables. Nine psychometric clusters and ten descriptive clusters were identified in the respective analyses. The psychometric clusters showed high levels of consistency in the cross-validation analysis. Classification accuracy for descriptive clusters was lower for the psychometric clusters, possibly due to distributional problems with descriptive variables.

The psychometric typology was compared to the Donovan and Marlatt (1982) typology and the Steer et al. (1979) typology. Several subtypes from earlier studies had counterparts in the psychometric typology. For instance, Donovan and Marlatt's (1982) "depressive" subtype was suggested to have similarities to a "DWI alcoholic" subtype in the California study (Arstein-Kerslake & Peck, 1986). This latter subtype was characterized by the highest levels of depression as well as high levels of alcohol problems. It was also suggested that some subtypes from earlier studies were subdivided into additional subtypes within the larger California study. For example, Donovan and Marlatt's (1982) "risk-enhancing" subtype had similarities to three subtypes in the California study (Arstein-Kerslake & Peck, 1986), suggesting further differentiation in the latter study. Subtypes with no clear counterpart in earlier studies were also identified. In comparing the two typologies derived in the California study, significant correspondence was found between the psychometric scheme and the descriptive scheme, although some specific clusters appeared to be unique to the particular domain. These comparisons suggest that derived subtypes from different domains and databases are not random. However, some subtypes are probably unique to specific domains or databases.

Empirical delineation of multivariate typologies represents a relatively new trend within the DWI research area. In order for these typologies to have practical relevance, additional replication and cross-validation of typologies are necessary. Studies that explicitly compare typologies developed from different domains would be useful. Also, studies that identify variables that are essential for separating clinically relevant subtypes from variables that are non essential or redundant would help to provide more parsimonious schemes.

Additional domains that are theoretically relevant to DWI behavior and that have been excluded from previous typologies need to be considered. For example, the sequence of driving after drinking is widely recognized as a product of the environment, the person, and interactions between the two (Vingilis & Mann, 1986). Newer theoretical models of DWI behavior emphasize that people develop representations or expectancies about specific environments and that these expectancies are important variables for predicting drinking-and-driving behavior (Pang, Wells-Parker, & McMillen, 1989; Snow & Anderson, 1987; Snow & Landrum, 1986; Snow & Wells-Parker,

1986). For example, young adults who receive approval from peers for risky driving after drinking in a particular social setting could develop an expectation of social reinforcement following drinking and risky driving only in a highly specific social setting (Snow & Landrum, 1986). As such environmental representations become better elaborated in models of DWI behavior, they could be useful in typology development by specifying environmental contingencies that have to be overcome within an intervention program for specific types of offenders. Also, multidimensional models of alcohol problems, as well as variables that have been found to specify treatment effects in the general alcohol treatment field, could be productive additions to DWI typologies. A study that incorporates variables from previous typologies and also includes additional domains is being conducted in the Social Science Research Center at Mississippi State University.

Typologies do appear to have considerable value for specifying the terms of the matching hypothesis. The use of problem behavior theory to suggest particular intervention strategies for "risk-enhancing" subtypes of young adults (Donovan et al., 1988) is an excellent example of how empirically derived subtypes could generate a specific hypothesis about appropriate intervention strategies. Typologies for DWI offenders have relied on such techniques as cluster analysis, and, as Morey and Skinner (1986) have emphasized, these typologies are categorical in nature. For describing DWI offender heterogeneity, categorical typologies should be compared to alternative models, such as dimensional models, regarding isomorphism, heuristic value, parsimony, and clinical utility. Indeed, Snowden and Campbell (1986) have suggested that more complex strategies, such as typologies, should always be compared to simpler strategies, such as simple linear combinations of variables, for predicting intervention outcome.

EVIDENCE FOR THE MATCHING HYPOTHESIS WITHIN THE DWI INTERVENTION FIELD

Miller and Hester (1986), in reviewing evidence for the matching hypothesis within the general alcohol intervention field, have identified three relevant research strategies. With the "predictor" strategy, client characteristics are used to predict a particular treatment outcome. This approach was used by Snowden and Campbell (1986) to conduct an external validation of the MMPI typology (Sutker et al., 1980). Among male DWI offenders, MMPI subtype membership predicted treatment outcome variables, which included levels of improvement in work adjustment, in family adjustment, and in motivation for treatment as well as decreased alcohol consumption; however, the typology was not superior to simpler linear combinations of the relevant MMPI scales for predicting those outcomes. Arstein-Kerslake and Peck (1986) used offender characteristics on which their typologies were based to predict compliance with several interventions, including chemotherapy, skills workshops, group therapy, and simple biweekly contacts. Client characteristics were significant predictors of compliance, with a small subset of descriptive characteristics, including age, nonmoving violations, number of license suspensions and revocations, and driving-related problems, accounting for most of the explained variance in compliance.

Although such predictor studies demonstrate relationships between client characteristics and treatment outcomes, they do not test the central matching hypothesis that client characteristics and type of intervention interact. Miller and Hester (1986) have suggested that, since the interaction hypothesis is not directly tested, the value of predictor studies is primarily heuristic in suggesting specific hypotheses about which characteristics are relevant to which aspects of intervention. As such, these studies are only valuable if relationships between client characteristics and specific outcomes are replicated across studies (Miller & Hester, 1986).

Another research strategy indirectly tests the matching hypothesis. Using this "modeling" strategy (Miller & Hester, 1986), treatment choices of clinical judges with high success rates are "modeled" by determining which client characteristics predict the clinicians' treatment choices. Although this approach could be applied, it has never been applied within the DWI intervention area. As with the "predictor" approach, the "modeling" approach does not directly test the matching hypothesis, and the value of both of these approaches is primarily heuristic.

In order to directly test the matching hypothesis using the "differential" approach suggested by Miller and Hester (1986), relevant offender characteristics would be measured and offenders randomly assigned to intervention strategies. Several analysis options could be adopted. Interaction terms between intervention strategies and client characteristics can be directly calculated and evaluated. If a multivariate typology has been developed, offenders first could be classified into subtypes, and appropriate contrasts could be developed to test the matching hypothesis. Adoption of this strategy is rare in the general alcohol field, and very few examples exist with the DWI intervention literature.

Interactions were evaluated in the Short Term Rehabilitation (STR) study, which was an early study of various intervention effects in 11 U.S. locations. Results were generally inconclusive; however, the effects of one intervention, Power Motivation Training, interacted with problem drinking levels at three locations in that the intervention was detrimental below a Mortimer-Filkins score of 16, but beneficial or without significant effect above a 16 score (Struckman-Johnson & Ellingstad, 1978).

The matching hypothesis was evaluated in a 2-year recidivism follow-up of the California DWI project (Reis, 1982a, 1982b). This project was a large-scale, controlled, random assignment study of the effects of several interventions on DWI offender traffic risk outcomes. The effect of each intervention was examined within several demographic groups. Home study programs reduced recidivism for Caucasian, but not minority, offenders. Biweekly unstructured counseling reduced recidivism rates for multiple offenders with a high-school education or less but not for multiple offenders with a year or more of college (Reis, 1982a, 1982b). Although the statistical analysis necessary to directly test the interaction hypothesis was not conducted, these findings certainly suggest that the effectiveness of the interventions varied across demographic groups.

Offender/intervention interactions have been directly examined within the context of another large-sample, controlled, random assignment study of DWI intervention effects. In the state of Mississippi, over 3,000 offenders were randomly assigned either to receive or not to receive monthly probation sessions for a year and either to receive or not to receive a short-term intervention. This design resulted in one group that received neither intervention (control), one group that received probation only, one group that received short-term intervention only, and one group that received both interventions. Prior to intervention assignment, offenders were screened as "high-problem" or "low-problem," using a traditional classification scheme that combined BAC, number of prior DWI and other drinking-related offenses, and scores on the Mortimer–Filkins Questionnaire. For the short-term intervention, the "high-problem" offenders received eight weekly 1 1/2- to 2-hour sessions of structured group therapy, whereas the "lower-risk" offenders received a traditional DWI educational school.

Within each intervention group, a subsample received the questionnaire portion of the Life Activities Inventory (LAI) at intake, at 6 months, and at 12 months after entry. This inventory was supposed to serve as a criterion measure against which the interventions could be evaluated; however, an early analysis indicated that receiving this questionnaire affected recidivism rates (Wells-Parker, Landrum, & Spencer, 1979) — a classic case of the measurement affecting the target behavior. Because of this early finding, the LAI has been evaluated as an intervention in subsequent analyses (Landrum et al., 1982; Neff & Landrum, 1983; Wells-Parker, Anderson, Landrum, & Snow, 1988).

The first analysis of intervention effects used 2-year recidivism and accident rates as outcome measures (Landrum et al., 1982). Intervention effects were reevaluated after a long-term follow-up in which 6 or more years of recidivism data were available for all offenders (Wells-Parker et al., 1988; Wells-Parker et al., 1989). Offender/intervention interactions were evaluated within both the 2-year and the long-term follow-up. In the 2-year follow-up, an exploratory interaction analysis was used to identify potential interaction terms. In this exploratory study, evidence suggested that receiving the LAI reduced recidivism rates for "low-problem" first offenders who either were Caucasian or were under the age of 25 at project entry. Further exploration of the effect of LAI administration on recidivism suggested that educational level was the critical variable that specified the LAI effect. Offenders with less than a 9th-grade education showed *higher* recidivism levels if they received the LAI. In contrast, offenders with at least a 9th-grade education showed markedly reduced recidivism rates if they received the LAI (Neff & Landrum, 1983).

Additional findings indicated that, for first offenders under 30 years of age at intake who also showed moderate levels of alcohol problems, receiving one of the short-term interventions actually increased recidivism rates. However, among multiple offenders who had three or more DWI arrests, structured group therapy benefited all except those offenders who were either separated or divorced.

In the long-term follow-up, it was possible to evaluate more directly the existence of interactions due to increased power of analysis. The long-term recidivism rate for the entire sample was approximately 46% as compared to 27% after 2 years. Higher recidivism rates greatly enhanced the sensitivity of the analysis for detecting interaction effects. Using a logit analysis and a factorial model in which interventions, screened risk groups, and demographics were treated as factors, interactions were evaluated (Wells-Parker et al., 1989). Overall, probation had a small positive effect; however, interactions between probation and demographic characteristics clearly altered the appropriate interpretation of this effect. Age specified probation's effect in that probation resulted in reduced recidivism for offenders who were under 30 years of age at project entry. For offenders 55 years of age or older who had 12 or more years of education ("better-education" offenders), probation was highly effective, reducing recidivism by over 40%. However, for less educated (under 12 years of education) older offenders, and for offenders between the ages of 30 and 55, probation was either ineffective or somewhat detrimental with respect to recidivism. The short-term interventions were modestly effective in reducing recidivism only for those with less than 12 years of education.

When the interaction hypothesis was examined only for offenders who were under 30 years of age at entry—the largest age group of offenders, which also had the highest overall recidivism rates—an additional finding indicated that ethnicity interacted with intervention to produce some rather dramatic results. Probation clearly benefited young minorities (most of whom were African-American) with 12 or more years of education by reducing recidivism rates more than 30%. No benefit from probation was found among young better-educated Caucasians. Also, combining short-term intervention with probation reduced recidivism rates by 24% for young, less educated offenders. Among offenders under 30 years of age, only the better-educated Caucasians failed to benefit from some form of intervention. These results are all the more intriguing in view of additional findings that the classification scheme, which was based on traditional alcohol problems screening criteria, was a poor predictor of recidivism for young offenders and utterly failed to predict recidivism for young minorities (Landrum, Snow, Wells-Parker, & Anderson, 1987), although the screening scheme significantly predicted recidivism for other groups. Indeed, the recidivism rates of young minorities screened into the "low-problem" group were identical to that of young minorities screened into the "high-problem" group. Furthermore, recidivism rates of young minorities who received no intervention exceeded 60% after 6 years—the highest rate of any demographic group. The failure of traditional recidivism predictors, coupled with the relatively large benefits of traditional interventions for these young minority offenders, suggests that traditional models of DWI behavior are inadequate for ethnic and minority groups in some cultural settings. Interventions that provide resources, such as education or interaction with supportive role models (e.g., probation counselors), could be especially effective in countering negative social factors, such as poverty, discrimination, or the negative labeling of minority offenders as "criminals," that may exist in some societies and exacerbate future traffic risk.

Interactions between administration of the LAI and demographics were also examined in the long-term study. As in the 2-year study, LAI administration was only effective in reducing recidivism for screened "low-problem" offenders (Wells-Parker et al., 1988). The most striking finding, however, resulted from adding gender to the evaluation model (Anderson & Wells-Parker, 1989). LAI administration generally reduced recidivism for men, especially those who were screened into the "low-problem" group. LAI administration was also beneficial for women who were better educated and who were screened as "low-problem" offenders; however, it was *detrimental* for women offenders who were less educated or who were screened as "high-problem" offenders. A very large detrimental effect of LAI administration was observed for women with arrest BACs that exceeded 0.199. For such women, receiving the LAI *increased* recidivism rates by more than 60%. In interpreting these findings, it was noted that the content of the LAI focuses on adjustment in such roles as marriage and family; however, the majority of DWI women are separated or divorced (Wells-Parker, Pang, Anderson, McMillen, & Miller, in press). Also, studies that have examined gender differences in drinking reasons have shown that females, especially females who drink heavily, drink to escape life's problems even more than do comparable males (Cahalan, Cisin, & Crossley, 1969). For female DWIs who may lack common sources of social support, such as marital role involvement, and who are experiencing severe drinking problems, the repeated examination of their current life circumstances (by completing the LAI questionnaire) possibly exacerbates a sense of distress, helplessness, and hopelessness that could, in turn, lead to increased escape drinking and increased drinking and driving (Wells-Parker et al., in press). The forced and repeated self-examination of one's current life situation, at least in the absence of intensive therapeutic support, appears to be counterproductive for female DWI offenders with relatively severe drinking problems (Wells-Parker et al., in press).

In summary, the findings of studies that have assessed interactions between demographic characteristics and type of DWI intervention are preliminary and in need of replication; however, they do suggest that current theories of DWI behavior and intervention strategies— developed primarily on the basis of a young or middle-aged Caucasian male, which is the modal demographic profile of DWI offenders in the United States—must be extended to account explicitly for gender and ethnic differences. The specification of intervention effects by age, ethnicity, educational background, and gender are especially relevant as the demographic profile of the population and social customs change. In the United States, the population is aging; women are found in increasing numbers in public drinking settings and in the DWI population; and ethnic groups in some areas are at particularly high risk of recidivism and accident involvement. These trends could have relevance for planning intervention strategies, given the apparent specification of intervention effects by demographics.

It should be noted that other studies have evaluated the effects of tailored treatment strategies (e.g., Kadell & Peck, 1984); however, the designs of these studies have not permitted an evaluation of the matching hypothesis per se. The mere demonstration that the outcomes for DWI clients who receive a tailored program differ (or fail to differ) from those receiving no intervention is not equivalent to demonstrating that different types of clients respond differently to intervention strategies.

CONSIDERATIONS FOR FUTURE RESEARCH

The matching hypothesis does provide some promising directions for understanding the effects of the various interventions and for improving intervention efficacy. However, the matching agenda presents many challenges to evaluators, and some of the common problems within the DWI evaluation literature, such as low statistical power, will become even more acute within this agenda. For example, the issue of appropriate criteria for measuring intervention success remains problematic. Technical problems, such as low recidivism base rates that reduce the statistical power, could be mitigated through better records, expansion of the criterion to incorporate DWI arrests as well as convictions (Landrum et al., 1982), or the inclusion of other types of relevant offenses besides DWI (Arstein-Kerslake & Peck, 1986; Perrine, 1970). Indeed, large sample sizes, and long follow-up periods will permit evaluation of interactions using a recidivism criterion when enough time and money are available to justify such an effort. However, the conceptual problems of commonly used criterion measures, such as failure of recidivism measures to reflect undetected, unsanctioned deviance (Mann et al., 1983), are not so easily solved.

Although considerable effort has been expended to identify and measure clinically relevant client characteristics and types of offenders, much less effort has been devoted to identifying and measuring clinically relevant dimensions of intervention. Indeed, the approach to identifying dimensions of interventions is often quite superficial, and evaluators are often content with assigning the interventions that they propose to evaluate to some nominal and vaguely specified category (Kunkel, 1983). If matching strategies are to be evaluated efficiently, the relevant characteristics of interventions themselves must be concisely defined and reliably measured. Also, even when sophisticated outcome evaluations are conducted, there is often no accompanying process evaluation to check whether or not what is actually done corresponds to what is described in the written protocols (Mann, 1988; Vingilis & Mann, 1986). Monitoring of "treatment integrity" (Boruch, Wortman, & Cordray, 1981) must improve in order for matching strategies to be adequately tested.

In spite of these challenges, the interaction model that is implied by the matching hypothesis cannot be abandoned if simpler (main effects) models inadequately account for intervention effects. The results of one test of the interaction model suggest that evaluation only of main effects is misleading and that interaction terms are necessary to complete the model (Wells-Parker et al., 1989). An alternative to expensive and large long-term studies for evaluating the matching hypothesis for all possible offender types would be the development of highly specific versions of the hypothesis that would suggest the utility of a particular intervention to a particular and relatively common offender-type profile. Donovan's work suggests the potential utility of this strategy in identifying common subtypes, such as "depressed" and "risk-enhancing" subtypes, and suggesting specific treatment alternatives for them.

The application of new analytic strategies also should be considered. Powerful quantitative review techniques summarily known as "meta-analysis" could assist the process of synthesis in the DWI evaluation field. Regarding the matching hypothesis, several possibilities exist for adapting meta-analysis techniques to provide relevant information. One straightforward adaptation of the technique would utilize a "study effects" approach in which the effects of an intervention could be calculated separately for several distinct and clinically relevant subgroups of DWIs (e.g., high-BAC females, or young minorities, or "risk-enhancing" subtypes) within each evaluation study. The effect sizes from the studies could then be cumulated separately for each *a priori* group. Although not directly comparing subgroups, this process could have considerable heuristic value in specifying promising matching hypotheses for specific groups. It is also possible that equivalent interaction terms from several studies could be cumulated using meta-analysis methods; however, this would require an extension of the technique beyond its current applications.

Although the current literature suggests that the matching hypothesis is more often discussed than tested, and in spite of the complexity of the necessary research for evaluating the hypothesis, adequate tests of the hypothesis do appear feasible and necessary.

ACKNOWLEDGMENTS

The chapter was supported, in part, by Grant No. 1R21 AA07598-01, ALCP-1 from the National Institute on Alcohol Abuse and Alcoholism, U.S.A. Dr. Ron Snow and Ms. Lisa Phillips assisted in editing and typing the manuscript.

REFERENCES

Anderson, B. J., & Wells-Parker, E. W. (1989). *The Life Activities Inventory as an intervention for DUI offenders: Interaction with demographic offender characteristics.* Unpublished manuscript.

Arstein-Kerslake, G. W., & Peck, R. C. (1986). *A typological analysis of California DUI offenders and DUI recidivism correlates* NTIS No. DOT-HS-806-994). Washington, DC: National Highway Traffic Safety Administration, Department of Transportation.

Boruch, R. F., Wortman, P. M., & Cordray, D. S. (1981). *Reanalyzing program evaluations.* San Francisco: Jossey-Bass.

Cahalan, D., Cisin, I. H., & Crossley, H. M. (1969). *American drinking practices: A national study of drinking behavior and attitudes* (Monograph No. 6). New Brunswick, NJ: Rutgers Center of Alcohol Studies.

Donovan, D. M., & Marlatt, G. A. (1982). Personality subtypes among driving-while-intoxicated offenders: Relationship to drinking behavior and driving risk. *Journal of Consulting and Clinical Psychology, 50,* 241–249.

Donovan, D. M., Marlatt, G. A., & Salzberg, P. M. (1983). Drinking behavior, personality factors and high-risk driving: A review and theoretical formulation. *Journal of Studies on Alcohol, 44,* 395–428.

Donovan, D. M., Queisser, H. R., Umlauf, R. L., & Salzberg, P. M. (1986). Personality subtypes among driving-while-intoxicated offenders: Follow-up of subsequent driving records. *Journal of Consulting and Clinical Psychology, 54,* 563–565.

Donovan, D. M., Umlauf, R. L., & Salzberg, P. M. (1989). Derivation of personality subtypes among high-risk drivers. *Alcohol, Drugs, and Driving, 4,* 233–244.

Glaser, F. B. (1980). Anybody got a match? Treatment research and the matching hypothesis. In G. Edwards & M. Grant (Eds.), *Alcoholism treatment in transition* (pp. 178–196). London: Croon Helm.

Hagen, R. E., Williams, R. L., & McConnell, E. J. (1979). The traffic safety impact of alcohol abuse treatment as an alternative to mandated licensing controls. *Accident Analysis and Prevention, 11,* 275–291.

Holden, R. T., & Stewart, L. T. (1981). *Tennessee DUI probation follow-up demonstration project final report* (DOT-HS-5-01199). Washington, DC: National Highway Traffic Safety Administration, Department of Transportation.

Jessor, R., & Jessor, S. L. (1977). *Problem behavior and psychosocial development: A longitudinal study of youth.* New York: Academic Press.

Kadell, D. J., & Peck, R. C. (1984). An evaluation of the alcohol reexamination program for drivers with two major traffic offenses. *Abstracts and Reviews in Alcohol and Driving, 5,* 3–12.

Kunkel, E. (1983). Driver improvement courses for drinking-drivers reconsidered. *Accident Analysis and Prevention, 15,* 429–439.

Landrum, J. W., Miles, S. M., Neff, R. L., Pritchard, T. E., Roebuck, J. B., Wells-Parker, E., & Windham, G. O. (1982). *Mississippi DUI probation follow-up project* (NTIS No. DOT-HS-806-274) Washington, DC: National Highway Traffic Safety Administration, Department of Transportation.

Landrum, J. W., Snow, R. W., Wells-Parker, E., & Anderson, B. J. (1987, November). *Six to nine year recidivism rates of DUI offenders.* Paper presented at the annual meeting of the Mid-South Sociological Association, Memphis, TN.

Mann, R. E. (1988, November). *Assessing and treating the convicted drinking driver.* Paper presented at the annual meeting of the American Society of Criminology, Chicago, IL.

Mann, R. E., Leigh, G., Vingilis, E. R., & DeGenova, K. (1983). A critical review on the effectiveness of drinking driving rehabilitation programmes. *Accident Analysis and Prevention, 15,* 441–461.

Mann, R. E., Vingilis, E. R., & Stewart, K. (1988). Programs to change individual behavior: Education and rehabilitation in the prevention of drinking and driving. In M. D. Laurence, J. R. Snortum, & F. E. Zimring (Eds.), *Social control of the drinking driver* (pp. 248–269). Chicago: University of Chicago Press.

McAllister, R. (1988). The drunken driving crackdown: Is it working? *American Bar Association Journal, 74,* 52–56.

Miller, W. R., & Hester, R. K. (1986). Matching problem drinkers with optimal treatments. In W. R. Miller & N. Heather (Eds.), *Treating addictive behaviours: Processes of change* (pp. 175–203). New York: Plenum.

Morey, L. C., & Skinner, H. A. (1986). Empirically derived classifications of alcohol-related problems. In M. Galanter (Ed.), *Recent developments in alcoholism* (Vol. 4) (pp. 145–168). New York: Plenum.

Mortimer, R. G., Filkins, L. D., & Lower, J. S. (1971). *Court procedures for identifying problem drinkers. Final report. Report on phase II.* Ann Arbor: Highway Safety Research Institute, University of Michigan.

Mulligan, M. J., Steer, R. A., & Fine, E. W. (1978). Psychiatric disturbances in drunk driving offenders referred for treatment of alcoholism. *Alcoholism: Clinical and Experimental Research, 2,* 107–111.

National Highway Traffic Safety Administration, Department of Transportation. (1986). *The drunk driver and jail: The drunk driver and the jail problem* (Vol. 1) (DOT-HS-806-761). Washington, DC: Author.

Neff, R. L., & Landrum, J. W. (1983). The Life Activities Inventory as a countermeasure for driving while intoxicated. *Journal of Studies on Alcohol, 44,* 755–769.

Nichols, J. L., Weinstein, E. B., Ellingstad, V. S., & Struckman-Johnson, D. L. (1978). The specific deterrent effect of ASAP education and rehabilitation programs. *Journal of Safety Research, 10,* 177–187.

Nichols, J. L., Weinstein, E. B., Ellingstad, V. S., Struckman-Johnson, D. L., & Reis, R. E. (1981). The effectiveness of education and treatment programs for drinking drivers: A decade of evaluation. In L. Goldberg (Ed.), *Alcohol, drugs and traffic safety* (Vol. 3) (pp. 1298–1395). Stockholm: Almgvist and Wiksell.

Pang, M. G., Wells-Parker, E., & McMillen, D. L. (1989). Drinking reasons, drinking locations, and automobile accident involvement among collegians. *International Journal of the Addictions, 24,* 215–227.

Peck, R. C., Sadler, D. D., & Perrine, M. W. (1985). The comparative effectiveness of alcohol rehabilitation and licensing control actions for drunk driving offenders: A review of the literature. *Alcohol, Drugs, and Driving: Abstracts and Reviews, 1,* 15–39.

Perrine, M. W. (1970). Identification of personality, attitudinal and biographical characteristics of drinking drivers. *Behavioral Research in Highway Safety, 2,* 207–225.

Perrine, M. W. (1975). The Vermont driver profile: A psychometric approach to early identification of potential high-risk drinking drivers. In S. Israelstam & S. Lambert (Eds.), *Proceedings of the 6th International Conference on Alcohol, Drugs and Traffic Safety* (pp. 199–223). Toronto: Addiction Research Foundation.

Perrine, M. W. (1987). Varieties of drunken and drinking drivers: A review, a research program, and a model. In P. C. Noordzij & R. Rosbach (Eds.), *Alcohol, drugs, and traffic safety—T86* (pp. 105–113). Amsterdam: Elsevier.

Popkin, C. L., Li, L. K., Lacey, J. H., Stewart, J. R., & Waller, P. P. (1983). *An initial evaluation of the North Carolina alcohol and drug education traffic schools: Volume 1. Technical report.* Chapel Hill: Highway Safety Research Center, University of North Carolina.

Reis, R. E. (1982a). *The traffic safety effectiveness of education programs for first offense drunk drivers* (NTIS No. DOT-HS-806-558). Washington, DC: National Highway Traffic Safety Administration, Department of Transportation.

Reis, R. E. (1982b). *The traffic safety effectiveness of educational counseling* programs for multiple offense drunk drivers (NTIS No. DOT-HS-806-557). Washington, DC: National Highway Traffic Safety Administration, Department of Transportation.

Ross, H. L. (1982). *Deterring the drinking driver: Legal policy and social control.* Lexington, MA: Lexington Books.

Sadler, D. D., & Perrine, M. W. (1984). *An evaluation of the California drunk driving countermeasure system: Volume 2. The long-term traffic safety impact of a pilot alcohol abuse treatment as an alternative to license suspensions.* Sacramento, CA: Department of Motor Vehicles.

Skinner, H. A. (1982). Statistical approaches to the classification of alcohol and drug addiction. *British Journal of Addiction, 77,* 259–273.

Snow, R. W., & Anderson, B. J. (1987). Drinking place selection factors among drunk drivers. *British Journal of Addiction, 82,* 85–95.

Snow, R. W., & Landrum, J. W. (1986). Drinking locations and frequency of drunkenness among Mississippi DUI offenders. *American Journal of Drug and Alcohol Abuse, 12,* 389–402.

Snow, R. W., & Wells-Parker, E. (1986). Drinking reasons, alcohol consumption levels, and drinking locations among drunken drivers. *International Journal of the Addictions, 21,* 671–689.

Snowden, L. R., & Campbell, D. (1986). Validity of MMPI classification of problem drinker-drivers. *Journal of Studies on Alcohol, 47,* 344–347.

Steer, R. A., Fine, E. W., & Scoles, P. E. (1979). Classification of men arrested for driving while intoxicated, and treatment implications: A cluster-analytic study. *Journal of Studies on Alcohol, 40,* 222–229.

Struckman-Johnson, L., & Ellingstad, V. S. (1978). *The Short-Term Rehabilitation Study Volume III: Site Specific Analyses of Effectiveness.* Washington, DC: National Highway Traffic Safety Administration. (DOT-HS-6-01366).

Surgeon General's Workshop on Drunk Driving: Background Papers. (1988), Washington, DC: U.S. Department of Health and Human Services, Public Health Service, Office of the Surgeon General.

Sutker, P. B., Brantley, P. J., & Allain, A. N. (1980). MMPI response patterns and alcohol consumption in DUI offenders. *Journal of Consulting and Clinical Psychology, 48,* 350–355.

Vingilis, E. R., & Mann, R. E. (1986). Towards an interactionist approach to drinking–driving behaviour: Implications for prevention and research. *Health Education Research, 4,* 273–288.

Waller, P. J. (1985). Licensing and other controls of the drinking-driver. *Journal of Studies on Alcohol,* (Suppl. 10), 150–160.

Wanberg, K. W., Horn, J. L., & Foster, F. M. (1977). A differential assessment model for alcoholism: The scales of the Alcohol Use Inventory. *Journal of Studies on Alcohol, 38,* 512–543.

Wells-Parker, E., Anderson, B. J., Landrum, J. W., & Snow, R. W. (1988). The long-term effectiveness of probation, short-term intervention, and LAI administration for reducing DUI recidivism. *British Journal of Addiction, 83,* 415–421.

Wells-Parker, E., Anderson, B. J., McMillen, D. L., & Landrum, J. W. (1989). Interactions among DUI offender characteristics and traditional intervention modalities: A long-term recidivism follow-up. *British Journal of Addiction, 84,* 381–390.

Wells-Parker, E., & Cosby, P. J. (1988). Behavioral and employment consequences of driver's license suspension for drinking driving offenders. *Journal of Safety Research, 19,* 5–20.

Wells-Parker, E., Cosby, P. J., & Landrum, J. W. (1986). A typology for drinking driving offenders: Methods for classification and policy implications. *Accident Analysis and Prevention, 18,* 443–453.

Wells-Parker, E., Landrum, J. W., & Spencer, B. G. (1979). *Analytic study: Preliminary analysis of the DUI probation follow-up project, December, 1979.* Mississippi State: Social Science Research Center, Mississippi State University.

Wells-Parker, E., Pang, M. G., Anderson, B. J., McMillen, D. L., & Miller, D. I. (in press). Female DUI offenders: A comparison to male counterparts and an examination of the effects of intervention on females' recidivism rates. *Journal of Studies on Alcohol.*

Wendling A., & Kolody, B. (1982). An evaluation of the Mortimer–Filkins test as a predictor of alcohol-impaired driving recidivism. *Journal of Studies on Alcohol, 43,* 751–766.

Wilson, R. J., & Jonah, B. A. (1988). The application of problem behavior theory to the understanding of risky driving. *Alcohol, Drugs, and Driving, 4,* 173–191.

INDEX

Accidents, alcohol-related, *see* Alcohol–crash problem; Crashes, alcohol-related

Accidents, incidence among drinking drivers, 19–20, 80

Adjudication of DWI in the U.S., 132–141

Administrative diversion, *see* Administrative per se laws

Administrative per se laws, 127, 133, 139–140, 236

Adolescents, *see also* Youth
and drinking and driving, 42–64
traumatic injury and traffic crashes among, 226–230, 242

Alcohol abuse, *see* Alcoholism, problem drinking

Alcohol availability, *see also* Availability theory
and per capita consumption, 205–220, 235
in Australia, 159–160, 196–197
natural experiments in decreased, 216–217
natural experiments in increased, 214–215

Alcohol beverage industry, advertising for, 45

Alcohol consumption, 42, 45, *see also* Drinking behavior; Drinking habits/patterns
and alcohol availability, 206–207

by youth, 229, 230, 231–236, 242
functions of, 46
quantity and frequency measures of, 69, 74–76

Alcohol–crash problem, 2, *see also* Crashes, alcohol-related
and alcohol availability, 205, 207–217, 218
methodological issues in measuring, 208
reductions in, 219

Alcohol dependence, *see* Alcoholism

Alcoholics
compared to nonalcoholics, 207
comparisons with impaired drivers, 20–21, 79–86
definition of, 144

Alcoholism
and DWI, 68–90, 269–271
incidence among impaired drivers, 20, 69, 104, 135
self-reports versus objective measures of, 76–79
treatment, 271, 277

Alcohol problems
among youth, 235
detection of in drinking–driving population, 70–79
relationship to alcohol consumption, 206–207, 219

Alcohol Safety Action Projects/Program (ASAP), 122, 129, 136

Alco-sensor™ *see* Preliminary breath test devices

Anti-plea-bargaining laws, 138–139

Arrests
history of by DWI offenders, 274
number of for DWI, 116–117, 121–122, 124, 128
serious alcohol problems and, 88–89

Automobiles
per capita ratio, 44
symbolic value of, 45

Availability theory, *see also* Alcohol availability
applicability to alcohol–crash problem, 207–217
approach to alcohol problems, 206–207

BAC, *see* Blood alcohol concentration

Behavioral-based enforcement system, *see* Enforcement system, behavioral-based

Blood alcohol concentration (BAC), 1–2, 3, 5, 17, 19, 23, 25, 78, 82, 88, 89, 108, 119, 122, 123, 125, 128–129, 133, 143, 152, 175, 182, 185, 187, 188, 190, 194, 208–209, 228, 236, 237, 250, 252–253, 256, 269, 271, 275, 279, 284
at arrest, 269, 279, 282
estimation of, 143, 250
legal, *see* Legal blood alcohol concentration
relationship to crash risk, 1, 228, 236

Breathalyzer™, Borkenstein, 119–120

British Road Safety Act of 1967, 123, 131, 152–153

Chemical testing of BAC, 119–120, *see also* Enforcement system, chemistry-based; *Breathalyzer*™; Illegal per se laws; Preliminary breath test

Citizen activist groups, 2, 86, 126–127, 133, 137, 150–151, 153
absence of in Australia, 194–195

Classical model of deterrence, 100–108, 163
assumptions of, 102–108
components of, 100–102

Community service, as a sanction for DWI, 149–150

Community-wide model, 240–241, 242

Corrections facilities, limitations in, 140–141

Cost recovery, of DWI adjudication, 148–149

Court monitoring programs, 137, *see also* Citizen activist groups

Crashes, alcohol-related, 1, 117, 140, 151–152, 196, 251, *see also* Alcohol–crash problem; Traffic safety
among youth, 226–230
police reports of, 209
reduction of during enforcement programs, 128–131
reductions in following RBT, 174–175, 180, 183, 187–188
surrogate measure of, 209

Department of Transportation, 122, 133, 149

Depressed affect, among DWI offenders, 82–85

Depression, *see also* Depressed affect
among impaired drivers, 27–29, 30, 272, 275, 276
and drug use, 24
deterrence doctrine/theory, 99, 130, 161, 162, 166

Deterrence, *see also* Classical model of deterrence; Social control model of deterrence
and RBT, 180, 184–185, 193–195
general, 100, 111, 146–148, 236
simple, 100, 111–112

Deviant/criminal behavior, 25, 80–82, 107

Diagnostic instruments for DWI, 70–74

Differential deterrability, 106, 107, 166–167, 188–191

Drinking behavior, relationship to DWI, 20–23, 59–60

Drinking habits/patterns
and RBT, 181, 185
of impaired drivers, 21–23, 254, 264
regional, 258

Driver education, 238

Driver improvement programs, in F.R.G.
evaluation of, 255–257

Driving behavior, relationship to DWI, 18–20, 270

Drug detection, by police officers, 123

Drug education, 232

Drug use
adolescent, 43, 64
and driving by youth, 227
relationship to alcohol-impaired driving, 24, 107

DSM-III/DSM-III-R, 73–74, 75, 83

Educational programs
  for impaired drivers, 136–137, 142–143, 270
  youth anti-drinking, 231–234
  youth DD, 62–64, 238
Enforcement
  of DWI in the U.S., 117–132
  programs in the U.S., evaluation of, 128–132
Enforcement system
  behavioral-based, 117–123
  chemistry-based, 123–126
Environment
  perceived (in PBT), *see* Problem Behavior Theory
  social, impact of RBT on, 167, 177, 180–181, 184–185
Environmental countermeasures, 196, 239–240
Evaluation(s)
  of driver improvement programs in the F.R.G., 255–257
  subjective, of legal interventions, 164–165, 167
Expectancies, role in predicting DD, 276–277
Eysenck Personality Inventory, 28, 271

Fear, of punishment in deterrence model, 105–106, 146, 165, 166, 184–185
Field theory, 14

Health-impairing behavior, relationship to impaired driving, 21, 62–63
Highway Safety Act of 1966, 133

Illegal per se laws, 123, 127, *see also* Legal blood alcohol concentration; Enforcement, chemically-based
Implied consent laws, 120, 139
Impounding of vehicles, 146
Interactionist model/theory/approach, 5–6, 14, 36, 102, 112, 276, 284

Jail, as punishment for DWI, 142, 252
  general deterrent effect of, 147–148
  means of incapacitation, 145

LEER model (of treatment), 252, 254, 260, 261, 262
Legal blood alcohol concentration (BAC), 17–18, 161, 194
  for youth, 236–237, 241
  lowering of, 250
  presumptive levels for, 119

License suspension/revocation, *see also* Administrative per se laws
  as a means of incapacitation, 145, 253, 267
  general deterrent effect of, 146
  licensing restrictions, for youth, 237, 242
Life Activities Inventory (LAI), 275, 280, 282
Life problems, 38–40, 82–85, 263
Life-skills approaches, 231–235

Matching hypothesis, 268–285
Meta-analysis, 284–285
Michigan Alcohol Screening Test (MAST), 21, 70–72, 77, 89, 90, 136
Minimum drinking age, 46
  laws, 133, 213–214, 217, 219, 226, 235
Minnesota Multiphasic Personality Inventory (MMPI), 28–29, 80, 83, 241, 272, 277, 278
Mortimer–Filkins Instrument, 71–72, 136, 269, 275, 279
Mothers Against Drunk Driving (MADD), 86, 126–127, 137, 156, *see also* Citizen activist groups

National Commission Against Driving Drunk (NCADD), 151, 237
National Committee on Uniform Laws and Ordinances (NCUTLO), 133
National Highway Traffic Safety Administration (NHTSA), 122, 144, 145, 149, 238, 239–240
National Institute on Alcohol Abuse and Alcoholism (NIAAA), 229

Passive alcohol sensor, *see* Preliminary breath test devices
PBT, *see* Preliminary breath test; Problem Behavior Theory
Peer intervention, 63
  programs, 238
Peer pressure, *see also* Social influence
  among youth, 47, 228, 234
  mandatory, 137–138
  penalties, for DWI, 127, 135, 139, *see also* Sanctions; Punishment
  reduced, 135–137
  to drink and drive, 176, 194, 277
  to use drugs, 232
Personality characteristics
  and DD, 54–55, 61
  of DWI offenders and alcohol abusers, 79–86

Plea bargaining, 135, *see also* Anti-plea-bargaining laws
Power Motivation Training, 279
Prediction of onset of drunk driving, 48–59
Preliminary breath test (PBT)
  devices, 5, 123–124, 126, 127
  in Australia, 194
  laws, 133
Prevention strategies for youth, 231–242
  multicomponent strategies, 240–241
  to limit morbidity/mortality (point 3), 239–240
  to reduce drinking (point 1), 231–236
  to separate drinking and driving (point 2), 236–239
Problem Behavior Theory (PBT), 14, 43, 49–52, 59, 64, 228, 274, 277
  Behavior System of, 15, 18–26
  conceptual framework of, 15–17
  Perceived Environment System of, 17, 31–34
  Personality system of, 15–16, 26–30
Problem drinking and DWI, 68–90, 104, 135, 144, 269–271, 279, *see also* Alcoholism; Alcoholics; Alcohol problems; Drinking behavior
Public policy, for the drinking driver with serious alcohol problems, 86–87
Punishment, 141–142, 164–166
  impact on drinking–driving, 100–102

Random breath testing (RBT), 108, 124–125, 152, 161–198
  civil rights considerations in, 197–198
  guidelines for, 192–193
  impact of, 174–175, 180–181, 183, 187–188, 192
  overview of in Australia, 170–171
  publicity of, 173, 182, 183, 192, 193
  public support for, 194
Random stopping programs, 161, 162, 198
  in Queensland, 187
  in Western Australia, 186
  overview of in Australia, 170–171
Recidivism, following treatment, 257–259, 262, 263, 280–282
Regression model of adolescent DD, 53, 56, 59
Rehabilitation
  as a sanction for DWI, 143–144
  effectiveness of, 264
  European approach to, 251–252
  of high risk drivers, 35

programs in the F.R.G., 250–264
programs in the U.S., 135–137, 143–145
Short Term (STR), 279
Relative risk to begin DD, 59
Remedial intervention, 267–269, 277–283, *see also* Rehabilitation; Educational programs
Remove Intoxicated Drivers (RID), *see* Citizen activist groups
Resistance training approaches, 234
Retribution function of sanctions, 150–151
Riding with impaired drivers (RWID), 63, 64, 227, 229–231, 238, 241–242
Risky driving, 19–20, 80, 104, 270, 272–273
  by youth, 228–229, 277
Roadblocks, *see* Random breath testing; Random stopping programs; Sobriety check points
Road safety, research, 13, *see also* Traffic safety
Roadside surveys, of drinking drivers, 19, 22, 106, 108, 116, 128, 183, 189–190, 211
Roadway design, *see* Environmental countermeasures

Sanctioning
  assumptions concerning, 106–108
  community and, 146–151
  of DWI in the U.S., 141–151
Sanctions
  informal (nonlegal), 162–165
  in Scandinavian countries, 123
  "Scandinavian model", 123
  "Scandinavian myth", 178
  Schmerber vs. California, 120
Seat belts (safety belts)
  effectiveness of, 239
  legislation, 178, 196
  relationship to DWI, 18–19
  use of by youth, 51, 53, 56, 239–240
Server intervention programs, 5, 197
Sitz vs. Michigan State Police, 132
Sobriety check points, in the U.S., 125, 131–132, 192
Sobriety tests, 118
  police officers' use of, 122
Social context
  of drinking, 31–32
  of drinking and driving, 277
Social control model of deterrence, 108–112

Social influence of drinking and driving, 33–34, 111, *see also* Peer pressure
Social surveys
  on drinking and driving, 22–23
  of high school seniors, 227, 229, 235
  on RBT, 179
Students Against Driving Drunk (SADD), 238, 240

Technological advances, in control of DWI, 5
Temperance movement, in Australia, 159–160
Traffic safety, 64, 152, *see also* Road safety
  effect of alcohol availability on, 213–217
  relationship with per capita consumption, 209–213

Treatment, *see* Rehabilitation
Trends in alcohol-related crashes, 3–4, 151–152
Typologies
  DWI offender, 271–277
  in alcoholism literature, 85, 271
  of arrest histories, 274–275
  of drinking–driving offense, 110

Uniform Vehicle Code, 133
U.S. Supreme Court, 125–126, 132

Vehicle design, *see* Environmental countermeasures; Seat belts
Violations, traffic
  incidence of among impaired drivers, 19–20, 53, 80